INCLUSION IN THE

AMERICAN DREAM

INCLUSION IN THE
AMERICAN DREAM

ASSETS, POVERTY, AND
PUBLIC POLICY

Edited by

Michael Sherraden

OXFORD
UNIVERSITY PRESS

2005

OXFORD
UNIVERSITY PRESS

Oxford University Press, Inc., publishes works that further
Oxford University's objective of excellence
in research, scholarship, and education.

Oxford   New York
Auckland   Cape Town   Dar es Salaam   Hong Kong   Karachi
Kuala Lumpur   Madrid   Melbourne   Mexico City   Nairobi
New Delhi   Shanghai   Taipei   Toronto

With offices in
Argentina   Austria   Brazil   Chile   Czech Republic   France   Greece
Guatemala   Hungary   Italy   Japan   Poland   Portugal   Singapore
South Korea   Switzerland   Thailand   Turkey   Ukraine   Vietnam

Copyright © 2005 by Oxford University Press

Published by Oxford University Press, Inc.
198 Madison Avenue, New York, New York 10016

www.oup.com

Oxford is a registered trademark of Oxford University Press

Library of Congress Cataloging-in-Publication Data

Inclusion in the American dream : assets, poverty, and public policy / [edited by] Michael Sherraden.
    p.   cm.
  Revisions of papers presented at a symposium held at Washington University in St. Louis.
  Includes bibliographical references and index.
  ISBN-13 978-0-19-516819-8; 978-0-19-516820-4 (pbk.)
  ISBN 0-19-516819-4; 0-19-516820-8 (pbk.)
    1. United States—Social policy—1993—Congresses. 2. Poor—Government policy—United
States—Congresses. 3. Saving and investment—Government policy—United
States—Congresses. 4. Marginality, Social—United States—Prevention—Congresses. 5.
Assets (Accounting)—Congresses.   I. Sherraden, Michael W. (Michael Wayne), 1948–

HN53.I43 2005
361.6'1'0973—dc22   2004063563

9 8 7 6 5 4 3 2 1

Printed in the United States of America
on acid-free paper

Preface

The seed for this book was planted during a symposium held at Washington University in St. Louis. First versions of the papers were presented and since then have been revised and updated extensively. I am grateful to all of the authors for their participation in the symposium and subsequent work. Also, I am grateful to other symposium participants whose essays did not end up in this book due to matters of emphasis, fit, and limitations of space. Their work is every bit as valuable as the chapters that appear here. Altogether, this is an outstanding group of scholars and policy analysts who have undertaken innovative and productive work.

The Ford Foundation provided resources that made the symposium and subsequent work possible. The vision of President Susan Berresford and former Vice President Melvin Oliver in reshaping the Ford Foundation to include a Division of Asset Building and Community Development has resulted in an emergent body of knowledge that is defining this area of work and informing policy. Many other foundations have contributed to this work as well. I am particularly grateful to the Charles Stewart Mott Foundation for supporting my time in completing this volume, and to the Common Counsel Foundation for providing a quiet place to write. I also thank the MetLife Foundation, F. B. Heron Foundation, Joyce Foundation, Annie E. Casey Foundation, Ewing Marion Kauffman Foundation, Lumina Foundation, W. K. Kellogg Foundation, Danforth Foundation, National Rural Funders Collaborative, State of Minnesota, United Way of Greater St. Louis, U.S. Department of Health and Human Services, and U.S. Department of Agriculture, all of whom have funded our research in asset building. Perhaps this is an example of the best use of American philanthropy—creating knowledge and innovations for application in the United States and around the world.

I thank Karen Edwards and other staff members of CSD who organized the logistics of the symposium. Lisa Morris, now at the University of Southern Maine, cochaired the symposium and provided valuable comments and suggestions for the book. Thanks go also to former Dean Shanti Khinduka, of the George Warren Brown School of Social Work, and Chancellor Mark Wrighton, of Washington University, for their steady support of this research agenda at CSD. Anupama Jacob assisted in editorial work, and Jenny Kraus-Smith helped prepare the manuscript.

Terry Vaughn and Mac Hawkins at Oxford University Press guided the project and made helpful suggestions. Comments from two anonymous reviewers improved the readability and usefulness of the book. Anne Rockwood and Catherine Rae assisted in moving the manuscript into production. Heather Hartman was an outstanding production editor.

Many other people helped as well. It would be impossible to thank everyone who made this book possible. I am fortunate to have had their support, and all remaining shortcomings can be attributed to me.

Contents

Contributors

Deborah Adams is associate professor at the School of Social Welfare, University of Kansas. She was a member of the research team on the American Dream Demonstration (ADD), the first systematic study of individual development accounts (IDAs). Dr. Adams is author of several articles from ADD research and other studies on asset-building strategies. She has particular interests in outcomes of asset holding for women and children. Dr. Adams is currently a principal investigator in a large study of children's savings accounts known as SEED (Saving for Education, Entrepreneurship, and Downpayment), where she has played the lead role in design of an impact assessment and other research methods.

Jared Bernstein joined the Economic Policy Institute in 1992, where he directs the living standards program. Formerly, he was deputy chief economist at the U.S. Department of Labor. His areas of research include income and wage inequality, technology's impact on wages and employment, low-wage labor markets and poverty, minimum wage analysis, and international comparisons. Dr. Bernstein has published extensively in popular and academic journals, and is the coauthor of seven editions of *The State of Working America.*

Sondra G. Beverly is assistant professor in the School of Social Welfare at the University of Kansas. Her areas of research include material hardship, saving and asset accumulation, and use of financial services by low-income individuals. Dr. Beverly has made contributions to saving theory and evidence in several articles. She has helped design and study an innovative savings-incentive program at ShoreBank in Chicago, and she has been a key member of the research teams for both ADD and SEED. She is currently working on a project with the Urban Institute and the Center for Social Development (CSD) at Washington University to assess the state of knowledge and research capacity to inform asset-based policy.

Ray Boshara directs the asset-building program at the New America Foundation. He was formerly policy director at the Corporation for Enterprise Development (CFED), and was also on the staff of the House Select Committee on Hunger. Mr. Boshara has led federal policy initiatives in IDAs and other asset-building strategies. He is the principal author of *Building Assets for Stronger Families, Better Neighborhoods, and Realizing the American Dream* (1998) and *Building Assets* (2001). In 2004 he was instrumental in introducing the ASPIRE Act in the U.S. Congress, which would create a universal and progressive children's savings account in the United States.

John P. Caskey is professor of economics at Swarthmore College. Over the past decade, his research has focused on financial institutions serving lower-income households. Among his publications are *Fringe Banking: Check-cashing Outlets, Pawnshops, and the Poor* (1994), *Lower Income Americans, Higher Cost Financial Services* (1997), and *Credit Unions and Asset Accumulation by Lower-Income Households* (1999, with David Humphrey). Taking a hiatus from his major research interest, Dr. Caskey is currently completing a study of the evolution of the Philadelphia Stock Exchange.

Ngina Chiteji is assistant professor of economics at Skidmore College. Among several other affiliations, she is a participant in the emerging scholars program at the Regional Poverty Center at University of Kentucky. Dr. Chiteji's fields of research and publication are monetary economics, development economics, and poverty and inequality. She has published articles in *Journal of International Development, American Economic Review Papers and Proceedings, Review of Black Political Economy,* and other journals. Her current research focuses on racial wealth inequality and interfamily transfers.

Margaret Clancy is project director at CSD, Washington University in St. Louis. A certified employee benefits specialist, Ms. Clancy formerly administered corporate 401(k) and defined benefit pension plans. She has been a key member of the research teams in both ADD and SEED, and has led a study of IDAs in Minnesota. At CSD Ms. Clancy has published several studies of college savings plans (529 plans), with a focus on inclusion of families with low incomes, and the potential of 529 plans as a structure for a universal children's savings account. Currently she leads planning and design of a universal children's savings account experiment in SEED.

Jami Curley is assistant professor at the School of Social Work, St. Louis University. Dr. Curley has studied asset-building strategies as a research team member in both ADD and SEED. She also undertook a background study of children's allowances in Western Europe with lessons for a children's savings account policy in the United States, published in *Child Welfare* (with Michael Sherraden). Dr. Curley focuses on program design features and their effects on savings and asset accumulation outcomes.

Robert Faris is a doctoral candidate in sociology at the University of North Carolina at Chapel Hill. He has served as assistant director of the Center for Community Capitalism on that campus, and is currently a research associate at the School of Public Health. His current work focuses on saving behavior and financial services.

Robert E. Friedman is the founder of CFED, which is known for innovations in community economic development and assessments of state and federal policies related to community and family development. Among Mr. Friedman's key publications is *The Safety Net as Ladder: Transfer Payments and Economic Development* (1988), which anticipated asset-based policy development. Mr. Friedman conceived of both ADD and SEED, garnered the funding to make them possible, and has guided implementation of these projects through CFED. He is currently directing the CFED West office in San Francisco.

Fred Goldberg is an attorney in the Washington, D.C., office of Skadden, Arps Slate, Meagher & Flom. Mr. Goldberg served as chief counsel of the Internal Revenue Service (1984–1986), IRS commissioner (1989–1992), and assistant secretary of the U.S. Treasury for tax policy (1992). He was executive director of the Kerrey-Danforth Bipartisan Commission on Entitlement and Tax Reform (1994–1995), a member of the National Commission on Restructuring the IRS (1996–1997), and a member of the National Commission on Retirement Policy (1997–1998). Mr. Goldberg is a longtime advocate of universal asset-building policy, with particular attention to the long-term potential of children's savings accounts.

Robert Greenstein is founder and executive director of the Center on Budget and Policy Priorities (CBPP), an independent, nonprofit organization established in 1981 to analyze federal and state budget and policy issues affecting low- and moderate-income Americans. In 1994, President Clinton appointed Mr. Greenstein to serve as a member of the Bipartisan Commission on Entitlement Reform. In 1979 and 1980 he served as administrator of the Food and Nutrition Service of the U.S. Department of Agriculture. Before that, he served as special assistant to the Secretary of Agriculture. Mr. Greenstein has contributed research reports and articles to many publications. Among many honors, he has received a public service achievement award from Common Cause (1991), a distinguished service award from the American Association for Budget and Program Analysis (1992), and a MacArthur Foundation fellowship (1996).

Michal Grinstein-Weiss is postdoctoral fellow at CSD, Washington University in St. Louis. During her doctoral studies, she received several awards, including a doctoral dissertation grant from the U.S. Department of Housing and Urban Development. Dr. Grinstein-Weiss was a member of the research team for ADD and has published several articles based on ADD research.

Her primary research interest is asset building among the poor, with attention to people of color and single mothers.

Darrick Hamilton is assistant professor in the School of Management and Urban Policy and affiliated with the Department of Economics at New School University. Dr. Hamilton was a Ford Foundation postdoctoral fellow at the Poverty Research and Training Program and the Program for Research on Black Americans at the University of Michigan at Ann Arbor, and a Robert Woods Johnson Foundation scholar in health policy research at Yale. His economic fields of study are health economics, economic development, poverty and inequality, and econometrics. Research articles have appeared in *American Economics Review, Journal of Economic Psychology, Social Science Quarterly,* and other journals. Dr. Hamilton's current research focus is on ethnic/racial inequality in economic and health outcomes.

Robert Haveman is John Bascom emeritus professor of economics and public policy at the University of Wisconsin at Madison. He is also a research affiliate at the Institute for Research on Poverty on that campus. Professor Haveman has served as director of the Institute for Research on Poverty (1970–1975), director of the Robert M. LaFollette Institute of Public Affairs (1988–1991), and chair of the Department of Economics (1993–1996). His books include *Starting Even: An Equal Opportunity Program to Combat the Nation's New Poverty* (1988) and *Succeeding Generations: On the Effects of Investments in Children* (1994, with Barbara Wolfe). He was coeditor of the *American Economic Review* from 1985 to 1991, and his work has been recognized by numerous appointments and awards, including the Harold Lasswell Prize in policy studies by the Policy Studies Association (1992). His current research concerns the assessment of resource adequacy of retired Americans and the intergenerational effects of growing income inequality.

Heather Beth Johnson is assistant professor of sociology at Lehigh University. Her research interests focus on intergenerational perpetuation of race and class inequality in the United States, the sociology of children and childhood, and dominant ideology. Dr. Johnson has a number of publications in these areas and she is currently completing her first book, *The American Dream and the Power of Wealth,* scheduled to appear in 2006.

Lissa Johnson is project director at CSD, Washington University in St. Louis, where she has been a member of several research teams. Ms. Johnson managed ADD research at CSD, and as part of this effort, she was the chief developer of the management information system for individual development accounts (MIS IDA), software used to manage IDA programs and simultaneously keep a database on participants and all savings transactions. Currently Ms. Johnson is working on research and information networks for a global project on civic service, and she is a member of the research team of "I Can Save," a children's savings study in a public school and one of the SEED study sites.

David Marzahl is executive director of the Center for Economic Progress in Chicago, a statewide organization that seeks to increase economic opportunities for low-income families and individuals by improving access to public, private and nonprofit programs and services. Previously, Mr. Marzahl was founding director of the Illinois Coalition for Immigrant & Refugee Rights, a statewide coalition of organizations promoting the rights of immigrants and refugees. Among many projects, he has helped to implement and study an incentivized savings program for the poor.

James Midgley is Harry and Riva Specht professor of public social services and dean of the School of Social Welfare at the University of California at Berkeley. He previously was on the faculty of Louisiana State University, the London School of Economics, and the University of Cape Town. He has published widely on issues of social policy, social development, and social work. His many book publications include *Social Welfare in Global Context* (1997), *The Handbook of Social Policy* (2000, edited with Martin Tracy and Michelle Livermore), and *Social Policy for Development* (2004, with Anthony Hall). Dr. Midgley's primary research interests are in social development and international social welfare.

Peter Orszag is Joseph A. Pechman senior fellow in economic studies at the Brookings Institution; codirector of the Tax Policy Center, a joint venture of the Urban Institute and Brookings Institution; director of the retirement security project; and research professor at Georgetown University. Dr. Orszag previously served as a special assistant to President Clinton, and as senior economist on the Council of Economic Advisers. Among many publications, he is coauthor of *Protecting the Homeland: A Preliminary Analysis* (2002) and coauthor of *Saving Social Security: A Balanced Approach* (2004, with Peter Diamond). He is also founder and president of Sebago Associates, Inc., an economic policy consulting firm. His current areas of research include pensions, budget and tax policy, Social Security, higher education, and homeland security.

Elaine C. Rideout is president of Economic Investment Strategies (EIS) Associates, a North Carolina consulting firm specializing in public investment issues and market-oriented public policies. She formerly served in the Reagan administration as the senior staff architect of the Federal Employee Retirement System and Thrift Savings Plan for federal employees. She also served as special assistant to the executive director of the Federal Retirement Thrift Investment Board, a federal agency she helped establish.

Jennifer L. Romich is assistant professor at the University of Washington School of Social Work. Her research interests are in working families and social policy. Dr. Romich engages in multi-method policy research, specializing in ethnography. Her research has appeared in *The National Tax Journal, Social Development Issues,* and other journals.

Edward Scanlon is associate professor at the University of Kansas School of Social Welfare. Dr. Scanlon is part of the research team for SEED, where he leads in-depth interviews with youth participants. In addition to SEED, his current research focuses on the relationship between housing conditions, housing tenure, home ownership, and child and family well-being.

Mark Schreiner is senior scholar at CSD, Washington University in St. Louis. He studies ways to help the poor build assets through both saving and credit. In the United States, his research interests are IDAs and micro-enterprise. He has been a key member of the research team in ADD and conducted the first cost study of an IDA program. He is lead author of *Can the Poor Save? Saving and Asset Building in Individual Development Accounts* (2005, with Michael Sherraden). In developing countries, Dr. Schreiner's research interest is microfinance, and he built the first credit-risk scorecards for microfinance organizations. He has published articles in *World Development, Savings and Development, Social Service Review, Economia,* and other journals.

Trina Williams Shanks is assistant professor at the University of Michigan School of Social Work, and formerly a Rhodes scholar. Her research interests include the impact of poverty and wealth on child development outcomes, community and economic development, and public policy affecting families. She has also studied estimated long-term effects of the Homestead Act. She is currently co-principal investigator in SEED, where she plays a key role in a quasi-experimental impact assessment of children's savings accounts in a Head Start program.

Thomas M. Shapiro is Prokross professor of law and social policy at the Heller School for Social Policy and Management, Brandeis University. Dr. Shapiro focuses primarily on wealth inequality by race. He coauthored *Black Wealth/ White Wealth* (1995, with Melvin Oliver), a book that received the C. Wright Mills Award from the Society for the Study of Social Problems (1995) and the Distinguished Scholarly Publication Award from the American Sociological Association (1997). Dr. Shapiro is also author of *The Hidden Cost of Being African American: How Wealth Perpetuates Inequality* (2004). He is editor of *Great Divides: Readings in Inequality in the United States* (third edition, 2004) and coeditor of *Assets for the Poor: The Benefits of Spreading Asset Ownership* (2001, with Edward N. Wolff). Dr. Shapiro's current project is a tenth-anniversary edition of *Black Wealth/White Wealth.*

Michael Sherraden is Benjamin E. Youngdahl professor of social development and founding director of CSD, Washington University in St. Louis.

In *Assets and the Poor: A New American Welfare Policy* (1991), he articulated the concept of asset-based development, which suggests that social policy should promote not merely consumption, but also savings and investment across the entire population. As a policy strategy, Dr. Sherraden suggested matched savings in the form of IDAs. At CSD he has led research teams for ADD and SEED and other projects intended to inform a more inclusive asset-based policy. His research interests in this area are how saving and asset accumulation occur and the effects of holding assets.

Timothy M. Smeeding is the Maxwell professor of public policy, director of the Center for Policy Research, and associate dean of the Maxwell School of Public Policy at Syracuse University. He is also director of the Luxembourg Income Study, which he founded in 1983. Dr. Smeeding's research is focused on economic inequality, poverty, and public policy toward vulnerable groups such as children, the aged, and the disabled. He has recently authored *Poor Kids in a Rich Country* (2003) and *The Economics of Aging* (2004), and edited *Future of the Family* (2004, with Daniel Patrick Moynihan). Two coauthored volumes are in preparation: *Supporting Children* and *Immigration in Europe.* Dr. Smeeding is currently working on a book that examines effects of inequality on social outcomes such as health, public goods, educational opportunity, and crime.

Michael A. Stegman is MacRae professor of public policy and business, chair of the Department of Public Policy, and director of the Center for Community Capitalism at the University of North Carolina at Chapel Hill. Previously he served as assistant secretary for policy development and research at the U.S. Department of Housing and Urban Development. Dr. Stegman has written extensively on housing and urban policy, and he was founding editor of *Cityscape*, a journal of urban policy research. Among his book publications are *Savings and the Poor: The Hidden Benefits of Electronic Banking* (1999) and *State and Local Affordable Housing Programs: A Rich Tapestry* (1999). He is currently leading studies of access to banking and financial services, with particular interests in mortgage financing for home ownership.

Jennifer Tescher is director of the Center for Financial Services Innovation, an initiative of ShoreBank Advisory Services (SAS), the research and consulting arm of ShoreBank, a leading community development bank. Previously, she worked in retail delivery of financial services, where she oversaw ShoreBank saving innovations such as IDAs and a program to link saving to the Earned Income Tax Credit. Under Ms. Tescher's direction, ShoreBank was one of the demonstration and research sites for ADD. She publishes, consults, and speaks widely on these topics, and she is president of the board of the Center for Economic Progress.

Edward N. Wolff is a professor of economics at New York University, senior scholar at the Levy Economics Institute at Bard College, and research associate at the National Bureau of Economic Research. He has served as managing editor of the *Review of Income and Wealth* (1987–2004) and president of the Eastern Economics Association (2002–2003). His principal areas of scholarship are income and wealth distributions and productivity growth. For many years Dr. Wolff has been the leading U.S. scholar in charting wealth distributions, and he has made contributions in alternative measures of well being. He is the author of *Growth, Accumulation, and Unproductive Activity* (1987), *Productivity and American Leadership* (1989), *TOP HEAVY: A Study of Increasing Inequality of Wealth in America* (1995), *Retirement Insecurity* (2002), and *Downsizing in America* (2003).

Min Zhan is assistant professor of social work at the University of Illinois at Champaign-Urbana. Her research interests are the impact of welfare reform on the well-being of women and poor children, and asset-building policy and programs. Dr. Zhan was a member of the research team for ADD. Based on ADD research and other data sets, she has published several articles on education, assets, and well-being outcomes among low-income single mothers. Dr. Zhan is currently designing an IDA-like demonstration and research project in Jinan, Shandong Province, China.

Introduction

Michael Sherraden

Asset building is a rapidly growing policy theme in the United States and in many other countries. The ideas of ownership and development are beginning to play a greater role in public policy, taking a place alongside the traditional welfare state ideas of income support and protection.

This change is not always well understood. Defenders of the welfare state may see asset-based policy as contrary to—or even as a threat to—traditional social policies. In fact, both protection and development are important; income-based and asset-based policies are complementary. Proponents of asset-based policy, especially on the political Right, may describe it as "privatization," but the policies are defined and regulated by government, often with large public subsidies. Much of the general public—and many authors of social policy books—seem not to notice asset-based policy at all because it operates largely through tax expenditures, which do not draw nearly as much attention as direct expenditures.

As demonstrated in this volume's chapters, asset-based policies are already extensively in place for the nonpoor in the United States. They operate through mechanisms such as public expenditures for higher education, property-enhancing public services, home mortgage interest tax deductions, tax deferments on retirement savings, and other mechanisms. In contrast, the poor in the United States are disproportionately left out of these asset-building policies.

This book is about *inclusion* in the American dream of asset holding and how public policy might promote and facilitate that dream for everyone, at every income level and of every color. The book examines patterns of saving and asset accumulation in multiple policy and program settings, as well as potential impacts of asset holding. Theoretical, measurement, and empirical issues are addressed, as is design of inclusive asset-based policies. The final chapters address critical questions regarding inclusion in asset-based policies and challenges for knowledge building.

A main purpose of this book is to bring together ideas, theory, measurement, analysis, and policy. This is an ambitious but necessary agenda if academic inquiry is to be relevant to application. Scholarship in asset-based policy over the past dozen years reflects this bridging. It is a good example of applied social science, emphasizing theory, measurement, and outcomes yet with an eye—and sometimes a hand—on policy. This book has excellent authors for both research and policy chapters, and most of the authors have worked across the research-to-policy bridge.

In part I, chapter 1 takes up in greater detail the policy context in which academic study and policy applications can be considered. It suggests Amartya Sen's seminal work on people's capabilities to attain what they have reason to value as a departure point for understanding the shift to asset-based policy; it also explains why greater inclusion is desirable and raises questions and challenges to this policy direction. The following chapter, "The Homestead Act: A Major Asset-Building Policy in American History," by Trina Williams Shanks, is a demographic assessment of who among the U.S. population living today had ancestors who benefited from the Homestead Act. Shanks's major and very early example of asset-based policy helps set the stage for the rest of the book, orienting the reader to the strength of this idea in the American experience. The Homestead Act arose from a Jeffersonian perspective on benefits of property holding for build- ing families, citizens, and the economy, and Shanks worked with demog- raphers at Oxford University and the University of California to develop estimates of its possible long-term impacts. This policy from 140 years ago may continue to have effects many generations later, even among those who have no knowledge that their ancestors were homesteaders. Next, James Midgley lays out the policy and political terrain in chapter 3, entitled "Asset- Based Policy in Historical and International Perspective." Midgley has a broad and comprehensive grasp of social policy. He provides an overview of policy theory and how asset building can be understood in historical con- text and in international comparison. This assessment is essential for placing the chapters that follow in perspective.

Part II, "Asset Holding and Well Being," consists of four empirical studies that address the meaning and measurement of asset holding and its potential effects on well-being. To begin, Robert Haveman and Edward Wolff present one of the first studies on measures of asset poverty, "Who Are the Asset Poor? Levels, Trends and Composition, 1983–1998." Following an asset-poverty measure by Melvin Oliver and Thomas Shapiro (1995), the Haveman and Wolff study is a more comprehensive attempt to measure asset poverty for the United States—and a necessary step if we are to define poverty in these terms and create public policies to build assets. Next, in their chapter "Family Matters: Kin Networks and Asset Accumulation," Ngina Chiteji and Darrick Hamilton look at kin networks and wealth, finding that asset deprivation in extended families of African Americans decreases asset accumulation in nuclear families. This finding may have important impli- cations for asset-building strategies across race. Following this, Thomas Shapiro and Heather Beth Johnson's "Family Assets and School Access: Race and Class in the Structuring of Educational Opportunity" details the role of wealth in educational options and choices among families of different racial backgrounds. Shapiro and Johnson's inquiries into asset holding and use by race, and into how public policy has shaped asset accumulation and de-accumulation for different racial groups in the past, inform our view of an appropriate role of the public sector in asset building. In this part's final chapter, "Home Ownership and Youth Well-Being," Edward Scanlon and Deborah Adams examine effects of homeownership on social outcomes for youth, finding modest positive effects, a pattern that is consistent with a growing body of research.

Turning to part III, "Saving and Asset Accumulation among the Poor," four chapters focus on how saving and asset accumulation occur, particularly among low-income, low-wealth populations. The first chapter here, "Reaching Out to the Unbanked," was written by John Caskey, who previously undertook pioneering research in this area in his book *Fringe Banking* (1994). His chapter provides insights and research-based proposals on financial services. The next chapter, "Linking Tax Refunds and Low-Cost Bank Accounts to Bank the Unbanked," coauthored by Sondra Beverly, Jennifer Tescher, Jennifer Romich, and David Marzahl, examines a program of saving incentives offered by ShoreBank in Chicago. Beverly and colleagues find that saving can be incentivized, at least for the short-term, and their chapter points to the potential of joining the Earned Income Tax Credit (EITC) with progressive savings policies. This analysis may have particular policy importance because the EITC, due to its large distributions (over $30 billion per year) and lump sum payout, might be a significant source of savings and asset building. In chapter 10, Mark Schreiner and his colleagues, Margaret Clancy, Lissa Johnson, Jami Curley, Min Zhan, Sondra Beverly, Michal Grinstein-Weiss, and I, discuss "Assets and the Poor: Evidence from Individual Development Accounts." [Individual development accounts (IDAs) are matched savings designed to include the poor.] They find that IDA participants can save, and the saving amount is only slightly related to income; indeed, it appears that institutional features of the IDA program, including match caps, financial education, direct deposit, and other features, play important roles in savings performance. The final chapter in this part, "The Impacts of IDA Programs on Family Savings and Asset Holdings," by Michael Stegman and Robert Faris, discusses effects of IDA programs on family savings and net worth. Stegman and Faris estimate that net worth does not increase. The studies of IDAs are among the first empirical assessments of saving behavior and outcomes among low-income individuals who participate in a subsidized savings program in the United States. Given growing policy interest in this concept, these empirical assessments have already contributed to legislative discussions and proposals.

Part IV, "Toward an Inclusive Asset-Building Policy," offers five chapters that could well inform a large-scale and inclusive U.S. asset-based policy. "Going to Scale: Principles and Policy Options for an Inclusive Asset-Building Policy" was written by Robert Friedman and Ray Boshara, who have provided leadership in asset-based policy discussions in Washington, D.C., including IDAs as well as proposals for universal savings accounts (USAs) and children's savings accounts (CSAs). The authors lay out a broad range of policy considerations and possible pathways. The next chapter, by Peter Orszag and Robert Greenstein, is entitled "Toward Progressive Pensions: A Summary of the U.S. Pension System and Proposals for Reform." These policy analysts point out the large inequalities in public benefits in pension coverage and offer suggestions for policy changes. In chapter 14, "The Thrift Savings Plan Experience: Implications for a Universal Asset Account Initiative," Elaine Rideout, one of the architects of the federal Thrift Savings Plan (TSP), examines the TSP for lessons that might apply to a large and inclusive asset-building policy. Chapter 15, "The Universal Piggy Bank: Designing and Implementing a System of Savings Accounts for Children" was written by Fred Goldberg, who served as commissioner of the Internal Revenue Service in the George H. W. Bush administration and has for many years proposed a universal children's savings account policy. Concluding this part, Timothy Smeeding presents his study, "The EITC and USAs/IDAs: Maybe a Marriage Made in Heaven?" Smeeding asks EITC recipients how they have used the tax refund and then considers policy implications for matched savings. He finds that EITC recipients view their lump sum payments differently from their ordinary income stream; they tend to use it for larger payments or purchases. The chapters in part IV, all by highly regarded analysts, deal with large-scale policy and provide design frameworks that could help guide future policy.

The final section of the book, part V, "Assessment and Directions," begins with valuable skepticism in Jared Bernstein's "Critical Questions in Asset-Based Policy," which offers concerns from a Left-liberal perspective. Bernstein's is not the only questioning voice in the book—many other authors also raise tough questions. In the next chapter, "Inclusion in Asset Building: Directions for Theory and Research," I join my colleagues at the Center for Social Development, Edward Scanlon, Deborah Adams, Sondra Beverly, and Mark Schreiner, in reviewing theory and research and suggesting directions in two important areas of scholarship: how savings and assets develop and the effects of asset holding. Analyzing how savings and assets develop may inform better policy design, while an assessment of the effects of asset holding may provide a potential rationale for asset-based policy. In both of these key areas, knowledge building has barely begun. The conclusion provides an assessment and commentary on the contents of the volume, its contributions, and the work that remains to be done.

Together, the chapters here contribute to academic and policy discussions on the nature and measurement of poverty, the historical context of asset inequality, family saving behavior, asset-holding dynamics within families, effects of asset holding, and implications and options for public policy. The book as a whole is part of a growing body of theory and research that examines assets as a measure of poverty and a potential tool for development.

It seems quite likely that broader definitions of poverty and more diverse policy responses will be emerging in the years ahead. This book's incisive essays question whether asset building should play a larger role in public policy, whether the poor can be included in asset-based policies that exist today, and whether and how new policies might be created in the future.

PART I

CONTEXT

Inclusion in the American Dream begins with a purpose and rationale. The purpose is inclusion of the poor in asset-building policies. The rationale is that assets are essential for long-term development of families and communities, and large asset-building policies already exist for the nonpoor. The introduction has already oriented the reader with an overview of the book, which combines leading scholarship, analysis of existing policy strategies, and policy design.

Chapter 1 provides a more in-depth look at the context for asset-based policy. Although this discussion began in the United States, it is noteworthy that some of the most exciting work in asset-based policy today is occurring in the United Kingdom, especially the creation of the Child Trust Fund, an account for every newborn with greater initial deposits for poor children. It seems likely that this policy, once implemented over several birth cohorts, will be very popular with the U.K. public and possibly copied by other countries. If so, fifty years from now scholars may look back at the Child Trust Fund as a turning point toward universal and progressive asset-based policy.

The next chapter, by Trina Williams Shanks, on the Homestead Act provides a key backdrop to American history. The Homestead Act was at once a major asset-based policy and a reflection of the social philosophy of property ownership upon which the United States was founded. Shanks's study is the first empirical assessment of the lasting impact of this act. She asks a simple and fundamental question: How many people living today have an ancestor who benefited from the Homestead Act? The estimated answer is surprisingly large. In many instances, the Americans affected do not even know they have a family heritage of publicly provided asset endowment. As Shanks documents, the Homestead Act benefited primarily European Americans, and the long-term impacts were not equal by race.

The chapter 3 contribution of James Midgley looks at asset-based policy in a larger context and offers his interpretation of it as a "productivist" policy, oriented toward "social investment." One or both of these terms may eventually become common in discussions of asset-based policy. Midgley is not starry-eyed in how he views asset-based policy, recognizing significant downsides, but he also sees the possibility of moving forward with a progressive agenda that has potential to attract broad political support.

1

Assets and Public Policy

Michael Sherraden

Poverty and development are determined by resources, broadly defined. But what constitutes "resources" is open to many alternative theories and measures. As noted by Robert Haveman and Edward Wolff in their chapter in this book, there is today growing discussion about conceptualizations and indicators of poverty and well-being, occurring in the wake of ideological and political challenges to the welfare state that evolved in the late twentieth century. This will likely be a fruitful inquiry and debate, though it is impossible to predict where the discussion and research will lead and what policies might eventually result. In this book, we explore one possible direction—a focus on tangible and financial assets as a measure of poverty and a strategy for household development.

INCOME POVERTY AND POLICY

Academic discussions of poverty and well-being have focused on measures of income, where income is considered a proxy for consumption and sometimes serves as a direct measure of consumption and/or hardship. This general approach has characterized research on poverty in the advanced economies during most of the past century and has markedly influenced social policy. Income support policy occurs mostly through social insurance, but also through universal grants ("demogrants") and means-tested social assistance ("welfare"), with different policy mixtures in different countries. The idea of income support to individuals and families, in cash or in kind, has been an almost singular idea of welfare states, making up 80 to 90 percent of social expenditures in economically advanced nations, where social expenditures typically comprise more than 50 percent of all public spending. Thus, income support may represent, in a fiscal sense, 40 percent or more of modern states' total public expenditures. By any standard, this is a stunning impact for a single idea. Remarkably, however, it has been largely taken for granted. Although the pathway is difficult to document, it seems likely that intellectual work in microeconomics, wherein consumption is considered equivalent to welfare, has had a huge impact on the policy content of welfare states. It is perhaps a sign of the overwhelming dominance of this perspective that it has gone steadily forward at such a large scale, and only a few scholars or policy analysts have found reason to question this viewpoint or raise other possibilities.

Nonetheless, income support policies have not worked very well from a development perspective. These policies have achieved large reductions in posttransfer poverty, for example, especially among the elderly in the United States, but by and large income policies have not reduced pretransfer poverty over time (e.g., Danziger and Plotnick, 1986). In other words, income transfers have not enabled poor households to develop. For this reason, income support by itself is not sufficient as a public policy.

TOWARD CAPACITY BUILDING

The past two decades have witnessed increasing attention to alternatives to income measures of poverty, and to income support as a singular strategy. Overall, these alternatives can be characterized as moving beyond the idea of consumption-as-well-being, toward what Amartya Sen (1985, 1993, 1999) identifies as increasing functionings or capabilities, such as increasing the capacity of people to attain what they have reason to value. In large measure, this thinking comes out of research and policy in social and economic development in less developed nations. Asset-based definitions of poverty have been prominent in development studies, which occur in "less developed" (that is, more impoverished) countries. In these countries, widespread income support policy is not affordable, and attention has been directed toward development. For the most part, "poverty" scholarship in the richer nations and "development" scholarship in the poorer nations have been distinct fields of inquiry and policy making. The subject matter is basically the same, but the policies, programs, measures, and research methods are mostly different. With Sen's reformulations, it could be that the boundaries between these fields of inquiry will not be as distinct in the future as they have been in the past.

In the language of social intervention, increasing people's capabilities as an approach to well-being focuses on *building capacities* for social and economic development more than on maintaining a certain level of consumption. Capacity building aims to increase individual and household resources, connections, knowledge, and abilities to function more effectively, to solve problems, and to increase well-being along multiple dimensions. The emphasis is on long-term development more than on maintenance of a current standard of living. The aim is to find interventions that provide a foundation for individuals' future growth and that eventually yield multiple positive outcomes.

Capacity building should not be considered a replacement or alternative to income support as a policy strategy. The two are complementary. Current income and consumption obviously matter, and so do long-term growth and development. The challenges for academics and policy makers are to specify the meaning of different approaches, gather empirical evidence, and make policy decisions that include an appropriate balance between short-term support and long-term development.

A major form of capacity building is development of human capital. There is little doubt that human capital is typically the single most important form of capital for individuals, households, business enterprises, and nations. Gary Becker has estimated that human capital may represent 75 percent of total wealth. Moreover, with the transition from the industrial era to the information era, human capital will play an ever greater role. If human capital is 75 percent of all wealth today, it will be 80 percent tomorrow. As Theodore Schultz (1959) suggested more than four decades ago, human capital should probably be the primary theme of social policy and programs. Beginning about mid-twentieth century, economists began pointing to the importance of human capital, but since that time only a few measures of human capital, other than years of education, have been created. One innovative approach is by Haveman and Andrew Berkshadker (1998), who offer a measure of net earnings capacity.

Others have focused on social capital, with key work by James Coleman (1988) and Robert Putnam (1995). Social capital refers to interpersonal relationships and the resources they provide. This is a widely appealing idea, and there is a beginning body of empirical work, but a well-specified theory of social capital has not yet developed. Quite likely there will have to be greater specification of what social capital is, what causes it, and what its effects are (that is, a theory or theories) before good measures of social capital at the individual or household level can be created, hypotheses tested, and policy applications designed and implemented.

Taking a different tack, Michael Sherraden (1988, 1991) suggests tangible and financial assets as a strategy for development and offers general propositions on likely welfare effects of asset holding, such as increased orientation toward the future, increased self-efficacy, increased civic participation, and improved welfare of offspring. These propositions are well short of an integrated theory or theories, but they suggest research agendas in which hypotheses can be specified and tested. The practical rationale behind this thinking is that the nonpoor seem to benefit from asset-building policies to which the poor, for the most part, do not have access.

Asset accounts as a policy instrument can, of course, be used for other forms of asset building, especially human capital. For example, one of the main purposes of proposals for children or youth accounts is to help finance education and training. In contrast to most economically developed nations, the United States has never enacted a monthly children's allowance, but a child savings account for education may have greater political potential (Curley and Sherraden, 2000).

WELFARE STATE IN TRANSITION

The welfare state, created in the twentieth century, may be undergoing a
major change. Gilbert describes a shift away from social entitlements and
toward private responsibility, with an "enabling state" treating individuals as actors who are capable of looking after themselves with some
assistance from the government, not as totally passive recipients of pubic
benefits and services (Gilbert, 1995; Gilbert and Gilbert, 1989). In a somewhat different but complementary interpretation, James Midgley (1999;
see also chapter 3 in this volume) describes the "productivist" nature
of current trends and the emergence of "social investment" as a policy
theme. It seems possible that twenty-first century social policy may move
beyond consumption support, aiming for social and economic development of households, communities, and societies as a whole (Sherraden,
1997, 2003).[1]

In conjunction with this shift in social policy, a reformulation of the
political-economic consensus of the welfare state may be underway, though
it is not yet well articulated. The consensus of the twentieth century was
that if the market economy was sufficiently productive, it could be taxed
to support social expenditures. These social expenditures were assumed to
be a diversion of capital from production and, therefore, a drag on economic growth. Using Sen's formulation, however, if social policy increased
people's capabilities, then it could be a sound investment. Going forward,
the assumed competition between social protection and economic growth
may be attenuated by a greater recognition that social spending for some
purposes and/or in some forms can contribute to economic growth.

The typical American middle-class household accumulates most of its
tangible and financial assets in home equity and retirement accounts, both
of which are subsidized through the tax system. These public policies are
highly popular and have little political opposition. Most everyone agrees
that asset accumulation is good for households and good for the country.
But the poor, for the most part, do not participate in these asset accumulation policies. Would everyone, particularly the poorest Americans, benefit
from asset-based policy? How can public policy promote asset accumulation for all Americans? These questions are being raised by a number of
scholars, and systematic studies of saving and asset accumulation by the
poor are underway.

THE TREND TOWARD ASSET ACCOUNTS

The original purpose of income-based policy was to support people when
they did not have income from industrial labor markets. But the world has
changed considerably since income-based policies were initiated. To be
sure, people still require income security when they are not employed, but
income alone is no longer enough; the labor market of the information age

requires that people have resources to invest in themselves throughout their lifetimes. In effect, people may require greater control in making their own "social policy" decisions across their life spans. With less stable employment, workers will need to carry fully portable benefits with them in and out of the labor market, from employer to employer, even across national boundaries. "Retirement" is likely to be redefined as a less rigid period of the life course, and Americans will want greater flexibility in how they live in their older years (Morrow-Howell, Hinterlong, and Sherraden, 2001). Also, policy should promote wealth accumulation across generations, so that more children begin life in households with at least some financial resources (Oliver and Shapiro, 1995). Asset accounts are better suited for these conditions.

In part for these reasons, a shift to asset-based policy is underway. Around the world it is uncommon to encounter a new or expanding policy of social insurance or social assistance but common to find a new or expanding policy of asset accounts. For a long time, provident funds (defined contribution pensions managed by government), with their very mixed record, were the major examples of social security based on individual accounts (Dixon, 1989). Today, the relatively successful provident funds of Singapore and Malaysia (Asher, 1991; Sherraden et al., 1995; Vasoo and Lee, 2001) have been joined by systems of individual accounts in much of Latin America (the most well-known example is in Chile; e.g., see Borzutsky, 1997). Australia has created a system of superannuation largely to replace its means tested retirement policy (Rosenman, 1997). Less remarked upon but perhaps most noteworthy is the rapid rise of individual accounts as "add on" policies in Western Europe and the United States. For the most part, these policies are not considered part of social policy systems. Nonetheless, asset-based policies are becoming an important form of social policy for many people in Western societies. This is true even in the traditional welfare states of Sweden and the United Kingdom.

In the United States, this shift can been seen in the introduction and growth of 401(k)s, 403(b)s, individual retirement accounts (IRAs), Roth IRAs, the Federal Thrift Savings Plan, educational savings accounts, medical savings accounts, individual training accounts, state college savings plans ("529 plans"), and proposed individual accounts in Social Security. Some of these are public, and some are called "private," but it is important to note that the "private" plans are defined by public laws and regulations and receive substantial subsidies through reduced tax obligations, which the Congressional Budget Office calls "tax expenditures." In an accounting sense, tax expenditures are not different from direct expenditures, only a different way of distributing public benefits. Looking at the purpose of existing asset accounts, primarily for retirement security, it would be appropriate to call these "welfare transfers" to the nonpoor elderly. Of course, this is not what we say. Most people with a 401(k) want to believe they have been prudent in saving for their retirement in a private-sector account, and that they are responsible for the accumulation of this wealth.

All of the above asset account policies have been introduced in the United States since 1970, and different uses are emerging. At present, asset accumulations in 529 plans for education are expanding rapidly. Overall, asset accounts, for various purposes, are a creative and expanding area of social policy, in contrast with new forms of direct social expenditures, which are relatively infrequent. In brief, direct social expenditures are under political attack, while tax expenditures for social benefits enjoy widespread, bipartisan political support. In this atmosphere, it seems likely that the shift to asset-based policy will continue.

ASSET-BASED POLICY IS REGRESSIVE

Unfortunately, asset-based policies as they have appeared to date are less inclusive and more regressive than income-based policies. There are major questions of both coverage and adequacy. For example, see the critiques of Singapore by Mukul Asher (1991), of Chile by Silvia Borzutsky (1997), and of Australia by Linda Rosenman (1997). To date, no country in the world has instituted a substantial asset-based policy that is universal and progressive.[2] Asset-based policies have greatly favored the rich and the middle class over the poor.

In the United States, the reasons for this favoritism toward the nonpoor are twofold: first, the poor typically do not participate in the asset-based policies that currently exist; for example, most of the poor do not have jobs that offer 401(k)s. And second, asset-based policies operate primarily through tax expenditures that benefit the poor little or not at all because the poor have little or no tax obligation (Sherraden, 1991). The tax policies could theoretically be refundable, meaning that those with no tax obligation could get a payment from the government (a form of negative income tax), but the U.S. Congress is very reluctant to enact refundable tax credits (the only major exception is the Earned Income Tax Credit).

All asset-based policies that we are aware of do not have refundable tax credits, and nearly all of the public benefits go the nonpoor. Tax expenditures to individuals for asset accounts, home ownership, and financial or business investments total more than $300 billion per year.[3] (To assess the scope of this, $300 billion is roughly equivalent to 25 percent of all direct federal social expenditures, including Social Security, Medicare, and all other programs; $300 billion is much more than we spend on all programs combined that are targeted to the poor, including Medicaid, food stamps, income transfers, rent subsidies, and others.) Well over 90 percent of this $300 billion goes to households that earn over $50,000 per year. For example, in 1999, two-thirds of tax benefits for pensions in the United States accrued to the top 20 percent of households, while only 2.1 percent went to the bottom 40 percent (Orszag and Greenstein, chapter 13 in this volume).

This point bears repeating: Public policies for asset building are making the comfortable more comfortable, the rich richer, and leaving the poor as they are. I emphasize this point because the common perception of social policy in the United States is that resources are redistributed downward from the rich to the poor by the federal government. This is to some extent true for direct expenditures, but it is decidedly not true for tax expenditures. There is a large and somewhat "hidden" asset-based policy in the United States (Howard, 1997; Seidman, 2001). Many people accumulate assets and do so in a manner that cannot accurately be described as "saving." Rather, for most Americans, most assets accumulate in structured systems that are defined, regulated, and subsidized by public policy.

Most Americans with retirement accounts, home equity, and financial and business investments seem to be largely unaware that they receive subsidies for these assets.[4] If the nature, scope, and effects of existing asset-based policies were better understood, would the general public support greater inclusion of the poor?

RATIONALES FOR AN INCLUSIVE ASSET-BASED POLICY

In my view, a major policy goal should be educating the general public about existing asset-based policy while working toward greater inclusion of the poor. The rationales are *fairness* and *practicality*. The reasoning for fairness is outlined above. If we are to have $300 billion per year in asset accumulation subsidies, why not distribute the money equally? Let us take a concrete example. The home mortgage interest tax deduction today subsidizes luxury housing. There is no good policy rationale for this; it is an inefficient use of scarce public funds, and it distorts investment flows into large, underutilized houses, an unproductive use of capital. As it stands, wealthy home owners may collect $20,000 or more in housing tax benefits per year, while poor home owners collect nothing. At a minimum, why not give everyone the same benefit? If distributed equally, the benefit would be about $1,000 per home owner. But even this would be questionable public policy. What is the rationale for assisting rich home owners? I would prefer a progressive policy, one that gave more to the poor, so that home ownership could be extended as broadly as possible.

The reasoning for *practicality* is that asset holding may have multiple positive effects beyond its potential for future consumption (Sherraden, 1991). Asset holding may lead to greater confidence, stronger families, more positive social relations, and increased civic participation. In Sen's (1999) language, assets may be one pathway to increase capabilities. Indeed, positive effects of asset holding are widely believed to be true. This is bedrock social philosophy in America and a reflection of the Jeffersonian idea of small property holding as the basis of a thriving democracy. If positive "asset effects" do occur, then inclusive asset-based policy would be a sound public investment. Unfortunately, the effects of asset holding have not been a central question in applied social research, as social scientists have focused more on the effects of income and education. Existing research, scattered across academic disciplines, indicates multiple positive effects of asset hold-ing, but as in much of social science, many studies have not been rigorous enough; thus, their results have to be considered tentative. Major intellec-tual challenges lie ahead in theoretically specifying how effects of assets might occur, as well as in undertaking sound research to test whether or not they do occur, for whom, and in what circumstances. This is a long-term project. In the interim, it may be prudent to assume that the American people and the nation are better off when asset holding is widely distrib-uted. Thomas Jefferson was probably on the right track about this, though Jefferson's vision of who should own property in America should be revised to include people of every race, gender, and nationality (see Conley, 1998; Oliver and Shapiro, 1990, 1995; Shapiro, 2004).

ASSET-BASED POLICY DISCUSSIONS IN THE UNITED STATES

The focus on asset-based policies for the poor is not to seek targeted poli-cies for the poor; in fact, the original proposal for individual development accounts (IDAs) was to include the poor in large-scale, matched savings policies. In this regard, there has been some degree of progress.

Influence of IDAs

In his State of the Union address on January 27, 2000, President Bill Clinton cited the experience of IDAs in proposing a large-scale, progressive asset-based policy:

> Tens of millions of Americans live from paycheck to paycheck. As hard as they work, they still don't have the opportunity to save. Too few can make use of IRAs and 401(k) plans. We should do more to help all working families save and accumulate wealth. That's the idea behind the Individual Development Accounts, the IDAs.[5] I ask you to take that idea to a new level, with new retire-ment savings accounts that enable every low- and moderate-income family in America to save for retirement, a first home, a medical emergency, or a college education. I propose to match their contributions, however small, dollar for dol-lar, every year they save.

Occasions when government leaders have made large and progressive asset-building proposals have been few, but they are becoming more com-mon. In the United States, President Clinton proposed universal savings accounts in 1999, which would be like a 401(k) for all workers, with deposits and matching funds for those with the lowest incomes, at a projected expenditure level of $33 billion per year. This was a huge vision of pro-gressive asset-based policy, but the proposal went nowhere in Congress during 1999. In 2000, it was reduced considerably in size and called retire-ment saving accounts, which also went nowhere. During the presidential campaign of 2000, Al Gore proposed a version of this plan called Retirement

Savings Plus, which was to be a progressive add-on to Social Security. In addition, both Republican and Democratic members of Congress have proposed universal children's savings accounts in recent years. However, none of these large-scale, progressive, asset-building proposals has yet become law in the United States.

During the 2000 presidential campaign, George W. Bush proposed $1 billion in tax credits to financial institutions that agreed to match savings of the poor in IDAs. His proposal was similar to a bill under consideration in the Congress known as the Savings for Working Families Act (SWFA).[6] During the campaign, Governor Bush (2000) said:

> If a low-income person is able to save up to three hundred dollars, we will encourage banks, with a federal tax credit, to match that amount. The money can then be withdrawn tax free to pay for education, to help start a business or buy a home.
> ... The great promise of our time is to fight poverty by building the wealth of the poor. A home to anchor their family. A bank account to create confidence. And, I believe, a personal Social Security account, which would give millions of low income Americans, not just a check, but an asset to own, a stake in our prosperity.

After taking office, President Bush has continued to support the SWFA during 2001, 2002, 2003, and 2004. At this writing it has not been enacted. The legislation has passed both the House and Senate, supported by the White House, but has yet to make it out of the House-Senate Conference Committee.

Social Security Commission

Following a campaign promise, President Bush created the Commission to Strengthen Social Security, whose members all favored some version of individual accounts, and the president charged them to produce a plan that included individual accounts (U.S. Commission to Strengthen Social Security, 2001a). The Commission reported in December 2001 with three options for allowing workers to establish individual investment accounts. They also acknowledged that the proposals would have to be accompanied by benefit cuts or tax increases to ensure that the retirement system would be able to avert a financial crisis.

Under the first option, workers could invest up to 2.0 percentage points of the 6.2 percent payroll tax on earnings up to $80,400, with retirement benefit reductions. Otherwise, there would be no change in the current system of benefits. Under the second option, workers could invest up to 4.0 percentage points, up to a maximum of $1,000 per year, with retirement benefit reductions. Under the third option, workers could contribute up to 1.0 percent of their earnings beyond their current payroll taxes, which would be matched by 2.5 percentage points of their payroll taxes, to a maximum of $1,000. The second and third options would also guarantee a minimum benefit package to low-income workers and widows/widowers with 30 or more years in the system, at 120 percent of the poverty line (U.S. Commission to Strengthen Social Security, 2001b).[7]

In the current political climate, which includes a return of federal budget deficits and a focus on fighting terrorism at home and abroad, the Commission's proposals have not attracted much attention. Any proposal that calls for reducing benefits or raising payroll taxes is unlikely to be embraced by members of Congress. Thus, proposals from the Commission were political nonstarters before they arrived. Nonetheless, the issue of individual accounts related to the U.S. Social Security system is unlikely to go away. It has great popular appeal, particularly among the young, and it will probably return to the political agenda. At the beginning of his second term in 2005, President Bush made this a priority.

As Sherraden (2001b) testified before the Commission, if there are to be individual accounts related to Social Security, they should be add-ons to (not carve-outs from) the existing social insurance policy, and there should be progressive funding of accounts of the poor.

PLANS FOR "SAVING AND ASSETS FOR ALL" IN THE UNITED KINGDOM

A serious discussion of asset-based policy began in the United Kingdom in 2000 (Institute for Public Policy Research, 2001; Kelly and Lissauer, 2000; Nissan and LeGrand, 2000). In a major policy development in April 2001, Prime Minister Tony Blair proposed a Child Trust Fund for all children in the United Kingdom, along with progressive funding. He also proposed a demonstration of a Saving Gateway, matched saving for the poor.[8] Blair (2001) said, "As a Government, we are committed to extending power, wealth, and opportunity to the many, not just the few." He offered a vision of inclusion in the following statements:

> I believe we have already made important strides in extending opportunity for all—through improving skills and work, through improving living standards and through improving the quality of public services.
>
> But now we want to add a fourth element: more people getting the benefit of assets and savings, so that we help spread prosperity and opportunity to every family and community.
>
> Because now too many young children are still excluded from the chance to go to university, to own their own home, to have financial security or a career, I want to see all children grown up knowing that they have a financial stake in society. I want to see all children have the opportunity of a real financial springboard to a better education, a better job, a better home—a better life. I want to see every child make the most of themselves.[9]

Child Trust Fund

The United Kingdom's Child Trust Fund is to be based on the principle of *progressive universalism*, wherein every baby would receive an endowment, but those in families on lower incomes would receive a larger lump sum. Following a Labour Party campaign promise and planning period, Prime Minister Blair announced in April 2003 that he would go forward with the Child Trust Fund.[10] Beginning in 2005 and retroactive to September of 2002, each newborn child will be given an account at birth with a deposit of at least £250. Children in families from the bottom third of the income distribution will receive an initial deposit of £500. Additional government deposits, as yet unspecified, are to be made as the child grows up. Contributions can be made by parents, relatives, or friends. Parents can invest in a wide range of investment options in the private sector that qualify under the Child Trust Fund policy (H. M. Treasury, 2001b, 2003). By the time a child reaches 18 years of age, his or her Child Trust Fund could be in the range of £7,000 (about $12,000).[11]

Saving Gateway

The Blair plan is also concerned with ensuring that adults are encouraged to save. The second program is a Saving Gateway, which would build on the universality of the Child Trust Fund and add progressive features, including matching funds. The Saving Gateway is much like IDAs in the United States; it targets lower-income households that have lower levels of savings and is intended to help "develop a saving habit." The government makes a 1:1 matching deposit for every pound saved up to a fixed limit. Financial education, information, and advice are part of the program. The Saving Gateway is available to individuals for a limited time. The account is invested for a minimum of three years and then is either cashed or transferred to existing savings instruments such as an ISA, a retirement pension, or the Child Trust Fund of a child of the person's choice (H. M. Treasury, 2001a, 2001b).[12] Currently, Saving Gateway is in operation at several sites in the United Kingdom in a pilot phase. The plan is to roll it out across the country.

If fully implemented as planned, the U.K. policy would possibly be the largest progressive, universal asset-building policy of any country in the world. It would signal a new direction in policy that might expand over time. As David Blunkett (2000), when he was Secretary of State for Education and Employment, observed: "We are on the cusp of a different way of looking at the welfare state—one which focuses on capital and assets." Noteworthy is the *progressive funding* in these universal proposals, wherein the poor receive more. This is in contrast to some proposals in the United States that call for equal deposits for all (e.g., Ackerman and Alstott, 1999). Also important is the *lifelong accumulation* that is embodied in the U.K. proposals, rather than one large lump sum at birth or at the age of 18 or 21.[13] Instead of equal lump sum deposits, the U.K. proposal for progressive funding and long-term asset accumulation with deposits at birth and throughout the growing up years may be preferable. In the United States, this has been suggested by Sherraden (1991) and Goldberg (see chapter 15 in this volume), and Duncan Lindsey (1994) has proposed a child social security account, wherein assets would build over time by government and private contributions.

ACADEMIC INQUIRY AND POLICY DISCUSSION

Until recently, there has been limited academic attention to asset-based policies for the poor. Nonetheless, some social science researchers have been focusing on asset distributions in the United States, especially Wolff (e.g., 1995, 2001), who deserves a great deal of credit for keeping wealth issues in the public eye. Melvin Oliver and Thomas Shapiro (1995) and Dalton Conley (1998) have very effectively opened the discussion of assets and race. Shapiro and Wolff (2001) bring together a number of studies on a range of topics related to assets and well-being. On the policy side, there have been several proposals for universal capital accounts, usually for youth (Haveman, 1988; Sawhill, 1989; Tobin, 1968). Proposals for capital accounts have usually been made to provide a lump sum to all youths at age 18 or 21.

Home ownership is another strategy for asset-building policy. Most low-income housing programs concentrate on rental housing. Home ownership for the poor has been a somewhat controversial strategy, but there is reason to believe that it can be effective. Since 1992, Presidents Clinton and Bush have emphasized the importance of home ownership for the poor, and federal policy has shifted somewhat in this direction. Evidence from research on IDAs suggests that there is demand for home ownership among the poor (Schreiner et al., chapter 10 in this volume).

Turning to financial services, John Caskey (1994) pioneered the study of second-tier financial services, such as pawnshops and check-cashing outlets. His book has brought attention to the prevalence and operations of these businesses, as well as the financial needs and practices of the customers. Michael Stegman (1999) recognizes that electronic banking will one day provide unprecedented opportunities to make saving instruments available to the poor.

With the shift to asset-based policy, the biggest challenge will be inclusion (Sherraden, 1991, 2001a). Hugh Heclo (1995) observes the welfare state of the twentieth century and concludes, "If there has been a direction to our century's struggle, it seems to have been mainly a question of expanding presumptions of inclusiveness." Unfortunately, at the beginning of the twenty-first century, the presumption of inclusiveness appears to be in retreat. As new asset-based policy regimes grow in many countries, the poor are being left behind, and the prospects for inclusion do not appear to be promising.

Nonetheless, we can be somewhat encouraged that thoughtful proposals for inclusion in asset-building policy and programs are becoming more common. For example, as one of eight strategies for policy action in the twenty-first century, C. Eugene Steuerle and colleagues list a proposal to "increase everyone's chances to build financial security" by "creating opportunities to accumulate assets for financial security, especially among those facing the greatest disadvantages. In this way society can give every-one a greater stake in the future and the common good. . . . We should look to the twenty-first century as a time to move beyond simple redistributive policy toward 'cumulative' policy" (1998, 7–8).

The idea of inclusion in asset accumulation is now on the table. The con-tributions in this book represent a marked change since the discussion began about fifteen years ago. However, the pathway to a universal policy is long and not clearly charted. There is a great deal to do, but we can begin by tak-ing small steps in the right direction. In this book, theoretical and measure-ment issues are considered; evidence of the effectiveness of asset-based policy is presented; and thoughtful policy options are outlined. Along the way, the authors raise numerous questions and challenges.

NOTES

1. This is discussed more thoroughly in Sherraden (2003).

2. The Blair government in the United Kingdom announced in April 2003 that it would proceed with a universal, progressive Child Trust Fund, an account for every newborn in the United Kingdom, with greater public deposits for children in the bottom third of the household income distribution. The policy is to go into effect in 2005, for all children born from 2002 on. After several generations of newborns, this could develop into a universal asset-based policy.

3. State governments provide additional tax benefits.

4. Not recognizing tax expenditures as benefits can be viewed in at least two ways. Possibly recipients are unaware or do not make the connection, or people may view tax benefits not as "benefits" but instead as less confiscation of their income by the government. This latter perspective hinges on whether the existing structure of taxation (before tax breaks) is viewed as legitimate or not. Some people do not think so. I suspect that, for most people, not recognizing tax breaks as public benefits is some combination of hazy awareness and underlying resentment of taxation.

5. Prior to Clinton's speech, the Center for Social Development (CSD) was working with the White House and Treasury Department, providing requested data from IDA research.

6. The SWFA was initiated in 2001 by Michael Stegman of the University of North Carolina, working with the office of Senator Joseph Lieberman. The Corporation for Enterprise Development (CFED) has led in the progress of the SWFA on Capitol Hill.

7. CSD provided data to the U.S. Commission to Strengthen Social Security from IDA research on savings by the poor and urged progressivity (Sherraden, 2001b). Some Commission members asked questions about where the money would come from to subsidize deposits for the poor, and they seemed reluctant to propose taking it out of general revenues. Subsequent e-mail correspondence with Commission staff members suggested that they were interested in some degree of progressivity. The final report cites data from research on IDAs, and there is an element of progressivity in the Commission's proposals, though it is very limited: The third option allows low-income workers to get greater matching deposits as a percentage of their income because the $1,000 maximum applies to all workers, regardless of income. Although far from satisfactory, this small progressive element in deposits and matches may

represent an important policy principle. However, a more universal and progressive element in the proposals is the minimum benefit guarantee in options two and three. The minimum benefit guarantee is excellent, though I would also like to see greater subsidy in asset accumulation *up front*. Under the current proposals, a two-tier system might result, wherein the well-off accumulate assets, and the poor get a minimum benefit guarantee, i.e., asset building for the nonpoor and means-tested income transfers to the poor. As Rosenman (1997) observes regarding the Australian system, this would be far from ideal. A better policy would be for all Americans to accumulate assets that are sufficient for their social protection needs, promoting household development, and making intergenerational transfers of assets more likely.

8. The Institute for Public Policy Research (IPPR) has led asset-based policy work in the United Kingdom (e.g., IPPR, 2001; Kelly and Lissauer, 2000). In June 2000, Sherraden was a respondent to a speech on asset-based policy in London by David Blunkett, then U.K. Secretary of State for Education and Employment. IPPR and CSD cohosted an international conference on asset-based welfare in London in January 2001. In October 2001, Sherraden joined Alistair Darling, U.K. Secretary of State for Work and Pensions, for speeches on "Wealth and Welfare" at the annual meeting of the Labour Party and consulted with Treasury Minister Ruth Kelly on design of the policies. All of this was organized by IPPR.

9. It is perhaps noteworthy that the words of Presidents Bill Clinton and George W. Bush and Prime Minister Tony Blair quoted in this chapter sound much the same. Were it not for contextual references, it would be difficult to determine which leader made which statement. What does this say about the political ideology of asset building? At a minimum it suggests that asset building does not fit neatly into traditional Right and Left political categories.

10. In September 2002, Prime Minister Blair organized a seminar at No. 10 Downing Street on the Child Trust Fund proposal. The session was chaired by Home Minister David Blunkett. Michael Sherraden from CSD, Bob Friedman for CFED, and Fred Goldberg participated. A dinner with Chancellor of the Exchequer Gordon Brown followed the seminar. Sherraden (2002) provided the opening remarks after dinner, relying significantly on findings from research on IDAs. Later, aides to Brown and Blair cited this dinner as crucial in the decision to go ahead with the Child Trust Fund; subsequently, Brown made the funding decision.

11. D. Nissan and J. LeGrand (2000) were influential in the Child Trust Fund proposal.

12. The Saving Gateway is much like IDAs, and it is to be implemented in only a few places as a demonstration, much like the American Dream Demonstration.

13. Those who have raised children through the teenage years might have reason to wonder if a large, lump sum, unrestricted payment to all 18-year-olds would be a wise national policy. For better versions of this idea, see Tobin (1968), Haveman (1988), and Sawhill (1989).

REFERENCES

Ackerman, B., and A. Alstott. (1999). *The Stakeholder Society*. New Haven, Conn.: Yale University Press.

Asher, M. (1991). *Social Adequacy and Equity of the Social Security Arrangements in Singapore*. Occasional Paper No. 8. Singapore: Centre for Advanced Studies, National University of Singapore.

Blair, T. (2001). "Savings and Assets for All." Speech. 10 Downing Street, London, April 26.

Blunkett, D. (2000). "On Your Side: The New Welfare State as an Engine of Prosperity." Speech. Department of Education and Employment, London, June 7.

Borzutsky, S. (1997). "Privatizing Social Security: Relevance of the Chilean Experience." In *Alternatives to Social Security: An International Inquiry*, eds. J. Midgley and M. Sherraden. Westport, Conn.: Auburn House, 75–90.

Bush, G. W. (2000). "New Prosperity." Speech. Cleveland, Ohio, April 11.

Caskey, J. P. (1994). *Fringe Banking: Check-Cashing Outlets, Pawnshops, and the Poor.* New York: Russell Sage Foundation.

Clinton, W. J. (1999). *State of the Union Address.* Washington, D.C.: U.S. Executive Office of the President.

Clinton, W. J. (2000). *State of the Union Address.* Washington, D.C.: U.S. Executive Office of the President.

Coleman, J. S. (1988). "Social Capital in the Creation of Human Capital." *American Journal of Sociology* 94, S95–S120.

Conley, D. (1998). *Being Black, Living in the Red.* Berkeley: University of California Press.

Curley, J., and M. Sherraden. (2000). "Policy Lessons from Children's Allowances for Children's Savings Accounts." *Child Welfare* 79(6), 661–687.

Danziger, S., and R. Plotnick. (1986). "Poverty and Policy: Lessons of the Last Two Decades." *Social Service Review* 60(1), 34–51.

Dixon, J. (1989). *National Provident Funds: The Enfant Terrible of Social Security.* Canberra: International Fellowship for Social and Economic Development.

Gilbert, N. (1995). *Welfare Justice: Restoring Social Equity.* New Haven, Conn.: Yale University Press.

Gilbert, N., and B. Gilbert. (1989). *The Enabling State: Modern Welfare Capitalism in America.* Oxford: Oxford University Press.

H. M. Treasury. (2001a). *Delivering Saving and Assets: The Modernisation of Britain's Tax and Benefit System.* Number Nine. London: Author, December.

H. M. Treasury. (2001b). *Saving and Assets for All: The Modernisation of Britain's Tax and Benefit System.* Number Eight. London: Author, April.

H. M. Treasury. (2003). *Details of the Child Trust Fund.* London: Author.

Haveman, R. (1988). *Starting Even: An Equal Opportunity Program to Combat the Nation's New Poverty.* New York: Simon and Schuster.

Haveman, R., and A. Berkshadker. (1998). *"Inability to be Self-Reliant" as an Indicator of U.S. Poverty: Measurement, Comparisons, Implications.* Working Paper No. 24, Jerome Levy Economics Institute, Bard College, Annandale-on-Hudson, N.Y.

Heclo, H. (1995). "The Social Question." In *Poverty, Inequality, and the Future of Social Policy*, eds. K. McFate, R. Lawson, and W. J. Wilson. New York: Russell Sage Foundation.

Howard, C. (1997). *The Hidden Welfare State: Tax Expenditures and Social Policy in the United States.* Princeton, N.J.: Princeton University Press.

Institute for Public Policy Research (IPPR). (2001). *The Centre for Asset-Based Welfare at the Institute for Public Policy Research.* London: Author.

Kelly, G., and R. Lissauer. (2000). *Ownership for All.* London: Institute for Public Policy Research.

Lindsey, D. (1994). *The Welfare of Children.* New York: Oxford University Press.

Midgley, J. (1999). "Growth, Redistribution, and Welfare: Towards Social Investment." *Social Service Review* 77(1), 3–21.

Morrow-Howell, N., J. Hinterlong, and M. Sherraden. (2001). *Productive Aging: Concepts and Controversies.* Baltimore: The Johns Hopkins University Press.

Nissan, D., and J. LeGrand. (2000). *A Capital Idea: Start-Up Grants for Young People.* Policy Report 49. London: Fabian Society.

Oliver, M., and T. Shapiro. (1990). "Wealth of a Nation: A Reassessment of Asset Inequality in America Shows That at Least One-Third of Households Are Asset Poor." *American Journal of Economics and Sociology* 49, 129–151.

Oliver, M., and T. Shapiro. (1995). *Black Wealth/White Wealth: A New Perspective on Racial Inequality.* New York: Routledge.

Putnam, R. (1995). "Bowling Alone: America's Declining Social Capital." *Journal of Democracy* 6(1), 65–78.

Rosenman, L. (1997). "The Social Assistance Approach and Retirement Pensions in Australia. In *Alternatives to Social Security: An International Inquiry,* eds. J. Midgley and M. Sherraden. Westport, Conn.: Auburn House, 17–32.

Sawhill, I. (1989). "The Underclass: An Overview." *The Public Interest* 96 (Summer), 3–15.

Schreiner, M., M. Sherraden, M. Clancy, E. Johnson, J. Curley, M. Grinstein-Weiss, M. Zhan, and S. Beverly. (2001). *Savings and Asset Accumulation in IDAs.* Research Report. St. Louis, Mo.: Center for Social Development, Washington University.

Schultz, T. M. (1959). "Investment in Man: An Economist's View." *Social Service Review* 33, 109–117.

Seidman, L. (2001). "Assets and the Tax Code." In *Assets for the Poor: Benefits and Mechanisms of Spreading Asset Ownership,* eds. T. Shapiro and E. N. Wolff. New York: Russell Sage Foundation, 324–356.

Sen, A. (1985). *Commodities and Capabilities.* Amsterdam: North-Holland Publishing Company.

Sen, A. (1993). "Capability and Well-Being." In *The Quality of Life,* eds. M. Nussbaum and A. Sen. Oxford, U.K.: Clarendon Press, 30–53.

Sen, A. (1999). *Development as Freedom.* New York: Knopf.

Shapiro, T. (2004). *The Hidden Cost of Being African-American.* New York: Oxford University Press.

Shapiro, T., and E. N. Wolff, eds. (2001). *Assets for the Poor: Spreading the Benefits of Asset Ownership.* New York: Russell Sage Foundation.

Sherraden, M. (1988). "Rethinking Social Welfare: Toward Assets." *Social Policy* 18(3), 37–43.

Sherraden, M. (1991). *Assets and the Poor: A New American Welfare Policy.* Armonk, N.Y.: M. E. Sharpe.

Sherraden, M. (1997). "Conclusion: Social Security in the Twenty-First Century." In *Alternatives to Social Security: An International Inquiry,* eds. J. Midgley and M. Sherraden. Westport, Conn.: Auburn House, 121–140.

Sherraden, M. (2001a). "Asset Building Policy and Programs for the Poor." In *Assets for the Poor: Benefits and Mechanisms of Spreading Asset Ownership,* eds. T. Shapiro and E. N. Wolff. New York: Russell Sage Foundation.

Sherraden, M. (2001b). "Assets and the Poor: Implications for Individual Accounts in Social Security." Testimony before the President's Commission to Strengthen Social Security, Washington, D.C., October 18.

Sherraden, M. (2002). "Opportunity and Assets: The Role of the Child Trust Fund." Notes for a seminar organized by Prime Minister Tony Blair, 10 Downing Street, and dinner speech with Chancellor of the Exchequer Gordon Brown, 11 Downing Street. London, September 19.

Sherraden, M. (2003). "Individual Accounts in Social Security: Can They Be Progressive?" *International Journal of Social Welfare* 12(2), 97–107.

Sherraden, M., S. Nair, S. Vasoo, T. L. Ngiam, and M. S. Sherraden. (1995). "Social Policy Based on Assets: The Impact of Singapore's Central Provident Fund." *Asian Journal of Political Science* 3(2), 112–133.

Stegman, M. (1999). *Savings and the Poor: The Hidden Benefits of Electronic Banking.* Washington, D.C.: The Brookings Institution.

Steuerle, C. E., E. Gramlich, H. Heclo, and D. S. Nightengale. (1998). *The Government We Deserve: Responsive Democracy and Changing Expectations.* Washington, D.C.: The Urban Institute.

Tobin, J. (1968). "Raising the Incomes of the Poor." In *Agenda for the Nation,* ed. K. Gordon. Washington, D.C.: The Brookings Institution, 77–116.

U.S. Commission to Strengthen Social Security. (2001a). *Interim Report.* August. Washington, D.C.: President's Commission to Strengthen Social Security.

U.S. Commission to Strengthen Social Security. (2001b). *Report.* December. Washington, D.C.: President's Commission to Strengthen Social Security.

Vasoo, S., and J. Lee. (2001). "Singapore: Social Development, Housing and the Central Provident Fund." *International Journal of Social Welfare* 10(4), 276–283.

Wolff, E. N. (1995). *Top Heavy: The Increasing Inequality of Wealth in America and What Can Be Done about It.* New York: Twentieth Century Fund.

Wolff, E. N. (2001). "Recent Trends in Wealth Ownership, from 1983 to 1998." In *Assets for the Poor: Spreading the Benefits of Asset Ownership,* eds. T. Shapiro and E. N. Wolff. New York: Russell Sage Foundation, 34–73.

2

The Homestead Act: A Major Asset-Building Policy in American History

Trina Williams Shanks

Land policy plays an important role in U.S. history. From frontier life, as exemplified by Laura Ingalls Wilder in her *Little House on the Prairie* books (Wilder, 1935) to key moments, such as the 1889 Land Run in Oklahoma, policy decisions about property shaped how and where people lived in early American society. One of the most enduring pieces of legislation shaped settlement in the western territories from 1863 to 1939. Signed into law on May 20, 1862, by Abraham Lincoln, the Homestead Act was one of the nation's first major domestic policies. The act is important for several reasons. It represents consensus culminating from a larger dialogue concerning the rights of citizenship, how the nation's land resources would be managed, and whether an opportunity should be provided for individuals other than the wealthy to own property in the western territories. In addition, it complements other policy and economic changes that were taking place simultaneously during the latter part of the nineteenth century.

This chapter will address three questions: What is the significance of the Homestead Act? Who benefited from the Homestead Act? What can we learn from the Homestead Act? After an introduction to the homestead legislation and an explanation of how it was implemented, there will be an empirical analysis that considers the long-term impact of the act. This will entail a calculation of the descendants each homestead family might have had, based on a few reasonable demographic assumptions, followed by an estimation of how many people living today may have ancestors who received property through this transfer of assets. Considering implications that follow from the Homestead Act, the chapter will discuss principles for policies that would provide genuine opportunities for all citizens while contributing to the long-term development of the nation's resources, particularly looking toward future generations.

SIGNIFICANCE OF THE HOMESTEAD ACT: HISTORICAL BACKGROUND

Land commonly known as the public domain was granted to or purchased by the U.S. government between 1781 and 1853.[1] This essentially included all land owned by the federal government that was not a part of the original thirteen states. Excluding Alaska, the total area of the public domain encompassed nearly 1.5 billion acres, obtained through the following territorial acquisitions: state cessions, the Louisiana Purchase, Red River Basin, cession from Spain, Oregon Compromise, Mexican cession, purchase from Texas, and the Gadsden Purchase (U.S. Department of the Interior, 1998; see map in figure 2.1). How to administer this public land that formed a continuous strip of territory from East to West Coast was an important part of early governmental policy. Congress passed 3,500 land laws between 1785 and 1880 (Gates, 1970).

The primary policies governing federal property were decided soon after the United States attained independence (Hughes, 1987; Robbins, 1976). The Land Ordinance of 1785 established a system of surveying to measure territories and divide them up for public sale. Townships of 36 square miles were marked off and divided into one-square-mile sections of 640 acres each. Congress reserved certain sections in townships for government use and for establishing common schools (Dick, 1970; Robbins, 1976). Complementing this arrangement, Congress passed the Northwest Ordinance in 1787, which established laws whereby territories could become states (Hyman, 1986; North and Rutten, 1987).

Opposing viewpoints arose on how best to distribute the property.[2] Initially, available land was to be auctioned as entire sections (640-acre lots) to the highest bidder at a minimum price of $1 to $2 per acre. There were complaints that the price was too high and the acreage too large, favoring the wealthy and speculators rather than small farmers. Politicians such as Thomas Jefferson, William Henry Harrison, and Albert Gallatin (who represented the frontier region of Pennsylvania) favored an agrarian republic made up of many small landholders and argued that the land should be sold in smaller plots at a reduced price to maintain economic democracy (Cross, 1995; Robbins, 1976). Numerous petitions were made to Congress for change, but the political reality was that raising revenue was the high priority. Since the "new government was practically bankrupt . . . one of the first thoughts of statesmen was to sell the public land and bolster the country financially" (Dick, 1970, 6).

However, attempts to sell land in large bundles at high prices did not always succeed. There were often owner resells and bounty warrants where land could be purchased at prices cheaper than $1 per acre (Gates, 1941; Lebergott, 1985; North and Rutten, 1987). In addition, many people on the frontier did not honor the official laws. Groups of settlers simply started living off the land, farming, cutting timber, and extracting natural resources. Some settlers even formed squatters' clubs to protect property, keep bidding at minimum levels, ensure their members got the best land,

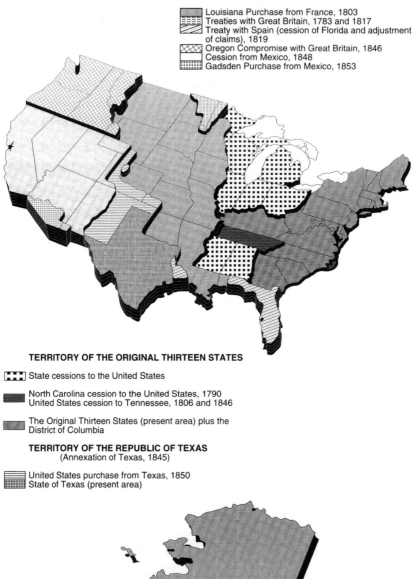

OTHER ACQUISITIONS OF THE UNITED STATES

Louisiana Purchase from France, 1803
Treaties with Great Britain, 1783 and 1817
Treaty with Spain (cession of Florida and adjustment of claims), 1819
Oregon Compromise with Great Britain, 1846
Cession from Mexico, 1848
Gadsden Purchase from Mexico, 1853

TERRITORY OF THE ORIGINAL THIRTEEN STATES

State cessions to the United States

North Carolina cession to the United States, 1790
United States cession to Tennessee, 1806 and 1846

The Original Thirteen States (present area) plus the District of Columbia

TERRITORY OF THE REPUBLIC OF TEXAS
(Annexation of Texas, 1845)

United States purchase from Texas, 1850
State of Texas (present area)

ALASKA

Purchased from Russia, March 30, 1867

Figure 2.1 Distribution of public land acquisitions by 1853 (Alaska not considered). *Source:* U.S. Department of the Interior, Bureau of Land Management.

and enforce their own informal norms. The eastern reaction to these practices was typically negative; laws were passed to fight against squatting and unauthorized occupancy (Dick, 1970; Robbins, 1976).

By 1832, raising revenue was no longer the most pressing priority because President Andrew Jackson had paid off the national debt. In addition, the very wealthy had other investment options, and their portfolios were more likely to include city lots rather than farmland (Lebergott, 1985). These changing competitive factors, along with new political concerns stemming from the growing political power of western states and territories, led to laws and institutional changes that shifted the balance from large landowners and eastern investors toward smaller landowners and independent farms. The Preemption Act of 1841 allowed squatters with an established claim guaranteed permission to purchase their land at the minimum price of $1.25 per acre once the area opened for survey and settlement. The Graduation Act of 1854 reduced the minimum fixed price from $1.25 to $1 per acre after ten years, and for plots of land not purchased for thirty years, prices were as low as 12.5 cents (Dick, 1970; North, 1974; Robbins, 1976).

The culmination of these incremental changes was the Homestead Act, passed in May 1862. The statute provided that heads of household, military veterans, and those over 21 years of age were entitled to 160 acres of unappropriated land as long as they had not borne arms against the U.S. government. Applicants had to be U.S. citizens or had to have filed intention of becoming one. After filing an application for surveyed land with the appropriate land office and swearing that the property was for one's own use with the purpose of cultivation and settlement, the person had six months to move onto the land and begin improvements. These plots of land were exempt from sale, taxes, and previous debt.[3] Any time after five years, the applicant was entitled to take out final papers and receive a patent for the land, after providing evidence that all conditions had been fulfilled and paying nominal charges to the appropriate land office. If the claimant abandoned the land or changed residence, the plot reverted back to the government. The Preemptive Clause of 1841 was still in effect, however, so if homesteaders wanted to pay the minimum price per acre before the five years expired, they could still buy title to the land. This was called the commutation of a homestead (Dick, 1970; Sloan, 1976).

The beauty of the Homestead Act was that anyone who was willing to move west and stake a claim was eligible to own public land. Wage earners, recent immigrants, young adults from large families desiring private property, those seeking adventure, those wanting to shape politics or culture in the "lawless" West, those seeking a new start, and thousands of others all were free to pursue their personal dreams and aspirations. Everett Dick (1970) writes that "land was the most important single social factor in frontier history"; it "became the lure that enticed immigrants to America and settlers farther westward" (ix).

Citizens with few or no assets could find an unoccupied 160 acres, file a homestead application and, after living on the land for five years, possess crops, land, and financial independence. In a sense, the government was not only giving away land, but also the opportunity for upward mobility and a more secure future for oneself and one's children. As Dick (1970) states, "Just as gaining an education is the surest way to rise in society today, in colonial days the acquisition of property was the key to moving upward from a low to a higher stratum. The property holder could vote and hold office, but the man with no property was practically on the same political level as the indentured servant or slave" (1–2).

Yet even with passage of the Homestead Act, the details of implementation would be the key to fulfilling its promise. It was a great opportunity but also entailed great risk. Gaining title to the available land was not a simple task and sometimes produced false hope. One of the biggest barriers to surviving five years and successfully attaining title was the need for at least some capital. More than land was necessary to build a farm. W. F. Deverell (1988) estimates that between $600–$1,000 was required. At minimum, the homesteaders needed money to travel, register with the appropriate land office, plant crops, and sustain themselves until harvest (Cross, 1995; Danhof, 1941). A bad crop or poor weather could cause setbacks that made surviving the winters difficult. In addition, moneylenders often charged exorbitant interest rates to settlers compelled to borrow. Initially optimistic homesteaders often became discouraged and returned home (Dick, 1970).

Understandably, farmers already living on western lands benefited the most. They knew the terrain and simply claimed the best homestead property nearby (Deverell, 1988). Due to a lack of information about certain areas and terrains, professional land agents arose who understood the legal process and tried to outmaneuver newcomers, sometimes charging fees to help people find good property or selling rights to contested land before it was actually surveyed (Gates, 1970). But in spite of such difficulties, the homestead policy of registering land claims on surveyed property and gaining title to land did provide a viable option for adults to attain independent living on a self-managed farm, to develop assets that might appreciate over time, and to provide an estate to pass on to their children. Indeed, a settler filing entry for a homestead with a land office was less likely to have his or her land dispossessed than a settler purchasing a similar plot of land from a private owner (Gates, 1996).

In his report for the Public Land Commission, Thomas Donaldson (1884, 350) summarized the benefits of the Homestead Act as follows:

> The homestead act is now the approved and preferred method of acquiring title to the public lands. It has stood the test of eighteen years, and was the outgrowth of a system extending through nearly eighty years, and now, within the circle of a hundred years since the Untied States acquired the first of her public lands, the homestead act stands as the concentrated wisdom of legislation for the settlement of the public lands. It protects the Government, it fills the States with homes, it builds up communities, and lessens the chances of social and civil disorder by giving ownership of the soil, in small tracts, to the occupants thereof. It was copied from no other nation's system. It was originally and distinctively American, and remains a monument to its originators.

Although the basic tenets of the Homestead Act remained the same throughout its seventy-five-year tenure, they were adjusted several times to deal with timber interests, mining interests, grazing interests, irrigation needs, and concern for the environment. For example, the area west of the one-hundredth meridian received insufficient rainfall to farm without special techniques, so adjustments were made in the allowable acreage and the time necessary to remain on the land prior to filing for ownership (Dick, 1970; Peffer, 1951). Also, when it appeared that forests were being harvested too quickly, some states created incentives for homesteaders to set aside part of their acreage to plant trees or required loggers to purchase land legally, according to the value of the timber it contained (Robbins, 1976).

By the 1920s, however, the land remaining in the public domain was less and less desirable for farming, due to severe climates and, in some cases, stripping of natural resources. Also, with an agricultural depression, it was difficult for novices to sustain themselves on small farms located in less fertile terrain (Dick, 1970). However, most scholars agree that the real end of frontier settlement came with a series of laws signed by President Franklin Roosevelt (Dick, 1970; Peffer, 1951; Robbins, 1976). Two executive orders, dated November 26, 1934, and February 5, 1935, withdrew all remaining land (aside from Alaska) from the "unreserved and unappropriated public domain" (Dick, 1970, 364). What was left could be reserved for uses such as logging and grazing but would be owned by all citizens of the United States, not given over as private property.

Overall, this process of land transfer provided a foundation for future growth both in terms of population and the economy. As the more western parts of the frontier were settled, the Homestead Act allowed development to occur in families and communities over time. With a legal title, the farmer could pass along accumulated assets and upward mobility to descendants. For example, the original homesteader might clear 80 of the property's 160 acres, build a house, and plant a few crops each year. The homesteader's children might make more improvements by clearing the other 80 acres and raising livestock, while continuing to sell crops. In addition, once enough farmers populated an area, there would be sufficient demand to establish a town, a school, retail stores, and other amenities, creating economic opportunities apart from agriculture. This one-time transfer of property provided a mechanism and incentives for growth over generations rather than limiting benefits to one person or lifetime.

NUMBER OF AMERICANS WHO HAVE BENEFITED FROM THE HOMESTEAD ACT

Number of Homesteads Granted

Building upon the narrative regarding the Homestead Act above, this section will be more empirical, focusing on the actual number of people who received a title to public lands through the policy. Data from a report by

Donaldson (1884), public land statistics (U.S. Department of the Interior, 1961), and historical statistics (U.S. Census Bureau, 1975) have been compiled in table 2.1 to summarize the basic information collected from land records. The first column records the dates of original entries, that is, applications that were accepted for land. The second column details the number of people who submitted accepted and properly entered applications to secure title to public domain lands. The third column lists the number of acres requested by these applications. The fourth column lists the number of people who made final entries (typically five years later) and were issued an equitable title (patent) to their homestead property after complying with the relevant legal requirements. The fifth column lists the final number of acres transferred from the federal government to those homesteaders. Upon paying the appropriate administrative fees, those making final entries owned the land and could use it as they pleased. As the original Homestead Act required homesteaders to live on the land for five years, there is a lag between the original entries in 1863 and the first homestead titles granted in 1868.

The numbers for each year have been tabulated into 10-year running totals. Comparing decades, the largest number of applications was submitted between 1900 and 1909, at 794,513 entries. The largest number of final titles (patents) was granted between 1910 and 1919, for 384,954 homesteads. Over the 76-year period in consideration, 3 million people applied for homesteads, and almost 1.5 million households were given title to nearly 246 million acres of land. This represents a remarkable transfer of wealth and assets. The total acreage is close to the land area of Texas and California combined.

A quick comparison makes it apparent that the number of original applications is much higher than the number of final titles issued. This may seem like a huge failure rate, and the reality is that some applicants were not able to survive or persevere for the required five years. There are other explanations, however. Although he cites some evidence of blacks who submitted preliminary entries being intimidated into leaving by white neighbors in the South, Roy Robbins comments that the primary reason for the discrepancy between the number of applications and patents was likely "dummy filings" (1976, 240–241). This occurred when wealthy individuals or corporations employed people to stake claims for agricultural homesteads so that the profiteers could cut the timber or mine the minerals therein. After stripping these lands of their resources, the claimants never concluded the transactions for final entry. Each local land district included thousands of square miles, making it impossible for officials to monitor and verify each entry. In addition to such possible instances of fraud, the final homestead numbers do not include commutations of the five-year residency requirement. That is, people who decided to buy their land outright at $1.25 an acre after six months could obtain an ownership title without filing a final homestead entry (Dick, 1970; Sloan, 1976). It is important to note, however, that even if one homestead application was unsuccessful, the farmer could make an entry on another plot of land. Some people made several entries before successfully attaining title to a homestead property (Dick, 1970).

Table 2.1 Homestead Totals: Number of Entries, Acres, and Final Patents

Year	Original Entries	Acres	Homestead Patents	Final Acreage
1863	8,223	1,032,872		
1864	9,405	1,247,171		
1865	8,924	1,141,443		
1866	15,355	1,890,848		
1867	16,957	1,834,513		
1868	23,746	2,332,151	2,772	355,086
1869	25,628	2,698,482	3,965	504,302
Total 1863–1869	108,238	12,177,480	6,737	859,388
1870	33,972	3,754,203	4,041	519,728
1871	39,768	4,657,355	5,087	629,162
1872	38,742	4,595,435	5,917	707,410
1873	31,561	3,760,200	10,311	1,224,891
1874	29,126	3,489,570	14,129	1,585,782
1875	20,668	2,369,782	18,293	2,068,538
1876	25,104	2,867,814	22,530	2,590,553
1877	18,675	2,176,257	19,900	2,407,828
1878	35,630	4,496,855	22,460	2,662,981
1879	41,005	5,267,385	17,391	2,070,842
Total 1870–1879	314,251	37,434,856	140,059	16,467,715
1880	47,293	6,054,709	15,441	1,938,235
1881	36,999	5,028,101	15,077	1,928,005
1882	45,331	6,348,045	17,174	2,219,454
1883	56,565	8,171,914	18,998	2,504,415
1884	54,982	7,832,000		2,946,000
1885	60,877	7,416,000	43,909	3,033,000
1886	61,638	9,145,000		2,664,000
1887	52,028	7,594,000		2,749,000
1888	46,236	6,677,000	115,264	3,175,000
1889	42,183	6,029,000		3,682,000
Total 1880–1889	504,132	70,295,769	225,863	26,839,109
1890	40,244	5,532,000		4,061,000
1891	37,602	5,040,000		3,955,000
1892	55,113	7,716,000		3,260,000
1893	48,436	6,809,000		3,477,000

(continued)

Table 2.1 (continued)

Year	Original Entries	Acres	Homestead Patents	Final Acreage
1894	56,632	8,047,000	116,178	2,930,000
1895	37,336	5,009,000		2,981,000
1896	36,548	4,831,000		2,790,000
1897	33,250	4,452,000		2,778,000
1898	44,980	6,207,000		3,095,000
1899	45,776	6,178,000	110,593	3,134,000
Total 1890–1899	435,917	59,821,000	226,771	32,461,000
1900	61,270	8,478,000		3,478,000
1901	68,648	9,497,000		5,241,000
1902	98,829	14,033,000		4,343,000
1903	80,188	11,193,000		3,577,000
1904	69,175	10,171,000		3,233,000
1905	70,344	12,896,000	144,121	3,419,000
1906	89,600	13,975,000		3,527,000
1907	93,957	14,755,000		3,741,000
1908	87,057	13,586,000		4,243,000
1909	75,445	12,302,000	130,430	3,699,000
Total 1900–1909	794,513	120,886,000	274,551	38,501,000
1910	98,598	18,329,000		3,796,000
1911	70,720	17,639,000		4,620,000
1912	52,991	13,624,000		4,306,000
1913	57,800	11,222,000		10,009,000
1914	62,229	12,117,000		9,291,000
1915	62,360	12,440,000	189,553	7,181,000
1916	65,282	13,628,000		7,278,000
1917	58,896	12,021,000		8,497,000
1918	35,875	7,420,000		8,236,000
1919	39,341	10,204,000	195,401	6,525,000
Total 1910–1919	604,092	128,644,000	384,954	69,739,000
1920	48,532	13,511,000		8,373,000
1921	43,813	13,662,000		7,727,000
1922	29,263	8,980,000		7,307,000
1923	18,942	5,524,000		5,594,000

Table 2.1 (continued)

Year	Original Entries	Acres	Homestead Patents	Final Acreage
1924	13,886	3,873,000	119,949	4,791,000
1925	11,010	3,041,000		4,049,000
1926	10,354	2,875,000		3,451,000
1927	10,500	3,237,000		2,584,000
1928	10,429	3,367,000		1,816,000
1929	11,598	4,178,000	39,439	1,701,000
Total 1920–1929	208,327	62,248,000	159,388	47,393,000
1930	12,708	4,723,000		1,371,000
1931	12,640	4,757,000		1,353,000
1932	10,639	3,914,000		1,210,000
1933	7,527	2,642,000		907,000
1934	7,507	2,787,000	20,501	1,124,000
1935	3,297	1,166,000		1,640,000
1936	1,209	357,000		1,765,000
1937	561	111,000		1,915,000
1938	447	78,000		1,362,000
1939	378	66,000	19,533	1,089,000
Totals 1930–1939	56,913	20,601,000	40,034	13,736,000
Grand total	3,026,383	512,108,105	1,458,357	245,996,212

Sources: Donaldson, 1970; U.S. Census Bureau, 1975; U.S. Department of the Interior, 1961.
Note: Homestead patents represent the number of households making final entry and receiving an equitable title to their land after complying with the relevant legal requirements, typically five years' residence.

The U.S. Department of the Interior (1998) lists that 287.5 million acres of the public domain were granted or sold to homesteaders. This is approximately 20 percent of public land and is comparable to the amount of land granted to states and the acreage sold or awarded to railroads and other corporate interests.[4]

Estimated Long-Term Impact

Even though the Homestead Act touched many aspects of American life as the western frontier developed and territories became states, the focus of this chapter is the families who acquired property as a result of this policy. This legislation provided many people the opportunity to relocate and begin new lives. Such choices not only affected the homesteaders and their immediate families, including children, but also their relatives and friends who were left behind. Acquiring a homestead created a distinct lifestyle and social situation, leaving a legacy for future generations.

Given that a homestead provided a real asset that could be developed and passed on to one's children, an interesting question is, how many people living today had ancestors who acquired property through the Homestead Act? This is not simply an intellectual curiosity, but rather a way to demonstrate the enduring legacy of early asset-building policy. The case can be made that after individuals successfully survived on a homestead for five years and obtained title (called "proving up"), they became active participants in the developing economy. Whether family members continued in farming or took on other professions, future generations could have a tie to property and obtain a positive externality from ancestors who had achieved upward mobility through the Homestead Act.

This section will calculate the descendants each homestead family might have had, based on a few fundamental demographic assumptions. This was done through demographic estimations with three scenarios. The demographic estimations were made according to the calculations outlined in table 2.1. The numbers are given in five-year increments because many of the relevant demographic statistics are listed as such and because it makes calculating a twenty-five-year generation easier. Starting with a single homestead family (taken from the total patents in column four from table 2.1),[5] calculations are made assuming a twenty-five-year generation. The number of homesteads granted in each five-year period is multiplied by the total fertility rate during that time to calculate the total estimated number of children.[6] The number of children is multiplied by the fertility rate twenty-five years later and the proportion of women ever married in that cohort.[7] This provides an estimate of the number of children in the second generation. The children of the second generation are multiplied by the fertility rate fifty years later and the proportion of women ever married twenty-five years later to provide an estimate of the number of children in the third generation. The children of the third generation are multiplied by the fertility rate seventy-five years later and the proportion of women ever-married fifty years later to provide an estimate of the fourth generation (if acquisition of the homestead occurred early enough for this data to be possible).

The first two scenarios assume that any benefit from a homestead would pass along to all children. Table 2.2 presents the first scenario and projects the total possible descendants, providing a high estimate for the number of persons living today with a homesteader in their ancestry. The two youngest generations will be considered as today's adults. Thus, for the homestead family obtaining title to property in 1878, enough time has passed for four generations to be born. The baby boomer great-grandchildren born around 1953 and the 20-something great-great-grandchildren born around 1978 will be counted as surviving descendants. Similarly, for a homestead family acquiring title to public land later (in 1926), enough time has passed for only two generations. Their children, born around 1951, and grandchildren, born

Table 2.2 Projected Beneficiaries of the Homestead Act: High Estimate

Years	Homesteads Awarded in Period	Total Fertility Rate	Estimated No. of Children	Percent Married (Cohort)	Second Generation	Third Generation	Fourth Generation
1867–1870	10,778	4.555	49,094	0.922	177,799	533,277	1,253,105
1871–1875	53,737	4.558	244,933	0.927	823,749	2,323,892	6,846,754
1876–1880	97,722	4.312	421,377	0.927	1,336,690	3,284,537	10,614,744
1881–1885	95,158	4.268	406,134	0.936	1,325,934	2,769,463	9,644,290
1886–1890	115,264	4.018	463,131	0.939	1,442,931	2,976,086	9,176,338
1891–1895	116,178	3.928	456,347	0.942	1,368,735	3,216,281	7,458,786
1896–1900	110,593	3.628	401,231	0.941	1,131,921	3,334,916	6,035,114
1901–1905	144,121	3.422	493,182	0.948	1,211,855	3,916,390	N/A
1906–1910	130,430	3.488	454,940	0.952	950,227	3,309,041	N/A
1911–1915	189,553	3.318	628,937	0.962	1,297,200	3,999,732	N/A
1916–1920	195,401	3.184	622,157	0.971	1,461,956	3,390,382	N/A
1921–1925	119,949	2.998	359,607	0.973	1,059,490	1,917,333	N/A
1926–1930	39,439	2.592	102,226	0.974	330,367	N/A	N/A
1931–1935	20,501	2.194	44,979	0.976	156,634	N/A	N/A
1936–1940	19,533	2.144	41,879	0.969	129,127	N/A	N/A
Grand total	1,458,357		5,190,154		14,204,616	34,971,331	51,029,131

Sources: Homesteads awarded taken from table 2.1, column 4 of this paper. Total fertility rate statistics taken from Coale and Zelnik, 1963. Percent married statistics taken from Ryder, 1986.

Note: High estimate: 51,029,131 + 34,971,331 + 6,785,940 = 92,786,402.

around 1976, would be counted as surviving descendants. In this high estimate, the two youngest generations' descendants of homesteaders would
range in age from 25 years to 80 years and number 93 million.

The second scenario is presented in table 2.3 and projects the potential
number of descendants using the same calculations but provides a medium
estimate. Rather than assuming the maximum possible number of children,
the numbers are divided in half. This is done to be conservative and to allow
for the very real possibility that the children of some homesteaders may have
applied for their own homesteads or married someone with a homestead,
thus duplicating numbers in downstream generations. In this medium estimate, the two youngest generations' descendants of homesteaders would
range in age from 25 years to 80 years and number 46 million.

The last scenario makes a more stringent assumption to provide a low
estimate. It is predicated upon the idea that only one inheritor (among multiple children) would maintain the homestead and retain a benefit that
could be passed along to descendants. This can be seen as a shift from equal
shares, with all future generations receiving comparable benefits, to a uni-
geniture system, meaning that in each generation one child receives the
entire benefit, which can be passed along to only one descendant. The children born to a homestead household would probably live on the homestead
at some point, so their children would be descendants of a homesteader,
but only one child would control the property and be able to pass accrued
benefits on to future generations.

Table 2.4 presents this third scenario. The fertility rates and proportion
of cohort ever married remain the same, as they are based on observed
demographic information, but this estimate is based upon the idea that
only one inheritor would maintain the homestead and thus have an asset
to pass on to his or her descendants. With this low estimate, the two youngest
generations of homesteaders potentially living today would range in age
from 25 years to 80 years and number 20 million.

These calculations of the number of homestead descendants living
today are based on a reasonable demographic foundation. Taking the
medium estimate of 46 million would mean that one-quarter of the current
U.S. adult population (age 25 and older) potentially has ancestors who
were homesteaders.[8] This would mean one-quarter of U.S. adults potentially have a legacy of property ownership and assets in their backgrounds
that can be directly linked to national policy. Of course, some of these
ancestors might have become property owners anyway, but a significant
portion likely utilized the Homestead Act as a means of enhancing their
upward economic mobility or of stabilizing their economic position. This
single policy, passed in 1862, leaves an enduring legacy.

The Situation of Blacks

The Homestead Act was passed as the country was on the brink of civil
war. Given its importance as a mechanism for acquiring property, a key

Table 2.3 Projected Beneficiaries of the Homestead Act: Medium Estimate

Years	Homesteads Awarded in Period	Total Fertility Rate	Estimated No. of Children	Percent Married (Cohort)	Second Generation	Third Generation	Fourth Generation
1867–1870	10,778	4.555	49,094	0.922	88,899	266,639	626,553
1871–1875	53,737	4.558	244,933	0.927	411,874	1,161,946	3,423,377
1876–1880	97,722	4.312	421,377	0.927	668,345	1,642,269	5,307,372
1881–1885	95,158	4.268	406,134	0.936	662,967	1,384,732	4,822,145
1886–1890	115,264	4.018	463,131	0.939	721,466	1,488,043	4,588,169
1891–1895	116,178	3.928	456,347	0.942	684,367	1,608,140	3,729,393
1896–1900	110,593	3.628	401,231	0.941	565,961	1,667,458	3,017,557
1901–1905	144,121	3.422	493,182	0.948	605,927	1,958,195	N/A
1906–1910	130,430	3.488	454,940	0.952	475,114	1,654,521	N/A
1911–1915	189,553	3.318	628,937	0.962	648,600	1,999,866	N/A
1916–1920	195,401	3.184	622,157	0.971	730,978	1,695,191	N/A
1921–1925	119,949	2.998	359,607	0.973	529,745	958,667	N/A
1926–1930	39,439	2.592	102,226	0.974	165,183	N/A	N/A
1931–1935	20,501	2.194	44,979	0.976	78,317	N/A	N/A
1936–1940	19,533	2.144	41,879	0.969	64,564	N/A	N/A
Grand total	1,458,357		5,190,154		7,102,308	17,485,665	25,514,566

Sources: Homesteads awarded taken from table 2.1, column 4 of this paper. Total fertility rate statistics taken from Coale and Zelnik, 1963. Percent married statistics taken from Ryder, 1986.

Note: Medium estimate: 25,514,566 + 17,485,665 + 3,392,970 = 46,393,201.

Table 2.4 Projected Beneficiaries of the Homestead Act: Low Estimate

Years	Homesteads Awarded in Period	Total Fertility Rate	Estimated No. of Children	Percent Married (Cohort)	Second Generation	Third Generation	Fourth Generation
1867–1870	10,778	4.555	49,094	0.922	177,799	117,075	75,962
1871–1875	53,737	4.558	244,933	0.927	823,749	509,849	446,646
1876–1880	97,722	4.312	421,377	0.927	1,336,690	761,720	776,017
1881–1885	95,158	4.268	406,134	0.936	1,325,934	648,890	692,139
1886–1890	115,264	4.018	463,131	0.939	1,442,931	740,688	733,023
1891–1895	116,178	3.928	456,347	0.942	1,368,735	818,809	633,101
1896–1900	110,593	3.628	401,231	0.941	1,131,921	919,216	589,654
1901–1905	144,121	3.422	493,182	0.948	1,211,855	1,144,474	N/A
1906–1910	130,430	3.488	454,940	0.952	950,227	948,693	N/A
1911–1915	189,553	3.318	628,937	0.962	1,297,200	1,205,465	N/A
1916–1920	195,401	3.184	622,157	0.971	1,461,956	1,064,819	N/A
1921–1925	119,949	2.998	359,607	0.973	1,059,490	639,537	N/A
1926–1930	39,439	2.592	102,226	0.974	330,367	N/A	N/A
1931–1935	20,501	2.194	44,979	0.976	156,634	N/A	N/A
1936–1940	19,533	2.144	41,879	0.969	129,127	N/A	N/A
Grand total	1,458,357		5,190,154		14,204,616	9,519,235	3,946,541

Sources: Homesteads awarded taken from table 2.1, column 4 of this paper. Total fertility rate statistics taken from Coale and Zelnik, 1963. Percent married statistics taken from Ryder, 1986.

Note: Low estimate = 3,946,541 + 9,519,235 + 6,785,940 = 20,251,716.

issue is how the legislation impacted the 4 million blacks who then lived as slaves. Blacks were ineligible for ownership of any public land prior to the Civil War because they were not considered citizens. After the Emancipation Proclamation and the end of the Civil War, the situation of black freedmen and women often depended upon local leadership and conditions.

As early as 1865, certain white Southerners put legal obstacles in place to prevent ex-slaves from acquiring property. Edward Magdol explains, "In the provisional state governments under President [Andrew] Johnson's protective leniency, planters not only prohibited black landownership but enacted extreme measures of social control that virtually restored slavery. The black codes struck directly at freedmen striving to escape their subordination and to obtain their communities. It was class and race legislation" (1977, 150). Claude Oubre (1978) acknowledges that the Freedmen's Bureau invalidated such black codes, but if no one enforced the directives, opposition to black ownership made acquiring any land difficult in some areas. Ironically, black men who served on the Union side during the war and even remained enlisted as Buffalo Soldiers to help protect settlers on the frontier from outlaws and Indian attacks were denied the opportunity to make land claims in some of the very communities they fought to defend (Cox, 1993).

Freed slaves, who were encouraged by words from President Lincoln and confiscation acts passed by Congress and fueled by a strong desire for land and schools, believed they would be given property along with freedom.[9] The myth of forty acres and a mule was never an official legislative promise, but there were moments of hope when it appeared that legal and political action would be taken to help recently freed slaves become economically independent from their former masters. Unfortunately, nothing permanent was created to help the former slaves acquire property or a better economic position.[10]

On June 21, 1866, Congress passed the Southern Homestead Act. Forty-six million acres of unsold public land in Alabama, Arkansas, Florida, Louisiana, and Mississippi were set aside for purchase as 80-acre plots, then later as 160-acre plots. The primary beneficiaries, at least in the first six months, were to be landless freedmen. This act was a rare, full-scale solution attempted to assist freed slaves. In addition, the land was to be for settlers, not sold to speculators or those with mining and timber interests. The desire for land among former slaves was strong, and they deluged local land officers with requests for homesteads (Lanza, 1990). This was true even though settlement would be difficult, given that most high-quality farmland had been claimed before the Civil War. What remained was primarily swamp land and pine trees that would have required much capital to improve (Gates, 1996; Magdol, 1977). Before much land had been distributed, the Southern Homestead Act, like most Reconstruction programs, was repealed in June of 1876. The "homestead only clause" was taken away, and the remaining land was opened for sale and preemption (Lanza, 1990).

Of the 67,600 homestead applications made under the Southern Home-stead Act, only 27,800 at most received final patent, which equates to the transfer of 2.9 million acres, about 6 percent of the land originally offered. Estimates from a sample of homestead claims in Mississippi reveal that about 23 percent of claimants under the Southern Homestead Act were judged to be blacks. In that sample, 35 percent of black claims were suc-cessful, compared to 25 percent of white claims (Lanza, 1990). Using these percentages, 5,440 of the 27,800 final patents may have been awarded to black homesteaders. Citing Magdol (1977), only 4,000 blacks even made homestead entries under the act (160). Either way, the reality is that few homesteads were granted to black claimants.

During a period when many citizens were given public land by the gov-ernment, blacks who wanted to be small farm owners had to pay for their land and struggle against obstacles that most of their white counterparts did not. This is especially unsettling, given that during the initial phase of the Homestead Act, from 1863 to 1880, most blacks had just been freed from slavery, faced active discrimination, and were not in a position to negotiate on equal terms. It was a missed opportunity for the post–Civil War United States that the Homestead Act was not used as a vehicle to encourage black self-sufficiency, to bring the freed slaves into the economy, using existing laws to establish them as productive farmers and ranchers. Many freedmen and women already had much more experience in farm-ing and raising cattle than the urban homesteaders. Melvin Oliver and Thomas Shapiro (1995) argue that outcomes of the Homestead Act are just one of many examples of the racialization of state policy, economic detours to self-employment, and sedimentation of racial inequality that shapes the inequality of wealth between blacks and whites even today.

REFLECTIONS ON POLICY IMPLICATIONS AND LESSONS LEARNED

Although there was political disagreement and ongoing debate, the pas-sage of the Homestead Act provided a voice and an opportunity for small landholders. Many other arrangements were possible at that time. Rather than becoming a nation of small farmers, the United States could have become a system largely comprising tenancy and sharecropping, which was the case in other developing economies of the time.[11] In light of possi-ble alternatives, the Homestead Act was a progressive policy, broadening the base of asset ownership beyond the wealthy.

Although many people were unable to or chose not to take advantage of the Homestead Act, there were no real restrictions as to who could apply. There was no means-testing or provision for special populations. Unfortunately, early descriptions of the advantages of becoming a homesteader were closer to propaganda than factual accounts. Had those who publicized the advantages of homesteading established more real-istic expectations, perhaps some of the fraud, abuses of the system, and unnecessary failures would have been prevented. But overall, becoming a homesteader was an opportunity available to practically anyone. Except for the racism that hampered nonwhite citizens, the Homestead Act was an inclusive policy.

The basic premise of the Homestead Act stayed constant over three-quarters of a century: Give land away in small parcels to persons who are willing to populate the western territories and develop the property. Although the overall goals remained consistent, there was flexibility to make minor changes based on local circumstances. In areas that were not as conducive to agriculture, concessions were made. Research made possible by the 1862 Morrill Land Grant Act and irrigation projects were financed to make unfamiliar terrains more productive. Raising cattle and increased acreage for grazing became acceptable land uses as well. However, even with such adjustments, the Homestead Act was a simple and enduring policy.

The nation's money and resources were invested to give people assets. Homesteads provided something of lasting value that potentially could change a person's economic status. Not only were crops produced and sold for money, but the land itself could increase in value as areas developed. The Homestead Act made it possible for a family of modest means to create a better life for the next generation. Nonetheless, it took ingenuity and hard work to survive on a homestead for five years. It was a participant-centered policy, requiring each homesteader to be an active contributor.

These lessons from the Homestead Act can help inform policy today. The Growing Wealth Working Group (GWWG)[12] advocates asset-building policy similar to that exemplified by the Homestead Act: progressive, inclusive, simple, enduring, and participant centered. This might entail several guidelines. Whenever possible, ways to assist the nonwealthy should be considered, and a voice should be provided to those who are currently asset-poor. Policies need to be created that are inclusive and not amenable to the stigmatization of visible groups; that is, policies must not target people by race, gender, religion, or nationality of origin. Policies must be pursued that are simple and enduring yet flexible enough to adapt to the unique circumstances of a person or locality. And participant-centered policies should be considered so that people can use their own ambition and creativity to create a future for themselves and their descendants. Taking these principles—embodied within the Homestead Act—into consideration, modern policy initiatives could provide positive opportunities for individuals and families, while contributing significantly to the economic development of the nation.

CONCLUSION

The Homestead Act was passed at a unique time in U.S. history. The populace was overwhelmingly rural, and the geography, politics, and racial dynamics familiar today were in the process of being formed. The nation chose to give up some immediate revenues in order to invest in its people and its future. As a result, 1.5 million families were offered a valuable asset. However, the homestead legislation did more than simply transfer property from the government to private ownership. It hastened the development of the western frontier and made the United States an attractive place for investors and new immigrants. The Homestead Act remained in force during a period of tremendous economic, demographic, and political growth, lasting through the Industrial Revolution and the start of World War II. It is part of the ancestry of many Americans currently living in the twenty-first century—even though they may be unaware of the fact.

Perhaps a more comprehensive understanding of the enduring legacy of asset-building policies, such as the Homestead Act and the G.I. Bill, will lead to more openness toward similar ideas as the bases for current policy making. What asset-building policies can be created today that will lead U.S. citizens into a productive future for themselves and subsequent generations? What would be the result if the government were daring enough to create policy that provides hope and opportunity for persons who otherwise are not likely to be successful (the poor, the uneducated, foster children, single mothers, the unemployed, and many others)? Ideally, an innovative domestic policy that provides opportunities to develop assets and turns hopelessness into meaningful futures for individual citizens and families will not just be a part of past U.S. history, but also a part of this generation's reality and heritage.

NOTES

I have benefited from comments by economist Douglass North as well as advice regarding estimation methods by demographers David Coleman and Eugene Hammel. The idea for this study was conceived by Michael Sherraden, who also guided and advised on the project. The research for this chapter was funded by the Ford Foundation and supported by the Center for Social Development at Washington University in St. Louis.

1. Prior to European colonization, land was occupied by various Indian tribes both north and south of what has become the Mexican border. Although wars and dishonesty were often the means of acquisition, by 1853 all the property being considered was the legal possession of the U.S. government. One author (Gates, 1976) explains how promoters, frontier settlers, and fur traders pushed the government to enter treaties with Indians that today would be regarded "as unconscionable" (223–224). Even those agreements that had been made were often honored only when reservations "did not contain land desired by the whites" (Robbins, 1976, 233).

2. In his overview of land policy, Gates (1976) discusses two major divisions of opinion: how to dispose of the land and how quickly the land should be surveyed and opened for settlement. The first concern was whether to grant large estates to influential people and whether the benefits from the sales revenue should go to the state or territory wherein the land was sold or to the federal government to distribute among all the states. The second concern was whether quick sale at favorable rates in the new territories would draw populations away from existing

eastern states, thus negatively impacting congressional representation, land values, and employment. The East and West typically had opposing opinions on these issues.

3. Before the Civil War, most states adopted this type of homestead exemption to provide security in a time of volatile market forces. A reasonable portion of property was exempt from seizure to pay debts, so that a household would be left with at least a place to live when facing destitution. For a good discussion of the legal, historical, and philosophical foundations for these laws, see Goodman, "The Emergence of Homestead Exemption in the United States" (1993).

4. Even after the Homestead Act was passed, there were other disseminations of the public domain outside of granting free land. Some land continued to be sold in larger plots and sold to private corporations (303,500,000 acres). Some land was granted to states for schools, public works, and other institutions (328,480,000 acres). The rest was granted to railroad corporations, veterans, or sold under special timber or desert laws (224,900,000 acres). (Data taken from the U.S. Department of the Interior [1998], *Public Land Statistics, 1961.*)

5. Column four from table 2.1 will be used as the relevant number of homestead families, representing the number of homestead patents granted to applicants who remained on the land for five years and "proved up." Although many others resided upon property applied for under the Homestead Act and may have benefited from the legislation, these calculations will only include those who fulfilled the requirements to attain full legal title to the land.

6. Data taken from the authoritative study on U.S. fertility by Coale and Zelnik (1963). Total fertility rate is a measure that summarizes the average number of children per woman that would be born to a hypothetical group of 1,000 who, as they pass through the reproductive ages, experience the birth rates observed in the population. The numbers represent births per white women in the United States over the given time period.

7. Data taken from an article by Ryder (1986) on cohort fertility in the United States. The statistic of proportion ever married by age 45 is based upon the census reports of women by age and marital status. Adjustments and corrections were made comparing between censuses. Thus, it provides a good estimate of how many of the homestead children born in the given five-year period ever married and were likely to bear children of their own.

8. The total U.S. population in 1998 was 270.3 million. The adult population (age 25 and over) was 175 million (U.S. Census Bureau, 1999).

9. Painter (1977) describes how thousands of freed slaves left the South in 1879, searching for land and assistance in Kansas. Some found jobs, and a few bought property or applied for homesteads, but most arrived poor and remained that way.

10. Cox (1958) does an excellent job discussing deliberations of the 38th Congress in 1865 on the Freedmen's Bureau bill, which would have taken abandoned and confiscated lands of the South for use in forty-acre allotments by freedmen or refugees to rent and eventually own. She demonstrates that there were persons interested in greater freedom, aid, and land ownership for former slaves, but the recommendations hinged upon an expected confiscation of large southern plantations, which never really took place.

11. Mosk (1951) compares historical institutional development in the United States (excluding southern states) and Latin America. He writes that the former developed a system of small landholdings, while the latter developed a landed aristocracy with tenancy or peonage systems. In his analysis, the wide distribution of

land ownership in the United States led to the development of a dominant middle-class, higher standards of living, attraction of more immigrants, and a less rigid social structure. Other scholars make similar points that U.S. land policies were consistent with economic growth (North, 1974) and increased "access to recognized avenues of mobility, opportunity, and success" (Hyman, 1986, 10).

12. The GWWG is a policy development "brain trust" convened by the Corporation for Enterprise Development (CFED) and the Center for Social Development (CSD). A more detailed description of principles for asset-building policy can be found in chapter 12 in this volume, written by Robert Friedman and Ray Boshara.

REFERENCES

Coale, A. J., and M. Zelnik. (1963). *New Estimates of Fertility and Population in the United States*. Princeton, N.J.: Princeton University Press.

Cox, C. (1993). *The Forgotten Heroes: The Story of Buffalo Soldiers*. New York: Scholastic, Inc.

Cox, L. (1958). "The Promise of Land for the Freedmen." *The Mississippi Valley Historical Review* 45(3), 413–440.

Cross, C. F. (1995). *Go West, Young Man!: Horace Greeley's Vision for America*. Albuquerque: University of New Mexico Press.

Danhof, C. H. (1941). "Farm-Making Costs and the 'Safety Valve': 1850–60." *The Journal of Political Economy* 49(3), 317–359.

Deverell, W. F. (1988). "To Loosen the Safety Valve: Eastern Workers and Western Lands." *The Western Historical Quarterly* 19(3), 269–285.

Dick, E. N. (1970). *The Lure of the Land: A Social History of the Public Lands from the Articles of Confederation to the New Deal*. Lincoln: University of Nebraska Press.

Donaldson, T. ([1884] 1970). *The Public Domain: Its History, with Statistics*. New York: Johnson Reprint Corp.

Gates, P. W. (1941). "Land Policy and Tenancy in the Prairie States." *Journal of Economic History* 1(1), 60–82.

Gates, P. W. (1970). "Introduction." For T. Donaldson [1884], *The Public Domain: Its History with Statistics*. New York: Johnson Reprint Corp., i–xi.

Gates, P. W. (1976). "American Land Policy." In *Two Centuries of American Agriculture*, ed. V. D. Wiser. Washington, D.C.: Agricultural History Society, 213–229.

Gates, P. W. (1996). *The Jeffersonian Dream: Studies in the History of American Land Policy and Development*. Albuquerque: University of New Mexico Press.

Goodman, P. (1993). "The Emergence of Homestead Exemption in the United States: Accommodation and Resistance to the Market Revolution, 1840–1880." *The Journal of American History* 80(2), 470–498.

Hughes, J. (1987). "The Great Land Ordinances: Colonial America's Thumbprint on History." In *Essays on the Economy of the Old Northwest*, eds. D. C. Klingaman and R. K. Vedder. Athens: Ohio University Press, 1–18.

Hyman, H. M. (1986). *American Singularity: The 1787 Northwest Ordinance, the 1862 Homestead and Morrill Acts, and the 1944 G.I. Bill*. Athens: University of Georgia Press.

Lanza, M. L. (1990). *Agrarianism and Reconstruction Politics: The Southern Homestead Act*. Baton Rouge: Louisiana State University.

Lebergott, S. (1985). "The Demand for Land: The United States, 1820–1860." *Journal of Economic History* 45(2), 181–212.

Magdol, E. (1977). *A Right to the Land: Essays on the Freedmen's Community.* Westport, Conn.: Greenwood Press.

Mosk, S. A. (1951). "Latin America versus the United States." *The American Economic Review* 41(2), 367–383.

North, D. C. (1974). *Growth and Welfare in the American Past: A New Economic History* (2d ed.). Englewood Cliffs, N.J.: Prentice-Hall.

North, D. C., and A. R. Rutten. (1987). "The Northwest Ordinance in Historical Perspective." In *Essays on the Economy of the Old Northwest,* eds. D. C. Klingaman and R. K. Vedder. Athens: Ohio University Press, 19–31.

Oliver, M. L., and T. M. Shapiro. (1995). *Black Wealth/White Wealth: A New Perspective on Racial Inequality.* New York: Routledge.

Oubre, C. F. (1978). *Forty Acres and a Mule: The Freedmen's Bureau and Black Land Ownership.* Baton Rouge: Louisiana State University Press.

Painter, N. I. (1977). *Exodusters: Black Migration to Kansas after Reconstruction* (1st ed.). New York: Knopf.

Peffer, E. L. (1951). *The Closing of the Public Domain: Disposal and Reservation Policies, 1900–50.* Stanford, Calif.: Stanford University Press.

Robbins, R. M. (1976*). Our Landed Heritage: The Public Domain, 1776–1970* (2d rev. ed.). Lincoln: University of Nebraska Press.

Ryder, N. B. (1986). "Observations on the History of Cohort Fertility in the United States." *Population Development and Review* 12(4), 617–643.

Sloan, I. J. (1976). *American Landmark Legislation: Primary Materials.* Dobbs Ferry, N.Y.: Oceana Publications.

U.S. Census Bureau. (1975). *Historical Statistics of the United States: Colonial Times to 1970.* Washington, D.C.: Government Printing Office.

U.S. Census Bureau. (1999). *Statistical Abstract of the United States: 1999* (119th ed.). Washington, D.C.: Government Printing Office.

U.S. Department of the Interior. (1961). *Public Land Statistics, 1961.* Washington, D.C.: Government Printing Office.

U.S. Department of the Interior. (1998). *Public Land Statistics, 1998.* Washington, D.C.: Government Printing Office.

Wilder, L. I. ([1935] 1953). *Little House on the Prairie.* New York: Harper and Row.

3

Asset-Based Policy in Historical
and International Perspective

James Midgley

Social welfare is a contested field in which very different ideas about human well-being are expressed. Divergent beliefs about the importance of individual responsibility, the contribution of markets, the support of family members, the role of charities and religious bodies, and the intervention of the state all compete to shape welfare policy. These beliefs are accompanied by different views about which policies, programs, and approaches are the most effective in promoting human well-being. While some contend that nonmaterial interventions such as professional counseling are the most useful, others believe that the transfer of cash benefits are a highly desirable means of addressing social needs. Yet others are critical of the provision of benefits and services to passive recipients and believe that steps should be taken to enhance the self-sufficiency and autonomous functioning of those in need.

It is in this context that debates about the role of asset-based policy in social welfare have become increasingly important. Proponents of an asset approach are critical of the emphasis that historically has been placed on income transfers through the payment of income benefits. Although the transfers are designed to increase consumption and, thus, to meet social needs and alleviate poverty, critics claim that they do not achieve these goals. They argue that income benefits are seldom sufficient to raise the consumption of needy people much above survival levels and that they do not create opportunities for mobility and sustained prosperity. They also argue that the provision of income benefits fails to address the root causes of poverty, and that often a culture of dependency is fostered. On the other hand, the asset approach encourages the accumulation of resources, which, in turn, generates economic returns. Resource accumulation also maximizes economic security by providing a reserve to deal with adverse events, promotes opportunity by fostering investments, increases economic flexibility, enhances economic status and social mobility, boosts self-confidence and esteem, supports risk taking, and promotes future-oriented action and other desirable behavioral qualities (Shapiro, 2001).

Asset-based policy has primarily taken the form of individual development accounts or IDAs, as they are known. The IDA is a matched savings account that subsidizes the savings of low-income people and helps them to acquire capital for socially approved purposes, such as housing, education, and retirement. The IDA was invented by Michael Sherraden, who first conceived of this idea in the 1980s, following his encounters with recipients of welfare benefits (Sherraden, 2001). Sherraden forged a successful collaboration with Robert Friedman, founder of the Corporation for Enterprise Development, and several IDA initiatives were introduced. The first IDA projects were established by community-based organizations and local social service organizations in the early 1990s. Federal and state legislation that supported the creation of IDA projects was also enacted. By the end of the 1990s, at least 200 IDA projects were in operation in different parts of the United States (Sherraden, 2001). Currently, thirteen IDA projects are being carefully evaluated by the Downpayment on the American Dream Policy Demonstration (also known as the American Dream Demonstration or ADD), and a good deal of useful information about how IDAs function is being obtained.

IDAs have also attracted attention at the highest levels of government. In 1992, President George H. W. Bush sympathetically reviewed IDA proposals and agreed to raise the asset limits of welfare recipients from $1,000 to $10,000 (Sherraden, 2001). The IDA idea was subsequently incorporated into housing programs by Housing and Urban Development (HUD) Secretary Jack Kemp. IDAs have also been incorporated into the Personal Responsibility and Work Opportunity Reconciliation Act of 1996, which replaced the country's traditional means-tested welfare program. A major achievement was the enactment of the Assets for Independence Act of 1998, which provides $125 million for asset-development projects for a five-year period. In addition, several states have introduced their own IDA programs. Toward the end of his term of office, President Bill Clinton proposed the introduction of universal savings accounts, or USAs, which were intended to encourage low- and moderate-income people to save for retirement. However, despite considerable publicity, this proposal was not implemented.

Although seldom recognized, the asset approach is controversial not only in the technical sense that there are differences of opinion about the advantages and disadvantages of assets as opposed to other interventions, but also in a wider ideological sense. As will be argued later in this chapter, the asset approach can be used to support quite different normative commitments in social welfare. The asset approach is also rooted in historical institutions and values that inform current debates about its role in welfare policy.

This chapter seeks to contextualize the asset approach by briefly reviewing the conceptual ideas attending the notion of assets, tracing the historical evolution of the asset approach, and describing asset policy innovations in some other countries. Hopefully, it will show that the asset approach is not merely a technical instrument of welfare policy, but that it represents a unique and viable perspective that enhances social well-being through social investments and the promotion of social development at the national level.

THE IDEA OF ASSETS

The *MIT Dictionary of Economics* (Pearse, 1992, 18) defines an asset as "an entity possessing market or exchange value and forming part of the wealth or property of the owner." This dictionary points out that assets are usually categorized by economists as either *real* (tangible) or *financial* (intangible). The former category includes assets such as land and buildings, while the latter includes money, bonds, and equities. In addition, the intangible assets of human, social, and cultural capital are increasingly being recognized as important. Just as real and financial assets have market value and can be converted into income, the knowledge, interpersonal skills and social networks that comprise intangible assets are critical for economic success.

As with many other terms in the social sciences, the complexity of the asset concept is not adequately expressed in the definition provided by dictionaries or in the classifications commonly used to categorize different types of assets. The fact that the term "asset" has many synonyms reveals the multifaceted nature of the concept, as well as the intricate way the notion of an asset is linked to other, closely related concepts, such as resources, money, income, property, wealth, capital, investments, holdings, and possessions, to name only a few. Despite the close link between asset and these other concepts, the term has a unique appeal, capturing the idea that certain possessions or, more accurately, rights to possessions, have value not only in the sense that they can be traded as entities in themselves but that they can be translated into income, and that income can, in turn, be translated into assets. However, for many, the ultimate value of an asset lies in its potential to generate additional income and wealth. When properly invested, financial assets can be increased in value. Tangible assets, such as land and buildings, also produce value-added gains. Similarly, intangible assets, such as human and social capital, also generate income returns (Shapiro, 2001).

Assets and Individual Development Accounts

Although IDAs represent a very tangible example of the asset approach, the asset idea is used in a loose and general way and has, as Sherraden (1991, 106) noted, been applied to "nearly everything of any conceivable value, concrete or abstract, including personal, social, cultural, and political characteristics, as well as all categories of tangible wealth." This complicates the application of the asset idea in the field of social welfare. Nevertheless, when translated into specific policies and programs, asset ideas—such as

IDAs, preschool interventions like the Head Start program, micro-enterprise and micro-lending projects, community development initiatives, and the like—become tangible and viable complements or alternatives to the income-transfer approach, which dominated social welfare policy for many years. It is important to recognize that IDAs are only one example of the asset approach. There are many other types of assets that people acquire and value and, although neglected by social welfare scholars, they have played an important role in promoting social welfare.

As noted earlier, an IDA is a matched savings account designed to help low-income and low-wealth families accumulate resources that can subsequently be used for education and job training, home ownership, and micro-enterprise investments. The magazine *Assets* (1998) explained that participants in IDA programs make monthly contributions into a designated account that is matched by a financial institution, philanthropic foundation, religious organization, or public agency by a factor ranging from one to four. Community organizations counsel and monitor participants and assist with financial management. They also authorize withdrawals. Usually, participants save for periods ranging from one to four years.

Thirteen IDA projects in different parts of the United States are currently being evaluated by the American Dream Demonstration project (ADD). These projects are managed by different types of community-based organizations and are supported by private foundations and individual donors. Preliminary findings from the ADD project were reported by Sherraden in 2001, and a more detailed account is included in this volume (see Schreiner et al., chapter 10 in this volume). The ADD evaluation project shows that by June 2000, the 1,326 participants in the thirteen projects had saved about $378,700, which had been matched by about $741,600. The median length of participation was nine months, and the mean amount saved per month was $33. The average saving per participant was $286. About two-thirds of the participants contributed regularly, and more than 70 percent were meeting their savings goals.

At the initiation of the project, more than half of the participants indicated that they intended to save to purchase a home, 17 percent stated that they intended to start a small business, and another 17 percent wanted to save to finance postsecondary education. By June 1999, ninety-two participants had made approved withdrawals, of which 33 percent were to finance small business start-ups, 27 percent for home purchases, 20 percent for home repairs, and 13 percent for education.

Although some will regard the amounts saved as meager and of limited consequence, the ADD project reveals that people with low incomes and few assets respond to incentives designed to promote asset accumulation and that they do, indeed, generate assets and use them for investments that create additional income and wealth. Further evaluations will be needed to determine whether these savings were successfully invested in the longer term and whether the economic and social goals of the IDA approach have, in fact, been realized.

Assets, Inequality, and Opportunity

Proponents of the asset approach believe that IDAs and similar asset programs take a tentative step in addressing the huge inequities that currently exist in American society. In a detailed study of the distribution of wealth in the United States, Edward Wolff (2001) reported that wealth is "extremely concentrated" among a small proportion of Americans. At the end of the 1990s, 1 per cent of families owned 38 percent of all marketable wealth. This same group owned an even larger share (47 percent) of all marketable wealth. When the asset ownership of the wealthiest 20 percent of Americans is taken into consideration, the situation is even more skewed. While the top 20 percent held 91 percent of marketable wealth, the remaining 80 percent held only 9 percent. Wolff points out that although income distribution is also highly skewed, with the top 20 percent earning 56 percent of all income, asset ownership is far more concentrated. He notes that both wealth and income inequality have become more skewed over the last two decades.

The concentration of income and wealth in the hands of relatively few people in any country is regarded by many as undesirable, not only on moral grounds but also on the premise that income and wealth concentration is economically and social harmful. Another problem is that public policy in the United States unfairly promotes asset accumulation among middle- and high-income earners but not among those with low incomes. Sherraden (1991) first emphasized the fact that the federal government operates two sets of welfare policy—one for the poor and one for the nonpoor—and that the costs of the latter far exceed that of the former. In 1990, he pointed out, the government spent $124 billion dollars or 8.5 percent of total expenditures on means-tested and similar welfare programs targeted at the poor. In contrast, government expenditures on social programs that are disproportionately utilized by the middle class, such as social security, civil service and military retirement pensions, Medicare, education, and similar provisions, together with fiscal welfare expenditures—including tax exclusions for employer pensions, tax deferred savings accounts, such as individual retirement accounts (IRAs) and Keogh plans, and mortgage relief—amounted to a staggering $651 billion or 44.5 percent of total federal expenditures (Sherraden, 1991).

More recently, Christopher Howard (1997) and Laurence Seidman (2001) have elaborated on these costs, showing that despite strident attacks on public expenditures, the "middle class welfare state" continues to prosper. In 1999, tax exclusions of employer contributions to medical insurance premiums amounted to $76 billion, while tax exclusions of employer contributions to pension funds amounted to $72 billion. Federal expenditures on mortgage deductions amounted to $54 billion. If the federal government is willing to use fiscal policy to promote asset accumulation among middle- and high-income earners, many believe that it is only fair that it do the same for the poor.

While some economists argue that these expenditures on behalf of middle- and high-income earners are a highly undesirable form of rent seeking, there is little electoral or political support for their abolition. Similarly, there is little support today for policies that are explicitly redistributional. The egalitarian commitment to steeply progressive taxation and high social expenditures that are designed to transfer resources to those with low incomes now has limited support. It is in this context that policies promoting asset accumulation among the poor may have merit. These policies would address the blatant inequities of current public policy, enhance opportunities, and reduce social divisions. This argument has particular cogency when the situation of people of color is taken into account. Melvin Oliver and Thomas Shapiro (1997) have shown that income and wealth inequality between African Americans and other Americans is highly skewed and that it cannot be explained by class position alone. Asset ownership among the black middle class is far lower than among the white middle class. This fact, Oliver and Shapiro contend, is not because of a lack of resources or a lack of interest in asset accumulation but in attitudinal and social structural factors that impede asset ownership. They believe that the problem can be countered by creating opportunities for full participation in society not only for people of color but for all. And, asset accumulation, the authors argue, can promote this goal (Oliver and Shapiro, 1997).

The idea that asset accumulation can promote opportunity, enhance participation and social solidarity, and foster the ideals of the "Good Society" have not been adequately debated by scholars and policy makers involved in the formulation of asset-based policies and programs. However, in recent times, more attention has been paid to the conceptual ideas attending the asset-based approach, and these have been linked to other social policy concepts such as social investment and social development (Midgley, 1995; Midgley and Sherraden, 2000; Midgley and Tang, 2001). These concepts may be relatively new in social welfare, but they are based on ideas that have an ancient provenance.

THE HISTORY OF THE ASSET-BASED APPROACH

Different societies at different times have developed complex social arrangements for the accumulation and ownership of assets. In some societies, assets were held in common, while in others, asset ownership was viewed as the prerogative of certain groups and particularly elite groups. In many societies, certain human beings were prohibited from accumulating assets, while in others, they themselves were viewed as assets. Slavery, which legitimated the ownership of human beings by others, has been common throughout history, and indeed it persists in some places even today. This is also true of feudalism, which legitimated the ownership of vast assets, particularly land, by aristocratic families, while severely restricting the rights of most people to hold property.

The decline of feudalism in Europe and its gradual transformation into a more fluid system of asset ownership has been explained by historians with reference to the rise of towns and the emergence of a new, independent merchant class; the destructive role of civil wars, which undermined the authority of feudal nobles; the effects of the Protestant reformation; and the growth of international trade. The popularization of new ideas associated with the writings of scholars who advocated the ownership of property as a condition for liberty was equally important. Among these writers was John Locke (1632–1704), whose ideas exerted a powerful influence on social and political thinking at the time. Locke argued that individuals were the unconditional proprietors of their own persons and that, in addition, they were the owners of the fruits of their labor. The individual accumulation and ownership of property was, therefore, an inalienable right that could not be restricted or expropriated by others, particularly by those in political authority. Indeed, Locke contended that property ownership was the best means of limiting political power. He argued that those who had acquired property could be expected to defend their assets against acquisitive rulers. However, like other contractarians, he recognized that the singular pursuit of personal advantage over the interests of others was likely to be destructive. For this reason, he argued that individuals should give their "tacit consent" to being governed and that they obey the rules they themselves had established within the bounds of natural law.

Locke's revolutionary ideas helped institutionalize liberal democracy, legitimate the emerging capitalist order, and establish the foundation for modern conceptions of asset ownership. His writings were particularly influential in the North American colonies that had been largely populated by yeoman settlers intent on acquiring land and protecting their possessions. In addition to invoking biblical injunctions about the sanctity of agrarian life, they turned to Locke's ideas to legitimate their rights to land ownership. Other writers had an equally important influence. Adam Smith's (1723–1790) criticisms of mercantilism and his ideas on the advantages of markets and the need for an institutional order that promoted economic exchange were also influential. Also significant was James Harrington's (1611–1677) utopian account of the Commonwealth of Oceana, in which agrarian property ownership formed the basis for political participation. Some of Harrington's recommendations for promoting land ownership were subsequently implemented by the newly independent American states.

The American Revolution gave impetus to the institutionalization of popular beliefs about land ownership. Alan Zundel (2000) reports that Harrington's attack on primogeniture found application in the enactment of constitutional provisions in several states which required the equal division of land among heirs. Other land ownership provisions derived from feudal traditions were also abolished. At about this time, Thomas Jefferson campaigned for the allocation of a minimum of fifty acres of pubic land to anyone willing to settle and cultivate it.

However, some of the revolutionary leaders were concerned that falling agricultural prices resulting from European boycotts would prevent settlers from securing a livelihood. While Jefferson remained in favor of settlement,

Alexander Hamilton advocated urban-based investments in manufacturing as a means of absorbing the growing labor force.

But the westward expansion of the nation's frontier could not be halted and, by the mid-nineteenth century, the Mississippi Valley had been settled, and a nation of agrarian landowners had emerged, even though the seeds of the economy's subsequent transformation were already evident in the cities where industrial development was gathering pace. Nevertheless, it was at this time that the ideals of what Zundel calls "Civic Republicanism" were fully realized. This notion encapsulates the idea that individuals and their families should be independent and self-sufficient and that government should encourage attitudes and behaviors conducive to self-reliance. Indeed, at the time of the founding of the Democratic Party, Andrew Jackson proclaimed that "it should be the policy of republics to multiply their freeholders, as it is the policies of monarchies to multiply tenancy. We are a republic . . . then multiply the class of freeholders; pass the public lands easily and cheaply into the hands of the People" (Zundel, 2000, 33).

These sentiments paved the way for the passing of the Homestead Act of 1862, as well as subsequent legislation, the Land Grant Acts, that distributed more than 200 million acres of public land to farmers and ranchers and another 200 million to the railroads (Sherraden, 1991; Stern, 2001; Zundel, 2000). In addition, the Land Grant Acts established a number of public universities with an explicit mission to promote agriculture and mechanical innovations. These were major asset investment programs that, as Sherraden (1991) suggests, had a significant impact on the well-being of the population. However, some scholars have shown that many settlers abandoned their allotments because the land was not suitable for cultivation (Zundel, 2000). In addition, fraud was widespread, and many of the settlers were not poor but members of successful eastern farming families seeking to enhance their family wealth. Particularly problematic was the failure of the federal government to honor its promise to dismantle the large plantations in the South at the end of the Civil War and to redistribute the land to former slaves. As Mark Stern (2001) points out, tepid support for the Southern Homestead Act failed to change existing economic institutions and accounted for the persistence of poverty and sharecropping exploitation well into the twentieth century.

Nevertheless, the notions of independence and self-sufficiency—the central normative tenets of the Civic Republican tradition—have continued to exert a powerful influence in American culture for more than two hundred years. During the late nineteenth century and into the twentieth century, the Civil Republican tradition was endorsed by the rise of agrarian populism, and its popularity was further reinforced by a number of policy innovations introduced during the Great Depression in the 1930s. These included New Deal innovations, such as home mortgage loans for those facing foreclosure, federally insured low interest rate mortgages and, probably of greatest impact, the introduction of mortgage tax deductions. The creation of the Federal Housing Administration (FHA) in 1934 was, as Zundel (2000) reported, specifically intended to link employment creation with home ownership. Although the success of this policy is disputed, there is no doubt that home ownership increased dramatically from about 45 percent of all dwellings before the Depression to more than 65 percent in the decades following World War II.

Similar asset accumulation proposals were also being advocated at the time of the New Deal. One was put forward by Dr. Francis Townsend, whose proposal to provide every worker over the age of 65 with a federal pension of $200 per month was extremely popular. The pension would be funded by a national sales tax, and recipients would be required to spend the pension or forfeit any remaining balance. By 1935, Townsend had collected more than 25 million signatures in support of this proposition. Another proposal came from flamboyant U.S. Senator Huey Long, the former governor of Louisiana, who advocated a program of share the wealth redistribution, by which every citizen would receive a guaranteed income. Long was a major presidential contender and might have secured the presidency if he were not assassinated in 1935. Some historians believe that both Townsend's and Long's proposals accelerated the implementation of Roosevelt's own social policy proposals.

Welfare Statism and the Civil Republican Tradition

The New Deal also made provision for the introduction of European-style social insurance for retirement, disability, and survivor's benefits through the enactment of the 1935 Social Security Act. This act also created a federally subsidized, nationwide social assistance program directed primarily at women with needy children. Social insurance had been advocated by a number of social policy writers since the late nineteenth century, and their proposals were supported by the labor unions and various advocacy organizations. With the introduction of social insurance and the expansion of means-tested benefits, the Civil Republicanism which had characterized American welfare policy now faced competition in the guise of a large-scale, consumption-based system of income transfers characteristic of European state welfarism.

Although state welfarism characterized and dominated American social policy in the years following World War II, asset-based provisions were not abandoned. Asset enhancing social programs, such as mortgage tax relief, continued to function through the fiscal system, even though they attracted little attention from mainstream social policy scholars. Instead, mainstream social policy scholarship was preoccupied with advocating the expansion of universal instead of means-tested benefits. This concern with universality and comprehensiveness revealed a strong commitment to the redistributive role of social policy. Universal programs were also regarded by social policy scholars as an expression of collectivist values, based on notions of altruism, social rights, and solidarity. Many were inspired by the writings of British writers, such as T. H. Marshall and Richard Titmuss, whose ideas offered an eloquent legitimation of state intervention and social welfare provision (Midgley, 2000). Enthused by these ideas, few American social policy writers paid much attention to the expansion of asset-enhancing social policies, such as those provided through the Servicemen's Readjustment Act of 1944 or the G.I. Bill, as it was popularly known. The introduction of various fiscal provisions, such as IRAs, in the 1980s, which are designed to encourage savings for old age retirement, also received little attention.

The neglect of these asset-based social welfare policies resulted in the unfortunate neglect of the powerful cultural force of the Civil Republican tradition that characterized popular attitudes toward social welfare in the United States. As David Stoesz (2000) and other critics have shown, European welfare statism, based on collectivist thinking, is hardly suited to American cultural beliefs, which are rooted in individualism and beliefs about liberty, autonomy, and self-reliance. Consequently, mainstream social welfare scholars were unprepared to address the countercultural attacks on state social provision that emerged during the Ronald Reagan era and have since dominated social welfare thinking in policy circles. Had these scholars been aware of the "hidden welfare state," or of the huge fiscal costs of the "non-poor welfare state," as Sherraden (1991) calls it, they may have been able to reveal the way opponents of government social provisions represented sectional interests and sought to legitimate the very rent seeking they condemned.

There is little doubt that American social welfare policy has moved away from the statist entitlement approach and that programs based on ideas of self-sufficiency and social responsibility now feature much more prominently. These ideas have found application in the Temporary Assistance to Needy Families (TANF) program, introduced in terms of the Personal Responsibility and Work Opportunity Reconciliation Act of 1996, which requires employment as a condition for benefits and has placed a time limit on the provision of assistance. In recent years, proposals for the partial privatization of Social Security have attracted more support and, in addition, asset-based policies and programs based on the individual savings account approach now feature prominently in social welfare policy thinking.

Although it was shown earlier that the IDA was developed by Sherraden, many variations and extensions of the IDA idea have since been proposed, and some have been implemented. In 1988, Robert Haveman advocated the creation of publicly funded human capital accounts of $10,000 to be used for educational purposes for each qualifying individual who reached the age of 18. Echoing this idea, Bruce Ackerman and Anne Alstott (1999) proposed that young adults who complete high school be given a capital sum of $80,000 each as a stake they can use for a variety of purposes: higher education, home ownership, a business start-up, or simply for investment. Although the cost of the program is prodigious, the authors propose that it be financed by a wealth tax on assets over $80,000, as well as a pay-back tax imposed at the time of each recipient's death (1999).

Another variation on the IDA idea is the child savings account (CSA), which was proposed by Duncan Lindsey (1994) as a way of transcending the nation's traditional remedial child welfare system. As Sherraden (2001) reports, this idea has attracted political support that resulted in a legislative proposal by former Senator Bob Kerrey of Nebraska, which, if enacted, would create an account for each child into which the federal government would make deposits until the recipient reaches the age of 18 years. Withdrawals would be permitted for education and subsequently for retirement. Medical savings accounts (MSAs), introduced in 1999, are accounts that encourage savings for medical expenditures by permitting tax deferred contributions. Proposals for the introduction of mandatory retirement savings accounts, funded by diverting a proportion of the current social security payroll tax, are also being debated with strong support from the George W. Bush administration and the business community.

As these examples reveal, asset-based policies and programs, particularly in the form of savings accounts, are gaining momentum and deserve much closer attention from social policy scholars. Although many scholars view these accounts as an unobjectionable policy instrument, their potential linkage to quite different normative positions in social welfare suggest that their ideological implications require further scrutiny and analysis. Their potential to form an integral component of a social investment approach to social welfare, designed to enhance stakeholding and promote social development, also deserves much more extensive debate.

ASSETS IN INTERNATIONAL PERSPECTIVE

Although the asset-based approach to social welfare has strong roots in American culture, the value of asset accumulation is also accepted in other countries. As discussed earlier, the conceptual ideas on which asset ownership are based have their roots in the writings of Locke, Smith, and other European enlightenment thinkers, and, although diluted by the pervasive influence of social democratic state welfarism during the twentieth century, beliefs about the virtues of asset ownership are hardly alien to Europeans. Many European countries have encouraged asset accumulation, and, until recently, mortgage tax relief was a major component of public expenditure in Britain. In addition, recent British governments have adopted policies designed to promote asset accumulation.

Perhaps the most strident and successful campaign for increased asset ownership was mounted by former British Prime Minister Margaret Thatcher in the 1980s. Mrs. Thatcher initiated a radical process of privatization by breaking the consensus that had legitimated the nationalization of key British industries, such as mining, steel manufacture, transportation, and utilities, for many decades. She did so on the basis that stock holding by ordinary people would not only spread the financial benefits of asset ownership, but also would be a desirable and necessary element in the creation of a vibrant, capitalist society. Her public statements about the virtues of popular capitalism were electorally popular, and, indeed, many individuals who had never invested in the stock market secured ownership in the newly privatized state industries. Stocks in major and profitable state enterprises, such as British Gas and British Petroleum, were sold at discounted rates, and it seemed that the nation was indeed being transformed into one in which everyone had a stake in the economy.

Additionally, in the United Kingdom, policies were introduced to transfer public housing to private ownership at heavily discounted prices. Tenants were encouraged to purchase the homes they rented, and desirable properties were soon snapped up. The Thatcher government also adopted policies to encourage the purchase of commercially managed "personal pensions," as they were known. These were intended to wean workers away from the State Earnings-Related Pension Scheme (SERPS), introduced by the Labour government to supplement the basic social insurance retirement system for those who did not have occupational pensions and would be entirely dependent on the basic state pension when they retired. However, while the Thatcher government proposed to replace SERPS with commercially managed pensions, unscrupulous promotion and sales activities by sections of the insurance industry resulted in widespread negative press publicity and discredited the proposed private program. Despite this debacle, the government was not deterred and vigorously continued to promote its social insurance privatization plans.

Some political commentators believe that the policy that advocated commercially managed pensions was unwise and that it contributed to the defeat of the Conservative Party in 1997. However, contrary to expectations, Prime Minister Tony Blair's Labour government did not oppose the creation of private pensions and soon began to promote what it called "stakeholder pensions" for those who did not belong to an approved occupational pension scheme. In addition, under pressure from the Labour Party's rank and file, the government agreed to strengthen the basic state retirement pension and to redress the devaluation of its retirement benefits by the previous Conservative government. The Blair government has used the rhetoric of assets and particularly the idea of stakeholding to promote its policies. Informed by the writings of newspaper columnist and editor, Will Hutton (1995, 1997), the idea of stakeholding emerged as a key element of New Labour thinking. This idea was consonant with the views of Frank Field (1996), the government minister appointed to initiate a radical transformation of the British welfare system. However, the failure to articulate these ideas in ways that could be translated into policies and programs that would be acceptable to the party's rank and file caused much confusion and criticism and contributed to Field's resignation. Nevertheless, the Blair government continues to make reference to the idea of stakeholding, and it has also expressed a strong interest in IDAs and particularly in establishing CSAs. In 2000, the Fabian Society, which is affiliated with the Labour Party, published proposals by David Nissan and Julian LeGrand (2000) for the introduction of a universal capital grant to be paid to young people when they reach 18 years of age. Based on Ackerman and Alstott's idea (1999), they proposed that the grant be financed from inheritance taxes.

Perhaps the most radical asset creation program in recent times was the introduction of commercially managed individual retirement accounts by General Augusto Pinochet's military government in Chile in 1981. These accounts replaced the country's venerable social insurance retirement system that had been created in the early decades of the twentieth century. Driven by the same ideological beliefs that inspired Prime Minister Thatcher in the United Kingdom and President Reagan in the United States, the Pinochet government deplored the welfare statism that characterized Chile's social policies, which, it argued, was responsible for the nation's economic and social decline. The introduction of commercially managed individual retirement accounts would, it claimed, not only solve the various fiscal, managerial, and other technical difficulties that had plagued the social insurance system for many years, but also would support a wider and more radical project to change popular attitudes and reconstruct the economy and the wider society (Borzutsky, 1991).

The privatization of the Chilean social insurance system has been extensively documented, and there are sharp differences of opinion among social security experts on whether workers will be able to accumulate sufficient resources in their individual retirement accounts over their lifetimes to ensure the accumulation of sufficient funds to provide adequate pension benefits. In the 1980s and early 1990s, rates of return for these accounts in Chile were high, averaging about 12 percent per annum (Williamson and Pampel, 1993), but they have since declined, and by the late 1990s, yields had fallen to less than 2 percent per annum (*The Economist*, 1998). This trend will negatively affect lower-income workers and particularly lower-paid women workers who are unlikely to save enough for retirement because they often cycle in and out of employment. In addition, as Carmelo Mesa-Lago (1994) has reported, the exceedingly high administrative charges levied by commercial providers has also reduced the amounts saved. Another problem is that contribution avoidance has become common, with as many as 40 percent of Chilean workers failing to contribute to their accounts (Queisser, 1995). The result is that the state continues to subsidize retirement and other income contingencies through its conventional social assistance system. Contrary to predictions that the public burden of caring for the needy would decline significantly, the government of Chile continues to provide income benefits and social services on a substantial scale (*The Economist*, 1998).

Despite these challenges, the Chilean privatization has been widely emulated in other Latin American countries (Queisser, 1995), and proposals to replace social insurance programs with individual retirement accounts continue to be advocated in many parts of the world, including the United States. The World Bank (1994) has aggressively promoted individual retirement accounts, while the International Labour Office has continued to urge that social insurance be maintained. A compromise position has been adopted by the Chinese government, which has begun to replace its employer liability approach, in which state-owned enterprises were required to pay retirement and other benefits for their workers, with a combined social insurance and individual retirement account approach. Launched on an experimental basis in several provinces, the combined approach ensures that a proportion of workers' contributions are paid into a conventional, income-pooled social insurance fund, while another proportion is deposited into their individual retirement accounts. The Chinese system is currently being evaluated by the Chinese government (Tang and Ngan, 2001).

The widespread attention given to these innovations obscures the fact that publicly managed individual retirement accounts, known as provident funds, have been in existence in many developing countries for many years. These funds were introduced by the British colonial authorities in the post–World War II years, when nationalist movements were campaigning for independence. With the expansion of state welfare in Europe, many nationalist leaders aspired to introduce social insurance and similar programs, but it was obvious that the lack of an industrial base and mass wage employment precluded the creation of these programs. Instead, individual retirement accounts were introduced. As the labor force was young, accounts of this type were expected to provide most workers sound opportunities to accumulate adequate resources for retirement (Dixon, 1993).

One of the most successful and most widely reported provident funds was established in Singapore in 1955. Although the country's Central Provident Fund (CPF) was initially intended to accumulate savings for retirement, the government of Singapore subsequently used the fund to finance the country's ambitious and extensive housing program (Vasoo and Lee, 2001). In 1968, the regulations governing the fund were modified to permit workers to withdraw deposits to finance the purchase of a home, usually an apartment. By 1995, the home ownership rate had reached 90 percent, largely as a result of this decision together with other policies designed to promote home ownership. In addition to permitting withdrawals for housing, accumulations in CPF accounts may be withdrawn to pay for higher education, medical expenses, and even investments in the equity market. These asset accumulation policies have resulted in about US$52 billion now invested in Singapore's CPF, and asset ownership, particularly in housing, has increased exponentially (Sherraden, 1997). The government believes that these policies have also promoted individual self-reliance, social stability, and other desirable values among its citizens (Singapore, 1998).

THE FUTURE OF ASSETS

The clear trend toward the adoption of asset-based social policies in different parts of the world reflects the declining popularity of state welfarist, income transfer programs. As various writers have suggested (Gilbert,

2002; Goldberg and Rosenthal, 2002), the post–World War II social demo-cratic tide that created an extensive system of income benefit and social service programs has turned, and today there is far more emphasis on individual responsibility, the use of markets, and the involvement of both secular and religious philanthropy in social welfare than before. This does not mean, as some believe, that government involvement in social welfare has effectively come to an end. Even though policies designed to increase access to commercial provisions and to promote employment are now more prominent, most Western industrial countries maintain their social insurance and social assistance programs, and collective responsibility con-tinues to characterize their welfare systems.

Nevertheless, the pluralism that now characterizes official social policy thinking in many parts of the world is challenged by competing ideas about the role of the state, markets, families, and philanthropy in the provision of welfare. As noted at the beginning of this chapter, social policy today is a vigorously contested terrain. Socialists, marketizers, regulationists, tradi-tionalists, and neo-institutionalists have very different ideas about how social welfare should be promoted. It is important, therefore, to articulate a clear and coherent vision for how an asset-based approach should be imple-mented in relation to these divergent normative approaches.

There is a tendency among some advocates of the asset approach to rep-resent asset programs as ideologically neutral. Although IDAs have been commended by those on both the political Right and Left, it is clear that those of different ideological persuasions would link them to quite differ-ent conceptions of social policy and of what constitutes the Good Society. Socialists will emphasize the redistributive role of IDAs, while market-izers would stress their contribution to enhancing market participation among the poor. Regulationists would approve of IDAs for promoting thrift and sobriety. Traditionalists would commend them for being com-patible with cherished American values such as ambition and self-reliance. Developmentalists view IDAs as a form of social investment that enhances participation and social solidarity, and neo-institutionalists.

Since IDAs and similar asset programs can be and, indeed, have already been used to give expression to quite different ideological beliefs, some writers have argued that the asset approach should be regarded as an inte-gral part of a wider commitment to promoting social welfare through social investment and social development (Midgley, 1999; Midgley and Sherraden, 2000). By linking asset programs to the social developmental approach, these scholars stress the programs' roles in enhancing human capabilities and promoting social inclusion and social solidarity. These writers call on policy makers to use asset programs to promote wider social welfare goals in ways that stress social change, interventionism, inclusiv-ity, participation, and the harmonization of economic and social policy (Midgley, 1995). A developmentalist interpretation of this kind, they con-tend, offers the most effective and congenial normative framework for the implementation of asset policies and programs.

It is within the context of a developmentalist perspective that asset programs can make a significant contribution to social welfare in the future. As government responsibility for social welfare is increasingly debilitated, it is important that assets are not used to legitimate public neglect. At the same time, assets should be promoted not only to complement conventional state welfare approaches, but also to transcend them and to facilitate the realization of a new and vibrant approach in social policy that will invest in human capabilities, promote economic participation, address social needs, and enhance the well-being of all.

REFERENCES

Ackerman, B. A., and A. Alstott. (1999). *The Stakeholder Society.* New Haven, Conn.: Yale University Press.

Assets. (1998). "What Are IDAs?" *Assets* (Fall).

Borzutsky, S. (1991). "The Chicago Boys, Social Security and Welfare in Chile." In *The Radical Right and the Welfare State: An International Assessment,* eds. H. Glennerster and J. Midgley. Savage, Md.: Barnes and Noble, 79–99.

Dixon, J. (1993). "National Provident Funds: The Challenge of Harmonizing Their Social Security, Social and Economic Objectives." *Policy Studies Review* 12(1/2), 197–209.

The Economist. (1998). "Chile: The Not Quite Pensions Miracle." April 18.

Field, F. (1996). *How to Pay for the Future: Building Stakeholder Welfare.* London: Institute of Community Studies.

Gilbert, N. (2002). *The Transformation of the Welfare State: The Silent Surrender of Public Responsibility.* New York: Oxford University Press.

Goldberg, G. S., and M. G. Rosenthal, eds. (2002). *Diminishing Welfare: A Cross-National Study of Social Provision.* Westport, Conn.: Auburn House.

Haveman, R. H. (1988). *Starting Even: An Equal Opportunity Program to Combat the Nation's New Poverty.* New York: Simon and Schuster.

Howard, C. (1997). *The Hidden Welfare State: Tax Expenditures and Social Policy in the United States.* Princeton, N.J.: Princeton University Press.

Hutton, W. (1995). *The State We're In.* London: Jonathan Cape.

Hutton, W. (1997). *Stakeholding and Its Critics.* London: Institute of Economic Affairs.

Lindsey, D. (1994). *The Welfare of Children.* New York: Oxford University Press.

Mesa-Lago, C. (1994). *Changing Social Security in Latin America and the Caribbean. Towards Alleviating the Costs of Economic Reform.* Boulder, Colo.: Lynne Rienner.

Midgley, J. (1995). *Social Development: The Developmental Perspective in Social Welfare.* Thousand Oaks, Calif.: Sage Publications.

Midgley, J. (1999). "Growth, Redistribution and Welfare: Towards Social Investment." *Social Service Review* 77(1), 3–2.

Midgley, J. (2000). "The Institutional Approach to Social Policy." In *Handbook of Social Policy,* eds. J. Midgley, M. B. Tracy, and M. Livermore. Thousand Oaks, Calif.: Sage Publications, 365–376.

Midgley, J., and M. Sherraden. (2000). "The Social Development Perspective in Social Policy." In *The Handbook of Social Policy,* eds. J. Midgley, M. B. Tracy, and M. Livermore. Thousand Oaks, Calif.: Sage Publications, 435–446.

Midgley, J., and K. L. Tang. (2001). "Social Policy, Economic Growth and Developmental Welfare." *International Journal of Social Welfare* 10(4), 242–250.

Nissan, D., and J. LeGrand. (2000). *A Capital Idea: Start-Up Grants for Young People.* London: Fabian Society.

Oliver, M., and T. M. Shapiro. (1997). *Black Wealth/White Wealth: A New Perspective on Racial Inequality.* New York: Routledge.

Pearse, D. W. (1992). *The MIT Dictionary of Economics.* Cambridge, Mass.: The MIT Press.

Queisser, M. (1995). "Chile and Beyond: The Second Generation Pension Reforms in Latin America." *International Social Security Review* 48(1), 23–40.

Seidman, L. S. (2001). "Assets and the Tax Code." In *Assets for the Poor,* eds. T. M. Shapiro and E. N. Wolff. New York: Russell Sage Foundation, 324–356.

Shapiro, T. M. (2001). "The Importance of Assets." In *Assets for the Poor,* eds. T. M. Shapiro and E. N. Wolff. New York: Russell Sage Foundation, 11–33.

Sherraden, M. (1991). *Assets and the Poor: A New American Welfare Policy.* Armonk, N.Y.: M. E. Sharpe.

Sherraden, M. (1997). "Provident Funds and Social Protection: The Case of Singapore." In *Alternatives to Social Security: An International Inquiry,* eds. J. Midgley and M. Sherraden. Westport, Conn.: Auburn House, 33–60.

Sherraden, M. (2001). "Asset Building Policy and Programs for the Poor." In *Assets for the Poor,* eds. T. M. Shapiro and E. N. Wolff. New York: Russell Sage Foundation, 302–323.

Singapore, Central Provident Fund. (1998). *Annual Report.* Singapore: Government of Singapore.

Stern, M. J. (2001). "The Un(credit)worthy Poor: Historical Perspectives on Policies Expand Assets and Credit." In *Assets for the Poor,* eds. T. M. Shapiro and E. N. Wolff. New York: Russell Sage Foundation, 269–301.

Stoesz, D. (2000). *Poverty of Imagination: Bootstraps Capitalism, Sequel to Welfare Reform.* Madison: University of Wisconsin Press.

Tang, K. L., and R. Ngan. (2001). "China: Developmentalism and Social Security." *International Journal of Social Welfare* 10(4), 253–259.

Vasoo, S., and J. Lee. (2001). "Singapore: Social Development, Housing and the Central Provident Fund." *International Journal of Social Welfare* 10(4), 276–283.

Williamson, J. B., and F. C. Pampel. (1993). *Old Age Security in Comparative Perspective.* New York: Oxford University Press.

Wolff, E. N. (2001). "Recent Trends in Wealth Ownership, from 1983 to 1998." In *Assets for the Poor,* eds. T. M. Shapiro and E. N. Wolff. New York: Russell Sage Foundation, 34–73.

World Bank. (1994). *Averting the Old Age Crisis. Policies to Protect the Old and Promote Growth.* Washington, D.C.: Author.

Zundel, A. (2000). *Declarations of Dependency: The Civic Republican Tradition in U.S. Poverty Policy.* Albany: State University of New York Press.

PART II

ASSET HOLDING
AND WELL-BEING

This second part of the book addresses the meaning and measurement of asset holding and its potential effects on well-being. The Center for Social Development (CSD) at Washington University in St. Louis commissioned the chapter 4 study by Robert Haveman and Edward Wolff on measures of asset poverty. This is the first systematic effort to create, assess, and compare multiple measures of asset poverty. The authors point out trade-offs in using one measure versus another, thoughtfully explicating theoretical assumptions that underlie alternative measures of asset poverty. Given the primacy of how poverty is measured in policy discussion, this is a very important topic. We do not know if one of these definitions will one day be as influential as Molly Orshansky's definition of income poverty, which has defined the federal income poverty line for nearly forty years; regardless, this chapter is a pioneering contribution, both intellectually and practically.

In chapter 5, Ngina Chiteji and Darrick Hamilton document with quantitative evidence what Carol Stack identified with qualitative evidence in *All Our Kin* (1974), which is that African American nuclear families, perhaps especially in low- to middle-income households, may experience significant flows of assets to extended families. For many blacks, kin networks hold few assets; this is due primarily to historical factors and continuing barriers to wealth by race, as documented by Melvin Oliver and Thomas Shapiro in *Black Wealth/White Wealth* (1995). At the same time and also for historical reasons, family obligations are strong to ensure survival. These factors set up a pattern of assets flowing from nuclear families to extended families to a greater extent for blacks than for whites. This finding may have important implications for asset-building strategies across race.

Thomas Shapiro and Heather Beth Johnson study family educational options for children in chapter 6: how class and particularly wealth affect such options and how racial differences in options operate in part through wealth. They document through informative case studies how family wealth can ensure or fail to ensure educational opportunity. These inquiries into asset holding and its effects on education by class and race help to inform our view of how racial inequality operates and how class reproduces itself in the next generation. These insights can lead to more informed decisions about what matters in pubic policy. For long-term development, nothing is more important than education. If wealth largely determines how educational opportunities play out, then asset building is a desirable direction for public policy.

Using data from the National Survey of American Families Child Data Set, Edward Scanlon and Deborah Adams study youth outcomes that might result from family asset holding in chapter 7. They focus on home ownership and its effects on children's behavioral problems and involvement in extracurricular activities. These authors also ask whether these patterns might be different for Hispanic, African American, and white children. They find modest positive effects of home ownership and different patterns by race. That effects of assets holding might vary by race, ethnicity, culture, or other factors may be important in the design of asset-based policies and programs.

4

Who Are the Asset Poor? Levels, Trends, and Composition, 1983–1998

Robert Haveman and Edward N. Wolff

The booming U.S. economy of the 1990s, particularly the big run-up in the stock market, created the impression that American households have done well, particularly in terms of wealth acquisition. As we shall show, this is decidedly not the case for many households. In this chapter, we introduce the concept of "asset poverty" as a measure of economic hardship, distinct from and complementary to the more commonly used concept of "income poverty." We develop several measures of asset poverty and use them to document changes from 1983 to 1998 in the extent to which American households are unable to rely on an asset cushion to sustain themselves during temporary hard times. These measures indicate that in the face of the massive growth in overall assets in the United States, the level of asset poverty has actually been rising. In addition to showing the trends in overall asset poverty in the United States, we describe the patterns of asset poverty rates for various socioeconomic (e.g., race, age, schooling, family structure) groups over the 1983–1998 period.

In the first two sections of this chapter, we briefly describe the current measure of official income poverty that serves as the basis for assessing the status of the nation's least well-off citizens, and we show the levels of official poverty for the years for which asset poverty measures are available. We also present the trend in median family income for these years. The third section presents our asset poverty concept, and the measures of this hardship indicator that we use; we also describe the data sources that we use in our analysis. These measures of asset poverty employ alternative concepts of wealth but use the same poverty cutoff thresholds. We also measure asset poverty by employing an absolute dollar cutoff, irrespective of family size. The chapter's fourth section presents our estimates of asset poverty for the entire population that flow from these definitions. In section five, we present more details on asset poverty in 1998 for the entire population, as well as subgroups of the population distinguished by race, age of the household head, education of the household head, tenure status, and family type. We then investigate trends in asset poverty over the entire 1983 to 1998 period for the entire population, as well as the various subgroups. The next section of the chapter shows the decomposition of these trends for subperiods of this entire period, namely for the period from 1983 (a recession year) to the recovery year of 1989 and from 1989 to a later peak year, 1998. In the final section, we summarize our results and offer a few conclusions.

THE CONCEPT OF POVERTY: RESOURCES AND NEEDS

Although reducing poverty is a nearly universal goal among nations and international organizations, there is no commonly accepted way of identifying who is poor. Some argue for a multidimensional poverty concept that reflects the many aspects of well-being. In this context, people deprived of social contacts (with friends and families) are described as being "socially isolated" and, hence, poor in this dimension. Similarly, people living in squalid housing are viewed as "housing poor," and people with health deficits as "health poor." Economists tend to prefer a concept of hardship that reflects "economic position" or "economic well-being," a situation that somehow can be measured. This economic concept underlies the official U.S. poverty measure, as well as its proposed revision, based on the National Research Council (NRC) Panel Report.[1]

The measurement of economic poverty seeks to identify those families whose economic position or economic well-being, defined in terms of command over resources, falls below some minimally acceptable level. Hence, any poverty measure requires both a precise definition of economic resources and the minimum level of well-being (or needs) in terms that are commensurate with the concept of resources that is used.[2] An acceptable measure must also allow for differentiation according to household size and composition. Such a measure, it should be noted, excludes many factors that may affect utility but are not captured by the concept of resources that is used.

Within this economic perspective, there are substantial differences regarding the specific economic well-being indicators believed to best to identify those whose economic position lies below some minimally acceptable level. For example, the official U.S. poverty measure relies on the annual cash income of a family and compares this to some minimum income standard or "poverty line." An alternative—and equally legitimate—position is that the level of annual consumption better reflects a family's access to resources or that a measure of a family's income generating capacity is a more comprehensive indicator.[3]

OFFICIAL U.S. POVERTY AND MEDIAN INCOMES: 1983–1998

The Official U.S. Poverty Measure

The official definition of poverty in the United States has played a very special role in the development of social policy in this country. A case can be—indeed, has been—made that the most important contribution of the War on Poverty era was the establishment of an official, national poverty line. Because of the official adoption of this measure in the late 1960s, the nation made a commitment to chart the nation's progress toward poverty reduction annually by publishing and publicizing a statistical poverty index. In fact, the official poverty statistics are published every year by the Census Bureau (U.S. Census Bureau, 2003).

The official U.S. poverty measure, including the recently proposed revision in it, has several distinct characteristics. First, it is a measure of income poverty; its purpose is to identify those families that do not have sufficient annual cash income (in some cases, including close substitutes to cash income such as food stamps) to meet what is judged to be their annual needs. As such, the measure compares two numbers for each living unit—the level of annual income and the level of income that a unit of its size and composition requires in order to secure a minimum level of consumption. By relying solely on annual income as the indicator of resources, this measure ignores many potential sources of utility or welfare (e.g., social inclusion or security) that may be weakly tied to annual income flows. Second, the official poverty measure is an absolute measure of poverty. As a result, even if the income of every nonpoor individual in the society should increase, the prevalence of poverty in the society would not be affected.

The economic resources concept on which the measure rests has been subject to many criticisms.[4] Similarly, the arbitrary nature of the denominator of the poverty ratio—the minimum income needs indicator—has also been criticized (Ruggles, 1990). Given its conceptual basis and the crude empirical evidence on which the dollar cutoffs rest, the U.S. official poverty lines are essentially arbitrary constructs. Finally, adjustments in the poverty line to account for different family sizes and structures also rest on weak conceptual and empirical foundations.

Official Income Poverty and Median Income, 1983–1998

In spite of criticisms of it, the official U.S. poverty measure provides a baseline against which to judge estimates of asset poverty. Table 4.1 presents estimates of the percent of families in the United States that were poor in those years over the 1983–1998 period for which we are able to study asset poverty, together with estimates of median family income for these years.

Both of these income-based indicators of well-being have closely followed macroeconomic conditions since the beginning of the 1980s. The official income poverty rate stood at over 12 percent at the end of the severe

Table 4.1 Official Income Poverty Rates for Families and Median Family Income, 1983–1998

Year	Poverty Rate for Families[a]	Median Family Income ($1999)
1983	12.3%	$41,100
1989	10.3%	$46,000
1992	11.9%	$43,400
1995	10.8%	$44,400
1998	10.0%	$47,800

Source: Survey of Consumer Finances (SCF). U.S. Census, 2003.
[a]Poverty rate for families indicates the percentage of U.S. families that were poor, according to the U.S. Census Bureau.

recession of the early 1980s. During the several years of economic growth following that recession, poverty fell steadily, reaching a level of 10.3 percent by 1989. By 1992, family poverty had again risen, as the recession early in that decade also took its toll. However, in the prolonged expansion of the 1990s, official poverty again fell, to 10.8 percent of the population in 1995, and to its lowest level since the 1970s—10 percent—in 1998.

This pattern parallels changes in median family income over this period. Median family income grew from $41,100 in 1983 to $46,000 in 1989 before falling to $43,400 during the recession of the early 1990s. Persistent growth during the 1990s led to growth in median family income to its highest level during the period of $47,800.

ASSET POVERTY: CONCEPTS AND DATA

With this background of trends in official poverty and median family income over the 1983–1998 period, we now turn to the definition and measurement of "asset poverty," a concept that was first advanced by Melvin Oliver and Thomas Shapiro (1997).

Definitions and Conventions

We define a household or a person as being "asset poor" if the access that the family members have to wealth-type resources is insufficient to enable them to meet their basic needs for some limited period of time. Clearly, this definition leaves open a number of issues on which judgments are required in order to develop a measure of asset poverty.

What Are "Basic Needs"?

We begin with the assumption that household needs can be met by access to financial resources or real assets (e.g., owned homes) that can be valued in monetary units. While there is no commonly accepted standard for the minimum amount of financial resources necessary to meet needs, we use the family size conditioned poverty thresholds recently proposed by a National Academy of Science panel as alternatives to the long-standing official thresholds.[5] The panel recommended that the thresholds should represent a dollar amount for food, clothing, shelter (including utilities), and a small additional amount to allow for other common, everyday needs (e.g., household supplies, personal care, and nonwork-related transportation). One threshold was developed for a reference family with two adults and two children, using Consumer Expenditure Survey data. The reference family threshold was then adjusted to reflect the needs of different family types and geographic differences in the cost of living. These thresholds are based on the three-parameter equivalence scale for reflecting the needs of families of various sizes and structures.[6] The 1997 threshold for a reference family of two adults with two children is $15,998, which is slightly lower than the 1999 official threshold of $16,276.[7]

What Period of Time?

The poverty thresholds indicate the level of basic resource needs for households of various sizes measured over the course of a year; it is an annual resource concept. When this standard is compared to the income flow over the course of a year, the resulting measure of poverty is clear. For our purposes, the questions are: How can these annual thresholds be used to indicate the adequacy of any stock of wealth-type resources? And how much of an asset stock would a household need to meet this annual minimum level of basic needs, were no other resources available?

We suggest, as a reasonable standard, that families should have an asset cushion that allows them to meet basic needs—the equivalent of the threshold poverty line—for three months (equal to 25 percent of a year), should all other sources of support fail. Hence, we compare the stock of asset holdings at a point in time to 25 percent of the annual family size specific poverty threshold. Hence, a four-person family would have asset needs equal to $4,000, which is 25 percent of the poverty threshold income (.25 × $15,998). With this standard, such a family that held net financial assets of less than $4,000 in 1997 would be declared "asset poor." Similarly, a one-person family with assets below $2,500 or a six-person family with assets below $6,900 would likewise fall below the basic needs threshold. In an alternative approach, we set an absolute standard of $5,000, implying that a household is poor if the family has wealth-type resources of less than that amount.[8]

What Is "Wealth"?

The third issue that we will employ in measuring asset poverty concerns the concept of wealth. In this study, we define the primary measure of wealth to be marketable wealth, which is also called net worth (NW), as the current value of all marketable or fungible assets less the current value of debts. NW is, thus, the difference in value between total assets and total liabilities (that is, total debt).[9] This NW concept is the primary measure of wealth because it reflects wealth as a store of value and, therefore, a source of potential consumption. We believe that this is the concept that best reflects the level of well-being associated with a family's holdings. Thus, only assets that can be readily marketed, that is, those that are "fungible" can be included as part of a household's NW.[10]

Alternatively, we present estimates of asset poverty that are based on two more restrictive definitions of wealth. In the first case, we use NW minus home equity (HE). In this definition, we presume that it would be untoward to require a household to sell the family's home in order to secure the financial resources necessary to tide them over a period without income sources. Finally, we use an even more restrictive definition of assets, namely, liquid assets (Liquid), defined as cash or easily monetizable financial assets; liquid assets exclude individual retirement accounts (IRAs) and pension assets. This measure, however, ignores all forms of debt, including mortgage and consumer debt. These two measures, net worth and liquid assets, are defined more completely in the appendix at the end of this chapter.

Data Sources

The data that we use in this study are the 1983, 1989, 1992, 1995, and 1998 *Surveys of Consumer Finances* (SCF), conducted by the Federal Reserve Board.[11] Each survey consists of a core representative sample combined with a high-income supplement. The supplement is drawn from the Internal Revenue Service's *Statistics of Income* (SOI) data file. For the 1983 SCF, for example, an income cutoff of $100,000 of adjusted gross income is used as the criterion for inclusion in the supplemental sample. The advantage of the high-income supplement is that it provides a much "richer" sample of high income and, therefore, potentially very wealthy families. The SCF also has the advantage of providing exceptional detail on both assets and debt (several hundred questions are asked). For example, it asks each household to identify both first and second mortgages and home equity credit lines, as well as the institutions granting the loans and the interest rates charged. Credit card balances are asked for for each credit card held by the family, as well as interest charges.

ASSET POVERTY IN THE UNITED STATES: 1983–1998

Our overall estimates of the level of asset poverty in the United States are provided in table 4.2 for the years 1983–1998. We present estimates for all three of the definitions of assets mentioned above and show the rate for the liquid assets below the $5,000 absolute standard as well.

Table 4.2 Asset Poverty Rates by Definition and Year, 1983–1998

Year	NW < .25 Poverty Line	[NW – HE] < .25 Poverty Line	Liquid < .25 Poverty Line	Liquid < $5,000
1983	22.4%	36.9%	33.2%	40.1%
1989	24.7%	37.3%	36.4%	39.2%
1992	24.0%	37.9%	37.5%	40.5%
1995	25.3%	40.0%	43.8%	51.5%
1998	25.5%	36.8%	39.7%	45.3%

Source: Authors' calculations based on the 1983, 1989, 1992, 1995, and 1998 SCF. Federal Reserve Board, 1983, 1989, 1992, 1995, and 1998.
Note: NW = net worth; HE = home equity.

As expected, the most inclusive measure of assets, NW, yields the lowest poverty rates among the four measures shown; the values range from 22.4 percent in 1983 to 25.5 percent in 1998. Subsequent to the recession of the early 1980s, NW asset poverty rose by about 2 percentage points by 1989, then fell slightly during the recession of the early 1990s, and again rose during the prolonged period of growth during the decade of the 1990s. By this standard, the level of asset poverty in 1998 is the highest level recorded over the 1983–1998 period.

When home equity is excluded from the definition of assets, the asset poverty rate rises to 35 to 40 percent. By this measure, asset poverty is lowest in 1982 and 1998 and reaches a peak of 40 percent in 1995. The two liquid asset poverty measures have their lowest levels during the 1980s, with substantial increases from 1989 to 1995. Even at the end of the 1990s growth period, liquid asset poverty stood at nearly 40 percent when the poverty thresholds are used to measure basic needs, and at more than 45 percent when the absolute $5,000 standard is set as the norm.

In the final year of this study, 1998, over 35 percent of the nation's households were asset poor, according to the NW less HE definition, combined with the three-month cushion standard. The liquid asset definition of wealth-type resources placed about 40 percent of the nation's families in asset poverty in 1998. The most expansive definition of wealth-type resources—NW—indicates a national asset poverty rate of nearly 30 percent in 1998. Using the absolute definition of asset poverty, over 35 percent of the nation's households were asset poor in the final year of our analysis.

For all of the measures except the NW – HE measure, asset poverty at the end of the period exceeded both its 1983 level and its level during the recession of the early 1990s. Interestingly, the time pattern of asset poverty rates does not reflect macroeconomic conditions and does not parallel that of income poverty or median family income.

THE STRUCTURE OF ASSET POVERTY IN 1998

In this section we present descriptive statistics on asset poverty for different demographic and labor market groups in 1998, the final year of our study. The population groupings that we discuss include divisions by (a) race/ethnicity, (b) age group, (c) education, (d) housing tenure status, and (e) marital status and presence of children (family type).

1998 Asset Poverty Rates by Race

Table 4.3 presents the racial breakdown of asset poverty rates for households in 1998. The racial disparities are enormous, with the poverty rate for minorities (blacks/Hispanics) being about double those for whites.[12] Using the three-month cushion criterion, the rates for whites range from 21 percent to 34 percent; the range for blacks/Hispanics is 45 percent to 65 percent. Using the absolute cutoff of $5,000, about 40 percent of white households have liquid assets below this cutoff, while nearly 70 percent of black/Hispanic households have less than this amount of financial reserves.

1998 Asset Poverty Rates by Age of Household Head

Table 4.4 shows the 1998 asset poverty rates for households headed by various age groups. As with the racial comparisons, the gaps here are enormous. Irrespective of the measure used, households headed by people younger than 25 years of age have remarkably high asset poverty rates—for example, more than 75 percent do not have a stock of asset wealth in any form sufficient to support poverty line consumption for a three-month period. Eighty one percent of these young households have less than $5,000 of liquid assets. These poverty rates fall monotonically by age. For households headed by a person age 35 to 49, asset poverty rates are one-half or less of the rates for the young households. Those age 62 or older have asset poverty rates using the quarter-year cushion criterion, which ranges from 11 to 26 percent.

Table 4.3 Asset Poverty by Race, Four Definitions, 1998

Poverty Concept	Households	
	Whites	Blacks/Hispanics
NW < .25 Poverty Line	20.5%	45.3%
[NW – HE] < .25 Poverty Line	30.8%	60.5%
Liquid < .25 Poverty Line	33.5%	64.7%
Liquid < $5,000	39.6%	69.0%

Source: Authors' calculations based on the 1998 SCF, 1998 dollars. Federal Reserve Board, 1998.

Table 4.4 Asset Poverty by Age of Household Head, Four Definitions, 1998

Poverty Concept	Households				
	<25 years	25–34 years	35–49 years	50–61 years	>62 years
NW < .25 Poverty Line	70.7%	46.8%	23.5%	15.0%	11.0%
[NW – HE] < .25 Poverty Line	75.3%	59.8%	33.8%	27.4%	22.9%
Liquid < .25 Poverty Line	70.0%	59.2%	39.7%	29.8%	26.2%
Liquid < $5,000	81.2%	64.9%	44.2%	36.3%	31.5%

Source: Authors' calculations based on the 1998 SCF, 1998 dollars. Federal Reserve Board, 1998.

1998 Asset Poverty Rates by Education of Household Head

Table 4.5 presents the asset poverty rates by the education level of the household head. As with age, the asset poverty rates fall monotonically by the education of the head. Asset poverty rates for households headed by a person with four or more years of college are about one-third of those of families with a head who has not completed a high school degree. While over two-thirds of families headed by a person with less than a high school degree have less than $5,000 of liquid assets, less than 24 percent of the college graduates have so low an asset cushion.

1998 Asset Poverty Rates by Housing Tenure

The pattern of 1998 asset poverty rates by housing tenure is shown in table 4.6, and it is revealing. For home owners, using the asset measure that includes the value of home equity, the asset poverty rate is less than 10 percent, compared with rates of over 60 percent for renters. While the rates between these tenure categories become closer when asset concepts that exclude home equity are used, the asset poverty rates of renters remain

Table 4.5 Asset Poverty by Education of Household Head, Four Definitions, 1998

Poverty Concept	Households			
	<High School	High School	1–3 Years College	College Grad
NW < .25 Poverty Line	40.2%	26.5%	24.5%	15.3%
[NW – HE] < .25 Poverty Line	58.7%	39.6%	34.8%	20.8%
Liquid < .25 Poverty Line	64.8%	45.6%	36.5%	19.1%
Liquid < $5,000	68.7%	51.9%	43.8%	23.8%

Source: Authors' calculations based on the 1998 SCF, 1998 dollars. Federal Reserve Board, 1998.

Table 4.6 Asset Poverty by Housing Tenure, Four Definitions, 1998

	Households	
Poverty Concept	Home Owners	Renters
NW < .25 Poverty Line	6.4%	63.0%
[NW – HE] < .25 Poverty Line	23.5%	63.0%
Liquid < .25 Poverty Line	26.6%	65.4%
Liquid < $5,000	31.4%	72.7%

Source: Authors' calculations based on the 1998 SCF, 1998 dollars. Federal Reserve Board, 1998.

more than double those of home owners. Indeed, nearly three-fourths of renters have less than $5,000 of easily accessible assets, in contrast with about one-third of home owners. It seems clear that home ownership provides more than home equity and is associated with the ownership of a wide range of financial assets.

1998 Asset Poverty Rates by Family Type

Asset poverty rates in 1998 varied substantially by family type, as shown in table 4.7. The lowest asset poverty rates were observed among married couple families age 65 years or older. Using the three-month cushion standard, asset poverty rates for nonelderly married couples range from 4 percent when home equity is included in the asset definition to 19 percent using the most liquid assets definition. The rates for two-parent families with children range from about 25 percent to 44 percent, while the rates for families with children and a female single parent range from 54 percent to 70 percent. For male-headed single-parent families, the poverty rates range from 37 percent to 54 percent. The comparable rates for households headed by men and women but with no children present are in the 35 percent to 50 percent range (not shown); interestingly, the asset poverty rates for such families are somewhat higher for male-headed families than those headed by a female.

TRENDS IN ASSET POVERTY: 1983–1998

In table 4.8, we summarize the patterns of asset poverty in both 1983 and 1998 for our four definitions of asset poverty. Table 4.8 also shows the percent change in asset poverty rates between 1983 and 1998, a fifteen-year period. Note that the first year, 1983, is a recession year, while 1998 is the sixth year of a sustained recovery with the economy at full employment. Given these different macroeconomic conditions, it is expected that the rates of asset poverty would have fallen over this period.

Table 4.7 Asset Poverty by Family Type, Four Definitions, 1998

				Households			
Poverty Concept	<65 years, Married, Children	<65 years, Married, No Children	<65 years, Female Head, Children	<65 years, Male Head, Children	>65 years, Married	>65 years, Single, Female	>65 years, Single, Male
NW < 25 Poverty Line	25.3%	19.0%	53.7%	36.8%	4.0%	17.3%	13.1%
[NW – HE] < .25 Poverty Line	39.3%	28.9%	64.4%	47.8%	12.8%	30.3%	30.8%
Liquid < .25 Poverty Line	44.4%	27.9%	69.8%	53.9%	19.1%	31.9%	32.7%
Liquid < $5,000	45.9%	34.9%	74.2%	63.3%	20.7%	39.9%	38.9%

Source: Authors' calculations based on the 1998 SCF, 1998 dollars. Federal Reserve Board, 1998.

Table 4.8 Asset Poverty Rates, 1983 and 1998, and Percent Changes, 1983–1998

	1983				1998				Percent Changes, 1983–1998			
	NW < .25 Poverty Line	[NW – HE] < .25 Poverty Line	Liquid < .25 Poverty Line	Liquid < $5,000	NW < .25 Poverty Line	[NW – HE] < .25 Poverty Line	Liquid < .25 Poverty Line	Liquid < $5,000	NW < .25 Poverty Line	[NW – HE] < .25 Poverty Line	Liquid < .25 Poverty Line	Liquid < $5,000
Total	22.4%	36.9%	33.2%	40.1%	25.5%	36.8%	39.7%	45.3%	14.0	-0.3	19.5	12.9
Race												
White	17.1%	30.0%	26.9%	33.5%	20.5%	30.8%	33.5%	39.6%	19.8	2.6	24.7	18.4
Black/Hispanic	47.4%	69.9%	63.8%	71.8%	45.3%	60.5%	64.7%	69.0%	-4.4	-13.4	1.0	-3.9
Age												
<25	55.6%	63.0%	56.1%	70.7%	70.7%	75.3%	70.0%	81.2%	27.1	19.6	24.7	14.8
25–34	36.3%	51.4%	44.8%	53.6%	46.8%	59.8%	59.2%	64.9%	29.1	16.3	32.1	21.0
35–49	17.7%	36.2%	30.9%	35.4%	23.5%	33.8%	39.7%	44.2%	33.1	-6.7	28.3	24.9
50–61	13.8%	27.8%	26.2%	29.5%	15.0%	27.4%	29.8%	36.3%	8.6	-1.5	13.9	23.1
62+	9.9%	21.9%	22.5%	30.5%	11.0%	22.9%	26.2%	31.5%	11.6	4.5	16.5	3.2
Education												
<High school	29.8%	50.0%	50.0%	56.9%	40.2%	58.7%	64.8%	68.7%	35.1	17.3	29.6	20.7
High school	20.9%	36.1%	33.6%	40.6%	26.5%	39.6%	45.6%	51.9%	26.7	9.8	35.9	27.9
1–3 years college	25.5%	37.8%	31.1%	38.8%	24.5%	34.8%	36.5%	43.8%	-4.1	-7.8	17.4	12.8
College grad	11.3%	19.3%	11.8%	17.6%	15.3%	20.8%	19.1%	23.8%	34.9	7.8	62.0	35.2

	1983				1998				Percent Changes, 1983–1998			
	NW <.25 Poverty Line	[NW−HE] <.25 Poverty Line	Liquid <.25 Poverty Line	Liquid <$5,000	NW <.25 Poverty Line	[NW−HE] <.25 Poverty Line	Liquid <.25 Poverty Line	Liquid <$5,000	NW <.25 Poverty Line	[NW−HE] <.25 Poverty Line	Liquid <.25 Poverty Line	Liquid <$5,000
Tenure												
Home owner	3.6%	26.5%	22.6%	27.6%	6.4%	23.5%	26.6%	31.4%	76.9	−11.5	17.9	13.6
Renter	54.8%	54.8%	51.7%	61.7%	63.0%	63.0%	65.4%	72.7%	14.9	14.9	26.5	17.8
Family type												
<65 years, married, children	21.6%	42.2%	37.6%	40.6%	25.3%	39.3%	44.4%	45.9%	16.9	−6.8	18.1	13.0
<65 years, married, no children	12.9%	25.0%	19.9%	25.1%	19.0%	28.9%	27.9%	34.9%	46.9	15.7	40.1	38.9
<65 years, female head, children	48.1%	67.0%	63.4%	68.4%	53.7%	64.4%	69.8%	74.2%	11.6	−3.8	10.0	8.5
65+ years, married	5.5%	16.3%	17.4%	22.6%	4.0%	12.8%	19.1%	20.7%	−27.8	−21.6	10.1	−8.5
65+ years, female head	15.3%	28.0%	29.0%	41.7%	17.3%	30.3%	31.9%	39.9%	13.1	8.3	10.0	−4.4
65+ years, male head	21.1%	40.2%	40.2%	49.6%	13.1%	30.8%	32.7%	38.9%	−37.8	−23.4	−18.7	−21.6

Source: Authors' calculations based on the SCF for 1983 and 1998. Federal Reserve Board, 1983, 1998.

For three of the asset poverty measures—NW/Poverty Line, Liquid/ Poverty Line, and Liquid/$5,000—our expectation regarding the change in the level of poverty was not met. Increases in asset poverty of 14, 20, and 13 percent, respectively, are recorded for these definitions. Only for [NW – HE]/Poverty Line—the measure that excludes home equity while maintaining other (primarily financial and pension wealth) holdings— does the prevalence of asset poverty not increase (though it remains virtu- ally unchanged). In spite of the enormous increase in financial and pension wealth holdings over this period, 37 percent of the nation remained in wealth poverty by this definition.

While this pattern holds for the white population, the situation is quite different for blacks and Hispanics. For blacks/Hispanics, decreases in asset poverty rates are observed for all of the measures except Liquid/Poverty Line, which remains virtually unchanged. The decreases range from 4 per- cent to 13 percent.

Irrespective of definition, households headed by people younger than age 25, ages 25–34, and ages 35–49 experienced the largest increases in asset poverty. Using the broadest and the narrowest definition of assets— NW/Poverty Line and Liquid/Poverty Line—the increases in asset poverty ranged from 25–27 percent for the youngest group and from 29–32 percent for the 25–34 year olds, and it ranged from 28–33 percent for the 35–49 year olds.

Across education groups, all of the groups except those with some col- lege education experienced an increase in asset poverty over this fifteen- year period. For the NW/Poverty Line and [NW – HE]/Poverty Line measures, both of which include pension plan and IRA assets, the two low schooling groups and the college graduates experienced a substantial increase in asset poverty. However, using these measures, the group with some college but not a degree experienced decreases in asset poverty. Using the measure based on a liquid asset measure of wealth—Liquid/ Poverty Line—a very large increase in asset poverty over the period is recorded for all of the schooling groups. However, the increase was sub- stantially smaller for the group with some college than for the remaining groups. The increase in liquid asset poverty is exceptionally large for fam- ilies headed by a college graduate; Liquid/Poverty Line asset poverty grew by 62 percent over the period, from 12 percent to 19 percent.

Irrespective of the asset measure used, asset poverty for renters grew by between 15 to 27 percent over the period. However, the patterns of asset poverty change are substantially different for home owners. Using the asset measure that includes home owner equity, the rate of poverty increased by 77 percent over the period, albeit from a very low base of 4 percent in 1983. The ostensible reason is the very high growth in mortgage debt as a percent of house value, which almost doubled over the period from 1983 to 1998. When the net asset value of the owned home is excluded from the asset base ([NW – HE]/Poverty Line), the rate of asset poverty for home owners actually fell. Relatively small increases in asset poverty—

14 to 18 percent—are recorded for home owners using the liquid asset-based measures.

Among families headed by a person younger than 65 years, the largest increases in asset poverty are recorded for childless married couples—the increases range from 16 percent to 47 percent. Young female-headed families experienced the lowest percentage increases in asset poverty—ranging from 4 percent to 12 percent. Among families headed by a person age 65 years or more, the change in asset poverty levels varies substantially by type. Female-headed families in this category—primarily widows—experienced modest increases in asset poverty. However, for both aged (older than 65 years) married couples and older single male households, decreases in asset poverty are recorded for most measures. For older single male households, the reductions in asset poverty range from 19 to 38 percent.

In sum, then, overall asset poverty grew modestly over this fifteen-year period from 1983 to 1998. Among population subgroups, however, the patterns of growth vary substantially—large increases in asset poverty are recorded for the following groups:

- Whites relative to racial minorities
- Families headed by a person younger than 50 years relative to older families
- Families headed by a person with little schooling and for college graduates, relative to those with some college (the result for college graduates reflects the low base from which the percentage change is calculated)
- Renters relative to home owners
- Families headed by a person younger than 65 years (irrespective of marital status and the presence of children), relative to families headed by a person 65 years or older

SUBPERIOD ASSET POVERTY TRENDS—1983–1989 AND 1989–1998

The trends discussed in the previous section and shown in table 4.8 summarize asset poverty developments over the entire period from 1983 to 1998, from a distant recession year to a recent full employment year. In this section, we decompose these long period trends into trends over two separate periods—from the recession year 1983 to a relatively full employment year later in that decade, 1989, and from that year to 1998. The latter comparison, between two full employment years, should be revealing in terms of the underlying structure of asset holdings over the decade of the 1990s.

Table 4.9 presents the pattern for the entire population and for racial groups within the population. For all households, asset poverty rose somewhat for three of the four asset measures during the early period and fell slightly for the Liquid/$5,000 measure. Basically, little change in overall

Table 4.9 Asset Poverty Rates: Total, by Race, and Percent Changes

	Year					Percent Changes		
	1983	1989	1992	1995	1998	1983–1989	1989–1998	1983–1998
Total								
NW < .25 Poverty Line	22.4%	24.7%	24.0%	25.3%	25.5%	10.3%	3.2%	14.0%
[NW – HE] < .25 Poverty Line	36.7%	37.3%	37.4%	40.0%	36.8%	1.6%	–1.4%	–0.3%
Liquid < .25 Poverty Line	33.2%	36.4%	37.5%	43.8%	39.7%	9.6%	9.1%	19.5%
Liquid < $5,000	40.1%	38.7%	40.5%	51.5%	45.3%	–3.6%	17.1%	12.9%
White								
NW < .25 Poverty Line	17.1%	16.6%	19.1%	20.2%	20.5%	–2.9%	23.4%	19.8%
[NW – HE] < .25 Poverty Line	30.0%	26.7%	31.0%	34.1%	30.8%	–11.1%	15.4%	2.6%
Liquid < .25 Poverty Line	26.9%	25.9%	29.8%	38.2%	33.5%	–3.7%	29.5%	24.7%
Liquid < $5,000	33.5%	28.5%	32.5%	46.0%	39.6%	–14.9%	39.0%	18.4%
Black/Hispanic								
NW < .25 Poverty Line	47.4%	53.6%	43.2%	46.1%	45.3%	13.1%	–15.5%	–4.4%
[NW – HE] < .25 Poverty Line	69.9%	74.7%	64.3%	64.8%	60.5%	6.4%	–19.0%	–13.4%
Liquid < .25 Poverty Line	63.8%	72.9%	66.8%	66.3%	64.7%	14.3%	–11.2%	+1.0%
Liquid < $5,000	71.8%	76.2%	70.4%	74.1%	69.0%	6.1%	–9.4%	–3.9%

Source: Authors' calculations based on the SCF for 1983, 1989, 1992, 1995, and 1998. Federal Reserve Board.

asset poverty is recorded over this period. Similarly, for most of the asset poverty measures, rather small increases in asset poverty occurred from 1989 to 1998 over the two recent full employment years. However, for the absolute asset standard definition—Liquid/$5,000—a substantial increase of 17 percent is recorded over this recent peak-to-peak period.

The difference in the patterns of asset poverty growth over the two periods between whites and blacks is unexpected and surprising. During the 1980s, asset poverty for white families decreased by all of the measures. However, over this same period, asset poverty among blacks/Hispanics increased. Precisely the reverse pattern exists over the 1989–1998 period. During this period, asset poverty for whites reversed course and grew substantially, increasing from 15 to 39 percent, depending on the measure of asset poverty used. However, for blacks/Hispanics, asset poverty declined substantially over this peak-to-peak comparison period. Depending on the asset measure, asset poverty for black families fell by from 9 to 19 percent during this last decade. This divergent pattern is noteworthy, and the reasons for it are not immediately obvious. However, the results do accord with findings reported in Wolff (2001), that the home ownership rate among black families rose during the 1990s and the share of black households with zero or negative net worth declined.[13]

Table 4.10 presents similar results for age groups. For the youngest and oldest age groups, substantial growth in asset poverty occurred during the 1980s, in spite of the move from a deep recession to full employment. During the 1989–1998 period, asset poverty remained nearly constant at rates around 70–75 percent for families headed by young people, but it fell substantially from rather low rates of from 15–30 percent for the families headed by a person age 62 or older. The picture is more mixed for the intermediate age groups. For families headed by a person age 25–34, asset poverty rose in both subperiods, irrespective of the measure used. For families headed by a person in the age range of 35–61, asset poverty growth patterns vary substantially between the subperiods, depending on the measure used.

The subperiod pattern of asset poverty changes for educational groups is shown in table 4.11. For each of the schooling groups considered individually, asset poverty grew substantially during the recent 1989–1998 peak-to-peak period, with especially large growth rates recorded for families headed by a college graduate.[14] This contrasts with the growth pattern during the 1980s, during which time asset poverty declined substantially for the two groups with some college education, while it either fell or rose modestly for the two groups with no more schooling than a high school degree. Again, the substantial growth in asset poverty for each of the educational groups over the recent decade is surprising and unexpected. Clearly, the fabled run-up in financial asset holdings for those with education and schooling has bypassed the lowest wealth holders of this group.

Table 4.12 presents the subperiod growth patterns for renters and home owners. For renters, asset poverty levels increased by all of the measures

Table 4.10 Asset Poverty Rates by Age and Percent Changes (1983, 1989, and 1998)

	Year			Percent Changes		
	1983	1989	1998	1983–1989	1989–1998	1983–1998
Ages < 25						
NW < .25 Poverty Line	55.6%	70.1%	70.7%	25.9%	0.9%	27.1%
[NW – HE] < .25 Poverty Line	63.0%	73.9%	75.3%	17.3%	1.9%	19.6%
Liquid < .25 Poverty Line	56.1%	76.1%	70.0%	35.5%	−8.0%	24.7%
Liquid < $5,000	70.7%	76.7%	81.2%	8.5%	5.9%	14.8%
Ages 25–34						
NW < .25 Poverty Line	36.3%	42.7%	46.8%	17.6%	9.6%	29.1%
[NW – HE] < .25 Poverty Line	51.4%	54.1%	59.8%	5.2%	10.6%	16.3%
Liquid < .25 Poverty Line	44.8%	50.4%	59.2%	12.5%	17.5%	32.1%
Liquid < $5,000	53.6%	53.6%	64.9%	0.0%	21.1%	21.0%
Ages 35–49						
NW < .25 Poverty Line	17.7%	22.1%	23.5%	25.1%	6.4%	33.1%
[NW – HE] < .25 Poverty Line	36.2%	35.0%	33.8%	−3.4%	−3.4%	−6.7%
Liquid < .25 Poverty Line	30.9%	32.1%	39.7%	3.6%	23.8%	28.3%
Liquid < $5,000	35.4%	33.2%	44.2%	−6.2%	33.2%	24.9%
Ages 50–61						
NW < .25 Poverty Line	13.8%	11.2%	15.0%	−18.8%	33.7%	8.6%
[NW – HE] < .25 Poverty Line	27.8%	27.6%	27.4%	−0.9%	−0.6%	−1.5%
Liquid < .25 Poverty Line	26.2%	27.9%	29.8%	6.6%	6.8%	13.9%
Liquid < $5,000	29.5%	31.1%	36.3%	5.5%	16.6%	23.1%
Ages 62+						
NW < .25 Poverty Line	9.9%	13.1%	11.0%	32.6%	−15.9%	11.1%
[NW – HE] < .25 Poverty Line	21.9%	25.6%	22.9%	16.8%	−10.6%	4.5%
Liquid < .25 Poverty Line	22.5%	28.1%	26.2%	24.9%	−6.7%	−16.5%
Liquid < $5,000	30.5%	32.4%	31.5%	6.2%	−2.8%	3.2%

Source: Authors' calculations based on the SCF for 1983, 1989, and 1998. Federal Reserve Board.

Table 4.11 Asset Poverty Rates by Education, and Percent Changes (1983, 1989, and 1998)

	Year			Percent Changes		
	1983	1989	1998	1983–1989	1989–1998	1983–1998
< High school						
NW < .25 Poverty Line	29.8%	32.3%	40.2%	8.6%	24.4%	35.1%
[NW – HE] < .25 Poverty Line	50.0%	48.2%	58.7%	–3.7%	21.8%	17.3%
Liquid < .25 Poverty Line	50.0%	49.7%	64.8%	–0.6%	30.4%	29.6%
Liquid < $5,000	56.9%	53.5%	68.7%	–6.1%	28.5%	20.7%
High school graduate						
NW < .25 Poverty Line	20.9%	25.4%	26.5%	21.6%	4.2%	26.8%
[NW – HE] < .25 Poverty Line	36.1%	36.6%	39.6%	1.4%	8.3%	9.8%
Liquid < .25 Poverty Line	33.6%	34.9%	45.6%	4.0%	30.6%	35.9%
Liquid < $5,000	40.6%	38.0%	51.9%	–6.3%	36.5%	27.9%
1–3 years college						
NW < .25 Poverty Line	25.5%	19.2%	24.5%	–25.0%	27.9%	–4.1%
[NW – HE] < .25 Poverty Line	37.8%	32.7%	34.8%	–13.4%	6.4%	–7.8%
Liquid < .25 Poverty Line	31.1%	26.4%	36.5%	–15.0%	38.2%	17.4%
Liquid < $5,000	38.8%	29.6%	43.8%	–23.9%	48.2%	12.8%
College graduate						
NW < .25 Poverty Line	11.3%	9.6%	15.3%	–15.2%	59.2%	34.9%
[NW – HE] < .25 Poverty Line	19.3%	15.3%	20.8%	–20.9%	36.2%	7.8%
Liquid < .25 Poverty Line	11.8%	13.5%	19.1%	14.7%	41.2%	62.0%
Liquid < $5,000	17.6%	13.2%	23.8%	–25.0%	81.0%	35.2%

Source: Authors' calculations based on the SCF for 1983, 1989, and 1998. Federal Reserve Board.

Table 4.12 Asset Poverty Rates by Housing Tenure and Percent Changes

	Year			Percent Changes		
	1983	1989	1998	1983–1989	1989–1998	1983–1998
Home owner						
NW < .25 Poverty Line	3.6%	3.3%	6.4%	−9.7%	95.8%	76.9%
[NW – HE] < .25 Poverty Line	26.5%	23.5%	23.5%	−11.6%	0.1%	−11.5%
Liquid < .25 Poverty Line	22.6%	22.2%	26.6%	−1.8%	20.0%	17.9%
Liquid < $5,000	27.6%	23.9%	31.4%	−13.4%	31.2%	13.7%
Renter						
NW < .25 Poverty Line	54.8%	60.8%	63.0%	10.9%	3.6%	14.9%
[NW – HE] < .25 Poverty Line	54.8%	60.7%	63.0%	10.6%	3.9%	14.9%
Liquid < .25 Poverty Line	51.7%	60.5%	65.4%	17.0%	8.1%	26.5%
Liquid < $5,000	61.7%	64.9%	72.7%	5.2%	12.0%	17.8%

Source: Authors' calculations based on the SCF for 1983, 1989, and 1998. Federal Reserve Board.

during both subperiods. However, while asset poverty fell during the 1980s for home owners by all of the measures, sizable increases in asset poverty, using the NW or Liquid definitions, are recorded over the recent decade. These increases ranged from 20 percent to 95 percent. During this period, only the measure based on the NW – HE asset concept indicates no increase in asset poverty.

Finally, we present the subperiod patterns of asset poverty for families of various structures in table 4.13. Consider, first, families headed by a person younger than age 65. During the 1980s, asset poverty fell by all measures for two-parent families with children; however, for childless families and especially for female-headed families, asset poverty rose during the 1980s. Again, a surprising and unexpected twist occurred during the most recent decade, from 1989 to 1998. In this period, asset poverty rose for intact families with children by all measures. For families without children, asset poverty continued its growth but at an accelerated rate. However, for female-headed families with children, asset poverty fell by all measures during the recent decade, by from 4 to 17 percent.

Some surprising twists are also seen for the families headed by a person age 65 years or older. For female-headed older families, asset poverty increased during the 1980s but fell by most of the measures over the peak-to-peak years spanning the 1990s. Just the reverse pattern is observed for older families headed by a male. Rapid decreases in asset

Table 4.13 Asset Poverty Rates by Family Structure and Percent Changes

	Year			Percent Changes		
	1983	1989	1998	1983–1989	1989–1998	1983–1998
<65 years, married, children						
NW < .25 Poverty Line	21.6%	21.3%	25.3%	−1.7%	19.0%	16.9%
[NW − HE] < .25 Poverty Line	42.2%	36.8%	39.3%	−12.6%	6.7%	−6.8%
Liquid < .25 Poverty Line	37.6%	36.9%	44.4%	−1.9%	20.4%	18.1%
Liquid < $5,000	40.6%	36.5%	45.9%	−10.1%	25.6%	13.0%
<65 years, married, no children						
NW < .25 Poverty Line	12.9%	13.5%	19.0%	4.2%	41.0%	46.9%
[NW − HE] < .25 Poverty Line	25.0%	25.4%	28.9%	1.7%	13.7%	15.7%
Liquid < .25 Poverty Line	19.9%	20.9%	27.9%	5.0%	33.4%	40.1%
Liquid < $5,000	25.1%	22.7%	34.9%	−9.8%	54.0%	38.9%
<65 years, female head, children						
NW < .25 Poverty Line	48.1%	63.0%	53.7%	30.9%	−14.8%	11.6%
[NW − HE] < .25 Poverty Line	67.0%	77.2%	64.4%	15.3%	−16.6%	−3.8%
Liquid < .25 Poverty Line	63.4%	75.0%	69.8%	18.2%	−6.9%	10.0%
Liquid < $5,000	68.4%	77.3%	74.2%	13.1%	−4.0%	8.5%
>65 years, married						
NW < .25 Poverty Line	5.5%	5.7%	4.0%	3.1%	−30.0%	−27.8%
[NW − HE] < .25 Poverty Line	16.3%	16.4%	12.8%	0.5%	−22.0%	−21.6%
Liquid < .25 Poverty Line	17.4%	17.2%	19.1%	−0.9%	11.0%	10.1%
Liquid < $5,000	22.6%	19.5%	20.7%	−14.0%	6.3%	−8.5%
>65 years, single female						
NW < .25 Poverty Line	15.3%	16.8%	17.3%	10.0%	2.9%	13.1%
[NW − HE] < .25 Poverty Line	28.0%	33.2%	30.3%	18.6%	−8.7%	8.3%
Liquid < .25 Poverty Line	29.0%	38.4%	31.9%	32.1%	−16.8%	9.9%
Liquid < $5,000	41.7%	43.3%	39.9%	3.8%	−7.9%	−4.4%

(continued)

Table 4.13 (continued)

	Year			Percent Changes		
	1983	1989	1998	1983–1989	1989–1998	1983–1998
>65 years, single male						
NW < .25 Poverty Line	21.1%	24.3%	13.1%	15.3%	−46.0%	−37.8%
[NW – HE] < .25 Poverty Line	40.2%	26.6%	30.8%	−34.0%	16.0%	−23.4%
Liquid < .25 Poverty Line	40.2%	24.6%	32.7%	−38.9%	33.1%	−18.7%
Liquid < $5,000	49.6%	36.6%	38.9%	−26.3%	6.4%	−21.6%

Source: Authors' calculations based on the SCF for 1983, 1989, and 1998. Federal Reserve Board.

poverty are recorded for the 1980s, but by most measures these were reversed in the 1990s.

SUMMARY AND CONCLUSIONS

The patterns of asset poverty over the period from 1983–1998 are both discouraging and confusing. They are discouraging because of the very high rates of asset poverty for the U.S. population, irrespective of the definition used. In 1998, one-fourth of the U.S. population had insufficient net worth to enable them to get by for three months at a poverty-line level of living, and nearly one-half had liquid assets of less than $5,000.

These high levels of asset poverty for the entire population disguise even higher rates for various groups. Using the [NW – HE]/Poverty Line standard, the following list indicates asset poverty rates in 1998 for some of the groups most disadvantaged in terms of wealth holdings:

- Total population, 37%
- Blacks/Hispanics, 61%
- Head age younger than 25 years, 75%
- Heads aged 25–34 years, 60%
- Heads with less than a high school degree, 59%
- Renters, 63%
- Nonaged female heads with children, 64%

The growth in asset poverty over time is also discouraging. Of the four asset poverty measures shown here, three indicated growth in the prevalence of asset poverty over the 1983–1998 period, ranging from 13–20 percent (the [NW – HE]/Poverty Line indicator showed no change over this period).

The confusing part of the story concerns the pattern of growth in asset poverty over the two subperiods—1983–1989 and 1989–1998. For the population as a whole, asset poverty did not change substantially during the

Table 4.14 Percent Change in Asset Poverty for Selected Demographic Groups, 1983–1989 and 1989–1998

	Percent Change: 1983–1989	Percent Change: 1989–1998
Whites	−11	+15
Blacks/Hispanics	+6	−19
Less than high school degree	−3	+22
Some college	−13	+6
College graduate	−21	+36
Nonaged families with children	−13	+7
Nonaged female head with children	+15	−17
Nonaged/aged female head	+19	−9

Source: Authors' calculations based on the SCF for 1983, 1989, and 1998. Federal Reserve Board.
Note: Nonaged means less than 65 years. Aged means 65 years or more.

1980s, in spite of the recovery from a severe recession. However, during the peak-to-peak prosperity years from 1989–1998, asset poverty for the total population unexpectedly increased for three of the four measures.

When looking at several of the subgroups of the population, we can see surprising twists in the patterns of asset poverty change over the 1980s and 1990s. Table 4.14 summarizes some of the most surprising of these twists, using the [NW – HE]/Poverty Line measure of asset poverty.

For groups that are generally viewed as not financially vulnerable— whites, college-educated people, families with children—the recovery from the recession of the early 1980s resulted in reductions in asset poverty. However, for these same groups, the prosperity of the 1990s saw an unexpected increase in asset poverty.

The reverse pattern holds for groups generally viewed as vulnerable— blacks/Hispanics, female-headed families with children, and aged (>65 years) single women. In these cases, the recovery of the 1980s, which took place during Ronald Reagan's administration, led to unexpected increases in asset poverty, while the peak-to-peak prosperity period of the 1990s witnessed sizable reductions in asset poverty.[15]

Explanations for these unexpected patterns are not obvious and await further investigation.

APPENDIX: DEFINITION OF ASSET CONCEPTS

Net worth = the gross value of owner-occupied housing

+ other real estate owned by the household
+ cash and demand deposits

+ time and savings deposits
+ certificates of deposit and money market accounts
+ government, corporate, and foreign bonds, and other financial securities
+ the cash surrender value of life insurance plans
+ the cash surrender value of pension plans, including IRAs, Keogh, 401(k)s
+ corporate stock and mutual funds
+ net equity in unincorporated businesses
+ equity in trust funds
− mortgage debt
− consumer debt, including auto loans and credit card balances
− other debt

Liquid assets = cash and demand deposits

+ time and savings deposits
+ certificates of deposit, and money market accounts
+ government, corporate, and foreign bonds, and other financial securities
+ the cash surrender value of life insurance plans
+ corporate stock and mutual funds

NOTES

The authors would like to gratefully acknowledge the financial support of the Russell Sage Foundation and the Ford Foundation.
    1. This proposed revision is described in the report of the Panel on Poverty and Family Assistance, which was appointed by the Committee on National Statistics of the National Research Council of the National Academy of Sciences (Citro and Michael, 1995).
    2. Sen (1992) considered the needs standard (or poverty line) to have "some absolute justification of its own," it being a level below which "one cannot participate adequately in communal activities, or be free of pubic shame from failure to satisfy conventions" (167).
    3. Haveman and Mullikin (2001) discuss the advantages and disadvantages of these alternatives.
    4. The most fundamental criticisms of the official measure focus on the basic social objective on which it rests; perhaps actual cash income is not the most salient indicator of well-being or position. Similarly, in assessing poverty trends over time, perhaps the general trend in the overall level of living should be taken into account. Aside from taking exception to the social objective that underlies the official measure, most other criticisms of it focus on the adequacy of the annual income measure of "economic resources." While the current cash income numerator of the poverty ratio may reflect the extent to which the family has cash income available to meet its immediate needs, it indicates little about the level of consumption spending potentially available to the family. For many families, annual income fluctuates substantially over time. Unemployment, layoffs, the decision to undertake midcareer training or to change jobs, health considerations, and especially income flows from farming and self-employment may all cause the money income of a household to change substantially from one year to the next. Even as an indicator of a family's ability to meet its immediate needs, the current cash income measure

is flawed—it reflects neither the recipient value of in-kind transfers (e.g., food stamps and Medicaid, both of which are major programs in the United States supporting the economic well-being of low-income families), nor the taxes for which the family is liable. The Earned Income Tax Credit (EITC), a component of the tax system, has expanded into a major form of income support for the low-income working population. However, because the refundable payments are viewed as negative taxes, they are not reflected in the definition of income used in the official poverty measure. Similarly, whereas current cash income—and hence the official poverty measure—reflects financial flows in the form of interest and dividends from the assets held by individuals, the assets themselves are not counted; nor is the value of leisure (or voluntary nonwork) time reflected in the measure. This is less the case for the NRC-proposed revision to the official poverty measure, as it attempts to account for some in-kind benefits in assessing the relationship of resources to needs. The official poverty measure is also silent on the differences in the implicit value that families place on income from various sources. Sources of income from public transfers, market work, and returns on financial assets are treated as being equivalent in contributing to the family's well-being. As an absolute measure of poverty, the U.S. official measure also implicitly assumes that it is the circumstances of those at the bottom of the distribution of income that matter and not income inequality per se. A growing gap between those with the least money income and the rest of society need not affect the official poverty rate.

5. See Citro and Michael (1995).

6. Three-parameter scale = (ratio of the scale for 2 adults to one adult is 1.41). For single parents (adults + .8 + .5 × children − 1)^7; all other families (adults + .5 × children)^7.

7. Our poverty line calculation is drawn from the U.S. Census Bureau (1999), "Experimental Poverty Measures 1990 to 1997," table C1, CPI-U adjustment, and table C2, three-parameter scale.

8. Note that no other source of resource support, such as earnings from work or other forms of income, are considered in measuring asset poverty.

9. Note that net worth excludes the value of vehicles that may be owned. The rationale for excluding vehicles is that for most families, particularly poor families, autos tend to be necessary for work-related transportation and, therefore, not readily available for sale to meet immediate consumption needs.

10. Note that neither social security nor pension wealth, defined as the present value of future expected social security and pension benefits, respectively, are included in this definition of wealth, as they cannot be drawn against to meet immediate consumption requirements.

11. The official data are published every three years by the Federal Reserve Board (see References). Its Web site gives the following information: "The Survey of Consumer Finances (SCF) is a triennial survey of the balance sheet, pension, income, and other demographic characteristics of U.S. families . . . The links to the surveys provide summary results of the surveys, codebooks and related documentation, and the publicly available data."

12. We have combined African Americans and Hispanics into a single group for two reasons. The first is the relatively small sample sizes for these two groups and the associated sampling variability. The second is due to some changes in the wording of questions on race and ethnicity over the five SCF surveys. In particular, in the 1995 and 1998 surveys, the race question does not explicitly indicate non-Hispanic whites and non-Hispanic blacks for the first two categories, so that some Hispanics

may have classified themselves as either whites or blacks. In the case of the former, there is no way to correct the classification.

13. Because of the rather unexpected turnaround trends starting in 1989, we also used a second set of weights in the calculations for 1989—those labeled X42001. This variable is a partially design-based weight, constructed at the Federal Reserve using original selection probabilities and frame information, along with aggregate control totals estimated from the Current Population Survey. The results for 1989 were almost identical with the new set of weights.

14. It should be noted that the high growth rates record increases from rather low levels of asset poverty for this group.

15. The pattern for families headed by a person with less than a high school degree does not follow this pattern. For these families, asset poverty fell during the recovery of the 1980s but rose substantially during the 1990s.

REFERENCES

Citro, C. F., and R. T. Michael, eds. (1995). *Measuring Poverty: A New Approach.* Washington, D.C.: National Academy Press.

Federal Reserve Board. (1983, 1989, 1992, 1995, 1998). *Survey of Consumer Finances* (SCF). Available at http://www.federalreserve.gov/pubs/oss/oss2/scfindex.html. Last updated December 12, 2003.

Haveman, R., and M. Mullikin. (2001). "Alternative Measures of National Poverty: Perspectives and Assessment." In *Ethics, Poverty and Inequality and Reform in Social Security,* ed. Erik Schokkaert. London: Ashgate Publishing Ltd., 77–104.

Internal Revenue Service (IRS). (2004). *Statistics of Income* (SOI). Available at http://www.irs.gov/taxstats/. Last updated October 13, 2004.

Oliver, M. L., and T. M. Shapiro. (1997). *Black Wealth/White Wealth.* New York: Routledge Press.

Ruggles, P. (1990). *Drawing the Line: Alternative Poverty Measures and Their Implications for Public Policy.* Washington, D.C.: Urban Institute Press.

Sen, A. (1992). *Inequality Reexamined.* Cambridge, Mass.: Russell Sage Foundation and Harvard University Press.

U.S. Census Bureau. (1999). "Experimental Poverty Measures 1990 to 1997." *Current Population Reports* (June), 60–205.

U.S. Census Bureau. (2003, September). *Poverty in the United States: 2002.* Washington, D.C., 60–222. Available at http://www.census.gov/hhes/www/poverty02.html.

Wolff, E. N. (2001). "Recent Trends in Wealth Ownership, 1983–1998." In *Assets for the Poor: The Benefits of Spreading Asset Ownership,* eds. Thomas M. Shapiro and Edward N. Wolff. New York: Russell Sage Foundation, 34–73.

5

Family Matters: Kin Networks
and Asset Accumulation

Ngina Chiteji and Darrick Hamilton

Social science research has long recognized that the characteristics of an individual's family and the relationships among family members can have important implications for an individual's economic outcomes. For example, research has noted that the number of siblings a child has can influence the child's life chances by affecting the amount of resources that parents are able to devote to the child during critical phases of his or her childhood. More siblings can mean poorer outcomes during adulthood due to resource dilution. Researchers also have investigated the relationships between parents and their adult children, revealing that the desire and ability to control children can affect bequests and that individuals' labor market prospects and wealth outcomes are influenced by parental bequests and inter vivos transfers. The research in this area offers ample evidence to suggest that significant and transformative transfers are often made from parents to children when the children are adults—in the forms of "gifts" of tuition assistance, down payment assistance for home purchases, or transfers of wealth at death (e.g., Kotlikoff and Summers, 1981; Laitner and Juster, 1996; Oliver and Shapiro, 1995).

Other research has examined a broader range of family relationships, taking a particular interest in economic and noneconomic transfers and exchanges among all types of kin (Schoeni, 1992; Stack, 1974). This literature suggests that family resources are not necessarily expended solely on behalf of the nuclear family.

The vast, provocative literature on connections among different family members and on the bearing that family situations can have on individuals' lives serves as the inspiration for our research. We ask whether ties among adult relatives affect their abilities to accumulate wealth. More specifically, we seek to determine whether having poor relatives has any effect on asset accumulation for nonpoor families. We arrived at this research question because the aforementioned literature provides ample evidence that many economic outcomes are affected by the family situation. Accordingly, it seems critical to ask whether the family-based forces that shape individuals' labor market outcomes and educational levels also affect saving. We posed this question because research on kin networks suggests that the concept of the individual or nuclear family may be too narrow to characterize decision making in practice. We also suspected that acknowledging the presence of poverty in some extended families may help explain some of the race differences in asset ownership that permeate the literature on wealth inequality (see Hurst, Luoh, and Stafford, 1998; Oliver and Shapiro, 1995).

This chapter is organized as follows. The next section briefly reviews the separate literatures on the family and wealth inequality; this is followed by an examination of economic theories of saving. We present our empirical work in the following section, which includes descriptive statistics covering asset accumulation among U.S. families and data on the extent of poverty within the family by race, along with the results of regression analysis that examines the effects that poverty among siblings and parents has on a number of dimensions of asset accumulation. We then discuss the policy implications of our research and the relevance of this work for debates about social justice. The chapter's concluding remarks summarize our findings and emphasize their relevance to policy.

THE LITERATURE ON FAMILY RELATIONSHIPS AND THE LITERATURE ON WEALTH INEQUALITY

Ours is not the first study to demonstrate an interest in the existence of connections among different family members, although the way that we think about family relationships ultimately will differ somewhat from the existing literature. Economics typically explores and models family relationships in the context of altruism—the interdependence of utility among different agents. The research of Gary Becker (1981), which specifies utility as being a weighted combination of an individual's own felicity function and a family member's utility function, is representative of the framework used in economics to introduce concern about other family members into economic analyses. Much of the research in economics has focused either on two-sided altruism, in which both agents whose utility functions are represented exhibit some concern for one another, or on one-sided altruism on the part of parents, who are concerned about their children's outcomes in life (Laitner and Juster, 1996; Masson, 1997; Stark, 1995). Our research marks an effort to examine altruism on the part of adult children—therefore necessitating a shift toward thinking about adults who exhibit concern for the plight of their parents and their siblings.

Outside of economics, the concern that individuals exhibit for other family members has led researchers to challenge the notion that the concept of a "selfish" or self-contained individual agent represents the appropriate unit of analysis for studies of actual behavior. This may be particularly true for minorities, as research suggests that nonwhite families are frequently embedded in networks that tie them financially, socially, and emotionally to others (Stack, 1974; Taylor, Chatters, and Mays, 1988). Such research provides an additional impetus for modifying the standard economic representation of "individual" choice. Evidence that individual resources may be spent on a variety of family members (be they individuals inside the nuclear family or extended family members) not only suggests that the circumstances of different family members influences individual decisions; it also introduces the possibility that some relatives' needs may serve as a constraint on others' behavior and purchases. Social ties to less fortunate relatives may create a basis for economic ties that inhibit nonpoor family members' ability to engage in "traditional" or "expected" middle-class activities, such as wealth accumulation.

Because the existing literature documenting the presence of wealth inequality in the United States is vast, our study does not attempt to provide any new, detailed evidence to prove that wealth is unevenly distributed.[1] Instead, we simply note that regardless of the measure of wealth chosen, substantial differences by class and by race are found in this literature. For example, Melvin Oliver and Thomas Shapiro report that, on average, black families hold about 25 cents for every dollar in net worth held by white families and only about 11 cents if the analysis is restricted to financial assets (Oliver and Shapiro, 1995). Robert Haveman and Edward Wolff (chapter 4 in this volume) reveal that minorities have higher rates of "asset poverty" than white families. There are similar race differences in ownership rates for individual assets, such as stocks and bank accounts, and these differences remain even when the demographic and economic variables believed to determine wealth accumulation are accounted for (Chiteji and Stafford, 1999; Hurst, Luoh, and Stafford, 1998).

Why is this important? An individual's (or family's) wealth level can affect that individual's quality of life. Wealth is a stock of savings that can be used to guard against shocks to income, allowing the individual to continue to consume in instances in which the normal flow of income is disrupted (due to job loss or retirement, for example). Savings also can be instrumental in ensuring that one has access to credit because many loans require collateral. Additionally, saved funds can be used to facilitate large purchases whose price exceeds one's current income flow, when outside financing is unavailable or insufficient, for example, educational investments. Wealth also can have important implications for a child's outcomes. An individual's parents' wealth holdings can influence that individual's life prospects if parental savings are used to ensure that a child has access to postsecondary schooling or to prestigious private schooling at the elementary and secondary levels (Conley, 1999; Shapiro and Johnson, chapter 6 in this volume). This discussion highlights an important connection between living standards and asset accumulation. For those with assets or those whose parents have assets, asset ownership can improve the individual's standard of living. For this reason, research that focuses on the role of family variables such as family size, marital status, or "having a rich uncle" in shaping wealth accumulation is enlightening. Yet there is another dimension to the connection between living standards and asset accumulation. A second, less recognized connection is that the living standards of others may affect one's ability to accumulate assets.

ECONOMIC THEORIES OF SAVING

The central hypothesis to be examined in this chapter is whether the circumstances of poor relatives affect a nonpoor individual's saving behavior. We know from the research of other scholars that being poor has significant implications for a poor individual's ability to accumulate assets—because of what it means for that individual's personal resources and for the individual's access to savings-building institutional devices (Sherraden, 1991). In our research, we have tried to determine whether the poor individual's status also has implications for the person's nonpoor relatives. To assess these implications from the standpoint of economic theory, we turned to simple, standard models of saving, and we asked how the incorporation of altruism affects each model's predictions regarding saving.

Consideration of this issue requires us first to specify a model of altruism, so that it can be applied to different theories of saving. The static utility function (V_s) that forms the basis for our analysis is the following:

$$V_s = U_s(C_s) + B_s \, (\bar{C} - C_{RE})V_R(C_{RF}) \tag{1}$$

where U_s represents a standard felicity function for the nonpoor individual and $V_R(C_R)$ is the utility function of his poor relative.

C_s represents the consumption level of primary agent s, whose utility is the focus of the optimization problem; agent s is presumed to be nonpoor. C_{RE} represents the consumption endowment of this person's relative. A relative is considered poor if his endowment is low. B_s is a function such that for $C_{RE} < \bar{C}$, B_s is positive, and the interpretation given to its arguments is that $\bar{C}$ represents some minimal standard of consumption that the nonpoor agent s views as acceptable for his less fortunate relative. A natural interpretation might be the official poverty line. The variable C_{RF} represents the poor relative's final consumption level.

A few words about this specification are warranted. First, as is standard in economic models of altruism, we assume that the relative's utility function enters into the primary agent's utility function with a weight, represented by the B_s term. This allows the possibility that the primary nonpoor agent does not view his own well-being and that of his relative as completely interchangeable. Second, in the above framework, the utility of the poor relative is not dependent on the utility of the nonpoor agent. This reflects the assumption that the nature of altruism is such that nonpoor individuals are concerned about members of their family who have low consumption endowments, while a poor person is presumed to have no reason to worry about the welfare of well-to-do relatives. Intuitively, it is possible to view this as one nonpoor person having an interest in the other party, and in whether this relative will starve to death (in an extreme case), rather than an interest in completely sharing his resources. Third, this model of altruism allows for the weight attached to the relative's utility to vary. In fact, we hypothesize that it will vary such that if one's relative's consumption endowment does not fall below some minimum standard, a nonpoor individual will not worry about the welfare of his relative. Hence B_s is an increasing function of the gap between $\bar{C}$ and C_{RE} (which can be thought of as a gap between the poverty line and the poor relative's personal resources). Additionally, $B_s = 0$ if $C_{RE} \geq \bar{C}$. This implies that it is only if the poor relative falls below the poverty line, that his well-being will affect the utility of his nonpoor relative and, more specifically, the nonpoor person receives satisfaction from raising his poor relative's standard of living. To the contrary, if the relative's consumption level exceeds the poverty line, the nonpoor individual no longer receives satisfaction from helping the relative. Finally, for simplicity, it is assumed that when $C_{RE} < \bar{C}$ (that is, when the poor relative's endowment falls below the poverty line), the nonpoor relative will make a fixed transfer—"t"—to his poor relative in order to make up for the shortfall. This implies that t = $\bar{C} - C_{RE}$.[2] We next examine the implications of an individual's having the utility function specified in equation (1) for the individual's saving behavior.

Incorporating equation (1) in a simple two-period model of saving, in which the motive for saving is to secure funds for retirement and solving for the optimal levels of consumption and saving, yields a mixed prediction as to how saving will be affected.[3] Because $\bar{C}$ (poverty line) and C_{RE} (poor relative's endowment) are constants, concern about the poor relative ultimately affects individual s's saving decision by entering the constraint on s's optimization exercise. An individual who assists a poor relative experiences a reduction in the amount of resources that are available for his own use. This puts downward pressure on s's own consumption in both periods (C_s), and the reduction in second period consumption necessarily leads to a reduction in the amount the nonpoor individual desires to save. However, in a situation in which the nonpoor individual anticipates making a transfer to his poor relative in the second period, there also will be upward pressure on current saving. It will have to rise (relative to the case in which there is no altruism) in order to provide for the second period consumption of the poor relative. One can think of such a case as one in which the nonpoor individual now has two people to support during the retirement years, himself and his poor relative. How savings behavior is affected by the presence of altruism depends, therefore, upon which effect is stronger. The conclusions emerging from the model are somewhat sensitive to the assumptions one makes regarding the discount rate, the interest rate, and the number of periods in which the nonpoor individual will make transfers to his poor relative.[4] The ambiguity of this situation is interesting. Intuition might suggest that transfers to poor relatives would always displace or "crowd out" savings. However, analysis of economic theory indicates that this is not always the case.

For example, in the simplest case in which there is no discounting, a zero interest rate and a relative who is poor in both periods, concern about the poor relative does not affect the level of savings. In the absence of discounting and no ability to earn interest on savings, the nonpoor individual will want his consumption levels to be equal across time. Therefore, the "reductions" to income represented by his desire to make transfers to his poor relative are spread evenly between his first period consumption and his second period consumption. If the rate of transfers is constant, period two consumption falls and depresses the nonpoor individual's need to save for his own retirement by the exact amount that savings are raised to help finance the second period consumption of the poor relative. With a positive discount rate but no ability to earn interest, however, the effect of introducing concern about a poor relative is ambiguous. It is not possible to tell how much second period consumption falls unless one has precise information about the individual's preferences.[5]

In a world in which the interest rate is positive and agents discount future utility, and the subjective rate of time preference is equivalent to the interest rate, concern about poor relatives has no net effect on overall savings—if that concern extends for both periods, but it leads to a decrease in savings if the nonpoor agent only has to assist his relative during the first period. Under this scenario, the nonpoor individual will prefer that his consumption levels be equal across the two time periods. However, the ability to earn interest on savings implies that he will reduce first period consumption by more than he reduces saving for his own retirement. If the nonpoor individual also has an obligation to save to make a transfer to his relative in the second period (which can be thought of as saving for his relative's second period consumption), first period consumption and saving for own retirement must fall enough to allow for a current transfer and a future one. However, the fall in saving for his or her own retirement ends up being exactly offset by the amount that saving must rise to permit a fixed transfer in the amount of "t" to the poor relative during the second period. Hence, the net effect on saving is zero. If, to the contrary, the nonpoor individual only needs to assist his relative during the first period, the nonpoor individual simply reduces savings to account for the smaller consumption level that is desired for period two, and there is no countervailing upward pressure on saving. Concern for poor relatives creates a situation in which the need to make transfers crowds out saving.

It is interesting that such simple models can yield such a variety of results. The theoretical analysis suggests there is no a priori reason to expect that the need to make transfers will necessarily "crowd out" saving. How saving is affected appears to be more of an empirical question, depending upon what the relative strengths of the two different sources of pressure on saving are in practice. Having examined the theoretical elements of the argument that concern about poor relatives will affect saving, we now turn to an empirical investigation of the research question.

EMPIRICAL RESEARCH: DATA, METHODOLOGY, DESCRIPTIVE STATISTICS, AND REGRESSION RESULTS

We use data from the Panel Study of Income Dynamics (PSID) to explore the relationship between poverty in the family and asset accumulation empirically. The PSID is a nationally representative, longitudinal survey of U.S. households that began in 1968. It has followed its original families and the newly formed families that have emerged, as children from the original families reached adulthood, since 1968.[6] Because of the way that the survey is constructed, the PSID offers researchers the ability to examine a set of families, as well as the families of their adult siblings and parents concurrently. Data from the core survey and from the special 1984, 1989, and 1994 Wealth Supplements are used in this analysis.

Our study is not the only one that presents data covering poverty in the family, nor is it the only research that empirically investigates the relationship between such poverty and wealth. Colleen Heflin and Mary Pattillo-McCoy (2002) examined data on middle-class families from the National Longitudinal Survey of Youth (NLSY), and found that (a) the black middle-class is more likely than the white middle class to experience sibling poverty, (b) having a poor sibling affects home ownership and bank account ownership, and (c) having come from a family that was once poor is also negatively associated with these outcomes. As the NLSY only contains data on siblings and presents less data on wealth holding than the PSID, our empirical research provides a unique opportunity to add to the understanding of family circumstances and their effects on a variety of measures of asset accumulation.[7]

Our analysis focuses on middle-class families, and as is standard in the social sciences literature, it invokes three different measures of class—income, education, and occupation. Economists regularly use income to group and categorize households because income represents the primary type of resource that most families have to meet their needs. Elsewhere in the social sciences, it is also common to use occupation and education to define class status (Landry, 1987). Using occupational status as an alternative way to conceptualize class recognizes heterogeneity among workers in the degrees of power that they exercise over their work conditions. Use of education acknowledges the status attainment literature's argument that education serves as a mechanism for positioning oneself in the productive sphere of the marketplace.

Our sample of middle-class families is obtained from the 1994 PSID, and it includes about 1,700 to 3,000 middle-class families (depending upon the definition of middle class that is employed).[8] The middle-class income sample includes families whose incomes fall within the middle 60 percent of the income distribution. The middle-class education sample is constructed by selecting families in which the head or the "wife" possesses a college degree (at least). Our middle-class occupation category is constructed by selecting families in which the head or the wife possesses a job that is classified as managerial or professional by the U.S. Census.

Examination of data on the proportion of middle-class families holding individual financial assets reveals that middle-class black families differ from middle-class white families in terms of their "success" in accumulating assets. As shown in table 5.1, middle-class black families exhibit lower rates of asset ownership than white families when specific individual financial assets are examined, and the black families possess lower wealth than their white counterparts. For example, about 87 percent of middle-income white families have a bank account, while only about 54 percent of middle-income black families hold this type of financial asset. On average, white families have from three-and-one-half to five times as much net worth as black families.

Asset ownership rate differences are even more striking for stocks. Among middle-income whites, about 35 percent of families own stock. This is more than twice the number of similarly situated black families that own stock. In the middle-class occupation and middle-class education categories, the differences are also great. Over one-half of white families in white-collar occupations own stock, and about three-fifths of college-educated white families own stock, while less than one-third of black families in white-collar occupations hold stock, and only one-fifth of college-educated black families hold this particular financial asset.

Our data also allow us to comment on the extent to which there is poverty among kin within black and white middle-class families. As shown in table 5.2, an examination of the economic status of the parents, as defined by the middle-income category, reveals that the average income of the parents of middle-class black families is a little over $22,000, and that the average income of parents among middle-class white families is about $49,000 (both expressed in constant, 1996 dollars). Additionally, among parents, poverty rates are higher for blacks than they are for whites. For example, slightly over one-third (35.7 percent) of the parents of middle-income blacks are poor when poverty is defined as falling below the poverty threshold that is specified by the U.S. Census Bureau, while fewer than one-tenth (8.3 percent) of the parents of middle-income white families are in this position. Additionally, about one-fifth (18.6 percent) of the parents of middle-income black families receive Aid to Families with Dependent Children (AFDC) or food stamps, while only 3.7 percent of the parents of middle-income whites are poor, according to this indicator. When receipt of public housing is used as an indication of low economic status, 25.2 percent of the parents of middle-income black families are found to be poor, while 4.2 percent of the parents of middle-income white families are in a similar position. Significantly, the rate of unemployment for black parents (6.9 percent) is about four times as large as the white

Table 5.1 Summary Statistics for the Middle Class

Variables	PSID		Middle Decile		White Collar		College Educated	
	Black	White	Black	White	Black	White	Black	White
Sample statistics								
Sample N	3,113	6,483	1,434	2,737	252	1,499	264	1,432
Race composition (%)	14.0	84.1	13.1	86.9	6.1	92.0	5.8	92.3
Mean age	43.8	48.2*	42.2	46.8*	41.5	43.5	42.8	45.2
Family								
Married (%)	25.3	55.5*	31.0	53.4*	32.7	67.2*	29.5	63.0*
Sep./div./wid. (%)	39.1	28.0*	35.2	27.4*	36.2	15.1*	37.0	15.4*
Never married (%)	35.7	16.4*	33.8	19.2*	31.1	17.7*	33.4	21.6*
Single mothers (%)	29.4	7.1*	24.9	7.3*	21.4	4.9*	16.4	3.7*
Mean family size	2.4	2.4	2.4	2.3	2.3	2.7*	2.1	2.5*
Measures of middle-class status								
Mean family income	$24,066	$49,359*	$30,640	$35,040*	$44,511	$81,748*	$39,461	$79,352*
College graduate (%)	10.7	27.5*	15.3	22.4*	38.3	58.3*	—	—
White collar (%)	12.5	30.4*	17.0	24.2*	—	—	53.3	67.3*

(continued)

Table 5.1 (continued)

Variables	PSID		Middle Decile		White Collar		College Educated	
	Black	White	Black	White	Black	White	Black	White
Measures of wealth								
Business ($)	$1,077	$25,275*	$1,348	$12,148*	$3,486	$53,600*	$734	$43,281*
Transaction accounts (%)	41.3	83.1*	54.7	85.7*	78.7	92.1*	78.7	94.4*
Transaction accounts ($)	$4,548	$22,164*	$6,258	$18,934*	$8,598	$29,006*	$16,356	$31,336
Stock (%)	10.7	37.8*	13.1	34.6*	27.5	57.3*	20.6	59.8*
Stock ($)	$2,867	$34,341*	$2,221	$18,473*	$5,293	$69,930*	$12,039	$81,545*
Vehicles ($)	$5,090	$11,082*	$6,212	$10,178*	$7,400	$13,824*	$8,354	$13,149*
Other savings/assets ($)	$4,742	$9,341*	$6,348	$6,662	$12,244	$16,244	$5,373	$16,783*
Portfolio composition								
Financial wealth share	24.8	32.2*	25.9	31.0*	38.1	38.1	30.4	41.9*
Consumable wealth share	74.7	63.0*	73.8	65.0*	59.5	55.5	69.1	53.3*
Net worth	$34,540	$173,892*	$36,000	$124,514*	$55,354	$292,782*	$75,685	$305,766*

Source: Authors' own calculations using data from the Panel Study of Income Dynamics (PSID), available at http://psidonline.isr.umich.edu.
*p-value < 0.10.

Table 5.2 Summary Statistics for Relatives of Middle-Class Families

Variables	Middle Decile		White Collar		College Educated	
	Black	White	Black	White	Black	White
Sample statistics for parents						
Sample N	472	984	131	597	136	546
Race composition (%)	10.4	88.4	4.8	94.6	6.6	92.4
Mean age	60.2	60.9	63.8	64.1	63.2	63.8
Measures of parents' economic status						
Mean family income	$22,267	$48,663*	$23,717	$56,472*	$22,307	$60,890*
Income to needs ratio	2.3	5.1*	2.5	6.0*	2.4	6.5*
Poverty status (%)	35.7	8.3*	31.5	8.9*	35.3	6.0*
AFDC/food stamps (%)	18.6	3.7*	20.7	2.4*	15.9	1.6*
Public housing (%)	25.2	4.2*	24.2	3.2*	19.3	2.1*
Unemployed (%)	6.9	1.7*	2.2	1.0	5.0	0.9
Net worth	$47,385	$266,397*	$55,907	$387,442*	$96,317	$420,987*

(continued)

Table 5.2 (continued)

Variables	Middle Decile		White Collar		College Educated	
	Black	White	Black	White	Black	White
Sample statistics for siblings						
Sample N	1,671.0	2,159.0	528.0	1,412.0	530.0	1,194.0
Race composition (%)	17.9	80.7	9.2	88.6	11.4	86.9
Mean age	34.8	35.3	35.9	36.6	35.6	36.6
Measures of siblings' economic status						
Mean family income	$24,337.0	$50,599*	$33,264.0	$63,493*	$26,261.0	$67,300*
Income to needs ratio	2.3	4.4*	3.2	5.5*	2.4	5.8*
Poverty status (%)	33.6	8.0*	21.4	5.8*	30.6	4.7*
AFDC/food stamps (%)	27.0	6.1*	16.6	3.8*	21.3	3.5*
Public housing (%)	23.1	4.7*	19.9	2.2*	19.3	2.2*
Unemployed (%)	13.3	5.3*	10.1	5.0*	12.2	5.0*
Net worth	$22,099	$98,324*	$34,970	$142,516*	$27,737	$157,587*

Source: Authors' own calculations using data from the Panel Study of Income Dynamics (PSID), available at http://psidonline.isr.umich.edu.
Note: US$ are in constant 1996 dollars.
*p-value < 0.10.

parental unemployment rate (1.7 percent). The race differences are similar in the other middle-class categories.

The lower half of table 5.2 depicts the economic status of siblings of the middle-class families. Among siblings of middle-income families, mean family income is higher for whites than it is for blacks—$50,599 compared with $24,337. The average income to needs ratios are also greater—4.4 for whites compared with 2.3 for blacks. Furthermore, the proportion of siblings who fall below the poverty line, the rate of AFDC or food stamp program participation, reliance on public housing, and the rate of unemployment are all greater for blacks than they are for whites. These differences exist across the board—when any category (income, occupation, or education) is used to denote middle-class status.

Regression Results

To determine whether there is an empirical connection between a family's asset accumulation and the economic circumstances of its kin, we estimated probit regressions for bank account ownership and for stock ownership and an ordinary least squares regression, using overall wealth (net worth) as the dependent variable. While it was an awareness of the literature on black families' participation in kin networks that motivated our research question, there seems no reason to expect that white families that have poor relatives are immune from pressure to assist these relatives. We, therefore, report the results from regressions using data for all families.[9]

Tables 5.3, 5.4, and 5.5 list the regression results for bank account ownership, stock ownership, and wealth, respectively. Each of the tables provides a series of results that include baseline controls for the economic and demographic variables that are standard in the literature—along with additional regressions that also include indicators of parental and sibling poverty status. Respondents' AGE and age-squared (AGESQ) are used to capture life-cycle effects. Additional economic controls are the respondents' years of schooling (EDUCATION), a five-year average income measure (AVG LIFETIME INCOME), and an indicator of managerial or professional occupational membership (MGR AND PROF OCCUPATION).[10] The demographic controls are the respondents' number of children (CHILDREN) and indicators of whether the household head is FEMALE, MARRIED, and/or self-identifies as racially black (BLACK).

Each of the tables also includes results from specifications of the model that include a parental or sibling poverty indicator. PNEED represents a composite measure of the pressure that a middle-class family faces to assist its parents. This measure indicates whether the respondent had a parent who satisfied at least one of the following in 1994: (a) lives in a household classified in poverty according to the family's income-to-needs, (b) lives in public housing or received a public housing or heating subsidy, and (c) is enrolled in the AFDC or the food stamp program. SNEED is a similar measure that gauges pressure to assist siblings. It includes all three criteria of

Table 5.3 Probit Regressions for Bank Account Ownership with Parental Controls

Variables	dF/dx	dF/dx	dF/dx	dF/dx
AGE	0.0027	0.0021	0.0022	0.0024
	(0.00997)	(0.00991)	(0.00994)	(0.01000)
AGESQ	−0.0005	0.0000	0.0000	0.0000
	(0.00013)***	(0.00013)	(0.00013)	(0.00013)
FEMALE	0.0660	0.06997***	0.0716***	0.07345***
	(0.02970)	(0.02954)	(0.02936)	(0.02935)
MARRIED	0.0698***	0.07436***	0.0759***	0.0779***
	(0.03073)	(0.03082)	(0.03074)	(0.03082)
BLACK	−0.2607****	−0.2078****	−0.1996****	−0.1979****
	(0.02343)	(0.02726)	(0.02864)	(0.02857)
CHILDREN	−0.0269****	−0.02415***	−0.02428***	−0.0247***
	(0.00980)	(0.00995)	(0.00997)	(0.01000)
EDUCATION	0.0339****	0.03058****	0.03010****	0.0302****
	(0.00641)	(0.00653)	(0.00654)	(0.00654)
AVG LIFETIME INCOME*	0.0062****	0.0057****	0.0056****	0.0056***
	(0.00078)	(0.00078)	(0.00078)	(0.00078)
MGR AND PROF OCCUPATION	0.0445*	0.04407*	0.04431*	0.0448*
	(0.02787)	(0.02812)	(0.02809)	(0.02808)

(continued)

PNEED for each respondent's sibling(s)—plus an additional indicator of whether the sibling was looking for employment.[11] We also construct a dummy variable to measure the combination of both a parent and a sibling experiencing economic hardship (BPSNEED), as well as another to reflect instances in which need was experienced either by parents or siblings (but not both—ORPSNEED—with neither parents nor siblings in need as the omitted reference category). There are also separate specifications that contain measures of relatives' participation in the AFDC and/or food stamps programs. PAFDC measures receipt of AFDC and/or food stamps by the parents of the middle-class family. SAFDC tracks receipt of these two types of public assistance among siblings. These two indicators are interesting because they offer information concerning how one of the largest publicly supported poverty programs can indirectly impact the wealth accumulation of the middle class.[12]

In order to parse out the effects of poverty in the family from other potential family-based effects, we include additional controls so that we can better isolate the effects of transfers to worse-off relatives from the positive asset-generating effects of transfers from better-off relatives. The additional

Table 5.3 (continued)

Variables	dF/dx	dF/dx	dF/dx	dF/dx
PPBANK		0.0865****	0.0797****	0.07627***
		(0.02757)	(0.02860)	(0.02831)
BEQUEST		0.0297514	0.0279909	0.0275396
		(0.06569)	(0.06602)	(0.06595)
PNEED[a]			−0.0268	
			(0.02642)	
SNEED[b]		−0.05615**	−0.05397***	
		(0.02300)	(0.02292)	
BOTH PARENT & SIBLING NEED (BPSNEED)				−0.0883***
				(0.03732)
EITHER PARENT/ SIBLING NEEDS (ORPSNEED)[c]				−0.03795*
				(0.02629)
NUMBER OF OBSERVATIONS	2,042	2,032	2,032	2,032
WALD STATISTIC	308.75	347.27	348.54	347.25

Source: Authors' own calculations using data from the Panel Study of Income Dynamics (PSID), available at http://psidonline.isr.umich.edu.
*$p < 0.15$, **$p < 0.10$, ***$p < 0.05$, ****$p < 0.01$. All regressions were estimated using the Stata cluster procedure to account for the fact that there will be some correlation across observations for any middle-class families who have more than one sibling in the sample. All regressions are unweighted regressions that include a constant term.
[a] Dummy indicator that takes on a value of 1 if the observation has a parent or parents who satisfies at least one of the following criteria: (1) lives in a household below the poverty line, (2) receives AFDC/food stamps, (3) lives in public housing/received housing or heating subsidy.
[b] Dummy variable that takes on a value of one if the observation had a sibling or siblings who satisfy at least one of the following criteria: (1) live in a household below the poverty line, (2) receive AFDC/food stamps, (3) live in public housing/receive housing or heating subsidy, (4) is looking for employment.
[c] The omitted categories are those observations coded as not having either parental or sibling pressure.

controls are whether the middle-class family received a bequest and parental ownership of the respective dependent variable asset(s). The argument for including the indicators of parental asset ownership is that existing research indicates that some parents may teach their children about individual assets and about the mechanics of asset ownership, making those whose parents do not expose them to certain assets less likely to acquire them (Chiteji and Stafford, 1999). Therefore, analysis of account ownership incorporates a dummy variable for parental account ownership (PPBANK)

Table 5.4 Probit Regression for Stock Ownership with Parental Controls

Variables	dF/dx	dF/dx	dF/dx	dF/dx
AGE	0.02248***	0.02109***	0.0211***	0.0207***
	(0.09114)	(0.00930)	(0.00938)	(0.00946)
AGESQ	−0.00023**	−0.00021**	−0.00021**	−0.00021*
	(0.00012)	(0.00013)	(0.00013)	(0.00013)
FEMALE	−0.0303	−0.0332	−0.0329	−0.0336
	(0.03051)	(0.03028)	(0.03060)	(0.03052)
MARRIED	0.04678**	0.04547**	0.04599**	0.04537**
	(0.02686)	(0.02670)	(0.02693)	(0.02691)
BLACK	−0.1453****	−0.11598****	−0.1114****	−0.1090****
	(0.01873)	(0.02060)	(0.02106)	(0.02119)
CHILDREN	−0.0119	−0.0106	−0.0111	−0.0116
	(0.00844)	(0.00840)	(0.00840)	(0.00843)
EDUCATION	0.03116****	0.02925****	0.0291****	0.0294****
	(0.00526)	(0.00530)	(0.00531)	(0.00538)
AVG LIFETIME INCOME	0.00256***	0.00234****	0.002371****	0.0023****
	(0.00086)	(0.00084)	(0.00085)	(0.00084)
MGR AND PROF OCCUPATION	0.03721*	0.0304	0.0291	0.0267
	(0.02372)	(0.02345)	(0.02338)	(0.02338)
PPSTOCK		0.0664****	0.06555****	0.06505****
		(0.02545)	(0.02544)	(0.02574)

(continued)

to eliminate the possibility that the poverty in the family measures would be capturing this type of effect. Similarly, the analysis of stock ownership among middle-class families includes a dummy variable for parental stock ownership (PPSTOCK), and the analysis of wealth incorporates a control for parental wealth.[13] All regressions also include a dummy variable indicating whether the middle-class family has received an inheritance. This modification is done to eliminate the possibility that the parental poverty measures would reflect poor parents' lesser tendency to leave bequests than rich parents.

The estimates listed in tables 5.3 and 5.4 describe the marginal effects (dF/dX) of each regressor on the respective probabilities of account and stock ownership, evaluated at the mean value of the other regressors. Table 5.5 lists the coefficients for the household wealth regressions. The first column of each table lists the baseline parameter estimates without any measures of bequest receipt, parental asset ownership, or parental or sibling poverty. Subsequent columns report the results of other models that incor-

Table 5.4 (continued)

Variables	dF/dx	dF/dx	dF/dx	dF/dx
BEQUEST		0.20208**** (0.05941)	0.20053**** (0.05926)	0.20005**** (0.05894)
PAFDC[a]		−0.0507* (0.02916)		
PNEED[b]			−0.0357026* (0.02284)	
BOTH PARENT & SIBLING NEED (BPSNEED)				−0.0493* (0.02915)
EITHER PARENT/ SIBLING NEEDS (ORPSNEED)[c]				0.0010 (0.02070)
NUMBER OF OBSERVATIONS	2042	2042	2042	2032
WALD STATISTIC	226.98	261.46	250.66	249.25

Source: Authors' own calculations using data from the Panel Study of Income Dynamics (PSID), available at http://psidonline.isr.umich.edu.
*$p < 0.15$, **$p < 0.10$, ***$p < 0.05$, ***$p < 0.001$. All regressions were estimated using the Stata cluster procedure to account for the fact that there will be some correlation across observations for any middle-class families who have more than one sibling in the sample. All regressions are unweighted regressions that include a constant term.
[a] Dummy variable that takes on a value of one if the observation has a parent or parents who receive AFDS/food stamps.
[b] A dummy indicator that takes on the value of one if the observation had a parent or parents who satisfy at least one of the following criteria: (1) lives in a household below the poverty line, (2) receives AFDC/food stamps, (3) lives in public housing/receives housing or heating subsidy.
[c] Omitted category is those observations coded as not having parent or sibling pressure.

porate bequests, parental asset ownership, and various measures of poverty in the family.

Most of the demographic and economic variables that typically are entered into regressions for asset accumulation have the standard effects found throughout the literature. In the case of stock ownership for example, the life-cycle parameters, AGE and AGESQ, appear statistically significant with the expected signs—positive for AGE and negative for AGESQ. For account ownership, both signs are in the expected direction, although only the quadratic term is statistically significant. Neither variable is statistically significant in the wealth regressions. As expected, the remaining economic parameters, EDUCATION, MGR AND PROF OCCUPATION, and AVG LIFETIME INCOME, have positive coefficients for all three outcomes. However, the effect of EDUCATION on wealth was surprisingly not statis-

Table 5.5 OLS Regressions for Wealth Holdings with Parental Controls

Variables	Coefficient	Coefficient	Coefficient
CONSTANT	−58591.10	−57930.85	−51215.59
	(46652.640)	(46059.900)	(47336.950)
AGE	1666.31	1996.26	1866.08
	(2409.639)	(2397.257)	(2445.979)
AGESQ	8.27	3.18	4.57
	(33.802)	(33.605)	(34.188)
FEMALE	−16374.03****	−17264.87****	−16887.51****
	(5139.527)	(5133.771)	(5074.457)
MARRIED	5348.08	4833.27	4221.02
	(6858.392)	(6796.747)	(6870.556)
BLACK	−24357.15****	−18674.51****	−17883.73****
	(5699.390)	(5231.629)	(5011.496)
CHILDREN	5346.57	5346.62	5725.51
	(4603.728)	(4573.107)	(4692.744)
EDUCATION	1389.49	710.31	507.40
	(1831.880)	(1823.718)	(1874.495)
AVG LIFETIME INCOME	531.2305**	493.0418**	494.7423**
	(276.925)	(278.150)	(278.509)
MGR AND PROF OCCUPATION	18588.38**	17955.71**	17749.87**
	(9297.820)	(9303.958)	(9403.628)
PPWEALTH		19.50211**	19.35156**
		(10.048)	(10.014)
BEQUEST		25482.59**	24885**
		(14647.650)	(14699.260)
PAFDC[a]		−8921.122***	
		(4181.931)	
SAFDC[b]			−10563.66***
			(4884.945)
NUMBER OF OBSERVATIONS	2042	2042	2032
F-STATISTIC	13.19	11.11	11.3
R-SQUARED	0.0674	0.0796	0.08

Source: Authors' own calculations using data from the Panel Study of Income Dynamics (PSID), available at http://psidonline.isr.umich.edu.

$*p < 0.15$, $**p < 0.10$, $***p < 0.05$, $****p < 0.01$. All regressions were estimated using the Stata cluster procedure to account for the fact that there will be some correlation across observations for any middle-class families who have more than one sibling in the sample. All regressions are unweighted regressions that include a constant term.

[a] Dummy indicator that takes on a value of one if the observation had a parent or parents who received AFDC/food stamps.

[b] Dummy variable that takes on a value of one if the observation has a sibling or siblings who receive AFDC/food stamps.

tically significant, and the effect of occupation on account ownership appears marginally significant at best (p-values in the range of 0.12 to 0.15 in the different models). The demographic control of being MARRIED yields a positive effect on asset accumulation, although its effect on stock ownership ranges from being statistically significant to marginally significant (p-values in the range of .090 to 0.104 for the different models). Having a household head that is FEMALE and having CHILDREN yields mixed effects in tables 5.3, 5.4, and 5.5. In the account ownership regressions, the variable FEMALE household head has a positive effect, while having CHILDREN has the expected negative effect. For stock ownership, neither variable is statistically significant, though both signs are negative, as would be expected. Finally, in the wealth regressions, both parameters have the expected negative sign, although the gender variable is the only one that attains statistical significance.

As shown in tables 5.3 and 5.4, race affects the probability of both account and stock ownership. In the first instance, being black reduces the probability of ownership by about 26 percent in the baseline model. In the second instance, being black reduces the probability of asset ownership by about 14 percent in the baseline model. As shown in table 5.5, race has a similar negative and statistically significant effect on wealth accumulation. All else being equal, black families are estimated to have accumulated close to $15,000 less than their white counterparts.

Tables 5.3, 5.4, and 5.5 also report the results of models that include bequests, parental assets, and various measures of kin poverty status, in addition the baseline controls. Beginning with table 5.3, which illustrates the regression results for account ownership, the parental account ownership variable (PPBANK) and BEQUEST both have positive coefficients; however, only PPBANK is found to be statistically significant. As shown in table 5.3, columns 3, 4, and 5, the signs found for our marginal effects suggest that both the composite measure of parental poverty and the composite measure of sibling poverty (PNEED and SNEED respectively) reduce the likelihood of account ownership; however, only SNEED was found to be statistically significant. Having siblings in dire circumstances appears to reduce the likelihood of account ownership for the nonpoor family roughly between 5 and 6 percent. In the last model of table 5.3 (column 5), having both parents and siblings who are poor (BPSNEED), relative to having neither, leads to almost a 9 percent reduction in the probability that the nonpoor family possesses a bank account.[14]

Table 5.4 reports the results for the stock ownership regressions. Both bequest receipt (BEQUEST) and parental stock ownership (PPSTOCK) were found to have statistically significant effects on the likelihood of stock ownership, with the former reducing the likelihood of stock ownership by 20 percent and the latter reducing it by about 6.5 percent. As for the effects of poverty in the family, PNEED is marginally significant in this regression. And, as shown in column 5 of table 5.4, having both parents and siblings who are poor (as opposed to neither) reduces the probability of stock ownership by about 5 percent, although this parameter also was only marginally significant (p-value = 0.106). Stock ownership was found to be somewhat sensitive to parents' AFDC/food stamps receipt when this specific measure of parental poverty was considered separately. As shown in column 3 of table 5.4, PAFDC reduces the likelihood of owning an account by about 5 percent, and this regressor is marginally statistically significant.

In the wealth regressions in table 5.5, BEQUEST and PPWEALTH each have the expected effects of raising wealth. The hypothesis that poverty among kin also affects wealth accumulation finds support when the more direct measures of poverty—PAFDC and SAFDC—are used. Each has a negatively signed and statistically significant coefficient.[15]

In summary, we find evidence to support the hypothesis that both parental and sibling poverty pressures adversely affect asset accumulation among middle-class individuals. Furthermore, we find that the addition of the various controls for poverty in the family reduces the size of the race effect in all three sets of regressions. This suggests that some of the race effects, found in the existing literature covering wealth inequality, may actually reflect differences in black and white families' tendencies to experience pressure to assist relatives who are in need.

A PERSPECTIVE ON THE RESULTS

James Midgley (chapter 3 in this volume) notes that it is possible to view assets and asset-oriented policy in both a positivist and a normative light. Furthermore, he argues that it is important to avoid shying away from contextual considerations, such as the way that a focus on assets fits into society's values and beliefs. The results of our analysis submit themselves to both positive and normative interpretation, as they have implications for debates about the appropriate structure of welfare policy and social justice.

The regression analysis offers evidence to support the hypothesis that poverty in the extended family serves as a constraint on asset accumulation. How does one discern the importance or economic *and* sociopolitical significance of this result? From the standpoint of social welfare policy, the results suggest that policy makers and social commentators must remember that policies for the poor can have implications for the nonpoor. Hence, it is not clear that welfare policy should be evaluated solely from the perspective of its effects on the poor. Considering the recent changes to the structure of welfare programs, for example, to the extent that the reforms that were instituted upon the passage of the Personal Responsibility and Work Opportunity Reconciliation Act of 1996 reduce the amount of publicly provided support that is available to poor families, the reforms may increase the strain on the nonpoor relatives of former welfare recipients. As John Caskey (chapter 8 in this volume) notes, the lives of the poor are filled with vulnerability and financial uncertainty. This may cause little concern for those who believe that family-based assistance and other sources of private charity are preferable to public assistance. In fact, some might argue that this is how the world should be—that family members, not governments, should bear responsibility for the poor. However, it is important to note that such a view implicitly accepts the proposition that it is appropriate for some citizens who "play by the rules" to be rendered less able to accumulate wealth than other citizens. Our results suggest that nonpoor individuals who ascribe to the same values of thriftiness, future orientation, and willingness to delay gratification that those on the Right argue should be rewarded, as evidenced by their having endured the sacrifices required to obtain college degrees and by their having worked diligently enough to obtain middle-class incomes and middle-class occupations, nevertheless, will become disadvantaged relative to their counterparts who do not have poor relatives. Whether one views this outcome as acceptable clearly depends on one's definition of fairness. Less troublesome for policy makers, our results suggest that changes in policy that promote saving and asset accumulation among the poor may enable the poor to build up sufficient reserves to allow them to avoid having to turn to their nonpoor relatives in times of trouble.

Our results also have implications for the public discussion of social justice. The finding that poverty in the family constrains asset accumulation among the nonpoor potentially explains why black families have less wealth than white families do, on average. The greater likelihood of asset poverty among minorities that is found by Haveman and Wolff (chapter 4) may be tied to differences in the poverty rates within the extended family, as our research reveals that even the nonpoor may struggle to accumulate assets if they have poor relatives who rely on them for support. This certainly has negative consequences for the ability of middle-class black families to engage in the kind of leveraging and use of assets to ensure better educational opportunities and success for their offspring that Shapiro and Heather Beth Johnson (chapter 6) describe as being important for many middle-class white Americans. It also provides further suggestion that not all families who "play by the rules" will necessarily attain the outcomes that many expect the hardworking and the thrifty to attain automatically. Those who are born into families with poor relatives—by chance and certainly through no actions of their own—will not reap the same rewards from their diligent behavior as those who are fortunate enough to have middle-class or rich relatives.

CONCLUSION

The primary theme emerging from this research is that there are important connections among family members—particularly poor and nonpoor kin—that need to be recognized by researchers and policy makers. Regression analysis indicates that poverty among siblings and parents reduces the probability that their nonpoor relative will own both bank accounts and stock. Assistance to poor relatives depresses overall wealth accumulation.

This suggests that a factor that has not traditionally been recognized may be an important constraint on individuals' decisions and outcomes in practice. These findings may help explain the wealth gaps that currently are observed in the United States because they suggest that some low-wealth families may have a hard time accumulating assets due to the precarious positions of their extended family members. Accordingly, it is unclear that low-wealth status can be interpreted as evidence of profligate spending or failure to take an interest in the future, positions that are sometimes tempting to take in public discussions about minorities and the poor.

As for policy implications, our research suggests that policies that reduce public support for poor people may have unintended consequences for the nonpoor and that these consequences need not be evenly distributed throughout the U.S. population. Families with many poor kin, such as newly minted middle-class families who emerge from humble circumstances, stand to bear a greater portion of the cost of caring for the poor in cases when the responsibility of providing for the poor shifts from the public sector to private individuals. Accordingly, when evaluating policy changes such as welfare reform, it is not only important to ask what has happened to the families that have vanished from the welfare rolls, but equally important to ask how their relatives are faring, to determine whether nonpoor relatives are becoming low-wealth relatives due to a need to provide assistance to poor family members. Poverty appears to be not entirely isolated in its effects. The fates of ascriptively and financially different family members appear to be somewhat intertwined.

NOTES

We wish to thank Sheldon Danziger, Colleen Heflin, Joseph Lupton, Mary Pattillo, and participants at the Washington University Center for Social Development Symposium on Inclusion in Asset Building. This research also has been presented at the Research Seminar of the Program for Research on Black Americans Research Seminar and at the Wealth Inequality-Global Impacts and Local Prospects Conference at the University of Maryland. Participants at these institutions are owed thanks for providing constructive commentary on our work. We also thank Rucker Johnson for his research assistance. This research was supported by a grant from the Ford Foundation, and both authors express much gratitude for the Ford Foundation's financial assistance. Any mistakes are the sole responsibility of the authors.

1. Oliver and Shapiro (1995) and Hurst, Luoh, and Stafford (1998) provide a discussion of the wealth gap. Chiteji and Stafford (1999) provide a comparison of the findings from these and other works.

2. The astute reader will note that a rational agent will only make a transfer if the reduction in utility due to a decrease in his own consumption is offset by the boost to utility that emerges from helping a poor relative. We do not derive such a result as a condition of the maximization exercise. Instead, we note that our analysis applies only to the group of individuals for whom this condition holds. If there

is sufficient heterogeneity in the population, particularly in terms of the consumption levels of the type s agents and the C_{RE} endowments, it is reasonable to argue that there will be some agents who satisfy this criterion.

3. Models that examine saving to acquire an indivisible good and precautionary saving also yield varied predictions. Formal mathematical representations of the theoretical analysis are available in an appendix (upon request).

4. Economics allows for the possibility that individuals attach less weight to the future than to the present. The discount rate denotes the rate at which the future is discounted.

5. If preferences are homothetic, for example, one can use the resulting knowledge that first and second period consumption are proportional to draw inferences about the magnitude of the reduction in second period consumption that occurs when income "falls," due to the need to make transfers. If the ratio of second and first period consumption is a fixed proportion, it can be shown that the change in second period consumption (brought about by the reduction in income) is proportional to the change in first period consumption, and the value of the proportionality constant can be used to determine whether the change in second period consumption is less than or greater than "t" (the amount that needs to be transferred to the poor relative in the second period). It then is possible to determine whether the upward pressure on saving resulting from the need to make a transfer during the second period exceeds the downward push attributable to the decrease in desired second period consumption.

6. Annually through 1997 and biannually beginning in 1997.

7. This is particularly true, given that the "having come from a poor family" (in 1978) measure used in Heflin and Pattillo-McCoy (2002) would not capture the present circumstances faced by parents. Using the PSID allows us to obtain the current measures of the parents' economic circumstances that our analysis requires.

8. More details about the construction of the different measures used in the analysis are available in an appendix available from the authors upon request. One important point, however, is that the PSID allows us to follow one side of the family tree only. This means that we have a rich array of information about parents and adult siblings of the sample member, but no information about his or her spouse. Accordingly, our empirical results may be subject to attenuation bias, due to the potential presence of an errors-in-variable problem. Our coefficient estimates may actually be lower bounds on the true size of the effects.

9. This chapter discusses the full sample results only. Regressions for split samples were run, and the results are available from the authors. In the separate regressions for blacks, poverty in the family is not found to be statistically significant; yet, sample size limitations prevent us from placing much confidence in these results.

10. The income measure is a five-year average of labor income over the period 1987–1991. It is averaged to provide a long-term measure of income, and it uses years prior to 1994 to avoid contemporaneous simultanity bias with the outcome variables.

11. An employment indicator was not included for parents because, given the age of the middle-class families, the parents of these families are expected to be too old to have regular employment.

12. While we employ AFDC support as an indicator of poverty status and financial burden for middle-class kin, the program may actually serve to relieve some of the burden experienced by middle-class families by substituting public support for

110	Asset Holding and Well-Being

private assistance. To the extent that it also has this latter effect, the real effect of having kin with low endowments may be stronger than our analysis will suggest.

13. These variables are taken from the 1984 Wealth Supplement, so that the time of the observation is closer to the time that current middle-class adults of interest would have been children in their parents' homes. Additionally, making them contemporaneous with the parental poverty measures creates the danger of introducing collinearity.

14. The models also were run without controls for bequest receipt and parental account ownership. In these models, PNEED did have a statistically significant effect. This opens the possibility that multicollinearity may be a factor in its lack of significance here.

15. The broader measures of poverty were not found to be statistically significant in the net worth regressions that contained controls for parental wealth and bequests, though they were highly significant in regressions that did not include these two variables. It is unclear whether this means that the broader measures of poverty (PNEED, SNEED, BPSNEED, and ORPSNEED) are insignificant or whether multicollinearity is present.

REFERENCES

Becker, G. (1981). *A Treatise on the Family*. Cambridge, Mass.: Harvard University Press.
Chiteji, N. S., and F. P. Stafford. (1999). "Portfolio Choices of Parents and Their Children as Young Adults: Asset Accumulation by African-American Families." *The American Economic Review* 89(2), 377–380.
Conley, D. (1999). *Being Black, Living in the Red: Race Wealth and Social Policy in America.* Berkeley: University of California Press.
Heflin, C., and M. Pattillo-McCoy. (2002). "Kin Effects on Black-White Account and Home Ownership." *Sociological Inquiry* 72(2), 220–239.
Hurst, E., M. C. Luoh, and F. Stafford. (1998). "Wealth Dynamics of American Families, 1984–1994." *Brookings Papers on Economic Activity* (Spring 1998), 267–337.
Kotlikoff, L., and L. Summers. (1981). "The Role of Intergenerational Transfers in Aggregate Capital Accumulation." *Journal of Political Economy* 89(4), 706–732.
Laitner, J., and T. Juster. (1996). "New Evidence on Altruism: A Study of TIAA-CREF Retirees." *American Economic Review* 86(4), 893–908.
Landry, B. (1987). *The New Black Middle Class.* Berkeley: University of California Press.
Masson, A. (1997). "Bequest Motives and Models of Inheritance: A Survey of the Literature." In *Is Inheritance Legitimate: Ethical Aspects of Wealth Transfers,* eds. G. Erreygers and T. Vandevelde. New York: Springer Verlag, 54–88.
Oliver, M. L., and T. M. Shapiro. (1995). *Black Wealth/White Wealth: A New Perspective on Racial Inequality.* New York: Routledge.
Panel Study of Income Dynamics (PSID). (1968, 1984, 1987–1991, 1994). Data from the core study and from the Wealth Supplements. Available at http://psidonline.isr.umich.edu.
Schoeni, R. (1992). "Essays on Interhousehold Transfers and the Family." Doctoral dissertation. University of Michigan.
Sherraden, M. (1991). *Assets and the Poor: A New American Welfare Policy.* Armonk, N.Y.: M. E. Sharpe.

Stack, C. (1974). *All Our Kin.* New York: Harper & Row.

Stark, O. (1995). *Altruism and Beyond: An Economic Analysis of Transfers and Exchange within Families and Groups.* New York: Cambridge University Press.

Taylor, R., L. Chatters, and V. Mays. (1988). "Parents, Children, Siblings, In-Laws, and Non-Kin as Sources of Emergency Assistance to Black Americans." *Family Relations* 37, 298–304.

6

Family Assets and School Access: Race and Class in the Structuring of Educational Opportunity

Thomas M. Shapiro and Heather Beth Johnson

In *The Black-White Test Score Gap* (1998), Christopher Jencks and Meredith Phillips argue that reducing black-white educational inequality would do more to promote racial equality than any other politically plausible strategy. Reducing racial inequality in education and, subsequently, in earnings, according to Jencks and Phillips, would go a long way toward eradicating other inequalities that flow from the educational gap. Debunking both traditional liberal and conservative arguments about innate abilities, family structure, and funding, for example, they strongly suggest that policy and research reorient to cultural and behavioral related approaches to learning. Specifically, their clarion call, which fits neatly with the current educational reform agenda, pulls attention away from highly inequitable conditions of education in the United States. While they have done an admirable job in clarifying much of this literature, and there clearly is much wisdom in their work and in what they say, in our view, the death knell for equity-based structural reform is premature.

One could review and learn from the burgeoning educational reform literature, reframe the issues, and attempt to shift the balance in one direction or another. Indeed, much can be learned that can guide efforts to improve classroom learning. The Tennessee class size experiment, for example, shows that reducing class size (by even seven students) makes a big difference for young black students. A consistent story is emerging from the empirical data, demonstrating compelling support that additional monies and resources matter greatly for minority and disadvantaged students but much less or little for advantaged students. A RAND (Grissmer, 2000) study of "Improving School Achievement" reports "remarkable" one-year gains in some states that have rigorous testing programs. One recent report touts school vouchers, reporting that two years of intervention by switching from public to private schools erases about one-third of the black-white test score gap. From Chicago, we learn that families living in the wealthiest sections of the city have access to many more magnet schools than families that live in other areas, while Latino neighborhoods and very low-income African American areas have access to the fewest magnet schools. Middle-income white neighborhoods also tend to have access to fewer magnet schools, and there are no magnet schools in predominantly Latino areas. In California, most charter schools are not yet being held accountable for enhanced academic achievement of their students. They exercise considerable control over the type of students and families they serve, and the federal requirement that charter schools reflect the social/ethnic makeup of their districts has not been enforced. These studies (Levin, 1998; Wells, 2002; Wells et al., 2000), and their implications, will please some, anger others, and no doubt guide future reforms.

We are not educational experts; rather, our interest comes from an asset-based sociological perspective, which, we believe, offers significant insights into the contemporary school reform debate. This is an important challenge to the meritocracy-labor market-earning paradigm presumed by Jencks and Phillips and by most others. The best-case scenario goal of educational and earnings equality is undeniably important and commendable; however, there is much work ahead that needs to be supported. Nonetheless, in *Black Wealth/White Wealth: A New Perspective on Racial Inequality,* Melvin Oliver and Thomas Shapiro demonstrated that college-educated whites possess about four times as much wealth as college-educated blacks: $67,000 compared with $15,000 (1997). An examination of more recent wealth data reveals no alteration in this relationship (Oliver and Shapiro, 2000). In other words, whites and blacks who have achieved similar education levels and similar earnings in the labor market have significantly different levels of assets. Income does not parallel wealth in similarly situated black and white families in the United States. This alone should make us pause to reconsider the goals of policy agendas that are exclusively earnings and income based, including those for education.

Furthermore, while the number of high-income-earning black families has grown substantially since the 1960s, their children's test scores still lag far behind those of white children from similar income-bracket families (Jencks and Phillips, 1998). In 1968, Otis Dudley Duncan noted that high-achieving black families did not necessarily pass their status along to their children, which stood in direct contrast with white families' ability to pass status to theirs (Duncan, 1968). Thirty years later, we revisited this dilemma and found that the tale of two mobilities continues. *Black Wealth/White Wealth* speculated that this was because black families, regardless of income achievement, lacked the wealth assets used by white families to optimize their children's opportunities and life chances. This is where our current work is focused. A central premise of our research is that the educational arena is a prime institutional site in which inequality is passed along from one generation to the next. Specifically, we are trying to understand how, within families, parents use assets (or the lack thereof) to pass along advantages or disadvantages to their children.

RESIDENTIAL LOCATION, SCHOOL SEGREGATION, AND SCHOOL CHOICE

In the United States, the traditional egalitarian ideals of merit and equality of opportunity apply best perhaps to the labor market, and even that arena typically is associated with a complex system of stratification. Through the lens of wealth, we see a dual, intersecting, and conflicting stratification system—based on nonmerit factors—that coexists. For example, inheritance upon a family member's death, family assistance with down payments on houses, and major cash gifts at weddings (just to name a few) are resources not gained through individual achievement. Family wealth, in terms of broad intergenerational resource assistance, institutionalizes existing inequalities and privilege across generations. Our research shows that families use assets to perpetuate advantages or disadvantages through the opportunity resources they are able or unable to offer their members; this is a major dynamic in sedimenting inequality (embedding inequality by transmitting it to the next generation) into the social structure.

The growth and dispersion of wealth over several decades, along with the transition to a service economy and the diminishing civic role of the state, have heightened the salience of wealth in determining opportunities, life chances, and capacities for families. Federal budget cutting over the past twenty years has weakened and diminished the public's role in basic civic duties. The power of the political Right and the acquiescence of others have reduced and weakened the state's role in housing, education, and health care. Families have to spend more to provide shelter, schooling, and medical coverage in 2004 than they did in the 1980s, and with a diminishing state presence, these additional costs must come out of family resources. In this changing context, we believe that assets carry a greater burden than ever before. While wealthy Americans have always been able to purchase opportunities, for the first time, many families possess financial resources that can alter their social mobility opportunities, especially through access to superior educational environments. By accessing quality school systems, parents ensure specific kinds of schooling for their children and in this way help to pass their own social position along to the next generation.

Specifically, educational markets are not neutral, meritocratic distributors of opportunities; instead, they are expressions of power relations and the resources families bring to that market (Henig, 1994). This observation is borne out by the different ways in which choice is exercised. One in five school children, that is, 20 percent, attend a private school or a particular school from a public education choice plan chosen by their parents; 9 percent of these children attend private schools, and 11 percent attend magnet, charter, or exam schools chosen from within the public system. These private and public school choices starkly reveal race and class dynamics. Black families exercise choice within the public school system more often than white families do (National Center for Educational Statistics [NCES], 1995). That is, a higher percentage of black families participate in magnet schools, special education programs, or voluntary desegregation programs ("choice" programs, which are disproportionately available in urban school districts). And whites select private schooling much more frequently than blacks: One in ten whites attends private school compared with one in twenty-five blacks (NCES, 1995).

The class dynamics at play are layered with the racial ones: Five times as many families with incomes over $50,000 opt for private schools as those with incomes of $15,000 or less, which is 16 percent versus 3 percent (NCES, 1995). Our own examination of the Panel Study of Income Dynamics (PSID) data indicates that 19.6 percent of all families with children have sent a child to private school, 22.3 percent of white families, and 14.8 percent of black families. When we asked who goes to private school, the answers were even more revealing; nearly one in three high earning (>$75,000) families have placed a child in private school. In contrast, 21.6 percent of children from middle-income families ($21,000–$75,000), and only 9.8 percent of the children from low-income families (<$21,000) go to private schools. To view this from another perspective, we examined the assets of those families that have ever sent children to private school compared to those who have not. Here, we find a disturbing pattern: Families that have used private schools possess a median net worth of $50,900 compared with a median net worth of $22,950 among families that have only used public schools. The net financial assets (not including home equity) differential between these categories of families is even starker, with a median of $20,000 compared with $7,000.

Selecting schools based on private or public status and using choice plans within a school district represent decisions that parents make to attempt to improve their children's life chances and provide them with greater educational opportunities. Selection of residential neighborhoods is an even more significant sorter of educational quality. Nearly half (47 percent) of parents say their choice of residence is strongly influenced by where their child would go to school (NCES, 1995). The potential significance of this parental concern is enormous because, according to one study, 29.1 percent of white households move during a three-year period, with over half of them buying a home (Yinger, 1995). Not only do many families select where to live, in part, on the basis of the perceived school environment and reputation, but many white households purposefully avoid locations with integrated or minority schools (Schuman, Steeh, and Bobo, 1985).

Access to public schools is tied directly to residential location and, therefore, residential segregation has a direct impact on access to schools. In *American Apartheid: Segregation and the Making of the Underclass* (1993), Douglas Massey and Nancy Denton describe hypersegregation as the extent to which blacks are isolated from other groups, clustered in contiguous areas, concentrated in a small area, and centralized within an urban area. More than one-third of blacks live in hypersegregated areas. John Yinger's *Closed Doors, Opportunities Lost: The Continuing Costs of Housing Discrimination* investigates the causes of residential segregation and concludes that it remains high "because of the predominance of complete racial and ethnic transition: most neighborhoods into which minorities enter eventually become dominated by minorities" (1995, 134). Black-white residential seg-regation indexes have been high for many decades (Massey and Denton, 1989; Yinger, 1995). Since 1970, residential segregation has declined slowly but steadily. This downward trend in segregation continued during the 1980s in those urban areas where most blacks live (Farley and Frey, 1994). Despite some decline, racial residential segregation in the United States remains extremely high. In metropolitan areas with large black popula-tions, three-quarters of the black residents (or white residents) would have to move for an even population distribution to be achieved (Yinger, 1995).

Residential segregation restricts minority households' access to high-quality schools. Therefore, one must examine the relationship between res-idential segregation and school quality and the subsequent consequences of school segregation for the educational environment and achievement of minority children. Racial disparities in educational outcomes are linked closely to the well-documented fact that schooling for minorities still is largely separate and unequal. Complicating matters further, school segre-gation has actually been increasing in recent years, offsetting earlier declines, and segregation for blacks is back to 1971 levels (Orfield et al., 1993; Yinger, 1995). In industrial states, over 50 percent of black children attend schools with minority populations higher than 90 percent. In large cities, over 90 percent of black children attend schools where a predominant number of students are nonwhite (Orfield and Yun, 1999). While not as extreme as in smaller cities, suburbs, small towns, or rural areas, levels of residential and school segregation in large cities are still disturbingly high.

THE ASSETS AND INEQUALITY PROJECT

The Assets and Inequality Research Project examined the processes by which parents in American families use wealth resources to place their children in socioeconomic positions similar to themselves. We are inter-ested in the role of wealth in framing a family's basic capacities. We argue that how much a family owns increasingly defines opportunity and suc-cess in contemporary America and that families acquire a substantial por-tion of this wealth from nonmerit sources; that is, it is not earned from the labor market. Families with assets consciously use this property and wealth to leverage advantages for their children, thereby introducing inequality into the social structure. Here we will focus on how, in the con-text of the educational arena, the ways that families use their assets can reproduce structures of inequality. As a part of this focus, we will share a bit of what we've learned about the role of race in the ways that white Americans make decisions about community and school preference.

The data we are reporting on come from the Assets and Inequality Research Project, a study in which 182 black and white families (232 parents) from three U.S. cities were interviewed in depth about their assets, income, and decision making about where they live and send their children to school.

The interview sample was chosen based on a snowball sampling method. Census tract data was used to identify residential neighborhoods in the metropolitan areas of Boston, St. Louis, and Los Angeles, based on the race and class identity of its residents. The sample included approximately one-half black and one-half white families from an evenly distributed, broad socioeconomic spectrum, ranging from poor to working class to middle and upper middle class. From January 1998 through June 1999, we interviewed couples and single heads of households in the three cities. Interview participants were all parents of school-age children. Approximately one-fifth of the families were sending their children to private schools (secular and parochial), and the rest were sending their children to public schools (both urban and suburban). Interviews took place in the participants' homes or in another place of their choosing and lasted one to three hours each.

The interviews were recorded and transcribed and were coded using NUD*IST qualitative data analysis software. The interview transcripts produced over 7,000 pages of reading and make up the foundation of the first qualitative research database on this subject (see Shapiro, 2004). Here we will discuss some of the patterns and themes revealed through our interviews.

ASSETS AND THE STRUCTURING OF OPPORTUNITY

Families expend a lot of time, energy, emotional investment, and money to find enriching, high-quality public and private educational environments for their children. For middle-class white families, this process also typically results in placing the family in predominately white communities. But the stories of the lengths to which most parents (of all classes and races) will go to provide their children the best opportunities are heartening and revealing. Because families choose schools primarily by where they choose to live, at critical moments in a family's life course, financial assets become a prime arbiter of school quality. Knowingly or not, these individual family decisions typically reinforce neighborhood and school segregation. Perhaps more than anything else in our conversations with families, we were continuously struck by how important it is for parents to get their children into particular schools. One theme from the interviews is that the class, racial, and educational characteristics of a community may be more important than owning a home, per se. Home ownership may be becoming more about choosing a community and cloaking the family in the identity of that community than anything else. Parents' hopes for their children disclose deep-seated class and racial anxieties. Rather than evidence of abstract racism or classism, the current and long-standing American context of communities and schools separated by race and class puts parents in a cruel dilemma: Using financial assets or other means to do the best they can for their children by navigating the class and race school landscape reinforces inequality and passes it along the next generation.

In an era of educational reform, a dizzying array of school choices, and high-stakes testing, our data capture the ways in which families navigate this new and changing environment. When we listened to families talk about their school choices and plans, we thought they often sounded like they were buying a product in the open market. We were struck, for example, by the individualistic strategies families adopted for their own good, as opposed to seeking to improve educational conditions and quality for all— all the public talk about educational reform notwithstanding. Educational aspirations also seem to be constructed differently by class. Poorer families, both white and black, were most concerned about finding a place where their children could learn, thrive, and acquire skills. The more affluent families seemed quite concerned with acquiring and keeping educational advantages for their children. In our interviews, some parents explained how they attempt to find educational advantages that will give their children an edge over the competition, while other parents described fighting to jump ahead of each other on massive waiting lists for programs that allow black children to attend suburban schools.

Distinct themes emerged from our interviews with middle-class families. The important difference is how they attempt to use assets to secure the kinds of education that pass along their advantages by placing their children in the richest possible educational environment. High-quality education, at least its perception, is the resource in question. Families with abundant assets search out educational environments that potentially maximize advantages to their children. This is a consistent theme among upper-middle-class families. The mechanisms varied, from using assets to purchase homes to gain access to highly reputed schools, to capturing magnet and charter schools, to demanding that children be placed in advanced learning classes, to paying large tuition bills for private schools. Whether the route is creative or crude, families invested much time, energy, emotion, and hope—as well as money—into securing the kinds of opportunities that put their children ahead. This theme is so pervasive that it seems as if we could excerpt almost any middle-class interview from our sample at random and illustrate the idea of leveraging advantage.

Equality of opportunity clearly does not characterize the distribution of opportunity resources. Schools are stratified, and, by one means or another, families use assets (or lack of them) to perpetuate existing inequalities by passing along advantages or disadvantages to the next generation. We see how working-class and poor families struggle just to find educational opportunities, while families with assets leverage advantages through exceptionally high-quality educational environments for their children. The educational scenario renders equality of opportunity problematic at best. For this aspect of life in the United States, merit clearly is not what determines opportunities. The matching of families to residential and school location is not by merit but by wealth.

HOW FAMILIES USE ASSETS TO ACCESS EDUCATIONAL OPPORTUNITIES

A significant racial wealth gap translates into a significant difference between black and white parents in the benefits that wealth confers to them and their children. Because of their asset ownership, the whites in our sample repeatedly had relatively more choices and were relatively more able to act on them. In this chapter, we will focus on illustrating some themes from our interviews with families who have assets and discuss some of the ways they use them to give advantages to their children and, in so doing, contribute to passing along inequality to the next generation. We will see some of the ways that the white families we interviewed use their assets to transmit cumulative advantages in the educational arena in ways that black families simply cannot compete with.

Indeed, in the case of white middle-class families, one of the most significant ways that children inherit the privilege that their parents' wealth confers is through the acquisition of quality education. Families with assets search out educational environments that ensure opportunity and potentially maximize advantages for their children. This is a consistent theme among the white middle-class families we interviewed. They may have differing wealth capacities or limitations, but we will see that even relatively small amounts of parents' assets reap large rewards for children. The opportunities and advantages created by wealth are dramatically different from those brought about by income alone. To illustrate the dynamics of these patterns, we will focus on three families from our sample who represent patterns and themes consistent with many others in our study.

Ensuring Opportunity: The Conway Family

Middle-class white families consistently told us about their desire to ensure opportunities for their children to receive the best possible education that they could afford. For these families, who tend to have at least some leverage through the assets they own, the options are numerous. Families plan and strategize ways to navigate the educational arena to ensure their children are placed in the highest quality educational environments. A striking theme is how even families with very young children think a lot about this process—they begin planning and strategizing very early on.

Fred and Sarah Conway are a white, middle-class couple from the Jefferson Park section of Los Angeles. They have one son, age four, whose name is Logan. Sarah is an operations supervisor for a capital management company. Fred is currently unemployed. He was laid off at a communications marketing firm, is currently changing careers, and is in the process of being certified to become an elementary school teacher. Their combined annual income is approximately $70,000. Very conservative estimates approximate their net worth to be $159,500, and their net financial assets total $139,500. Their inheritances have been significant. They receive gifts of $1,000 regularly from their parents and once received $85,000 in stock from them. In addition, they've received a $10,000 cash inheritance, and both Sarah and Fred expect to inherit wealth in the future.

The Conways bought their house one month before they were married eight years ago. Sarah's mother gave them $10,000 as a down payment. They looked around Los Angeles for a neighborhood that they could afford. They settled on the highly diverse Jefferson Park area because it was affordable, and they had friends living there. At the time, they did not yet have their son, and school options were not a part of their decision about where to buy. Things have changed now, with the addition of Logan to their family. They like their neighborhood, "However, now we are considering possibly moving because of the school district," Sarah says. When asked to elaborate on this, Fred turns to Sarah and says, "I think that's kind of your department." Sarah then explains that their local elementary school and several schools in the area recently "showed up on the worst schools in Los Angeles list." When asked where they would like to move, Sarah says they would be "very interested" in moving to South Pasadena because "I think it has a really great school district." When asked about the diversity of South Pasadena, Fred says, "I would guess that it's more Caucasian than anything else," and Sarah says, "Caucasian and Asian. Probably not as much of a mixture as we have now." Sarah also talks of her concerns about Logan being in the racial minority as a white child if he were to enroll in their current local school district. She says, "I do worry a little bit that he will be the only white kid in the class, and I don't want to put him in that position. I'd like to raise him with cultural diversity but not as big and as an extreme minority." Sarah says that for these reasons, "other than the school" they are "perfectly happy" in Jefferson Park.

However, because they are so concerned about providing quality educational opportunities for Logan, the Conways have decided that they will attempt to get Logan into a particular magnet school for "gifted" children, or else they will move. They say that "magnet schools are better than your regular schools" but that there is "a phenomenal demand" for admission. Although the waiting lists for admission are long and the chances of Logan getting in are slim, they will try for it. They say that if they stay in Jefferson Park, Logan is "definitely going to have to get into a magnet school or a private school." Otherwise, they will move to tony South Pasadena in order to "move into a better school district." (In South Pasadena, they can expect to spend at least $600,000 for an intact period house in clean condition with original floor plans on a quiet street.) Sarah feels strongly about Logan's education and says that she would "like to see him get a good all around education." They are prepared to move and to buy an expensive home in a financially and racially exclusive neighborhood in order to do so. If it were not for their significant unearned assets, that is, gifts from their parents, they would not be able to consider such an option.

Maximizing Advantage: The Yorrand Family

A major theme to emerge from our interviews with white middle-class families is that moving residential location is the most common way they use assets to maximize their advantage by securing the best possible public education for their children. It is important to note that the ability to own a home in a neighborhood with high-quality services like education typically requires significant assets. If one has such assets, this ownership can be the ticket to access the often well-endowed schools that these neighborhoods support. Buying a home in areas such as these is not affordable to most Americans and simply is not an option. However, for families with enough assets to afford a down payment, the key to their house can be the key to excellent schools for their children.

Anna and Elan Yorrand are a white middle-class couple from the Los Angeles area. They have two children, ages twelve and two. Anna works part time (15–20 hours/week) at a diner. Elan works in the film industry as a chief lighting technician. Their combined annual income is approximately $80,000. Their estimated net worth is $171,500, and their net financial assets are estimated to be about $32,500. The Yorrands have received gifts of cash exceeding $1,000 per gift from both sets of parents. They do not expect to receive an inheritance but feel they can rely financially on family if they need to.

The Yorrands own a house in Santa Monica. They chose Santa Monica because they wanted to get as close to the ocean as they could afford to, and they liked the Santa Monica schools. Anna says, "I mean, the first house that was in our budget in Santa Monica, we bought it, even though it was smaller. I mean, we saw bigger houses and nicer houses. But . . . it is in Santa Monica, for schools and for everything . . . schools and the good community. . . . It's just like Santa Monica has a good name and good schools." The purchase price of their house was $255,000, and they made a down payment of 20 percent, which they "borrowed" from family members and friends. They like their neighborhood and note that there are no black people living in their area.

Although the Yorrands moved to Santa Monica for the schools, their 12-year-old daughter does not go to their local school. She goes to Washington, which is not her assigned school but in a different zone within Santa Monica and considered much better than Jefferson, the school that is actually her assigned school. The daughter has six friends whose parents have all figured out ways to get their daughters into Washington with various strategies. The reason this group of parents all put their children in Washington was to avoid their assigned school, Jefferson, because its reputation is not as good. Anna explains there is a "bad" section of

Santa Monica, the kids from that area go to Jefferson, and they are "col-
ored" people—"black and Spanish." Anna says,

> I mean, there is a bad pocket in Santa Monica, that people think that that's the
> reason that Washington is better than Jefferson is. Because of the pocket that got
> a lot of the colored people, maybe. There is more like a drug or behaving prob-
> lem in Jefferson compared to Washington. Washington is completely white,
> very rich. That's the part I don't really like. I don't like that most of her friends
> live north of Montana, rich houses. I mean, she has a birthday party and I
> wanted to do it here in the house; she doesn't want me to do it in the house. So
> that's the part that I don't like. But I'm very happy [she's] in the school. I'm very
> happy with the school.

Anna's strategy was to lie about her address by using her friend's
address. She was caught doing this because the friend moved, and the
school found out. Apparently, the principal decided to let the daughter
stay in the school anyway. "We were really lucky," Anna says.

Indeed, they are lucky. Although both Jefferson and Washington are in
the same school district, are approximately the same size, and are only two
miles apart, they are significantly different. Washington scores significantly
higher on all measures of standardized testing and ranks significantly
higher by all accounts. Washington has only 14 percent of its students on
the free lunch program and only 13 percent considered socioeconomically
disadvantaged, while Jefferson has 37 percent of students on free lunch and
41 percent considered socioeconomically disadvantaged. Washington is
69 percent white and 16 percent Hispanic, while Jefferson is 40 percent
white and 43 percent Hispanic. At Washington, 8 percent of the students
are Asian, and 7 percent are black. At Jefferson, only 4 percent are Asian,
and 12 percent are black (California Department of Education, 2000).

Furthermore, the Yorrands are lucky because the principal did not
kick their daughter out of Washington. While, in our sample, using false
addresses to access schools was not uncommon, getting caught and not
being kicked out surely was. In this case, the Yorrands are not crossing
school district borders; they are only crossing neighborhood borders within
Santa Monica. We would guess that if the Yorrands were living in the
Los Angeles school district or perhaps if they were a nonwhite or poor
family and were caught with their child in a school in Santa Monica, the
child would have been expelled. However, the principal has allowed their
daughter to stay. We can only guess what the principal's thinking might
have been: that this is a nice, well-off Santa Monica white family, and the
parents are really committed to their children's education. Anna plans to
keep her daughter in Washington and then see that she continues within
the Santa Monica system.

While the Yorrands have ensured educational opportunity for their children by purchasing an expensive house in Santa Monica, they also maxi-
mized their advantage by falsifying their address to get their daughter into
the Washington School within the Santa Monica district. Clearly, they have
used their assets to make these moves.

Acquiring the Best: The Cummings Family

Taking advantage of specialized public schools or moving to access specific school districts are not the only ways that white middle-class and wealthy families use their assets to place their children in advantaged positions in the educational arena. For many of these families, their assets allow them to consider private schools as a viable option. Many families choose private parochial or secular schools for their children because they see them as a way to opt out of the public education system altogether. Some parents are willing to pay very large tuition bills to acquire what they see as the best possible education that money can buy.

Elizabeth and Blaine Wainwright Cummings are a white family from St. Louis. They have two children, ages nine and four. The family lives close to Washington University. Blaine is a teacher at a magnet school. Elizabeth is a part-time nurse, but she considers herself a "stay at home mom part-time." Their annual income is $95,000. Their net worth is approximately $328,000, and net financial assets are approximately $165,000. Elizabeth comes from an "old-money" family and has always received and will continue to receive very significant sums of money. "About half of our income is from my husband—well, more than half—and then some is from mine, but also a lot of it is inherited money that I invest. And that generates income." Elizabeth says that they receive about $30,000 annually from investment income from invested inherited money; in addition, at least $20,000 per year is gifted to Elizabeth from her family. Elizabeth says,

> My parents try to gift to the maximum amount allowed by law because they're sitting on a huge estate, and they don't need it and we do. And there are four kids in my family of origin, and they try to spread it around, especially to my sister and me, who have children. And it can cover anything. . . . I mean, they recognize births, graduations, and birthdays, or, on the other hand, they recognize if we need a new piece of furniture or appliance; they'll pay for that.

Elizabeth's family also gives them approximately $20,000 per year for their school-age son's private school tuition. Elizabeth expects a significant inheritance in the future. She says, ". . . there's more than a million sitting there with my name on it . . . chunks that we still will come into down the road. . . ." They have investments everywhere: stocks, bonds, mutual funds, home property, real estate, gold, cars, retirement, savings, CDs, inherited furniture and art, jewelry, and so on. This family is very wealthy, and very few of these assets are earned by their own merits.

When Elizabeth and Blaine married, they first lived in an apartment, but when Elizabeth became pregnant soon after (within a year), they knew immediately that they would buy a home. They moved into a "historic farm house" that they say is much more extravagant than the "starter homes" surrounding it. Despite the fact that they frown on the schools in the area, they felt good about moving there because they would be sending their children to private schools. This was understood between Elizabeth and Blaine from the start—". . . quite frankly, neither my husband or I would want to see our children in the city school system. . . . And that's why we chose it, because we knew we weren't going to be using the school district." Their down payment, which was inherited money, made up half the price of the home.

Their son, age 9, now goes to a private elementary school, Crossroads Preparatory—the same exclusive private school that Elizabeth, her father, and three generations of Wainwrights (Elizabeth's maiden name) have attended. This family has a legacy of elite education, including Ivy League colleges. When asked why her son attends Crossroads Preparatory, Elizabeth says,

> Because when my son was born and started to be school age, I looked at all my choices. And I found that despite looking at all the choices, that I really did like Crossroads Preparatory best. And so decided to go with that, not only because it's a very old choice of my family—and my family has very close ties to the school, going all the way back in its history—but I just like the place. I like the campus. I like the setting. It has a huge green space, and they use it well. And the teachers are really devoted. Really believe in instilling a love of learning, and taking children who already have a sense of wonder and drama, whatever their special interests are. They do a great job.

However, Elizabeth says that even before she became pregnant with her first child, she was committed to sending her own children to public high schools so that they would be exposed to different classes of people. She feels that a completely private education portrays a skewed vision of the world. She plans to move in a few years so that her children can attend public high schools in a "good" school district. At this point, she thinks they will move to Clayton, an expensive neighborhood with an extremely reputable school system. Elizabeth says, "I've got my eye on this area that's really close to our house but worlds away." (Clayton is one mile away from their house.)

For now, Elizabeth is happy with Crossroads Preparatory, a very well respected and expensive private preparatory school. In addition to the tuition (paid for by Elizabeth's parents), Elizabeth pays $1,000–$2,000 per month on extra activities for her son. She says, "We have a lot of expenses associated with our 9-year-old son. . . . He goes to a lot of extra activities. And they're starting to be pretty expensive. He goes to a group called High Achievers, which is social training. He has an occupational therapist that comes by the house. He's had tutors and private swimming instructors. And just all kinds of stuff. So he's gotten to be an expensive little guy." Elizabeth continues,

> No question about it. I mean, if my parents hadn't had the money to send my kids to Crossroads Preparatory, we couldn't have considered it. We would have had to really do belt tightening, and financial aid, and many more loans, more mortgages. It would have been very difficult and a real strain on us, especially with two. And we probably would have felt like we just couldn't swing it as a family. So, I don't know, I would have had to gone [sic] out and gotten a job that would pay enough to justify two kids in private school. With that it would have

meant not being able to mother them as much myself. Or my husband having to change work, and all the soul searching that would have meant for him. It's unimaginable.

What is "unimaginable" to Elizabeth is literally the norm for most American families.

TRANSFORMATIVE ASSETS

The Cummings family is illustrative of how the reservoir of wealth and expected inheritance open the door to opportunities and can make dreams come true more easily. As one parent we interviewed said, "Income supplies life support; assets provide opportunities." The stories these families tell are not extraordinary. We heard different versions of these themes repeatedly.

These cases illustrate a critically important concept—the idea of transformative assets. Transformative assets (increased prospects for well-being) are assets used in such a way that an individual's or family's capacity trajectory is significantly altered beyond labor market rewards to launch social mobility. In the cases presented here, inherited family assets are employed through home ownership to transform the community capabilities of one generation and the schooling capacities of still another generation. Among the white home owners we interviewed ($n = 53$), nearly two-thirds received substantial financial assistance from their families. In contrast, about one in four black home owners ($n = 25$) received similar family help. Assets, whether they are earned or unearned (given by parents or other family members), are powerful resources that can literally transform the basic opportunities of the families who possess them.

POLICY IMPLICATIONS

Families in the United States have been making critical educational choices throughout the history of our educational system. The traditional family move to suburbia often involves a choice to remove their children from urban educational environments. In addition, the percentage of children enrolled in private schools has increased modestly (8 percent) since 1970. "Choosing schools" is not a new phenomenon, then, but an old one. What is new, however, is the rapidly changing and uneven educational environment of the past few years that includes an array of charter, magnet, pilot, vouchers and other school reform experiments. This does not mean that families suddenly face choices for the first time; it just means that more selections have been added to the public menu. In our view, which is corroborated by educational researchers, the new educational reform menu has not diminished educational inequality, nor is it providing enhanced educational opportunities for traditionally disadvantaged groups. Equity is not a major concern for the current educational reform movement.

High-stakes testing is another important element of this rapidly chang-ing environment. The perception of dwindling commitment to public edu-cation, coupled with the twilight of court-mandated desegregation plans, intensifies equity concerns. In addition, in a technologically driven service economy, human capital investments take on even greater importance in preparing people for citizenship. The idea of educational choice is not new. What is different is that the public discourse around choice today is ideo-logically driven in a rapidly changing, more highly charged context, where the outcomes may have even greater consequences than they had in the past. Thus far, equity (and perhaps even quality) is being sacrificed at the altar of "reform."

We would like to sketch briefly some policy directions that follow from our work. The first concerns the community-school nexus. Simply, children receive stratified educational opportunities because of the communities their parents can afford to buy into. We need to do much more to facilitate communities that are better integrated by race and class.

Second, we need to make quality schooling actually accessible to all chil-dren regardless of background. We believe strongly that the advantages conferred by assets in educational markets can—and should—be mini-mized. A family's bank account may determine the community and size of house they can afford; however, a community's wealth should not deter-mine the quality of that school district's education. Democracy demands no less. In our view, a full-fledged commitment to rebuilding America's schools in an equitable manner to the highest possible quality is the right approach. This educational equity approach focuses on important features such as facilities; advancement placement classes; class size, especially in elementary school; teachers' qualification, certification, and pay; computers and technological support; and educational materials. We also should take the best lessons from the recent spate of educational reforms and apply them to this noble task.

Third, we think there is a message in our interview findings for asset-based social policy. Our goal should be to ensure that low-resource families are able to use assets in a transformative manner and not for life supports. Many of the families we interviewed spent considerable time, energy, and money on seeking and providing educational opportunities for their chil-dren. Families and their children should not suffer from or have to make up for a flagging state commitment to high quality and equitable public education.

There is a challenge for asset-based policy in our stories from families as well. Conceptually, the challenge is to articulate asset-generative policies for private use more closely with public capacity-enhancing policies. We believe that the concept of transformative assets best captures this hope. This poten-tial is compromised if these newly acquired assets must be used for life sup-ports like medicine, health care, ensuring adequate resources at retirement, or paying for schooling because the state has failed. If asset policies are suc-cessfully enacted, then we need to be watchful that states not get away with the temptation of shifting civic cost burdens from the public to families simply because formerly resource-poor families are growing "pockets."

REFERENCES

California Department of Education. (2000). "Great Schools" Web site. Available at http://www.cde.ca.gov/psaa/.

Duncan, O. D. (1968). "Inheritance of Poverty or Inheritance of Race?" In *On Understanding Power,* ed. Daniel P. Moynihan. New York: Basic Books, 85–109.

Farley, R., and W. H. Frey. (1994). "Changes in the Segregation of Whites from Blacks during the 1980s: Small Steps toward a More Integrated Society." *American Sociological Review* 59 (February), 23–45.

Grissmer, D. (2000). *Improving School Achievement.* Santa Monica, Calif.: RAND Corporation.

Henig, J. R. (1994). *Rethinking School Choice: Limits of the Market Metaphor.* Princeton, N.J.: Princeton University Press.

Jencks, C., and M. Phillips, eds. (1998). *The Black-White Test Score Gap.* Washington, D.C.: The Brookings Institution Press.

Levin, H. (1998). "Educational Vouchers: Effectiveness, Choice, and Costs." *Journal of Policy Analysis and Management* 17, 3.

Massey, D. S., and N. A. Denton. (1989). "Hypersegregation in U.S. Metropolitan Areas: Black and Hispanic Segregation along Five Dimensions." *Social Forces* 26 (August), 373–391.

Massey, D. S., and N. A. Denton. (1993). *American Apartheid: Segregation and the Making of the Underclass.* Cambridge, Mass.: Harvard University Press.

National Center for Educational Statistics (NCES). (1995). *Use of School Choice.* Washington, D.C.: U.S. Department of Education, June.

Oliver, M., and T. M. Shapiro. (1997). *Black Wealth/White Wealth: A New Perspective on Racial Inequality.* New York: Routledge.

Oliver, M., and T. M. Shapiro. (2000). "Wealth and Racial Stratification." In *America Becoming: Racial Trends and Their Consequences,* eds. N. Smelser and W. J. Wilson. Washington, D.C.: The National Academies Press, 222–251.

Orfield, G., S. Schley, D. Glass, and S. Reardon. (1993). *The Growth of Segregation in American Schools: Changing Patterns of Separation and Poverty since 1968.* A report of the Harvard Project on School Desegregation to the National School Boards Association (NSBA). Alexandria, Va.: NSBA/Council of Urban Boards of Education (CUBE).

Orfield, G., and J. T. Yun. (1999). *Resegregation in American Schools.* Cambridge, Mass.: The Civil Rights Project, Harvard University.

Schuman, H., C. Steeh, and L. Bobo. (1985). *Racial Attitudes in America.* Cambridge, Mass.: Harvard University Press.

Shapiro, T. (2004). *The Hidden Cost of Being African American: How Wealth Perpetuates Inequality.* New York: Oxford University Press.

Wells, A. (2002). *Where Charter School Policy Fails: The Problems of Accountability and Equity.* New York: Teachers College Press.

Wells, A., A. Vasudova, J. Holmes, and C. Cooper. (2000). "The Politics of Accountability: California School Districts and Charter School Reform." *The Stanford Law and Policy Review* 11(2) (Spring).

Yinger, J. (1995). *Closed Doors, Opportunities Lost: The Continuing Costs of Housing Discrimination.* New York: Russell Sage Foundation.

7

Home Ownership and Youth Well-Being

Edward Scanlon and Deborah Adams

Interest in asset-based social welfare proposals has grown among anti-poverty scholars since the early 1990s. Advocates of this perspective argue that U.S. policy is overly reliant on income transfers to promote economic security. They contend that income transfers, which tend to be consumed almost immediately, do not provide poor families with resources they can draw upon when they face difficult economic times. Instead, asset-based advocates recommend welfare policies that would assist low-income citizens to accumulate wealth in the form of personal savings and home and business ownership (Sherraden, 1991). In addition to arguing that this approach is more effective for poverty reduction than are income transfer strategies, they also claim that asset holding has positive sociobehavioral outcomes: increased household stability, stronger future orientation, greater personal efficacy, higher levels of social and civic participation, and improved intergenerational welfare (Page-Adams and Sherraden, 1997; Sherraden, 1991). Asset-based welfare policy resonates with many policy makers and citizens, due to its consistency with the historical U.S. emphasis on property owning and the clarity with which these policy concepts have been articulated (Zundel, 1995).

Scholars have begun to test empirically whether asset holding promotes beneficial household outcomes. Recent literature reviews contend that the well-being of children may be promoted through asset-based social welfare (Boshara, Scanlon, and Page-Adams, 1998; Page-Adams and Sherraden, 1997), despite an empirical literature limited to a small handful of studies. Further empirical work must be undertaken if social welfare scholars are to evaluate adequately claims that asset-building policies will promote child well-being. This study uses the 1997 "Child Data Set" of the National Survey of America's Families (NSAF) to examine whether home ownership affects child behavioral problems and extracurricular involvement and whether such effects are equivalent across racial and socioeconomic groupings.

THEORETICAL PERSPECTIVES AND EMPIRICAL EVIDENCE

One of the most widely cited scholars of asset-based social welfare is Michael Sherraden (1990, 1991). Sherraden argues that U.S. social welfare policy overemphasizes the benefits of income consumption and that asset holding promotes a form of well-being that reflects a lifetime of stored efforts and accrued wealth. He contends that it is impossible to spend one's way out of poverty and that effectively exiting poverty requires the cushioning and security afforded by accumulated wealth. Further, he suggests that when the poor are able to accumulate assets, they experience cognitive shifts that transform them into "stakeholders" who develop more efficacious views of self, world, and future. When they begin to accumulate assets, present-oriented consumers are transformed into savers and investors who possess longer-term time horizons. This "stakeholder mentality" leads to behaviors that increase personal stability and commitments to family, home, and community. In this sense, asset holding is hypothesized to create a "virtuous cycle" that reduces the likelihood of poverty. Households with assets are more likely to promote the well-being of their children, through their capacity to pass on wealth and through the development of a greater sense of future orientation (Page-Adams and Sherraden, 1997).

Scholars in the sociology of tenure tradition also hypothesize that housing tenure effects operate, but for different reasons than those posited by Sherraden. Robert Rakoff (1977) states that owner occupation is not inherently a social good but is valued because it is associated with domesticity and the raising of children. Owner occupation is a source of status and economic success in U.S. society, and homes are a symbol of achievement. This view is shared by Constance Perin (1977), who suggests that the value of home ownership is rooted in cultural preferences, which are reinforced by preferential tax and legal arrangements. These scholars suggest that homes symbolize order and safety and that home ownership promotes a sense of control over one's personal space and boundaries. Peter Saunders (1978, 1990) refers to this control of housing space as "ontological security." Parents' increased sense of control over their own space may contribute to more effective parenting and, in turn, could enhance children's feelings of well-being (Green and White, 1997).

Only a very limited number of empirical studies examine the effects of asset holding on child well-being. The most widely cited study is Richard Green and Michelle White's (1997) examination of four national, longitudinal data sets. The authors test the hypotheses that parental home ownership reduces offspring's levels of criminal activity, delays childbearing by adolescent girls, and increases high school completion rates. They find that home ownership reduces arrest rates and increases high school completion rates. However, their findings are reevaluated by Daniel Aaronson (2000), who suggests that much of the variance in children's outcomes that Green and White attributed to home ownership actually results from decreased residential mobility. Martha Hill and Greg Duncan's (1987) analysis of the Panel Study of Income Dynamics (PSID) finds that assets have positive effects on school attainment, even controlling for income. Li-Chen Cheng's (1995) work suggests that asset holding reduces the likelihood of the replication of intergenerational poverty. This is consistent with studies that demonstrate that, even controlling for income and parental wealth transfer, the adult children of home owners are more likely to own homes than are the adult children of renters (Henretta, 1980).

Some scholars argue that the empirical claims made for the effects of home ownership are due to methodological limitations found in the existing body of research. Among other concerns, they suggest that home ownership is a quality that is "bundled" with other variables. That is, home owners are more likely to live in better neighborhoods, to live near other people with greater assets, to live in single family homes, and to move less often (Aaronson, 2000; Rohe and Stewart, 1996). Thus, it is unclear whether it is home ownership itself or one of these closely related variables that accounts for the positive well-being outcomes found in previous studies.

Moreover, the home ownership of large numbers of poor and minority citizens often occurs within an unequal and isolated social and spatial context; that is, minority and poor citizens who own homes are more likely to do so in racially segregated and economically distressed neighborhoods (Immergluck, 1998). To date, the literature does not explore whether home-ownership effects operate in the same way across neighborhood contexts or whether other social and economic conditions faced by the poor and racial minorities reduce the positive impacts of asset holding. The literature on concentrated poverty and residential segregation suggests that other conditions faced by low-income and minority citizens may provide a context that negates the positive effects of home ownership.

William Julius Wilson's (1987) theory of concentrated poverty suggests that the experiences of the urban poor in high poverty areas are marked by lack of employment, disrupted marital opportunities, exposure to high levels of welfare utilization, criminal involvement and drug use, and the absence of a strong middle class. Similarly, Douglas Massey and Nancy Denton (1993) have argued that the hypersegregation of poor urban minorities results in extraordinarily high levels of exposure to poverty, crime, joblessness, and welfare use for African Americans. Both hypersegregation and concentrated poverty are hypothesized to impact negatively the behavior of those citizens isolated by these conditions. Marta Tienda (1991) proposes that the theoretical relationship between poor neighborhoods and the behavior of their residents might be explained by contagion effects (that result from imitating peer behavior), socialization effects (the internalization of social norms), and institutionalization (behavioral regularities formed in patterned interaction with formal structures and organizations). These theoretical perspectives are supported by a large body of empirical research that indicates that race, socioeconomic status, and neighborhood conditions affect, among other well-being outcomes, children's school performance and drop-out rates (Case and Katz, 1991; Coulton and Pandey, 1992; Crane, 1991; Jencks and Mayer, 1990).

It seems plausible that these spatial and social inequities could reduce the beneficial aspects of owner occupation. Indeed, there is some empirical support for the idea that home ownership doesn't operate the same way for all owner occupiers. Peter Meyer, Jerry Yeager, and Michael Burayidi (1994) argue that home ownership for the poor may cause financial distress, due to unanticipated disruptions in income streams, property repair costs, or tax increases, all of which reduce the likelihood that low-income residents will continue to be owner occupiers over the long term. Descriptive data from a program evaluation funded by the U.S. Department of Housing and Urban Development (HUD) suggest that large numbers of Habitat for Humanity home owners must request emergency financial assistance to prevent foreclosure (U.S. HUD, 1997). Richard Buckhauser, Barbara Butrica, and Michael Wasylenko (1995) demonstrate that low-income elderly home owners can become stuck in distressed, high-crime, urban areas due to declining property values. Empirical scholarship has also documented that minority home owners purchase primarily in central city locations, and experience relatively lower property value increases over time (Immergluck, 1998; Long and Caudill, 1992; Oliver and Shapiro, 1995; Parcel, 1982).

Significant policy implications follow if empirical research can demonstrate that social and spatial inequities reduce asset effects. It may be that home ownership programs need to be combined with ongoing subsidies or financial supports in order to make them a feasible policy option for low-income households. That is, asset-based policy may need to be augmented by more traditional income supports or by other forms of housing subsidy that assist owner occupiers with mortgage payments. We currently have an example of such a policy in the U.S. HUD department's newly approved program that uses Section 8 vouchers for mortgage payments ("Creating Opportunities," 2000). Similarly, targeted community development activities or social service provisions may need to be combined with home-ownership programs, in order to surmount the negative effects of neighborhood conditions on child well-being and property values. For example, children of home owners who are living in distressed neighborhoods may need to be assisted with access to housing vouchers or preferences in admission to magnet schools.

METHODOLOGY

Conceptual Model and Research Questions

This study centers on two research questions: First, do children of owner occupiers demonstrate greater extracurricular activity and lower levels of behavior problems than children of nonowner occupiers? And, if so, do the

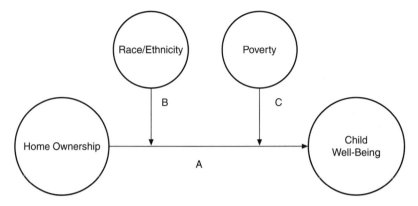

Figure 7.1 The moderating effects of race, ethnicity, and poverty status on the relationship between home ownership and child well-being.

effects of owner occupation on extracurricular activity and behavior problems vary by race and poverty status?

The conceptual model, presented in figure 7.1, is informed by Sherraden's (1991) propositions that asset holding enhances household stability and the well-being of off-spring. We hypothesize that home ownership will reduce the frequency and level of emotional and behavioral problems and increase children's extracurricular involvement (arrow A). However, asset-based welfare theory does not consider the potential behavioral impacts of the deleterious social and economic conditions facing poor and minority children. For minority and low-income citizens, owner occupation is riskier— they face greater financial stresses and often tend to live in more distressed and racially segregated neighborhoods than do white or nonpoor home owners. This results in more stress associated with home owning, more exposure to unfavorable social conditions, and fewer opportunities for wealth accumulation associated with home owning. Therefore, we hypothesize that these experiences will moderate the positive effects of home ownership on child behavior problems and extracurricular activity (arrows B and C). Moderation occurs when the effects of an independent variable on a dependent variable vary across the level of a third (or moderator) variable (Baron and Kenny, 1986). In this case, the effects of home ownership on child well-being will vary by ethnic group, racial group, and level of socioeconomic status (SES). For lower-income, African American, and Hispanic children, we hypothesize that the effects will be positive, but the associations will be weaker. Thus, our conceptual model includes African American racial status, Hispanic origin, and poverty as moderating variables. Our conceptual model for this study does not include neighborhood conditions such as poverty rate or residential turnover as controls because the NSAF is not geocoded and does not provide data on neighborhood conditions.

Data Set and Sample

The National Survey of America's Families Child Data Set is a random sample survey of 33,373 respondents, conducted in 1997 by the Urban Institute, a nonpartisan economic and social policy research organization. Respondents were drawn from thirteen states (Alabama, California, Colorado, Florida, Massachusetts, Michigan, Minnesota, Mississippi, New Jersey, New York, Texas, Washington, and Wisconsin). Taken together, the populations of these states total over half the population of the United States. The survey used random-digit dialing to survey households and subsampled randomly selected households without telephones. Detailed, 25 to 40 minute interviews were conducted in these households. If households had more than one child under 6 years old or more than one child from ages 6 to 17, only one child was used as part of the sample. No more than two children were used for the sample from each household, and responses were taken from a most knowledgeable adult (MKA). The data set was limited to those focal children from ages 12 to 17, reducing it to 10,434 cases (Urban Institute, 1997).

The sample consists of 5,360 males (51.4 percent) and 5,074 females (48.6 percent). There are 8,439 (80.9 percent) white respondents; 1,569 (15 percent) African American respondents; and 426 (4.1 percent) categorized as other. Hispanics make up 12.4 percent ($n = 1,292$) of the sample, with the remaining 87.6 percent ($n = 9,142$) categorized as non-Hispanic. There are 1,927 (18.5 percent) subjects below the poverty threshold and 8,507 (81.5 percent) with above poverty-level incomes. In 1997, the poverty threshold for a family of four was $16,300. Children in owner-occupied homes comprise 70.4 percent ($n = 7,342$) of the sample, with the remaining 29.6 percent ($n = 3,092$) categorized as children of renters. The mean age of focal children is 14.6 years.

Variables and Descriptive Statistics

Dependent Variables

The study includes two measures of child well-being: problem behaviors and extracurricular involvement. These are used in the study due to their relationship to child well-being, their frequent use in child outcomes literature, and their availability in the NSAF data set. Behavior problems are scored with a problem behavior index that asked MKAs about the presence or absence of a series of typical child behavior problems. These included the following: how often during the previous month the child did not get along with other children; could not concentrate or pay attention; and was unhappy, sad, or depressed. MKAs of children from ages 12 to 17 were asked how often during the past month the child had trouble sleeping, lied or cheated, and did poorly at schoolwork. The indices have a range of 1–13, with a higher score indicating more problems. The problem behavior index for 12- to 17-year-olds has an alpha reliability of .75, which indicates that the items are internally consistent.

Extracurricular activities are measured by asking parents whether or not in the last year the child had been on a sports team, taken lessons, or participated in a club. The measure is summative and ranges from 0–3. If the MKA answered "no" to all three questions, he or she was asked whether the child participated in any other organized activity in the last year. Comparisons of the measure to those used in the Survey of Income and Program Participation and the National Education Longitudinal Study of 1988 suggest that the measure is valid, although psychometric evaluations of the measure are not available (Urban Institute, 1997).

Independent and Moderating Variables

Home ownership is measured by asking, "Is this home or apartment owned by someone in the household, rented for cash, or occupied without payment of cash rent?" The values of 0 = renter, and 1 = home owner. Respondents occupying without payment are coded as nonowners. The term "nonowner" is used interchangeably with "renter" throughout the study. Other covariates include child age (12–17 years); sex of the child (male = 1); whether the focal child has two parents in the household (yes = 1); and legal family income as a percent of poverty (<50 percent of poverty line = .5; 50–100 percent = 1; 100–150 percent = 1.5; 150–200 percent = 2; 200–300 percent = 3; >300 percent = 4). We also include a parental mental health index, which ranges from 25–100. Higher scores indicate better mental health functioning. Because we are interested in the home ownership experiences of poor versus nonpoor families, we include a dichotomous variable measuring family income where 0 = greater than 100 percent of the poverty threshold and 1 = family income of 100 percent or less of the 1997 poverty threshold. The 1997 poverty threshold for a family of four was $16,400. Race is a three-level variable where 1 = white, 2 = black, and 3 = other. It is dummy coded for the analysis. Hispanic origin is a dichotomous variable where 0 = non-Hispanic and 1 = Hispanic. Table 7.1 presents the mean scores and standard deviations of the dependent variables for each of the subgroups of interest in the study.

FINDINGS

Reuben Baron and David Kenny (1986) describe methodological procedures for analyzing moderation effects. They recommend the use of two-way analysis of variance (ANOVA) to assess hypothesized main and interaction effects when the independent and moderator variables are both dichotomous. They state that the moderation effect of a continuously measured moderator (such as income) can be tested by dichotomizing the variable at the point that the function is presumed to accelerate. Because we hypothesize that home ownership's effects will operate differently for poor

Table 7.1 Subgroup Means and Standard Deviations on Problem Behavior
and Extracurricular Activities

Subgroups	Problem Behavior Means/Standard Dev.	Extracurricular Activities Means/Standard Dev.
Nonblack home owner ($n = 6{,}289$)	2.92 ± 2.07	$1.52 \pm .91$
Nonblack renter ($n = 2{,}150$)	3.48 ± 2.34	$1.17 \pm .88$
Black home owner ($n = 795$)	3.22 ± 2.07	$1.40 \pm .88$
Black renter ($n = 774$)	3.85 ± 2.46	$1.27 \pm .95$
Hispanic home owner ($n = 609$)	3.09 ± 2.13	$1.24 \pm .92$
Hispanic renter ($n = 683$)	3.31 ± 2.29	$1.07 \pm .88$
Non-Hispanic home owner ($n = 6{,}733$)	2.95 ± 2.06	$1.54 \pm .90$
Non-Hispanic renter ($n = 2{,}409$)	3.66 ± 2.38	$1.22 \pm .91$
Nonpoor home owner ($n = 6{,}539$)	2.91 ± 2.03	$1.55 \pm .90$
Nonpoor renter ($n = 1{,}968$)	3.44 ± 2.29	$1.25 \pm .90$
Poor home owner ($n = 803$)	3.33 ± 2.32	$1.18 \pm .88$
Poor renter ($n = 1{,}124$)	3.84 ± 2.47	$1.08 \pm .90$

and nonpoor households, we use a dichotomized measure of family income (poor vs. nonpoor) in the analysis. As the subgroups have different sample sizes, we use the similar general linear model (GLM) procedure, which corrects for unequal cell size. Next, interaction terms found to be significant in the GLM procedure were entered into hierarchical regression models conducted in three steps. In step one, demographic control variables were entered; in step two, the independent variable owner occupation is entered; and in step three, the interaction term(s) are entered. Finally, we run a regression analysis of each subgroup to determine the direction and magnitude of the interaction's effects.

Baron and Kenny (1986) state that a moderating effect is indicated by a significant interaction between the moderating variable and an independent variable on the strength or direction of a dependent variable. Consistent with our theoretical framework, we expect that the positive impact of owner occupation on problem behaviors and extracurricular activities will be reduced for African American respondents, Hispanic respondents, and poor respondents.

The results of the three GLM procedures for problem behavior are presented in table 7.2. Home ownership, African American racial status, and poverty status all have significant associations, but Hispanic origin does not. The interaction terms of home ownership × African American racial status and home ownership × poverty status are not significant. Only the interaction term of home ownership × Hispanic origin is significantly associated with problem behavior. That interaction term will be entered into a hierarchical regression model in which problem behavior is the dependent variable.

Table 7.2 General Linear Models Predicting Problem Behaviors from Home Ownership, Race, Ethnicity, and Poverty Status

Predictor Variables	F	R^2
Model one		
Home ownership	181.69***	
African-American	27.78***	
Home ownership × African-American	.27	.02
Model two		
Home ownership	181.49***	
Hispanic origin	2.15	
Home ownership × Hispanic	14.46***	.02
Model three		
Home ownership	182.08***	
Poverty status	50.83***	
Home ownership × poverty	.04	.02

***$p < .0001$.

In table 7.3, the results of the GLM procedure for the outcome of extracurricular activities are presented. In these models, there are significant associations for home ownership, poverty status, and Hispanic origin, but African American racial status is not significant. The interaction terms of home ownership × African American racial status, home ownership × Hispanic origin, and home ownership × poverty status are all significantly associated with extracurricular activity. All three of these interaction terms will be entered into the hierarchical regression model in which extracurricular activity is the dependent variable.

The results of the hierarchical multiple regression model for problem behavior are presented in table 7.4. In step one, we enter the demographic control variables and find marginal negative associations between problem behavior and age, parental mental health, and family structure. Marginal positive associations are found with male gender, African American, and other racial status. That is, problem behaviors decrease with age, and with having better parental mental health, and increase with being a child in a one-parent family, with being male, and with being a member of the racial groups African American or "other." In step two, home ownership is entered along with all of the variables in step one. Home ownership has a small negative association with problem behavior, suggesting that living in an owner-occupied home is associated with fewer problem behaviors among youth. In step three, the interaction term home ownership × Hispanic origin is entered into the regression equation along with the variables entered in steps one and two. The interaction term is marginally significant, suggesting that the relationship between

Table 7.3 General Linear Models Predicting Extracurricular Activities from Home Ownership, Race, Ethnicity, and Poverty Status

Predictor Variables	F	R^2
Model one		
Home ownership	274.03***	
African-American	.78	
Home ownership × African-American	22.09***	.03
Model two		
Home ownership	275.36***	
Hispanic origin	66.77***	
Home ownership × Hispanic	6.61*	.03
Model three		
Home ownership	226.144***	
Poverty status	104.99***	
Home ownership × poverty	14.70***	.04

*$p < .01$, ***$p < .0001$.

Table 7.4 Hierarchical Regression Model for Problem Behavior

Predictor Variables	β	R^2
Step one		
Age	−.0233*	
Parental mental health	−.0478***	
Family structure	−.4541***	
Sex	.3552***	
African-American	.2113**	
Other race	.2723*	
Hispanic	−.0708	
Poverty status	−.0055	.1370
Step two		
Step one variables		
Home ownership	−.2112	.1385
Step three		
Step two variables		
Home ownership × Hispanic	.3040*	.1393

*$p < .05$, **$p < .001$, ***$p < .0001$.

home ownership and problem behavior varies between Hispanic and non-Hispanic populations.

The results of the hierarchical multiple regression model for extracurricular involvement are presented in table 7.5. In step one, we enter the demographic control variables and find marginal negative associations between extracurricular involvement and gender, age, and poverty status. Marginal positive associations are found with parental mental health, family structure, and African American racial status. That is, extracurricular involvement decreases for older, poorer, and male children. The outcome increases with having better parental mental health, with being a child in a two-parent family, and with being African American. In step two, home ownership is entered along with all of the variables in step one. Home ownership has a small positive association with problem behavior, suggesting that living in an owner-occupied home is associated with greater extracurricular involvement among youth. In step three, the interaction terms of home ownership × African American, home ownership × Hispanic origin, and home ownership × poverty status are all entered into the regression equation along with the variables entered in steps one and two. The interaction terms are all marginally significant, which indicates that the relationship between home ownership and extracurricular involvement varies by race, ethnicity, and poverty status.

Table 7.5 Hierarchical Regression Model for Extracurricular Involvement

Predictor Variables	β	R^2
Step one		
Age	−.0796***	
Parental mental health	.0049***	
Family structure	.2015***	
Sex	−.0926***	
African-American	.0067***	
Other race	−.0017	
Hispanic	−.2543	
Poverty status	−.2199***	.0731
Step two		
Step one variables		
Home ownership	.1866	.0799
Step three		
Step two variables		
Home ownership × African-American	−.2014***	
Home ownership × Hispanic	−.1444**	
Home ownership × poverty status	−.1523**	.0831

$*p < .05, **p < .001, ***p < .0001.$

We illustrate the magnitude and direction of the interaction effects by running hierarchical regression models for each subgroup: African American, non–African American, Hispanic, non-Hispanic, poor, and non-poor children. For each, we report the significance and direction of the regression coefficient for home ownership, as well as the magnitude of the variance explained by owner occupation. Table 7.6 demonstrates that the effects of home ownership on problem behavior are in the expected direction for both Hispanic and non-Hispanic children, but the relationship does not reach significance for Hispanic children. Even for non-Hispanic children, the magnitude of the effect is small, explaining only 1 percent of the variance in the outcome.

Table 7.6 also demonstrates that the effects of home ownership on extracurricular activity are in the expected direction for all of the subgroups. However, home ownership is not significantly associated with the independent variable for African American or poor children. There is a significant association for Hispanic children, but that relationship is not as strong as that of non-Hispanic children. Again, while the relationship is significant for white, non-Hispanic, and nonpoor children, the association between home ownership and extracurricular involvement must be considered to be small even for those groups. Home ownership accounts for 1.1 percent of the variance in extracurricular activities among nonblack children, .7 percent of the variance among non-Hispanic children, and 1.0 percent of the variance among nonpoor children.

DISCUSSION

It was predicted that home ownership would have significant positive associations with both problem behaviors and extracurricular activity among adolescents. Our model also specified that those associations would

Table 7.6 Regression Coefficients and Contributions to R^2 of Home Ownership by Subgroup: Problem Behavior and Extracurricular Involvement

Subgroup	Coefficient for Problem Behavior	Increment to R^2	Coefficient for Extracurricular Involvement	Increment to R^2
Black			.0366	.04
Nonblack			.2433***	1.14
Hispanic	−.0280	.3	.1126*	.3
Non–Hispanic	−.2881***	1.0	.1960***	.7
Poor			.0770	.2
Nonpoor			.2234***	1.0

$*p < .05, ***p < .0001.$

be weaker for African American, Hispanic, and poor children. We briefly restate our findings and then discuss our interpretation of them.

Home Ownership and Problem Behavior

In general, our results indicate that home ownership has a significant positive association with the level of problem behaviors among children from ages 11–17. However, the effect size should be considered small, using Jacob Cohen's (1987) criteria that a small effect is one that explains from 1 to 10 percent of variance in an outcome. The relationship between home ownership and problem behaviors is moderated only for Hispanic children, for whom the relationship is nonsignificant. A significant interaction effect is not found on this outcome for African American and poor children, indicating that owner occupation operates similarly for those groups.

The finding that home owning is associated with lower levels of problem behavior is consistent with the assumptions of asset-based welfare theory and with empirical findings that children of home owners are more likely to achieve academically and complete school (Green and White, 1997; Hill and Duncan, 1987). Empirical research has suggested that a reduction in problem behaviors is causally related to school completion, and these findings complement Green and White's 1997 study. This analysis suggests that owner occupation status may be an overlooked variable in current theorizing about the risk and protective factors related to child and adolescent well-being (Smokowski, 1998). Of course, it is possible that our hypotheses should be reversed—it may be that unobserved characteristics of families are responsible both for home owner status and reduced teen problem levels. Either way, the results from this study should be considered conservatively, given the small amount of variance explained by owner-occupation.

That this association is not found for Hispanic children suggests support for our hypothesis that ethnicity does impact home ownership effects. Indeed, the finding exceeds our hypothesis—while we proposed that the association between owner occupation and problem behavior would be weaker for Hispanic children, in fact, the relationship is not significant. Several processes may explain this finding. Because of the pervasiveness of residential segregation, minority home owners accrue less equity than nonminority home owners, which may reduce the effects of home ownership for Hispanics (Rosenbaum, 1996). That minority home ownership occurs frequently in segregated neighborhoods also suggests that the children of minority home owners may be exposed to greater levels of crime, poverty, and residential turnover. This could also reduce the beneficial effects of owner occupation. It has also been noted that spells of unemployment, repair costs, and tax increases can make home ownership financially burdensome for low-income residents (Meyer, Yeager, and Burayidi, 1994). These race- and class-based experiences may reduce the beneficial effects of home ownership. This literature, coupled with our findings, suggest a need for a closer look at the differential home ownership experiences of each of these groups.

Home Ownership and Extracurricular Activities

The results of the GLM procedures and the moderated hierarchical regression indicate that there is a small, positive, significant association between home ownership and extracurricular involvement. The analysis also indicates that the significant association between home owning and extracurricular involvement varies by race, ethnicity, and poverty status. African American and poor children do not experience the positive effects of home ownership on levels of extracurricular involvement, and the relationship is not as strong among the sample of Hispanic youth as it is among non-Hispanic youth. As extracurricular involvement has been linked to academic achievement and school completion (Nettles, Mucherah, and Jones, 2000), this finding provides support for asset-based housing policies. Still, because the different experiences of poor, African American, and Hispanic home owners may be reducing these beneficial effects, our findings again suggest a need for more research and targeted home-ownership policies. Again, the reasons for the differential findings are likely the same that we offer above: residential segregation reduces wealth accumulation possibilities and exposes residents to multiple environmental deprivations, and lower income levels make home ownership a potentially stressful experience.

A cautionary note should be raised about the implications of findings regarding the extracurricular activities outcome. It may be problematic that the measure conflates three different types of extracurricular activities: outings, sports, and club participation. As some scholarship has suggested that sports involvement, unlike other extracurricular participation, is not predictive of school achievement, conclusions about the benefits of this broadly measured outcome must be made cautiously (Fisher, Juszczak, and Friedman, 1996).

These conclusions must be considered cautiously for other reasons as well. The data is cross sectional, which means that these associations are correlational and do not prove causation. It is plausible that home-owner families may have unobserved characteristics that account for differences in these outcomes and that make these families more likely to become home owners. Also, these small effects must be considered in relation to the large sample used in the study. Large sample sizes increase the likelihood that small or trivial effects will be found, increasing the risk of finding effects where none exist. To correct for this possibility, this study should be replicated using a smaller random sample of respondents.

IMPLICATIONS FOR RESEARCH AND POLICY

While this study adds empirical support to the theoretical claims of asset-based welfare, the relationship between housing tenure and personal well-being remains unclear. The sparseness of the literature suggests a need to build the empirical literature in this area by examining additional child well-being outcomes, such as academic performance, school completion, and emotional and physical health. Longitudinal data would be helpful in determining whether home ownership is causally related to, rather than simply correlated with, child well-being. This would also allow us to determine whether temporality matters in home ownership outcomes. It is plausible, for example, that home ownership effects intensify over a longer period of time or that there are time lags before effects become observable. Also, there is a need for research that focuses on the experiences of participants in low-income and minority home ownership programs. To date, only a limited number of studies have looked at such programs (Rohe and Stegman, 1994a, 1994b).

The study also suggests that there is merit to the idea that asset effects can vary by race, ethnicity, and SES. Future studies should explore these differences in greater depth, and asset-based welfare theory should consciously work to incorporate race and class variables. This work should also incorporate the concept of *spatiality;* that is, researchers should attempt to clarify how owner-occupation effects vary between specific spatial contexts, for example, by comparing home-ownership outcomes in suburban and distressed inner-city neighborhoods. Finally, and perhaps most important, empirical work should build asset-welfare theory by clarifying the theoretical mechanisms by which these effects occur. For example, a current research project of the authors examines whether the impacts of owner occupation on child well-being occur through the increased school stability associated with home ownership.

Our findings are consistent with claims that home ownership is beneficial for families and children—all of which provide support for the burgeoning number of federal, state, and local programs, such as HUD's Home Ownership for People Everywhere (HOPE), that are attempting to expand home ownership opportunities. These programs typically reduce the costs of home ownership, provide financial counseling, train potential home owners in home repair, and assist clients in the process of home loan application. However, the fact that some of the benefits appear to vary by race and social class suggests that home ownership programs should be structured with the needs of minority and low-income citizens in mind.

Those who design home ownership programs could structure them somewhat differently to make them more effective for minority and low-income citizens. In working with poor citizens, program staff should determine whether household income flows are steady and adequate enough to cope with the sudden expenses of home repair and tax increases (Meyer, Yeager, and Burayidi, 1994). Financial support could be built into these programs, assisting low-income home owners to deposit funds in matched savings accounts to be used for home repairs and unexpected housing expenses. Such an approach is currently being attempted by the Justine Peterson Housing Corporation in St. Louis (Scanlon, 1998). People who live and/or work in areas under consideration for home ownership programs should be consulted to evaluate the neighborhoods carefully before programs are set up. Planners need to make sure that new home owners will not become trapped in distressed, crime-ridden neighborhoods with negative housing equity (Buckhauser, Butrica, and Wasylenko, 1995).

Neighborhoods in transition toward becoming distressed might be the most logical candidates for targeting home ownership programs, providing residents the opportunity to increase the neighborhood's stability without asking new home owners to assume inordinate financial risk. Additionally, it is clear that low-income home buyers benefit from an extended, service-enriched relationship with those who administer home-ownership programs, as they advise low-income citizens on home maintenance and financial management, thus preventing foreclosure (U.S. HUD, 1997). Maintaining ongoing relationships with participants should become a standard feature of low-income home-ownership programs. Previous home ownership literature has suggested that these issues must be taken seriously. Outcome effectiveness and utilization can only be increased by tailoring home ownership programs to the circumstances of low-income and minority citizens.

CONCLUSIONS

The results of this study indicate that overall, owner occupation is positively associated with decreased problem behavior and increased extracurricular activity among adolescents. However, for African American, Hispanic, and poor children, these relationships are not found, or the associations are found to be less strong. The study provides support for the claims of asset-based welfare advocates who promote policies designed to extend home ownership to low-income and minority citizens. Asset-based welfare advocates should, however, consider how asset effects may operate differentially for historically disadvantaged populations and structure asset-based strategies accordingly. Carefully planned, asset-based housing policies may serve to enhance citizen well-being and reduce class and race inequality in the coming century.

NOTE

This study was made possible by financial support from the Center for Social Development at Washington University in St. Louis.

REFERENCES

Aaronson, D. (2000). "A Note on the Benefits of Homeownership." *Journal of Urban Economics* 47, 356–369.

Baron, R., and D. Kenny. (1986). "The Moderator-Mediator Variable Distinction in Social Psychological Research: Conceptual, Strategic, and Statistical Considerations." *Journal of Personality and Social Psychology* 51(6), 1173–1182.

Boshara, R., E. Scanlon, and D. Page-Adams. (1998). *Building Assets for Stronger Families, Better Neighborhoods, and Realizing the American Dream.* Washington, D.C.: Corporation for Enterprise Development.

Buckhauser, R., B. Butrica, and M. Wasylenko. (1995). "Mobility Patterns of Older Homeowners: Are Older Homeowners Trapped in Distressed Neighborhoods?" *Research on Aging* 17(4), 363–384.

Case, A., and L. Katz. (1991). *The Company You Keep: The Effects of Family and Neighborhood on Disadvantaged Youth.* Working Paper No. 3705. Cambridge, Mass.: National Bureau of Economic Research.

Cheng, L. (1995). "Asset-Holding and Intergenerational Poverty Vulnerability in Female Headed Families." Paper presented at the Seventh International Conference of the Society for the Advancement of Socio-Economics, Washington, D.C.

Cohen, J. (1987). *Statistical Power Analysis for the Behavioral Sciences.* Hillsdale, N.J.: Lawrence Erlbaum.

Coulton, C., and S. Pandey. (1992). "Geographic Concentration of Poverty and Risk to Children in Urban Neighborhoods." *American Behavioral Scientist* 35(2), 238–257.

Crane, J. (1991). "The Epidemic Theory of Ghettos and Neighborhood Effects on Dropping Out and Teenage Childbearing." *American Journal of Sociology* 96(3), 1226–1259.

"Creating Opportunities: HUD Program to Open Doors of Homeownership for Some of the 1.4 Million Families Nationwide Who Receive Federal Rental Assistance." (2000). *Boston Globe,* J-11, September 10.

Fisher, M., L. Juszczak, and S. Friedman. (1996). "Sports Participation in an Urban High School: Academic and Psychologic Correlates." *Journal of Adolescent Health* 18(5), 329–334.

Green, R., and M. White. (1997). "Measuring the Benefits of Home Owning: Effects on Children." *Journal of Urban Economics* 41(3), 441–461.

Henretta, J. (1980). "Parental Status and Child's Homeownership." *American Sociological Review* 49, 131–140.

Hill, M., and G. Duncan. (1987). "Parental Family Income and the Socioeconomic Attainment of Children." *Social Science Research* 16, 39–73.

Immergluck, D. (1998). "Progress Confined: Increases in Black Homebuying and the Persistence of Residential Segregation." *Journal of Urban Affairs* 20(4), 443–457.

Jencks, C., and S. Mayer. (1990). "The Social Consequences of Growing Up in a Poor Neighborhood: A Review." In *Concentrated Urban Poverty in America,* eds. M. McGeary and L. Lynn. Washington, D.C.: National Academy, 111–186.

Long, J., and S. Caudill. (1992). "Racial Differences in Homeownership and Housing Wealth, 1970–1986." *Economic Inquiry* 30, 83–100.

Massey, D., and N. Denton. (1993). *American Apartheid: Segregation and the Making of the Underclass.* Cambridge, Mass.: Harvard University Press.

Meyer, P., J. Yeager, and M. Burayidi. (1994). "Institutional Myopia and Policy Distortions: The Promotion of Homeownership for the Poor." *Journal of Economic Issues* 28(2), 567–576.

Nettles, S., W. Mucherah, and D. Jones. (2000). "Understanding Resilience: The Role of Social Resources." *Journal of Education for Students Placed at Risk* 5, 1–2, 47–60.

Oliver, M., and T. Shapiro. (1995). *Black Wealth/White Wealth.* New York: Routledge.

Page-Adams, D., and M. Sherraden. (1997). "Asset Building as a Community Revitalization Strategy." *Social Work* 42(5), 409–536.

Parcel, T. (1982). "Wealth Accumulation of Black and White Men: The Case of Housing Equity." *Social Problems* 30(2), 199–211.

Perin, C. (1977). *Everything in Its Place.* Princeton, N.J.: Princeton University Press.

Rakoff, R. (1977). "Ideology in Everyday Life: The Meaning of the House." *Politics and Society* 7, 85–104.

Rohe, W., and M. Stegman. (1994a). "The Effects of Homeownership on the Self-esteem, Perceived Control, and Life Satisfaction of Low-Income People." *Journal of the American Planning Association* 60, 173–184.

Rohe, W., and M. Stegman. (1994b). "The Impact of Homeownership on the Social and Political Involvement of Low-Income People." *Urban Affairs Quarterly* 30, 28–50.

Rohe, W., and L. Stewart. (1996). "Home Ownership and Neighborhood Stability." *Housing Policy Debate* 71, 37–81.

Rosenbaum, E. (1996). "Racial/Ethnic Differences in Home Ownership and Housing Quality." *Social Problems* 43(4), 403–426.

Saunders, P. (1978). "Beyond Housing Classes: The Sociological Significance of Private Property Rights in Means of Consumption." *International Journal of Urban and Regional Research* 18(2), 202–227.

Saunders, P. (1990). *A Nation of Homeowners.* London: Unwin Hyman.

Scanlon, E. (1998). "Low-Income Homeownership Policy as a Community Development Strategy." *Journal of Community Practice* 5(2), 137–154.

Sherraden, M. (1990). "Stakeholding: Notes on a Theory of Welfare Based on Assets." *Social Service Review* 64(4), 580–601.

Sherraden, M. (1991). *Assets and the Poor: A New American Welfare Policy.* Armonk, N.Y.: M. E. Sharpe.

Smokowski, P. (1998). "Prevention and Intervention Strategies for Promoting Resilience in Disadvantaged Children." *Social Service Review* 72(3), 337–364.

Tienda, M. (1991). "Poor People and Poor Places: Deciphering Neighborhood Effects on Poverty Outcomes." In *Micro-macro Linkages in Sociology,* ed. J. Huber. Newbury Park, Calif.: Sage Publications, 244–262.

Urban Institute. (1997). Child Data Set. *1997 Child Public Use File Documentation and Codebook.* In the National Survey of America's Families (NSAF). Washington, D.C.: Author.

U.S. Department of Housing and Urban Development (U.S. HUD). (1997). *Making Homeownership a Reality: A Survey of Habitat for Humanity International Homeowners and Affiliates.* Washington, D.C.: Author.

Wilson, W. J. (1987). *The Truly Disadvantaged: The Inner City, the Underclass, and Public Policy.* Chicago: University of Chicago Press.

Zundel, A. (1995). "Policy Frames and Ethical Traditions: The Case of Homeownership for the Poor." *Policy Studies Journal* 23(3), 423–434.

PART III

SAVING AND ASSET ACCUMULATION AMONG THE POOR

During the past decade, we have learned a great deal about saving and asset accumulation among the poor. Before that time, this was almost never a topic of inquiry by social scientists in the United States. It was not until publication of *Assets and the Poor* (1991) that this topic was named as important in advanced economies (asset building has long been a theme in "developing"economies), and then gradually became a focus of inquiry. In this part of the book are several examples of a growing body of research and empirical knowledge on asset accumulation among and financial services for the poor.

John Caskey was the first social scientist in the United States to study in detail the financial products and institutions that serve very low-income people in urban America. He documents in *Fringe Banking* (1994) that many of the poor do not use the same types of financial services or products as the middle class. While this may seem obvious today, it was not well-known before Caskey's research—it was not a topic that economists and policy makers were thinking much about. In Caskey's chapter 8 in this volume, he further specifies the financial needs of the "unbanked" and proposes an innovative strategy with elements that will provide them with familiar financial services and products at better rates than they currently pay, as well as ways to build savings, improve credit-risk profiles, and gain access to lower-cost mainstream credit.

In a detailed study of a saving innovation, Sondra Beverly, Jennifer Tescher, Jennifer Romich, and David Marzahl examine a pilot savings program in the private sector that was designed to link the Earned Income Tax Credit (EITC) and saving incentives. This program, called "Extra Credit Savings," was offered by ShoreBank in Chicago, perhaps the most successful community development bank in the country. The research finds merit in saving linked to lump-sum flows of resources and to incentives. However, challenges to saving among this population are considerable. This study illustrates the merits of applied research in illuminating both opportunities and barriers when policy ideas "hit the ground" with real people.

Similarly, Mark Schreiner and his colleagues at the Center for Social Development (CSD) discuss asset-accumulation evidence from individual development account (IDA) savings data. IDAs are special savings accounts with matching funds (from private and public sources) provided to vendors when withdrawals are used for development purposes, such as home purchase, education, and capitalization of a small business. IDAs were proposed as lifelong, universal, progressive accounts beginning at birth. However, as demonstration projects, IDAs are short-term (several year) savings plans. This study is based on monitoring data in the American Dream Demonstration (ADD), the first large study of IDAs. ADD, which was in operation from 1997 through 2001, has demonstrated that even the very poor who sign up for IDAs can save. These results have significantly changed the policy discussion, and research is continuing. Data from ADD have been influential in federal and state policy for IDAs and in proposals for large, inclusive policies in the United States and other countries. The data reported in this chapter are the most detailed data on a matched savings program and probably on any savings program tailored to the needs and aspirations of the poor.

In the final chapter in this section, Michael Stegman and Robert Faris begin with IDA data from ADD, then construct a model to answer a counterfactual question, using households with similar characteristics from the *Survey of Consumer Finances*. This strategy is not perfect—it does not control for the self-selection and program-selection that occurred in ADD—but it is an effort to ask whether IDA savings in ADD represent new household savings as assessed by changes in net worth. Using this strategy, Stegman and Faris find that ADD savings may not be new savings. This study asks a key question, and the results of ADD experimental data will later contribute more to answering this question.

Together, these studies are among the first empirical assessments of financial services and products, saving behavior, and outcomes among low-income individuals in the United States. With growing interest in this topic worldwide, these studies are contributing to academic discussions, advancing legislative proposals, and pointing the way toward additional research.

8

Reaching Out to the Unbanked

John P. Caskey

This chapter presents a strategy for helping the "unbanked"—those who do not have deposit accounts of any type—to join the financial mainstream. The purpose is to help these individuals build savings and improve their credit-risk profiles, in order to lower their cost of payment services, eliminate a common source of stress, and gain access to lower-cost mainstream credit. The proposed strategy has five elements. First, participating banks should open special branch offices, called "outlets," that are conveniently located for lower-income households and that provide fee-based, check-cashing services in addition to traditional consumer banking services. Second, these outlets should offer "starter" bank accounts that have low minimum-balance requirements, cannot be overdrawn, and include access to low-cost money orders for making long-distance payments.[1] Third, the outlets should offer accounts, similar to traditional "Christmas Club" accounts, designed to help people accumulate savings. Fourth, the outlets should offer deposit-secured loans to individuals whose credit histories would make them ineligible for mainstream credit. Fifth, banks should form partnerships with nonprofit community-based organizations to help promote the outlets and to offer budget-management and credit-repair seminars to interested clients of the outlets.

This chapter argues that a strategic approach is likely to be most effective in assisting the unbanked and, furthermore, that it is realistic to expect many banks to implement it. The proposed initiative will appeal to banks because it can be effective for the clients, while offering banks a reasonable rate of return on their investments. In addition, banks that implement the strategy can receive credit toward the "service" component of their federal Community Reinvestment Act obligations.

The section below describes people who are unbanked, noting their demographic characteristics, why they decide to remain outside the banking system, and the problems they face as a result of their status. The next section presents my strategy for bringing the unbanked into the financial mainstream and explains the rationale for the strategy. And in the final section, I explain why it is realistic to expect banks to implement the strategy.

A BRIEF DESCRIPTION OF THE UNBANKED

Several surveys have attempted to identify the socioeconomic characteristics of households without bank accounts and to ask individuals in these households why they do not have bank accounts. Although the details of these surveys differ, they all find that the unbanked are disproportionately represented among lower-income households, among households headed by African Americans and Hispanics, among households headed by young adults, and among householders who rent their homes. Table 8.1, based on data from the 2001 *Survey of Consumer Finances,* presents data supporting such generalizations.

The second issue that the surveys attempt to answer is why people do not have deposit accounts. Again, the details differ across the surveys, but there is a broad consensus in their findings. Families most frequently report that they do not have deposit accounts because they have almost no month-to-month financial savings to keep in the accounts. In 1996, a consulting firm working for the U.S. Department of the Treasury surveyed a large sample of recipients of federal benefit checks to inquire why they did not have deposit accounts (Booz-Allen, 1997). About half of the respondents cited as the primary reason, "Don't have enough money." In the same year, 1996, I commissioned a survey of 900 lower-income households to obtain information on their use of financial services (Caskey, 1997b). Of those without accounts, as shown in table 8.2, 53 percent cited, "Don't need account because we have no savings," which made this the most frequently cited reason.[2] Unfortunately, the *Survey of Consumer Finances* does not ask people why they do not have deposit accounts. Rather, it asks households without checking accounts to give the primary reason why they do not have a checking account. As shown in table 8.3, the most common (28.6 percent) reason cited is "Do not write enough checks to make it worthwhile." "Do not have enough money" is the third most common (14 percent) response.

In the surveys, other common responses for why people do not have deposit accounts include "Bank fees are too high," "Bank minimum balance requirements are too high," "We want to keep our financial records private," and "We are not comfortable dealing with a bank." The first two of these reasons are closely related to people's low level of financial savings, as depositors able to maintain a month-to-month balance of about $500 or more rarely pay account maintenance fees and rarely write checks that "bounce," leading to nonsufficient funds fees. The desire to keep financial records private could arise because (a) a creditor might seize the savings of a delinquent debtor, (b) a former spouse might pursue the savings of an individual behind on his child-support payments, (c) welfare eligibility could be threatened by a substantial account balance or by a history of

Table 8.1 Percentage of Families without Deposit Accounts, 2001 *Survey of Consumer Finances*

Family Characteristic	Percentage without Deposit Account
All families	9.1
Percentile of income	
Less than 20	29.1
20–39.9	10.6
40–59.9	3.9
60–79.9	1.2
80–89.9	0.3
90–100	0.8
Age of head (years)	
Less than 35	14.0
35–44	9.3
45–54	7.8
55–64	6.4
65–74	6.2
75 or more	6.3
Race or ethnicity of respondent	
Nonwhite or Hispanic	21.8
White non-Hispanic	5.1
Current work status of head	
Working for someone else	7.6
Self-employed	4.8
Retired	11.1
Other, not working	29.5
Housing status	
Owner	3.5
Renter or other	20.7

Source: Aizcorbe, Kennickell, and Moore, 2003.

deposits from under-the-table earnings, or (d) illegal immigrants might fear that a bank record would reveal their presence to the Immigration and Naturalization Service. The formal surveys have not delved into these reasons, but one ethnographic study finds evidence of these concerns even, in some cases, when there is little legitimate basis for the concerns (Caskey, 1997a). Less common reasons given for not having a deposit account include, "Banks won't let us open an account" (presumably because the per-

Table 8.2 Reasons Given in Caskey Survey for Why Households Do Not Have Deposit Accounts

Reason/Reasons Given	Percentage Giving This Reason
Don't need account because I have no savings	53.3
Bank account fees are too high	23.1
Banks require too much money just to open an account	22.1
I want to keep my financial records private	21.6
Not comfortable dealing with banks	17.6
Banks won't let us open an account	9.5
No bank has convenient hours of location	8.5
Problem fee/fees among those citing bank fees as a barrier	
Monthly account maintenance fee	28.4
Bounced-check fees	18.5
Check-writing fees	12.9
ATM fees	11.0

Source: Caskey, 1997b.

son has a history of writing bad checks or a severely impaired credit record) and, "No bank has convenient hours or location."

Many of the unbanked encounter few problems from their status (Prescott and Tatar, 1999). They have no financial savings, so there is no hardship from not having access to a financial institution to safeguard such savings. They cash paychecks for free at an accommodating deposit insti-

Table 8.3 Primary Reasons in 2001 *Survey of Consumer Finances* for Why Households Do Not Have Checking Accounts

Reason	Percentage Giving This Reason
Do not write enough checks to make it worthwhile	28.6
Do not like dealing with banks	22.6
Do not have enough money	14.0
Service charges are too high	10.2
Minimum balance is too high	6.5
Cannot manage or balance a checking account	6.6
Do not need/want an account	5.3
Credit problems	3.6
No bank has convenient hours or location	0.4
Other	2.1

Source: Aizcorbe, Kennickell, and Moore, 2003.

tution, grocery store, or other business. They purchase money orders from the post office or convenience stores to pay bills by mail. They have no immediate need for credit or do not find that their unbanked status excludes them from the credit that they do need.

Such a sanguine outlook is not, however, true for a significant fraction of the unbanked. In urban areas, surveys indicate that somewhere between 30 and 60 percent of the unbanked pay fees to cash their paychecks, and many of these patronize commercial check-cashing outlets, called CCOs (Caskey, 2002). CCOs cash people's paychecks or government checks for a fee that is usually expressed as a percentage of the face value of the check. Except in a small number of states that impose fee ceilings below 2 percent, typical fees for cashing low-risk checks range from 2 to 4 percent. Some CCOs will cash personal checks, usually for a higher fee to reflect the higher risk that such checks might bounce. CCOs also sell money orders, handle utility bill payments, serve as agents for firms that transfer money electronically, and sell related convenience items, such as photocopying services and prepaid calling cards.

The problem created by the regular use of a CCO is that CCOs are an expensive source for payment services. Over the course of a year, a family making $18,000 a year can easily spend $500 or more of this limited income obtaining basic payment services at a CCO. Nevertheless, there is little mystery as to why many individuals without financial savings go to a CCO. The CCO will cash their paychecks instantly. While standing at the service window, the customers can use some of the cash to purchase money orders for paying bills. The CCO also sells stamps and envelopes for mailing the payments. CCO customers will frequently use some of their cash to pay utility bills, cable television bills, and phone bills at the CCO. In communities with large numbers of recent immigrants, many CCO customers wire some of their funds to family members in home countries. After conducting these transactions, the customers walk out of the CCO with their remaining cash. They spend this down until the next pay period when they repeat this procedure.

Given this behavioral pattern, it is understandable why such customers do not go to a bank. Most banks in urban areas refuse to cash paychecks for people who do not have accounts at the bank or who do not have accounts with sufficient funds to cover the check. Banks typically require account holders without sufficient funds to deposit the check and wait a few days for it to clear before they gain access to the funds. Although the CCO charges fees for cashing a paycheck (a percentage of the amount), a money order (generally about $0.35 to $1), or transmitting a utility bill payment (commonly about $1), this can be less costly for someone with no month-to-month savings than relying on a bank. It is very easy for a person who runs his account balance down to nearly zero at the end of each pay period to bounce checks on the account. Each bounced check can cost the account holder $25 to $35.[3] It is also expensive and inconvenient for customers without checking accounts to make long-distance payments. Almost all banks charge at least $1 for money orders, and many charge as much as $3. Moreover, they do not sell stamps and envelopes, so the customer must go elsewhere to meet this need. Finally, banks generally do not transmit payments to utility companies, nor do they serve as agents for electronic money transfer services, such as Western Union.

Although most attention has gone to the relatively high fees that many of the unbanked incur for basic payment services, this may not be the major problem associated with their status. In 1997, in collaboration with a group of anthropologists, I conducted a series of detailed discussions with lower-income individuals, many of whom were unbanked, in two communities, San José, California, and a small town in Mississippi (Caskey, 1997a). In discussing their financial affairs, the unbanked rarely complained about the expense or inconvenience of obtaining payment services. Rather, they complained mainly about the insecurity and stress associated with living from paycheck to paycheck. This was also true of individuals with bank accounts who consistently ran down their account balances to nearly zero at the end of each pay period. In both cases, the interviewed individuals commonly spoke of feeling physically and emotionally drained from facing frequent personal financial crises and worrying about future unforeseen expenses.

Because so many of the unbanked live from paycheck to paycheck with no financial margin of safety, many have been forced by past personal financial crises to miss scheduled payment obligations, such as rental, debt service, or utility bill payments. In my 1997 survey of 900 lower-income families, for example, 42 percent of the families without deposit accounts reported that they had been two months late on some bills in the previous year (see table 8.4). Among lower-income families with deposit accounts, 28 percent reported being late paying some bills in the previous year. Similarly, 41 percent of the unbanked families and 25 percent of lower-income families with deposit accounts reported that they had been contacted by a bill collection agency in the past year.

Table 8.4 Indicators of Impaired Credit Records among Households with Incomes of $25,000 or Less

Indicator	% Families without Deposit Accounts Answering "Yes"	% Families with Deposit Accounts Answering "Yes"	Difference Is Statistically Significant?
Been more than 2 months late on some bills in the past year?	41.9	28.2	Yes
Contacted by a bill collection agency in past year?	40.9	24.8	Yes
Have a Visa, MasterCard, Discover, or Optima credit card?	13.6	58.7	Yes

Source: Survey conducted as part of Caskey, 1997b.

These data indicate that the unbanked are more likely to have impaired credit records than those in households with bank accounts. But they also indicate that problems with credit histories and debt service burdens are widespread among lower-income households generally, including those with bank accounts. As indicated in table 8.5, this impression is supported by data from the 1998 *Survey of Consumer Finances.*

Problems with credit histories and debt-service burdens leave a large share of the unbanked, as well as a significant share of lower-income households generally, cut off from mainstream credit.[4] When these households need short-term loans to meet emergencies, they find informal sources of credit or turn to high-cost, formal-sector lenders, such as pawnshops, car title lenders, payday lenders, and small-loan companies. Interest rates from these lenders are generally over 100 percent average percentage rate (APR) and often as high as 300 percent (Caskey, 1997b).

PROPOSED OUTREACH STRATEGY

This section sets out a strategy for bringing the unbanked into the financial mainstream. As noted earlier, the strategy has five elements, the details of which will be presented below. First, however, it should be emphasized that while the overall proposal is new, it embeds several other initiatives with similar goals that are already under way. For example, the proposed strategy includes efforts to design accessible, low-cost deposit accounts, to create institutional mechanisms that facilitate people's efforts to accumulate savings, and to increase financial literacy within lower-income communities.

Open Specialized Bank Branches That Provide CCO Services

The first step in the proposed strategy is for banks to open specialized branches that offer a full range of CCO services, as well as standard con-

Table 8.5 Indicators of Debt Burdens and Debt Payment Difficulties

Family Characteristic	% with Ratio of Debt Payments to Family Income above 40 Percent	% with a Debt Payment Late 60 Days or More in Previous Year
All families	12.7	8.1
Income (1998 dollars)		
Less than 10,000	32.0	15.1
10,000–24,999	19.9	12.3
25,000–49,999	13.8	9.2
50,000–99,999	5.7	4.5
100,000 or more	2.1	1.5

Source: Kennickell, Starr-McCluer, and Surette, 2000.

sumer banking services. To distinguish them from other bank branches, I call these specialized bank branches "outlets." An alternative approach would be for banks to form partnerships with existing check-cashing outlets and to offer basic consumer banking services through these outlets. For simplicity, the discussion below assumes that banks are opening their own outlets, but it could easily be adapted to fit a model based on a bank/CCO joint venture.

For an appropriate fee, the new bank outlets should cash low-risk local paychecks and government checks without placing a hold on the checks, even for individuals who lack deposits to cover the checks.[5] As people without checking accounts who cash their paychecks will need a means to pay bills, these outlets should sell money orders, stamps, and envelopes, and they should serve as an in-person payment point for utility bills, cable TV bills, and so on. They should also offer a service for transferring funds by wire, especially when the outlets are located in areas with large numbers of recent immigrants. Additionally, when unbanked people cash paychecks and pay bills, they frequently need to obtain convenience items and services such as photocopies, fax transmissions, prepaid telephone calling cards, and, in some regions, transit tokens. The outlets should provide such supporting products and services—in fact, the outlets would perform all CCO-type services but charge somewhat lower fees for all products and services than charged by the CCOs.

If the outlets are to be successful, banks must locate them at points likely to be convenient for large numbers of low- and moderate-income households. The outlets will need to maintain hours similar to those of check-cashing outlets, meaning that they should be open early evenings and on Saturdays. Banks should also post prominent signage indicating that the outlets offer check-cashing services. In many cases, giving the outlets a CCO-type name, such as "Cash Express Center of Bank X," will serve this purpose. It also distinguishes the outlets from a bank's regular branches that do not offer check-cashing services to those without deposit accounts.

Opening such outlets serves three purposes. First, by offering CCO services in a bank branch, the bank establishes direct contact with CCO customers. Over time, banks can develop relationships with unbanked individuals that they can use to encourage them to take steps to build savings and address credit record problems. Simply put, banks cannot help the unbanked if they do not get them in the door. Second, the establishment of such outlets recognizes that many CCO customers are likely to be slow to open deposit accounts. As noted earlier, many simply do not have month-to-month savings and see little advantage to a deposit account. Others do not want deposit accounts for fear that their savings might be seized by creditors or might make them ineligible for welfare. By offering check-cashing services, banks can provide high-quality, relatively low-cost payment services to individuals who remain outside the deposit system. Third, banks with branches in lower-income areas often report that it is difficult to cover the costs of these branches with traditional services because deposit mobilization is low, transaction levels are high, and loan opportunities are limited (Caskey and Humphrey, 1999). If these branches were able to find new sources of revenue, such as check-cashing fees, this could contribute toward making these branches profitable and encourage banks to open branches likely to attract large percentages of lower-income households.

Banks opening such outlets may be able to set fees for check-cashing services that are somewhat lower than those of most commercial check-cashing outlets and yet sufficiently high to be profitable for the banks. This is true for two reasons. First, bank outlets, which will offer traditional consumer banking services as well as check-cashing services, should benefit from economies of scope. Earnings from both services can cover many of the same fixed overhead expenses. Second, banks, unlike commercial check-cashing outlets, have direct access to check-clearing systems and have a relatively low cost of financial capital. This will eliminate some of the costs that check-cashers incur from the need to clear checks through the banking system and obtain working capital.

Offer "Starter" Bank Accounts That Have Low Minimum-Balance Requirements, Cannot Be Overdrawn, and Include Access to Low-Cost Money Orders for Making Long-Distance Payments

In addition to offering traditional, fee-based check-cashing services, these specialized outlets should provide the full range of consumer banking services offered at banks' traditional branches. This recognizes that even in very low-income communities, there will be significant numbers of people who desire traditional deposit and credit services and can qualify for them. To the extent that outlets can attract such customers, they will make banking services more convenient for some community members and help to cover the costs of operating the outlets. In addition, because the outlets are intended to help the unbanked become traditional bank customers, it will be helpful to have banking services offered in locations where unbanked individuals are already comfortable.

Beyond their traditional deposit accounts, the outlets should offer a low-cost, low-minimum-balance savings account, and account holders should be able to purchase at least ten money orders per month for no more than $0.75 each, as well as stamped envelopes for mailing the money orders. For qualifying households, the account should include automated teller machine (ATM) and debit-card access. If banks are able to block individuals' abilities to overdraw their accounts, then banks should be able to provide ATM access even to householders with severely impaired credit histories. Finally, the accounts should accept electronic deposits of wage payments and government transfers.

The proposed features of this type of account differ from those of two other prominent accounts that have been advocated as mechanisms to help the unbanked join the banking system. A number of advocates for the unbanked have sought to enact laws, called "basic" or "lifeline" banking laws, that would require banks to offer a low-cost checking account with a low minimum-balance requirement. A small number of states have enacted such laws, but the federal government has not. Although bank trade associations fought against such proposed laws, especially at the federal level, they called on banks to offer such accounts voluntarily. A majority of banks claim that they do (Krieger, 2000). In a second initiative, beginning in 1999, the U.S. Department of the Treasury asked banks to offer "electronic transaction accounts" (ETAs). The federal government wants banks to offer these accounts in order to encourage the use of direct deposit by unbanked recipients of federal transfer payments. Currently, the government must mail paper checks to individuals who do not have deposit accounts. In designing the ETA, the government had two concerns. First, it wanted to ensure that the account was inexpensive for account owners, even for individuals unable to maintain a month-to-month minimum balance. This was to provide the unbanked an incentive to open an ETA, making them eligible for direct deposit. Second, the government wanted the account to be at least moderately profitable for banks so that they would be willing offer the ETA. To meet these two goals, the government offers to pay banks $12.60 for each ETA they open. It permits the banks to charge account owners up to $3 a month and requires that the accounts accept electronic payments from the federal government, have no minimum balance requirement, and permit account owners to make up to four withdrawals per month from the account. The withdrawals can be from a proprietary ATM machine or through a teller. The accounts need not include the ability to draw checks on them or the ability to initiate electronic payments.[6]

There are good reasons to think that basic checking accounts and ETAs are unlikely to bring many of the unbanked into the banking system. A checking account can be very costly for someone who lives from paycheck to paycheck. Individuals who consistently run down their account balances to zero or nearly zero by the end of each pay period are likely to bounce checks frequently unless they are especially scrupulous account managers. Writing a check that bounces commonly results in fees of $25 to $35, so people who bounce a few checks every other month or so will quickly spend more for their bank accounts than they would for using a check-cashing outlet. In addition, because banks fear that people who bounce checks might not pay the fees that banks charge to cover the banks' costs of handling the checks, they generally do not permit people with histories of bouncing checks to open or maintain checking accounts.

Low-cost deposit accounts on which individuals cannot write checks, such as the ETA, have a different problem. These accounts do not include any means for account holders to make long-distance payments. Since most banks charge comparatively high fees for money orders, do not sell stamps and envelopes, and do not handle utility bill payments, account holders have to go elsewhere to obtain these services, a feature that makes the ETA unattractive.

Unfortunately, there are no data indicating whether or not basic checking accounts have drawn significant numbers of the unbanked into the banking system (Doyle, Lopez, and Saidenberg, 1999). Anecdotal information suggests that they have not. Complicating the analysis, however, several surveys of banks in states requiring basic checking accounts have found that banks do not publicize these accounts and frequently steer customers to more costly alternative accounts (Pristin, 1999). Such behavior is not surprising, as banks claim that the accounts are unprofitable. The ETA has also failed to have a significant impact. As the U.S. General Accounting Office (2002, 25) reported, "Despite Treasury's efforts to market the ETA program, since the program was initiated in July 1999, about 36,000, or fewer than 1 percent, of unbanked federal beneficiaries had opened ETAs by June 2002."

The account that I propose has two advantages over the basic checking account and the ETA. For one, banks can offer it to people who have a history of bouncing checks, and people who fear the expense associated with bounced checks will not be deterred from opening the account. In addition, unlike the ETA, it provides account holders with a convenient, low-cost means to make long-distance payments: inexpensive money orders with stamped envelopes. If they desire, banks can design the proposed account to qualify as an "electronic transfer account" in order to receive the $12.60 that the Treasury Department pays for each ETA that banks open.

Offer Accounts Specifically Designed to Help People Build Savings

In addition to the savings account described above, the outlets should offer a "savings-building" account. Although there can be many variations in the details of savings-building accounts, research on consumers' savings behavior indicates that these accounts should have several key features. First, in opening such an account, an individual should pledge to make regular, fixed-value contributions to the account over a specified time period, usually one year. The timing of these contributions should closely coincide with the individual's receipts of income. Second, the bank should permit the required periodic contributions to be small, perhaps as little as $20 per month. Third, if possible, contributions to the account should be automatic. The contributions, for example, could be linked to a member's direct deposit of his or her salary, or a check-cashing customer might agree to deposit $10 each time he cashes his biweekly paychecks. Fourth, a savings-building account should be separate from other accounts that the individual might own. This helps separate the funds psychologically from savings for short-term transaction purposes. Finally, there should be some financial penalty if the account owner closes the account early or fails to keep the commitment to make specified deposits at regular intervals. In imposing this penalty, such as loss of accumulated interest, the bank should probably show some flexibility. It might, for example, permit one or two missed deposits before the penalty takes effect.

The psychological basis of these rules is obvious. People have a hard time saving on a discretionary basis, so they save most effectively when the act of saving is relatively unconscious and the savings are viewed as "locked away" (Thaler, 1992).

This proposed savings-building account is similar in several of its features to the individual development accounts (IDAs) that some banks and credit unions have begun to offer in partnership with philanthropic foundations, community-based organizations, or government agencies. There are, however, two main differences. The IDAs offer matching funds to lower-income individuals who accumulate and maintain savings over a designated period of time. In addition, holders of IDAs, if they are to receive the matching funds, must use their IDA savings for an approved set of purposes, such as education or the down payment on a home.

When matching funds are available and administrative costs are not a problem, the outlets might consider offering IDAs in addition to the savings-building account advocated above. The IDA should not, however, replace the savings-building account. For one, the savings-building account is administratively simpler and has lower costs, making it more likely that banks will offer it. A bank can offer it to anyone and need not verify that an account holder has a sufficiently low income to qualify. The savings-building account also does not require the bank to find a source to provide matching deposits. More important, IDAs are intended to help people build medium- or long-term savings for a particular set of approved purposes. People living from paycheck to paycheck would benefit from such savings, but they also need short-term savings to dip into to handle periodic fluctuations in income and expenditures. Such short-term savings are a form of self-insurance, a financial margin of safety or "buffer" intended to prevent periodic personal financial crises.

Offer Deposit-Secured Emergency Loans to Individuals Whose Credit Histories Make Them Ineligible for Traditional Mainstream Credit

Although bank outlets can compete with commercial check-cashers, in most cases they will not be able to provide traditional loans to people currently borrowing from deeply subprime lenders, such as pawnshops, payday lenders, and small loan companies. These people generally have far higher risk profiles than would be prudent for depository institutions to underwrite. The deeply subprime lenders can provide credit to this population group by adopting labor-intensive risk-control procedures, such as prompt and persistent in-person debt collection. The outlets could try to follow a similar path, but pawnbroking and collecting unsecured subprime debt are specialized skills that bank outlet employees are unlikely to possess or would not choose to develop. In many cases, it is doubtful that a bank outlet would be providing a beneficial service if it were to make short-term, high-cost loans to financially hard-pressed individuals. This could simply worsen the borrowers' financial distress and the costs of the resulting consequences.

In some cases, however, bank outlets should be able to use creative means to meet customers' legitimate credit needs. Banks with branches in lower-income communities frequently report that many of their customers with good credit records occasionally seek unsecured, nonrevolving loans of under $1,000. Commonly, banks do not offer such loans because the processing and monitoring costs are high relative to the size of the loan. But with credit-scoring and other cost-saving technologies, the outlets may be able to make fast-disbursing, small-value loans with fees that are attractive to both the customers and the banks.

Customers with impaired credit histories will also have legitimate needs for credit. To help meet this need, the outlets should offer deposit-secured loans to customers unable to pass standard credit-risk assessments. An outlet could, for example, issue a deposit-secured credit card to a customer. Or it could make a loan against the balance that a member has accumulated in a savings-building account. When the customer repays the loan, his or her savings are still in place. Moreover, if outlets offer such loans, customers may be more likely to agree to lock away their savings in savings-building accounts (Caskey and Humphrey, 1999).

Seek Community-Based Partners and Offer Financial Literacy Programs

As the previous example makes clear, banks can benefit by forming partnerships with not-for-profit community-based organizations (CBOs) when launching outlets to serve the unbanked. Of course, in doing so, banks must tread carefully. Just because an organization is not-for-profit or declares itself to be "community-based" does not mean that it will be a good partner. Some CBOs operate primarily to promote the personal political or economic ambitions of their executives, some are well-meaning but incompetent, and others have severe shortages of human and financial resources. In most large urban areas, however, there are numerous well-managed CBOs dedicated to helping lower-income individuals and communities.

A partnership with an appropriate CBO can bring a number of benefits to a bank that is beginning to open outlets to serve the unbanked and to the CBO. Significantly, if the CBO is well respected and well connected in the community, it can help overcome any distrust that the community might have of the bank's motives. This role is especially important if a bank's managers and board of directors are separated from the target community by racial or ethnic barriers. In many cases, the CBO can help the bank find qualified community residents to staff the outlet, further tying the outlet to the community. The CBO also benefits from the partnership because it enables the CBO to bring sophisticated financial services to the targeted neighborhood in a short time period. Some CBOs have tried, as an alternative strategy, to start their own credit unions. Most of these credit unions, however, remain very small with limited management capacity and can offer only a very restricted range of consumer financial products.

In addition to forming a partnership with a CBO to launch outlets to serve the unbanked, banks should use the outlets as bases to promote appropriate financial literacy initiatives. Although there are no random assignment studies demonstrating the effectiveness of financial literacy programs, anecdotal information and some quasi-experimental studies suggest that financial management counseling can help individuals accumulate savings and improve their credit-risk profiles (Braunstein and Welch, 2002). Typically, the educational programs are one of two types. One is remedial, focusing on helping people reduce their debt service burdens and address outstanding credit problems. The other type is oriented toward wealth-building activities, such as identifying cost-savings in family budgets and accumulating savings for retirement, education, or the purchase of a home.

This is not to say that the outlets should conduct such financial counseling programs themselves. Not only are such programs costly to offer, but banks may not be the appropriate institutions to deliver the information. CBOs are likely to be more effective because well-run CBOs will understand the particular financial literacy needs of members of their communities and have staff who can communicate comfortably and effectively with them. In addition, as not-for-profit organizations, CBOs can apply to philanthropic foundations and government agencies to fund their financial counseling programs.

WHY IT IS REALISTIC TO EXPECT BANKS TO IMPLEMENT THE PROPOSED OUTREACH STRATEGY

If banks are to implement this outreach strategy, they must receive an acceptable financial rate of return on their investment. As delivering financial services to lower-income communities counts towards banks' Community Reinvestment Act obligations, banks may accept a slightly lower return on capital than normal. Naturally, the higher the expected returns from pursuing the outreach strategy are, the more likely banks will be to embrace it.

There are a number of measures that banks can take to ensure that they earn an adequate rate of return from their outlets. To keep their operating costs low, the outlets should have flexible staffing because demand for check-cashing services is closely tied to the paydays of local businesses and arrival dates for government transfer payments. In addition, the outlets should be small, perhaps taking no more than 1,000 square feet, as many check-cashing outlets do. Banks might also investigate using automated check-cashing machines to cash paychecks, dispense money orders, and initiate utility bill payments within the outlets. Several such machines have been developed, based around ATM platforms, and some preliminary reports of their performance and customer acceptance are favorable.

Well-located outlets should have strong revenues. Assuming that they attract a moderately high volume of check-cashing business and levy reasonable check-cashing fees in the neighborhood of 1.5 percent, the outlets should earn about $100,000 per year from check-cashing and other payment service fees.[7] In addition to this income, the outlets will earn income from their traditional banking services. If these two businesses can be combined in one outlet with substantial economies of scope, the outlets should be at least moderately profitable.

Reinforcing my argument that it is realistic to expect banks to implement all or many elements of this general approach, a small number of deposit institutions have already begun to do so. The pioneer in this regard is Union Bank of California (UBC). In 1993, UBC, a bank that currently has about $40 billion in assets, created "Cash & Save" outlets to offer check-cashing services and banking services in the same location.[8] Since that time, the structure and operations of these outlets have changed, and they will likely continue to change as UBC refines its initiative. As of early 2003, UBC had thirteen Cash & Save outlets, mostly located in Los Angeles and San Diego.

In addition to providing traditional consumer banking services, the Cash & Save outlets provide the full range of commercial check-cashing outlet services. They cash government checks and paychecks for non-depositors. The check-cashing fee is 1.5 percent of the face value of paychecks and 1.0 percent for government benefit checks. The outlets sell money orders (with stamped envelopes), originate domestic and international wire transfers of funds, handle the payment of utility bills, sell prepaid phone cards, provide fax and photocopying services, and in some locations sell bus tokens and passes.

Through its Cash & Save outlets, UBC offers ETAs; low-cost, low-minimum-balance checking accounts; and low-cost, low-minimum-balance savings accounts. The Cash & Save outlets also offer two plans to help check-cashing customers build savings. The first is the "Nest Egg" savings account. One can open this account with as little as a $10 deposit, but the account holder must also commit to depositing at least $25 per month for one year. The account does not include access to an ATM card, and it is not intended as a transaction account. Anyone can open this account, even people with a history of writing bad checks or with severely impaired credit records. Account holders pay no fees for the account, and they receive a passbook interest rate on their savings. They cannot withdraw funds from the account until the end of the year, but the bank, at its discretion, does allow some emergency withdrawals. An account holder can close the account at any time. The second savings-building account is the "Combo" account. This is the Nest Egg account combined with the bank's Money Order Plan. To open a Combo account, one must deposit at least $10 in a Nest Egg account and commit to depositing at least $25 per month into the account for one year. As a Combo account holder, one pays a 1.0 percent check-cashing fee and receives six free money orders each month.

The other approach that banks have taken to combine check-cashing and consumer banking services is to partner with existing check-cashing operations. This approach has much lower start-up and learning costs for the banks, but also limits the range of banking services that can be delivered through CCOs. In early 2000, UBC entered into a joint venture with Nix Check Cashing, a firm with numerous CCOs in Southern California. In this initiative, UBC placed ATM machines, capable of taking deposits as

well as dispensing cash, inside thirty of Nix's CCOs. It also placed telephones with direct connections to a UBC representative in the CCOs. Using
the telephone connection and assistance from a CCO teller, a customer can
open a UBC deposit account or complete a loan application. In New York
in early 2001, a small credit union, Bethex Federal Credit Union, which
serves a predominantly low-income population, formed a partnership
with a commercial check-cashing firm, RiteCheck Check Cashing. With its
11 CCO outlets, RiteCheck refers to Bethex its customers who might wish
to open a deposit account or to take out a small loan. RiteCheck will cash
the paychecks of Bethex members for a fee that is somewhat lower than its
normal fee. Bethex, in turn, pays RiteCheck a small transaction fee so its
members can, without charge, deposit checks at a RiteCheck outlet or
obtain cash from their Bethex accounts (Stegman and Lobenhofer, 2001).
Effectively, the RiteCheck outlets function as limited service branches for
the credit union. Another New York credit union, Actors Federal Credit
Union, has recently initiated a similar partnership with a second check-
cashing firm, Manhattan Money Branch. In addition, Bethex, RiteCheck,
and others have been working to implement a system that would enable
any check-casher that participates in a three-state, regional ATM-type network, known as Paynet, to provide basic payment services to the members
of participating credit unions.

CONCLUSION

This chapter proposes a strategy for bringing the unbanked into the banking system. I fully acknowledge that even if this strategy were widely implemented, it would not reach all of the unbanked. Nor would it succeed in
helping all those it does reach to build savings, improve credit histories, or
lower the cost of their financial services. Nevertheless, with over 10 million
unbanked households in the United States, even a modest rate of success
could mean significant improvements in the quality of life for hundreds of
thousands of lower-income families.

NOTES

1. Throughout this chapter, I use the term "bank" in its generic sense, meaning
that it includes commercial banks, saving banks, savings and loans, and credit
unions.
2. In the survey, respondents were allowed to give more than one reason.
3. As indicated in the report by the Board of Governors of the Federal Reserve
System (2000), in 1999, all banks imposed fees for writing a check with insufficient
funds to cover it. In that year, the average fee was $17.71. As banks generally also
charge a fee to businesses that deposit such checks (the average fee in 1999 was
$6.28), merchants will commonly impose a charge (usually $10 to $15) on customers
who write checks that bounce.

4. As indicated in table 8.4, among unbanked lower-income households, only 14 percent carry a major credit card. Among lower-income households with deposit accounts, 59 percent do. Data from the *Survey of Consumer Finances* are similar (as cited in Hogarth and O'Donnell, 1999).

5. Banks entering the check-cashing business should employ the standard software and operating procedures marketed to check-cashing outlets. These have been carefully refined over many years to speed check-cashing and related transactions, while minimizing fraud and the risk of cashing checks that bounce. Using standard software and operating procedures, most check-cashing transactions take less than one minute. CCOs that employ these procedures and that cash mainly payroll checks and government checks report that losses from cashing "bad" checks amount to well under 0.25 percent of the face value of the checks they cash.

6. Stegman (1999) provides an excellent discussion of the economics and politics behind the development of ETAs and a more detailed description of their features.

7. The largest publicly traded check-cashing firm is ACE Cash Express, Inc. Its 2002 SEC 10-K filing indicates that a mature store's annual revenues from check-cashing fees total about $130,000. Its revenues from bill payments, money transfers, and money order sales total about $30,000. ACE's typical fee for cashing a check is 2.2 percent of the face value of the check.

8. I thank Yolanda Scott Brown of Union Bank of California for the description of the operations of the Cash & Save outlets.

REFERENCES

Aizcorbe, A., A. Kennickell, and K. Moore. (2003). "Recent Changes in U.S. Family Finances: Evidence from the 1998 and 2001 Survey of Consumer Finances." *Federal Reserve Bulletin* (January), 1–32.

Board of Governors of the Federal Reserve System. (2000). *Annual Report to the Congress on Retail Fees and Services of Depository Institutions.* Washington, D.C.: Federal Reserve System, June.

Booz-Allen & Hamilton Shugoll Research. (1997). "Mandatory EFT Demographic Study." A report prepared for the U.S. Department of the Treasury, September 15.

Braunstein, S., and C. Welch. (2002). "Financial Literacy: An Overview of Practice, Research, and Policy." *Federal Reserve Bulletin* (November), 445–457.

Caskey, J. P. (1997a). "Beyond Cash-and-Carry: Financial Savings, Financial Services, and Low-Income Households in Two Communities." A report for the Consumer Federation of America, December.

Caskey, J. P. (1997b). *Lower Income American, Higher Cost Financial Services.* Madison, Wis.: Filene Research Institute.

Caskey, J. P. (2002). *Check-Cashing Outlets in a Changing Financial System.* Federal Reserve Bank of Philadelphia Working Paper #02-4, February.

Caskey, J. P., and D. B. Humphrey. (1999). *Credit Unions and Asset Accumulation by Lower-Income Households.* Madison, Wis.: Filene Research Institute.

Doyle, J. J., J. A. Lopez, and M. Saidenberg. (1999). "How Effective Is Lifeline Banking in Assisting the 'Unbanked'?" Federal Reserve Bank of New York, *Current Issues in Economics and Finance* 4(6), June.

Hogarth, J. M., and K. H. O'Donnell. (1999.) "Banking Relationships of Lower-Income Families and the Government Trend toward Electronic Payment." *Federal Reserve Bulletin* (July), 459–473.

Kennickell, A., M. Starr-McCluer, and B. Surette. (2000). "Recent Changes in U.S. Family Finances: Results from the 1998 Survey of Consumer Finances." *Federal Reserve Bulletin* (January), 1–29.

Krieger, D. L. (2000). Testimony on behalf of the American Bankers Association. Presented before the Committee on Banking and Financial Services, U.S. House of Representatives, June 27.

Prescott, E. S., and D. D. Tatar. (1999). "Means of Payment, the Unbanked, and EFT '99." Federal Reserve Bank of Richmond, *Economic Quarterly* 85(4) (Fall), 49–70.

Pristin, T. (1999). "Group Says Banks Don't Push Low-Cost Checking Accounts." *New York Times*, July 30, B8.

Stegman, M. A. (1999). *Savings for the Poor: The Hidden Benefits of Electronic Banking.* Washington, D.C.: The Brookings Institution Press.

Stegman, M. A., and J. Lobenhofer. (2001). *Bringing More Affordable Financial Services to the Inner City: The Strategic Alliance between Bethex Federal Credit Union and RiteCheck Check Cashing, Inc.* A working paper issued by the Center for Community Capitalism, in the Kenan Institute of Private Enterprise, University of North Carolina at Chapel Hill, August.

Thaler, R. H. (1992). "How to Get Real People to Save." In *Personal Saving, Consumption, and Tax Policy,* ed. Marvin H. Kosters. Washington, D.C.: American Enterprise Institute for Public Policy Research (AEI) Press, 143–150.

U.S. General Accounting Office. (2002). *Electronic Transfers: Use by Federal Payment Recipients Has Increased but Obstacles to Greater Participation Remain.* Washington, D.C.: Author, September.

9

Linking Tax Refunds and Low-Cost Bank Accounts to Bank the Unbanked

Sondra G. Beverly, Jennifer Tescher, Jennifer L. Romich, and David Marzahl

As chapters in this volume reveal, asset accumulation is increasingly viewed as an important, long-term antipoverty strategy. For the "unbanked"—those without a checking or savings account—asset accumulation is likely to be difficult. The unbanked are generally excluded from home owner-ship, a key route to asset accumulation. In addition, financial savings kept outside of formal financial institutions are less secure, are more sus-ceptible to consumption pressures and temptations (Beverly, Moore, and Schreiner, 2003), and do not earn interest or tax benefits. National data suggest that from 10 to 20 percent of all American households are unbanked (Aizcorbe, Kennickell, and Moore, 2003; Carney and Gale, 2001; Hogarth and O'Donnell, 1999; Hurst, Luoh, and Stafford, 1998). By linking tax refunds to low-cost bank accounts, the Extra Credit Savings Program (ECSP), developed by Chicago's ShoreBank and the Center for Economic Progress in 2000, aims to connect the unbanked to mainstream financial services and to facilitate ongoing saving and asset accumula-tion. This initiative is especially interesting because federal tax credits, such as the Earned Income Tax Credit (EITC) and the child tax credit, have expanded in recent years, and it is now common for low- and moderate-income working families to receive income tax refunds as large as $2,000 or $3,000.

This chapter summarizes results from an evaluation of the ECSP's first year. We describe ECSP participants and reasons for enrollment, uses of tax refunds, and saving and asset accumulation in ECSP accounts. We also summarize participants' comments about the effects of the program on their financial attitudes and behaviors.

BACKGROUND

The Earned Income Tax Credit

When the ECSP began in 2000, the federal EITC was the major tax credit for low- and moderate-income families. Although childless workers are eligible for a small refund, the EITC largely benefits working families with children. For the 1999 tax year, the maximum benefit was $2,312 for families with one child and $3,816 for families with two or more children. In 1998, the average EITC benefit for families with one child was about $1,500, and the average benefit for families with multiple children was about $2,300 (Johnson, 2001). The credit is refundable, so eligible individuals and families receive payments even if they do not owe federal income taxes. For several years, the Internal Revenue Service (IRS) has promoted the advance-payment option, which allows EITC-eligible individuals to receive a portion of the credits through their paychecks, but almost all EITC recipients receive a lump-sum refund after they file tax returns (Hotz and Scholz, 2001).

The Extra Credit Savings Program

The ECSP was developed by ShoreBank (formerly South Shore Bank), a community development financial institution in Chicago, and the Center for Economic Progress (CEP, formerly the Center for Law and Human Services), a nonprofit organization that seeks to improve access to public benefit programs for low-income families. Between January and April 2000, the Tax Counseling Project of CEP offered free tax preparation and electronic tax filing to EITC-eligible individuals two nights a week at a ShoreBank branch. On these evenings, ShoreBank bankers invited people to join the ECSP. Enrollees opened no-fee, no-minimum-balance savings accounts and arranged to have their 1999 federal tax refunds directly deposited. Funds in ECSP accounts earned a market rate of interest (2.5 percent), and a no-fee ATM card was available. As an extra savings incentive, participants received an additional 10 percent bonus on funds remaining in the account on December 31, 2000 (up to a maximum of $100). Enrollment in the ECSP was voluntary and was not limited to those without bank accounts.

We expected the ECSP to appeal to unbanked individuals for at least two reasons. First, allowing refunds to serve as opening deposits removes a fairly common barrier to account ownership for low-income families (Caskey, 1997). Second, electronic tax filing combined with direct deposit allows people to receive refunds quickly and free of charge and, thus, provides an alternative to the costly refund anticipation loans (known as "rapid refunds") marketed by commercial tax preparers. We also expected the ECSP to facilitate saving and asset purchases by the unbanked because accounts provide a safe place to store refunds and should help families save and prioritize spending out of refunds (Smeeding, Phillips, and

O'Connor, 2000). Moreover, automatic transfers into savings vehicles may reduce spending temptations by making money less accessible (Beverly, Moore, and Schreiner, 2003).

DATA AND RESEARCH QUESTIONS

This research uses six sources of data from ECSP participants. CEP intake forms provide demographic data. Data from federal tax returns compiled by CEP provide additional demographic data, as well as income and tax information. Monthly bank statements provide data on ECSP account transactions. Account holders completed twenty-minute surveys upon enrollment and five-minute follow-up telephone surveys in November and December 2000. The baseline survey included questions on planned EITC uses, saving-related attitudes, perceptions of banks and account features, and use of financial services. The follow-up survey asked participants about actual refund uses and about perceived effects of ECSP participation.

Finally, qualitative interviews were conducted with a subset of unbanked participants. The interview protocol included questions on participants' financial history, use of formal or informal banking services, and experience with ECSP. Interviews lasted from thirty-five minutes to just over one hour and were conducted either in the participant's home or at a neighborhood restaurant. Interviewees received a $20 gift certificate to a drugstore with many South Side locations.

With these data, we seek to answer several research questions:

1. Who chose to enroll in the Extra Credit Savings Program and why?
2. How did participants use their refunds?
3. How did participants use ECSP accounts?
4. Did participants believe the program changed their financial attitudes and behaviors?

For all questions, we report findings for the entire sample and note differences between banked and unbanked participants.

Out of 446 individuals who filed their taxes at the CEP-ShoreBank site, eighty-nine chose to open ECSP accounts for a take-up rate of 20 percent. Eighty-six of these account openers were adults and, therefore, eligible study participants. Seventy-two of these eligible individuals completed the informed consent process, resulting in an overall study participation rate of 84 percent. Sixty-nine individuals completed baseline surveys.

Some research questions pertain only to the subset of participants whose refunds were directly deposited into ECSP accounts. After we exclude two individuals who received refunds smaller than $15, our primary sample for questions regarding account activity and refund use consists of fifty-eight participants who received non-negligible refunds. Of these individuals, 59 percent completed follow-up phone surveys. Baseline demographic data reveal no clear pattern of advantage or disadvantage for follow-up survey respondents, relative to non-respondents.[1] Analysis of monthly statements revealed four patterns of account use, and we randomly selected three unbanked individuals from each of these groups for in-depth interviews. Nine (75 percent) were interviewed.

ENROLLMENT IN ECSP

Characteristics of ECSP Participants and Nonparticipants

Table 9.1 lists demographic characteristics and tax refund information. The second and third columns show percentages of each characteristic for ECSP "Participants" and "Nonparticipants," respectively. Participants

Table 9.1 Logistic Regression Results Predicting ECSP Enrollment

Characteristics	Participants[a]	Nonparticipants[a]	Parameter Estimate	p-value	Odds Ratio
Intercept	—	—	−0.81	0.24	—
Female	84%	77%	0.42	0.51	1.52
African American	99%	97%	—	—	—
Never married	72%	72%	−0.22	0.43	0.81
Children in household	63%	58%	−0.42	0.33	0.65
Social Security/ unemployment insurance recipient	9%	16%	−0.60	0.22	0.55
TANF recipient	29%	23%	−0.30	0.48	0.74
Food stamps recipient	51%	33%	1.17	0.003**	3.21
Medicaid recipient	27%	28%	−0.95	0.02*	0.39
Calendar week of tax return submission	7.5	8.6	−0.10	0.04*	0.91
AGI/500	$18.1	$21.5	−0.02	−0.10	0.98
Unbanked	61%	54%	0.23	0.47	1.26
Anticipated refund/500	$3.4	$2.9	0.10	0.17	1.11
N	70	357	385	—	—
−2 log likelihood	—	—	323.94	—	—
Chi-square ($df = 11$)	—	—	28.46*	0.003	—

Sources: ECSP baseline survey and tax returns and intake forms collected by CEP during the 2000 tax season.
*$p < 0.05$, **$p < 0.01$.
[a]Mean value unless otherwise noted.

were predominantly female, African American, and had never married. The median age was 34, and the median number of dependents was 1.2. The group was economically disadvantaged. Half had received food stamps in 1999, 29 percent had received Temporary Assistance for Needy Families (TANF), and 27 percent had received Medicaid. The median 1999 federal adjusted gross income (AGI) was $8,570, and the median antici-pated federal tax refund (based on return information) was $1,206. Sixty-one percent of participants were unbanked at enrollment. About one-third of these unbanked individuals had never had a checking or savings account, and one-third had not had either type of bank account in at least three years.

Table 9.1 also shows results of a logistic regression that estimates the independent effects of these variables on ECSP participation. Because there is so little variance (that is, 99 percent of the participants are African Americans), we omit race in these calculations. We divide AGI and antici-pated federal refund amount by 500 to make the odds ratios easier to inter-pret. Given the small sample, point estimates tend to be imprecise, and it is difficult to achieve statistical significance. Therefore, we note some dif-ferences that are not statistically significant at conventional levels and emphasize the need to reexamine correlates of program participation with a larger sample.

Three independent variables are significant at conventional levels. Controlling for other variables in the model, food stamp recipients were about three times more likely to enroll in the ECSP (odds ratio = 3.2) than nonrecipients. Those who did not receive Medicaid were 2.6 (1/0.39) times more likely to enroll than Medicaid recipients. It is difficult to explain these patterns. In addition, individuals who filed their taxes earlier were more likely to enroll. Perhaps early filers who came to the CEP-ShoreBank site were unwilling to pay the fees associated with refund anticipation loans but found the direct deposit of tax refunds appealing.

Two other variables have significance levels between .05 and .20. Higher-income individuals were less likely than lower-income individuals to enroll, but the estimated effect is small. Those who expected large refunds were more likely to enroll. The odds ratio implies that a $500-increase in anticipated refund is associated with an 11 percent increase in the odds of ECSP participation. This relationship is significant at the 0.17 level and is consistent with anecdotal evidence: ShoreBank employees noticed that individuals often wanted to complete their tax forms to deter-mine a refund amount before deciding whether to open ECSP accounts.

Reasons for Enrolling in ECSP

In the baseline survey, we asked participants why they decided to open an ECSP account. The first question on this topic was open-ended,[2] and the sixty-nine survey respondents mentioned a total of ninety-six reasons. Thirty-two respondents (46 percent) named some sort of saving motive, usually a general saving motive (e.g., "To learn to save money," "To try to save more money," "I need to save"). Twenty-eight respondents (41 percent) mentioned wanting a bank account, including twenty-one who expressed a general desire for an account (e.g., "I wanted to open up a savings account before," "This is something I've been meaning to do for awhile") and seven who expressed a specific desire to save in a formal institution (e.g., "Need an account to save money," "To have a secure place for money," "It's easier to save when money is in the bank and not in my hand"). These last responses reveal a saving motive as well as a desire for a bank account.

Responses from the in-depth interviews indicate that the ECSP offer nudged some unbanked individuals to act on preexisting desires for accounts and savings. However, many of these participants were not actively looking for an account. For instance, one young woman who was asked if she would have opened any account in the absence of the program replied, "Yes, eventually, I always said that I wanted to open another savings account, especially since I have a son now. . . . [The offer] was another good thing, because I had kinda been talking about getting it, and that just kinda pushed me on to do it." Another woman used very similar language, saying that the offer "helped me, pushed me a little."

In another portion of the survey, we asked participants which of nine account features was most important in their decision to open an account (table 9.2). Sixteen respondents (24 percent) cited the absence of fees, twelve (18 percent) cited the tax refund serving as opening deposit, and

Table 9.2 Most Important ECSP Account Features by Account Ownership

Account Features	Most Important		
	All ($N = 68$)	Unbanked ($n = 41$)	Banked ($n = 27$)
Account has no fees.	16 (24%)	8 (20%)	8 (30%)
Money earns interest.	11 (16%)	9 (23%)	2 (7%)
Money earns 10% year-end bonus.	8 (12%)	3 (8%)	5 (19%)
Account has no minimum balance.	8 (12%)	3 (8%)	5 (19%)
Tax refund is opening deposit.	12 (18%)	11 (27%)	1 (4%)
Tax Counseling Project cosponsored ECSP program.	1 (1%)	0 (0%)	1 (4%)
Account comes with free ATM card.	1 (1%)	1 (3%)	0 (0%)
Refund will arrive faster.	5 (7%)	3 (8%)	2 (7%)
Account provides access to other bank services.	4 (6%)	2 (5%)	2 (7%)
Other	2 (3%)	1 (3%)	1 (4%)

Source: ECSP baseline survey data collected during the 2000 tax season.

eleven (16 percent) cited interest payments. Table 9.2 also shows the most important account features separately for those with and without accounts at enrollment. For the unbanked, the most commonly cited feature was that the tax refund would provide the opening deposit. We believe many unbanked individuals chose to open ECSP accounts because the opportunity was presented when they anticipated having money available. The anecdotal evidence cited above also supports this proposition: Individuals often wanted to know their refund status before deciding whether to open ECSP accounts. Other important account features for the unbanked were that the money earned interest and the account had no fees.

For individuals who had bank accounts when they enrolled in the ECSP, the most important account feature was the absence of fees. Other important features were the 10 percent year-end bonus (that is, an additional interest payment of 10 percent of the amount left in the account is paid at the end of the year) and the absence of a minimum balance requirement. We suspect that banked participants compared ECSP features to features of their other accounts and decided that the ECSP account was a more attractive depository for tax refunds.

TAX REFUND USES

In the follow-up survey, we asked participants to name the most important uses of their refunds, and we coded these responses into ten categories (table 9.3). First, we created seven fairly broad categories: bills; housing-

Table 9.3 Categories of Refund Use, by Account Ownership

	All ($N = 34$)	Unbanked ($n = 19$)	Banked ($n = 15$)
Bills	22 (65%)	11 (58%)	11 (73%)
Personal and household purchases	14 (41%)	9 (47%)	5 (33%)
Vehicle-related uses[a]	11 (32%)	8 (42%)	3 (20%)
Other saving and investment	9 (27%)	3 (16%)	6 (40%)
Educational uses	6 (18%)	2 (11%)	4 (27%)
Housing-related uses[b]	5 (15%)	3 (16%)	2 (13%)
Special events	3 (9%)	1 (5%)	2 (13%)
Social network-related uses	3 (9%)	1 (5%)	2 (13%)
Any saving[c]	14 (41%)	6 (32%)	8 (53%)
Any asset[c]	22 (65%)	11 (58%)	11 (73%)

Source: ECSP follow-up survey.
[a]Excludes payments for vehicle insurance and loans, which are defined as bills.
[b]Excludes rent and utility payments, which are defined as bills.
[c]Items in this category overlap items in other categories. See text for definition.

related uses (excludes rent and utility payments, which are defined as bills); vehicle-related uses (excludes insurance and loan payments, which are defined as bills); educational uses; personal and household purchases; social network-related uses (e.g., pay back money owed to relative, make cash gift to relative, save for grandchildren); and special events (e.g., travel, "treat" for self or children). These categories include goods and services respondents had purchased and were saving for. For example, spending money on travel and saving for future travel were both coded as special events. Next, we created an eighth category, other saving and investment, for responses such as "save for a rainy day" and "save to establish a credit record" that did not fall into one of the seven categories just mentioned. We also computed the number of individuals giving responses that explicitly mentioned saving. These responses could fall into any of the eight categories. We refer to this cross-cutting category as "any saving." Finally, we created a tenth category, labeled "any asset," that includes saving, education-related uses, vehicle-related uses, housing-related uses, and computer purchases. This category is similar to the "social mobility" bundle of uses created by Timothy Smeeding and colleagues (2000).

For the full sample, the most common use for the tax refund was paying bills (65 percent), especially utility bills, credit card bills, and rent payments. Other common uses were personal and household items (especially clothing) at 41 percent, vehicle-related uses (primarily vehicle purchase) at 32 percent, and other saving and investment (primarily precautionary saving) at 27 percent. Fourteen participants (41 percent) mentioned "any saving," which overlaps several categories, and twenty-two (65 percent) named at least one use that we coded as an asset, another that overlapped categories. The average refund for participants with an asset use was $1,753 (median = $1,918), and the average refund for those without an asset use was $1,126 (median = $353). This difference in means, although not significant at conventional levels ($t = -1.37$, $df = 32$, $p = 0.18$), may suggest that larger refunds facilitate asset uses. Paying bills was the most common response for both banked and unbanked participants, although unbanked participants were less likely than banked participants to name this use. Unbanked participants were also less likely to name other saving and investment, education, any saving, and any asset use.

ECSP ACCOUNT ACTIVITY

In this section, we use data from account statements to describe deposit and withdrawal patterns for ECSP accounts. We use data from January 15 to November 15, 2000, to describe overall patterns of account activity following tax year 1999 refunds and data from January 15 to June 15, 2001, to describe use of ECSP accounts for tax year 2000 refunds. As noted above, we restrict our sample to the 58 participants who received nonnegligible refunds. Although we do not discuss them here, six of the twelve individuals who did not receive refunds deposited money into their ECSP accounts.

Most participants received their refunds in February or March 2000. Refunds ranged from $141 to $4,688. The mean amount was $1,808, and the median was $1,524. For these lower-income families, refund amounts were substantial. On average, anticipated refund amount was equal to 23 percent of adjusted gross income (median = 21 percent).

Initial Account Activity

In this section, we examine account activity in the first month (one month equals thirty days). These data reveal initial responses to anticipated tax refunds.

Withdrawals, Deposits, and Ending Balances in the First Month

The column of table 9.4 headed "Month 1" summarizes account activity in the first month following receipt of refund. The median number of withdrawals during the first month was 3, and the mean was 4.3. Withdrawals were fairly small. Fifteen individuals (26 percent) made at least one deposit (excluding interest payments) in the first month. Individual deposits (number of withdrawals = 23) ranged from $1 to $1,500. The median value was $150, and the mean was $292. Three individuals—including two who were unbanked at enrollment—received paychecks or public transfer payments via direct deposit within the first month. Arranging for direct deposit is important because it demonstrates some degree of comfort with a bank account and some commitment to using the account over time. By automatically converting money into a less liquid form, direct deposit may also facilitate saving and asset accumulation (Beverly, Moore, and Schreiner, 2003).

By the end of the first month, one individual had closed her account, and six others had less than $5. Thus, 12 percent had essentially depleted their accounts. The median ending balance after the first month was $206, and the mean was $649. The median ending balance as a percent of refund was 13 percent, and the mean was 39 percent. Ten participants (18 percent) had ending balances that were larger than their refunds.

Initial Patterns of Account Activity

To summarize account activity in the first month, we defined three general patterns: maintenance (first-month ending balance greater than or equal to 95 percent of refund amount), decline (first-month ending balance less than 95 percent but at least 15 percent of refund amount), and depletion (first-month ending balance less than 15 percent of refund amount). Table 9.5 shows the distribution of patterns for all participants and by account ownership. In the full sample, 19 percent of refund recipients left their refunds

Table 9.4 Cumulative Account Activity for Refund Recipients in First Four Months following Refund

Recipients' Account Activity	Month 1	Months 1–2	Months 1–3	Months 1–4
Withdrawals (N = 58)				
Number (percent) with no withdrawals	9 (16%)	5 (9%)	4 (7%)	2 (3%)
Median number of withdrawals	3	5	6	6
Median withdrawal amount[a]	$67	$61	$60	$60
Median withdrawal amount as percent of refund[a]	8%	6%	6%	6%
Deposits (excluding interest payments) (N = 58)				
Number (percent) with one or more deposits	15 (26%)	19 (33%)	22 (38%)	25 (43%)
Number (percent) who had received direct deposit paychecks or transfer payments	3 (5%)	4 (7%)	7 (12%)	8 (14%)
Ending balance (N = 57)				
Number (percent) with closed accounts	1 (2%)	1 (2%)	1 (2%)	1 (2%)
Number (percent) with ending balance less than $5[b]	7 (12%)	11 (19%)	13 (23%)	16 (28%)
Median ending balance	$206	$86	$36	$19
Mean ending balance	$649	$433	$379	$271
Median ending balance as percent of refund	13%	5%	4%	2%
Mean ending balance as percent of refund	39%	28%	41%	29%
Number (percent) with ending balance greater than refund	10 (18%)	7 (12%)	6 (11%)	4 (7%)

Source: ShoreBank account statements through November 15, 2000.
[a]Withdrawal amounts are calculated across the sample of withdrawals.
[b]Includes those with closed accounts.

Table 9.5 Patterns of Account Activity in First Month by Account Ownership

	All (N = 57)	Unbanked (n = 34)	Banked (n = 23)
Maintenance	11 (19%)	4 (12%)	7 (30%)
Decline	16 (28%)	10 (29%)	6 (26%)
Depletion	30 (53%)	20 (59%)	10 (43%)

Source: ShoreBank account statements through November 15, 2000.
Note: See text for definitions of patterns.

virtually untouched and/or had first-month ending balances that exceeded their refund amounts. Twenty-eight percent withdrew some of their refunds but did not deplete their accounts. Fifty-three percent depleted their accounts in the first month, including 21 percent who depleted their accounts within the first week. Unbanked participants may have been more likely than banked participants to deplete their accounts in the first month and less likely to have high (relative to refund amounts) ending balances.[3]

Subsequent Account Activity

We next describe withdrawals, deposits, and ending balances in the second, third, and fourth months and discuss overall patterns of account activity. In particular, we document the extent to which individuals used ECSP accounts for something more than a short-term holding place for tax refunds.

Withdrawals, Deposits, and Ending Balances

The third, fourth, and fifth columns of table 9.4 summarize cumulative account activity for months one–two, one–three, and one–four. As expected, the number of individuals with no withdrawals declined over time. Still, four participants (7 percent) made no withdrawals in the first three months, and two (3 percent) made no withdrawals in the first four months. The median withdrawal amount changed very little, in absolute and percentage terms.

The number of individuals who had made one or more deposits increased over time, as did the number who had received direct deposit paychecks. Seventeen of the twenty-five individuals who made deposits—including six of the eight who had received direct deposit paychecks or transfer payments—were unbanked at the time of enrollment. No additional accounts were closed in the second, third, and fourth months, but the number of individuals with less than $5 in their accounts increased to 16 (28 percent). The median ending balance declined substantially over time. After four months, half of the participants had ending balances of less than $19, and half had ending balances of less than 2 percent of the refund amount. The mean balance after four months was $271, and the mean balance as a percent of refund was 29 percent.

Overall Patterns of Account Activity

To identify overall patterns of account activity, we examined graphs showing daily balances between the date of refund receipt and November 15, 2000, for each individual.[4] Four patterns emerged: (a) rapid spend-down, (b) slow spend-down, (c) transaction, and (d) saving. For each account holder, we also computed the average daily balance (ADB) between date of refund receipt and November 15, 2000, the ADB as a percent of refund amount, and the number of account transactions per month.

Table 9.6 shows the number and percent of ECSP participants in each category. The most common pattern is rapid spend-down—the 24 individuals in this group (41 percent of the sample of 58) depleted their accounts (that is, their account balances fell below 15 percent of refund amounts) in the first month, and their accounts were largely inactive from this point on. Six of these individuals made at least one deposit, but they quickly withdrew their funds. To a large extent, these ECSP participants used their accounts solely as a short-term holding place for tax refunds.

The second pattern is slow spend-down. The 13 individuals in this group (22 percent of the sample) did not deplete their accounts in the first

Table 9.6 Account Activity, AGI, and Refund Amount by Overall Pattern of Account Activity

Patterns of Account Activity (N = 58)	Rapid Spend-Down	Slow Spend-Down	Transaction	Saving
Number (percent) of ECSP participants	24 (41%)	13 (22%)	13 (22%)	8 (14%)
ADB				
Median	$25	$618	$188	$537
Mean (SD)	$88 ($182)	$727 ($460)	$287 ($374)	$688 ($683)
ADB as percent of refund				
Median	4.1	31.9	9.7	55.1
Mean (SD)	5.4 (5.4)	38.6 (23.8)	43.7 (99.8)	54.5 (35.7)
Transactions per month				
Median	0.6	1.4	5.7	1.4
Mean (SD)	0.9 (0.8)	1.9 (1.5)	6.7 (4.3)	1.2 (0.7)
Adjusted gross income				
Median	$6,628	$10,198	$9,515	$13,702
Mean (SD)	$7,213 ($4,534)	$12,495 ($8,223)	$9,713 ($6,365)	$14,598 ($10,078)
Federal refund				
Median	$647	$2,661	$1,081	$1,462
Mean (SD)	$1,599 ($1,569)	$2,391 ($1,309)	$1,670 ($1,492)	$1,713 ($1,330)

Source: ShoreBank account statements through November 15, 2000, and tax returns and intake forms collected by CEP.
Notes: See text for definitions of patterns. SD = standard deviation.

month, but their account activity was dominated by withdrawals. Almost all had balances of at least $500 two months after refund receipt, and many had balances of at least $500 after three months. Like ECSP participants who spent their refunds very quickly, these individuals used their accounts to store tax refunds, but they held funds in the accounts longer. These individuals' postponed consumption might be viewed as saving, especially because ADBs were fairly high.

The third overall pattern of account activity is transaction. The 13 individuals in this group (22 percent of the sample) rapidly withdrew their tax refunds but in later months had frequent deposits and withdrawals. ADBs were fairly low. These individuals were essentially using their ECSP accounts like checking accounts. Nine of these individuals received direct deposit paychecks or transfer payments.

Eight individuals (14 percent) fell into the fourth pattern—saving. All of these individuals had periods of time when account balances were increasing, and all had account balances on November 15 that were greater than 15 percent of their refund amounts. The median ADB was $537, and the median ADB as a percent of refund was 55. We assume that these individuals were attempting to save in their ECSP accounts.

Because of the small sample size, we do not report results from a multivariate analysis designed to predict overall pattern of account activity. However, table 9.6 provides information on AGI and federal refund for each of the four groups, and table 9.7 shows overall patterns of account activity by account ownership. Participants in the saving and slow spend-down groups had higher incomes; therefore, they may have been better able to keep money in their ECSP accounts. Those in the slow spend-down group received relatively large refunds, and those in the rapid spend-down group received relatively small refunds. Because it is easy to spend small refunds, refund size may partly explain observed patterns of account activity. In addition, interview data suggest that participants were most likely to become active account holders if they could integrate the account into their established routines. Rapid spend-down and transaction appear to have been more common for the unbanked than for the banked, and saving and slow spend-down appear to have been less common for the unbanked.

Table 9.7 Overall Patterns of Account Activity by Account Ownership

Patterns of Account Activity	All ($N = 58$)	Unbanked ($n = 35$)	Banked ($n = 23$)
Rapid spend-down	24 (41%)	16 (46%)	8 (35%)
Slow spend-down	13 (22%)	6 (17%)	7 (30%)
Transaction	13 (22%)	11 (31%)	2 (9%)
Saving	8 (14%)	2 (6%)	6 (26%)

Source: ShoreBank account statements through November 15, 2000.
Note: See text for definitions of patterns.

Use of Accounts for Refunds in Tax Year 2000

One way to assess comfort with and commitment to ECSP accounts is to note whether participants arranged to have federal refunds for the 2000 tax year directly deposited into their accounts. By June 15, 2001, 28 percent of the ECSP participants who had received direct deposit refunds for tax year 1999 (16 out of 58) had also received 2000 refunds via direct deposit. Those who were unbanked at enrollment were less likely than the banked to receive 2000 refunds in their ECSP accounts (20 percent vs. 39 percent). In addition to the 16 people who received direct deposit federal refunds, 10 account holders did not receive direct deposit refunds but made deposits greater than $500 between February 15 and June 15, 2001. Some of these deposits may have come from refunds received by mail rather than by direct deposit.

PARTICIPANT PERCEPTIONS

Open-ended questions in the follow-up survey and in-depth interviews with unbanked participants provided additional insight into the effectiveness of the ECSP, from the participants' point of view. Two key findings from qualitative data are that financial constraints and spending temptations sabotaged efforts to save and make asset purchases. These findings are discussed in Sondra Beverly, Jennifer Tescher, and Jennifer Romich (2004). Despite these barriers, there is evidence that participation in the ECSP changed financial behaviors and attitudes.

Changes in Refund Use

In the telephone survey, we asked the following question: "Overall, did having the Extra Credit Savings Account at South Shore Bank change the way you used your tax refund?" Twenty-five respondents (74 percent) answered affirmatively. A follow-up question asked these individuals how the account had changed the way they used their tax refunds. We also asked all respondents if they had any other comments, positive or negative, about the program, and we classified a few of these comments as changes in refund use. Here, we summarize responses to both of these open-ended questions, and percentages refer to the entire follow-up survey sample of thirty-four people.

Twenty-one follow-up survey respondents (62 percent) implied that ECSP participation changed their spending patterns and/or helped them save. Three individuals (9 percent) suggested that the ECSP helped them save by creating an incentive or a goal. Four (12 percent) said that having an account helped them to save but did not say how or why. More, however, described changes in spending. For example, thirteen respondents (38 percent) said they had fewer spending temptations and/or spent the money more slowly than they otherwise would have. Here are comments from a few of the respondents: "Couldn't spend the money on a whim." "By keeping it in the bank, I had to go and get it instead of having it in hand; I didn't have the urge to spend it all at once." "Normally I would have done what I wanted to do with it and it would have been gone quicker." In addition, three individuals (9 percent) said ECSP participation helped them prioritize spending in favor of "more important things." Three individuals (9 percent) mentioned having other accounts and implied that physical accounting (that is, using separate accounts for specific purposes) helped them achieve financial goals.

Changes in Other Financial Behaviors and Attitudes

In addition to naming ways ECSP participation had changed refund use, some phone survey respondents described changes in other financial behaviors and attitudes. For example, one respondent said she was thinking about opening a checking account, and another commented on the benefits of direct deposit: "Now I have an account. I have my work check deposited. It's been a little better. It's helping me to save more." One respondent said the program "helps people get back on the right track." This notion of getting back on track was also mentioned in in-depth interviews. Five of the nine interviewees had previously closed or stopped using other checking or savings accounts, and most cited problems with bounced checks or maintaining minimum balances.

In-depth interviews revealed an increased familiarity with banks among those who had never had a bank account. For example, one respondent said, "I always thought all banks you had to put an amount of money in them, that you couldn't spend it or touch it, so it gave me another outlook on it." Another reported helping her mother open an account at a different bank and contrasted the features, noting that her mother opened a checking account to avoid the other institution's minimum balance on savings accounts. Two of the four "never-banked" participants spoke about positive interactions with ShoreBank tellers, calling them "helpful" and "classy."

In-depth interviews also suggest that some unbanked participants viewed the ECSP as a bridge to other mainstream financial products and services. One interviewee described her decision to sign up for direct deposit in this way, "I always knew that the school did it, you know, you have the check deposit, you know the safe deposit, but I never thought about it until I started going to [ShoreBank], and then I said, there is a good idea, because when I get paid in the summer I don't have to wait for the mailman."

Others said that having a savings account helped them establish credit histories, obtain leases, and obtain credit cards. One 21-year-old spoke of wanting to build her credit. The account was a springboard to another account and then a secured credit card. She described her next steps to an interviewer: "I'm just building my credit by paying [my secured credit card bill] on time." Two other mothers talked about opening IRAs, mutual funds, or college savings accounts for their children.

DISCUSSION

The ECSP allows participants to access refunds quickly, without check-cashing or rapid-refund fees. These are valuable services for low-income families. However, the ECSP also aims to help low-income individuals, especially those without bank accounts, to become more connected to mainstream financial services and to save and accumulate assets. Evidence regarding these goals is mixed.

About 60 percent of ECSP participants lacked a checking or savings account at the time of enrollment. In multivariate analysis, unbanked individuals were no more likely than banked individuals to enroll in the ECSP. However, qualitative data reveal that the ECSP offer tapped into preexisting desires to have accounts and to save but that many unbanked participants were not actively looking for an account. This suggests that the ECSP was an effective outreach tool for the unbanked.

Saving in ECSP accounts was quite limited in the first year, especially by previously unbanked individuals. Participants identified two key barriers to saving, financial constraints and spending temptations. At the same time, many of those who did not appear to be saving their tax refunds said that the account helped them spend their refunds more slowly and more thoughtfully. In addition, over half of unbanked participants reported using their refunds for some type of asset use. Because it is difficult to save and prioritize spending without a bank account, we believe that the ECSP facilitated asset uses of refunds for those who were unbanked at enrollment.

There is also evidence that some unbanked participants became more integrated into the financial mainstream. Data on overall patterns of account use suggest that over half of unbanked participants used their accounts for something other than short-term storage of tax refunds. Many participants spoke positively about the program and ShoreBank, and in interviews some unbanked participants said the program made them think more positively about banks. Some participants seemed to view the program as a bridge to other financial products and services, such as checking accounts, direct deposit of paychecks, and credit cards. It is important to note that ShoreBank did not market other bank products and services to ECSP participants, except through generic marketing materials sent with all account statements. The "bridge" or "gateway" function of programs such as the ECSP would probably be even more successful if banks marketed appropriate products and services directly to program participants.

Finally, some participants said that the program helped them get "back on track," and some described looking ahead to next year's refunds. These findings suggest that programs like the ECSP may have positive effects on saving and asset accumulation beyond any observed in the first year. We cannot say whether participants would have sought other ways to join the financial mainstream in the absence of the ECSP, but the program seems to represent an important step toward participation in a full range of financial services.

CONCLUSIONS

Asset accumulation is increasingly viewed as an important, long-term antipoverty strategy, and participation in mainstream financial systems is a principal prerequisite. This research suggests that the short-term effects on saving and asset accumulation of programs linking tax refunds to low-cost savings accounts will be small. However, by helping individuals spend money more slowly and more thoughtfully, introducing some to account ownership or direct deposit, and encouraging some to obtain other mainstream financial products, programs like the ECSP may help low-income families "get on track" for future saving and asset accumulation. For some ECSP participants, the account was a first step on the path toward establishing credit and making saving and investment a planned part of their lives.

We believe that programs like the ECSP are worthy of additional research, especially as expansions in tax credits for low-income families increase the number of low- and moderate-income families who receive sizable tax credits.

NOTES

The ECSP was made possible in part by a grant from the Ford Foundation. The Ford Foundation and the Joyce Foundation supported the evaluation research. Adele Botha, Dequiana Brooks, Emily Burkhalter-Blosser, Thamar King, Judy Martinez, Renell Morgan, Veronica Nelson, Seow Ling Ong, John Ottomanelli, Elizabeth Rossman, Kevin Ruland, Efrain Soto, Nicol Turner, and José Valdez helped collect and prepare the data.

1. Follow-up survey respondents were somewhat less likely than nonrespondents to receive cash assistance and food stamps, and they were less likely to be unbanked at the time of enrollment. However, mean and median adjusted gross incomes were lower for respondents.

2. We coded all open-ended survey questions in four steps: Two individuals separately developed coding schemes and then discussed each discrepancy until they reached consensus. The same two individuals separately assigned codes and then reached consensus on discrepancies.

3. The chi-square test for differences in patterns by account ownership is significant at the 21 percent level ($\chi^2 = 3.15$, $df = 2$, $p = 0.21$).

4. Sample graphs are available from the authors on request.

REFERENCES

Aizcorbe, A. M., A. B. Kennickell, and K. B. Moore. (2003). "Recent Changes in U.S. Family Finances: Results from the 1998 and 2001 Survey of Consumer Finances." *Federal Reserve Bulletin* 89(1), 1–32.

Beverly, S. G., A. Moore, and M. Schreiner. (2003). "A Framework of Asset-accumulation Stages and Strategies." *Journal of Family and Economic Issues* 24(2), 143–156.

Beverly, S. G., J. Tescher, and J. L. Romich. (2004). "Linking Tax Refunds and Low-Cost Bank Accounts: A Social Development Strategy for Low-Income Families?" *Social Development Issues* 25(1), 235–246.

Carney, S., and W. G. Gale. (2001). "Asset Accumulation in Low-Income Households." *In Assets for the Poor: The Benefits of Spreading Asset Ownership,* eds. T. M. Shapiro and E. N. Wolff. New York: Russell Sage Foundation, 165–205.

Caskey, J. P. (1997). *Lower Income Americans, Higher Cost Financial Services.* Madison, Wis.: Filene Research Institute.

Hogarth, J. M., and K. H. O'Donnell. (1999). "Banking Relationships of Lower-Income Families and the Governmental Trend toward Electronic Payment." *Federal Reserve Bulletin* (July), 459–473.

Hotz, V. J., and J. K. Scholz. (2001). *The Earned Income Tax Credit.* Working Paper No. 8078. Cambridge, Mass.: National Bureau of Economic Research.

Hurst, E., M. C. Luoh, and F. P. Stafford. (1998). "The Wealth Dynamics of American Families, 1984–1994." *Brookings Papers on Economic Activity* 1, 267–337.

Johnson, N. (2001). *A Hand up: How State Earned Income Tax Credits Help Working Families Escape Poverty in 2001.* Washington, D.C.: Center on Budget and Policy Priorities.

Smeeding, T. M., K. R. Phillips, and M. O'Connor. (2000). "The Earned Income Tax Credit: Expectation, Knowledge, Use, and Economic and Social Mobility." *National Tax Journal* 53(4, Part 2), 1187–1209.

10

Assets and the Poor: Evidence from Individual Development Accounts

Mark Schreiner, Michael Sherraden, Margaret Clancy,
Lissa Johnson, Jami Curley, Min Zhan, Sondra G. Beverly,
and Michal Grinstein-Weiss

The question of how to help the poor get rich is, in essence, the question of how to help them build assets. Poverty is a trap because resources are needed to produce resources. Poor people must consume most of their incoming resources, so they cannot save much. With low savings, they do not produce enough to increase their income enough to break the cycle.

To escape from poverty usually requires capital—human, physical, social, or financial. Many U.S. policies subsidize asset accumulation (Sherraden, 1991), sometimes to combat poverty. For example, the most important asset of the poor is their human capital, and the most widespread asset-subsidy policy is public education. Deductions for mortgage interest subsidize home ownership, the bedrock of the middle class and the second most important asset of the poor. Subsidized student loans, public colleges and universities, and subsidized retirement accounts are other common asset subsidies that reduce poverty. The Homestead Act (Shanks, chapter 2 in this volume) and the G.I. Bill subsidized assets for many poor people.

Most asset subsidies, however, go disproportionately to the nonpoor because these subsidies directly or indirectly require wealth. For example, local school finance places the best public schools in wealthy neighborhoods. Tax-advantaged retirement accounts link subsidies to the human capital required to reach a high tax bracket. Subsidized debt is indirectly linked to wealth because loans can finance only part of a purchase and because wealth signals creditworthiness.

Tax breaks for asset accumulation—such as tax deferments for individual retirement accounts (IRAs) and 401(k) plans and tax deductions for student loan interest and home mortgage interest—are weak incentives for poor people in low tax brackets. Furthermore, larger loans mean larger subsidies, so the poor, who go to less expensive colleges and buy less expensive homes, get smaller subsidies. Whatever the administrative, targeting, and incentive reasons for linking asset subsidies to wealth, loans, and taxes, the current system does less to include the poor than the nonpoor.

A new policy proposal designed to help the poor build assets, called individual development accounts (IDAs), does not require wealth, tax breaks, or debt. Withdrawals from IDAs are matched if they are used to buy a home, to pay for postsecondary education, or to finance self-employment. Participants in IDAs also receive financial education and support from IDA staff.

This chapter analyzes asset accumulation in IDAs by poor people in the American Dream Demonstration (ADD). The main results are the following:

- Poor people can save and build assets in IDAs. It is unknown, however, whether they save more than they would have without IDAs.
- Income and welfare receipt were not linked with net deposits in IDAs. The very poor saved a larger share of their income than the less poor. Also, members of all racial/ethnic groups saved in IDAs, although some saved more than others.
- Institutional characteristics mattered. In particular, greater financial education was associated with greater savings. Higher match rates were associated with a greater likelihood of saving something, but with lower savings, given that something was saved.
- IDAs in ADD were costly. A different program structure and a different bundle of services may be needed if access to IDAs is to become universal and permanent.

This chapter first presents IDAs and ADD and reviews relevant theory. It then discusses evidence from ADD on whether the poor can save in IDAs, who saves in IDAs, how IDAs work, and what IDAs cost. The final section discusses the main results from a policy perspective.

IDAs AND ADD

IDAs subsidize asset accumulation by the poor. IDAs differ from IRAs or 401(k) plans in that IDAs:

- Target the poor rather than the nonpoor
- Provide subsidies through matches rather than through tax breaks
- Require financial education

IDAs decouple the asset-subsidy mechanism from wealth, taxes, and debt. With IDAs, people who pass an income test may deposit posttax dollars in insured, interest-bearing passbook savings accounts. They receive monthly statements, financial education, and support from staff and peers. Withdrawals are matched if used for home purchase, postsecondary education, or small business. Some IDA programs also provide matching funds for home repair, investment in retirement accounts, job training, and cars or computers. Withdrawals for other purposes are allowed, but they are not matched. Matching funds are disbursed directly to vendors.

Michael Sherraden's (1991) original IDA proposal calls for permanent accounts for all, opened at birth, with greater subsidies for the poor. Regardless of balances or activity, the poor would not be "on" or "off" IDAs any more than the nonpoor are "on" or "off" IRAs. Funds for program costs and matches may come from public or private sources. As a simple way to subsidize saving for targeted goals, IDAs fit a wide range of public policy purposes.

Intellectual History of IDAs

Although development economics has long focused on saving as central to long-term improvement in well-being, public policy in the United States somehow overlooked the importance of saving for the poor (Sherraden, 1991). Public assistance provided just enough cash to meet subsistence requirements, but it stopped short of transfers whose amounts and forms could help people break free of a poverty orbit.

In the late 1980s, a movement began with the intention of including the poor in asset-subsidy policies. Robert Friedman's book, *The Safety Net as Ladder* (1988), proposed changes to public assistance to encourage development beyond mere subsistence. Robert Haveman's book, *Starting Even,* said that "transfer payments are necessary but not sufficient" (1988, 149). Sherraden's article, "Rethinking Social Welfare: Toward Assets" (1988), critiqued the subsistence paradigm and proposed IDAs as a step toward a development paradigm.

The movement to include the poor in asset-subsidy programs gained momentum (Ackerman and Alstott, 1999; Conley, 1999; Oliver and Shapiro, 1995; Shapiro and Wolff, 2001) and attracted support from many quarters. When Bill Clinton was governor of Arkansas, he wrote the foreword to *The Safety Net as Ladder.* He later supported IDAs in his 1992 presidential campaign and proposed a large matched savings program. In their 2000 platforms, both George W. Bush and Al Gore advocated for billion-dollar IDA proposals. As of 2004, 32 states have IDA legislation, and, at the national level, the Savings for Working Families Act—if passed—would fund 300,000 IDA accounts. Outside the United States, Canada is sponsoring its own version of an IDA demonstration, and the United Kingdom's Child Trust Fund will give an account and a deposit to each newborn, with larger deposits for children of poor families.

The American Dream Demonstration

The focal point of research on IDAs in the United States is the ADD. ADD was run by the Corporation for Enterprise Development from 1997 through

2003 with private and public funds. Data from ADD cover 2,353 participants in fourteen programs across the United States (excluding enrollees who died or those who had to quit because they moved). Mark Schreiner and colleagues (2001) describe ADD programs and their rules.

Program staff for ADD entered IDA deposits and withdrawals for each participant for all months from the date the IDA was opened until the last month for matchable deposits into the Management Information System for Individual Development Accounts (MIS IDA) (Johnson, Hinterlong, and Sherraden, 2001). In addition to monthly cash flows, MIS IDA records initial account structure parameters, demographic and economic data on participants at enrollment, and intermittent events, such as program exit or attendance at financial education classes.

MIS IDA provides what may be the only high-frequency data on matched saving by the poor. The cash flow data are unusually accurate; they come from records of depository institutions and satisfy accounting identities. All data were extensively cross-checked. Still, no data are perfect, and a few caveats are in order. IDA staff members are not researchers, and, despite a commitment to accurate data and support for the research, data quality varies through time and across programs. Time-constant demographics are very accurate. Time-varying economic data, regardless of accuracy, may change after enrollment, and, as in all surveys, income, assets, and liabilities are noisy and probably understated. Also, fields added to MIS IDA after ADD started were not always collected from all already enrolled participants, especially those who had left. At the program level, the account structure parameters in MIS IDA do not always match the rules used in practice or understood by participants. There is no foolproof way to know whether program staff recorded all intermittent events. Throughout this chapter, we take care to note when data issues might influence results. Schreiner et al. (2001) discusses the data at length.

The ADD data are unusually rich, but they cannot answer all questions. For example, the data cover only participants. In ADD, participants were both self-selected (they chose to join based on expected net benefits) and program-selected (most programs targeted people of color, the "working poor," and/or women). Thus, the effects of use are tangled up with the effects of preexisting characteristics correlated with selection. Without a credible way of determining what would have happened without IDAs, there is no way to measure the impact of use (nor of eligibility) of IDAs. One program in ADD did randomize across qualified applicants, but that data is not analyzed here.

Because of limited funds, ADD ran for a short time, and so it cannot tell us how poor savers would behave if they had permanent access to IDAs. If the goal is long-term improvement in well-being, if assets foster development, and if IDAs increase asset accumulation by the poor, then a permanent IDA program is probably better than one with a time limit.

Sherraden (1991) hypothesizes that saving—by poor and nonpoor alike—depends not only on rational choice but also on institutions. This research looks at how variations among institutions regarding items such as match rates, match caps, and financial education and across groups of participants in ADD are associated with variations in saving outcomes. Although programs set rules before enrollment, the rules may still have depended in part on expected participant behavior, so endogeneity bias may affect the results on institutional characteristics to some unknown extent.

The MIS IDA data show how participants saved in IDAs in ADD. These are not the grandest of questions, but they are quite important, especially because some believe that the poor cannot save at all.

SAVINGS THEORY AND IDAs

This section describes theories of saving and asset accumulation and how the institutional structure of IDAs takes advantage of insights from these theories.

Saving and Asset Accumulation

Income is defined as the inflow of resources in a period of time. Assets are stocks of resources held at a point in time. Whether seen as assets or income, resources may be consumed (changed into forms no longer useful) or moved through time.

Saving is an increase in assets (or net worth) in a period of time. Dissaving is a decrease in assets. Saving is not consuming income, and dissaving is consuming assets.

Asset accumulation is a long-lasting increase in assets. Saving that consistently exceeds dissaving leads to asset accumulation.

The concept of assets encompasses far more than financial assets as cash or as bank account balances. The chief asset of most people—especially the poor—is human capital. People also possess household durables (such as homes, cars, clothes, furniture, and appliances) and producer durables (such as tools for self-employment). People also use social capital (networks, norms, and trust) to produce information, reduce transaction costs, buffer shocks, and soothe psyches. Sherraden (1991) presents a typology of assets and their returns.

Asset accumulation matters because resources are required to earn income, smooth consumption, buffer risk, and make large purchases. In the absence of constant, massive transfers from government, long-term improvement in individual well-being requires increased productive capacity. Because assets beget assets, escaping from poverty requires asset accumulation.

Beyond these economic effects of resource use, Sherraden (1991) suggests that resource ownership has healthy effects on thoughts, behavior, goals, and overall well-being. People who own assets expect better future outcomes, and their expectations may spark hopes that, in turn, change current feelings, beliefs, and choices.

Three Theories of Saving and Asset Accumulation

Theories of saving relevant to IDAs are economic, social/psychological, and behavioral.

Economic Theory

Economic theory assumes that people seek to maximize long-term well-being subject to constraints. People are assumed to be forward looking and rational, with fixed preferences. Choices and the distribution of their probable consequences are known and fixed. Preferences are the deus ex machina of unobserved causes that drive observed outcomes.

For savings and the poor, the fundamental insight of economics is that people who must consume most of their incoming resources just to survive will not be able to save much. Also, because additional consumption is very valuable to people with low consumption, the poor pay more—in terms of foregone utility—to save. Because current savings (in human capital, financial assets, social networks, and producer and consumer durables) determine future production and, thus, future income, poverty can be a trap of low assets.

Economic theory also highlights the importance of indivisibilities. Some assets, such as houses, involve large, all-or-none purchases. Saving for such all-or-none purchases is more difficult than saving for purchases that can be made in bits and pieces.

Matches in IDAs address both rate of return issues and size of return issues. For example, the median match rate in ADD (2:1) may make saving a good choice for poor people despite the high cost in terms of foregone consumption. (Economic theory does not predict that greater rates of return will always lead to greater savings; this issue is taken up again below.) Also, the match changes a given level of savings into a higher level of asset accumulation, perhaps enough to purchase a large asset.

Social/Psychological Theories

These theories, which have been discussed in detail by Sondra Beverly and Sherraden (1999), emphasize that people are not always rational and that society shapes preferences. The theories look behind the deus ex machina of preferences to explain saving-related goals and expectations.

Social/psychological theories assume that people do not always form their own goals or even know what choices are available, let alone know all possible consequences of choices. For example, people who see family and friends save are more likely to view saving as a possibility (Lusardi, 2000). Likewise, cultural norms may affect saving goals. For example, U.S.

couples with children are more or less expected to own a home, but single and childless couples are not.

Broad social norms also mold saving expectations. Americans learn that Benjamin Franklin was wise and that he advised, "A penny saved is a penny earned." Many Japanese have acted upon their government's suggestion that they should save one-fifth of their income (Bernheim, 1994). In the United States, the home mortgage interest deduction suggests that a home is a good investment. Likewise, the existence of 401(k) plans in the United States signals not only that workers *can* save but also that they *should* save.

The institutional structure of IDAs builds on social/psychological theory in several ways. First, the existence of IDAs sends a message that the poor can (and perhaps should) save. In particular, the match attracts attention. Second, IDAs require financial education; people are not expected to know how to save or to know the consequences of saving. Third, IDA programs give feedback and social support via staff and peers. Fourth, planning for withdrawals encourages participants to make goals and to think about the benefits of saving. Fifth, participants receive monthly statements that remind them of their goals and help them track their progress.

Behavioral Theory

Like social/psychological theory, behavioral theory relaxes some assumptions in economic theory. It recognizes that people impose systems of mental accounts on their resources (Shefrin and Thaler, 1988). For example, small windfalls—such as lottery wins—may be assigned to splurges. Likewise, people may be comfortable with debt for assets such as homes or college education but not for eating out or for buying gifts.

Behavioral theory also recognizes that most people know that they can be their own worst enemy. People know that they are both forward-looking and shortsighted; they recognize that they will be tempted to spend even if saving would make them better off in the long term. Thus, they may create their own mental or external rewards and punishments that help them save rather than spend (Maital, 1986; Thaler, 1994). For example, they may commit to rules of thumb (and feel guilty when they break them), such as saving one spouse's income and paying oneself first. Payroll deduction, probably the most common self-commitment constraint, removes payday temptations. Christmas Clubs and time deposits help people stick to saving plans by offering a substantial penalty for early withdrawal.

IDAs fit behavioral theory because they help people to commit to save and to resist the temptation to dissave. First, IDAs create a new mental account: savings for a home, college tuition, or a business. The distinct account, together with reinforcements from staff that IDA funds are off-limits even though unmatched withdrawals are, in fact, freely and always available, helps participants avoid viewing IDA balances as spending money (Beverly, McBride, and Schreiner, 2003). Second, the expression of the match cap (a limit) in terms of a monthly savings target (a goal) may encourage participants to set monthly savings goals. Third, automatic deposits into IDAs—when available—may help to curb temptations to spend because cash cannot burn a hole in one's pocket. Fourth, the perceived obligation to save in IDAs may give participants a socially acceptable excuse to deny requests from members of social networks (Chiteji and Hamilton, chapter 5 in this volume).

CAN THE POOR SAVE IN IDAs?

ADD shows that the poor can save in IDAs. ADD does not address, however, whether the poor saved more with IDAs than they would have without IDAs.

Participation

ADD enrolled 2,353 participants (line Aa in table 10.1). The average length of participation was 26 months (line Ac).

About 53 percent of participants in ADD were defined as *savers* because they held net deposits of at least $100 as of the last month in the data. Low savers (47 percent of participants) may have saved and held balances for a time, but the maximum matched withdrawal that they possibly could make was less than $100.

Savings Outcomes

- Gross deposits: In an average month, the average participant deposited $47.07 (line Am).
- Unmatched withdrawals: About 67 percent of participants made an unmatched withdrawal (line Bp of table 10.2). The average participant in this group made 4.1 unmatched withdrawals, each worth an average of $127 (line Bn). In ADD, the average unmatched withdrawal per participant ($526, line Br) almost equaled average net deposits ($537.41, line Cd of table 10.3). Given the average match rate of 1.78:1 (line Dk of table 10.4), unmatched withdrawals represent lost potential matches worth about $936. The unexpected size and frequency of unmatched withdrawals in spite of their high opportunity cost highlights the difficulty of asset accumulation for the poor, even in the supportive institutional context of IDAs. At the same time, it highlights the importance of allowing poor savers to withdraw from their IDAs as they see fit.
- Net deposits: Average net deposits in ADD—defined as gross deposits minus unmatched withdrawals minus balances in excess of the match cap—were $537 ($998 for savers). If all net deposits as of the last month in the data were used in matched withdrawals

Table 10.1 Enrollment and Gross Deposits in ADD

Line	Item	Formula	Value
Enrollments			
Aa	# of participants	Data	2,353
Ab	# of participant-months	Data	61,066
Ac	Average months of participation	Ab/Aa	26
Gross deposits			
Ad	Gross deposits	Data	$2,874,311
Ae	# of deposits	Data	39,428
Af	Average gross deposit	Ad/Ae	$72.90
Ag	# of participants with a deposit	Data	2,341
Ah	Percentage of participants with a deposit	$100 \times (Ag/Aa)$	99%
Ai	# of deposits per participants with a deposit	Ae/Ag	16.8
Aj	Gross deposit per participants with a deposit	Ad/Ag	$1,228
Ak	# of participant-months with a deposit	Data	31,526
Al	Deposit frequency	$100 \times (Ak/Ab)$	52%
Am	Gross deposit per participant-month	Ad/Ab	$47.07
An	Gross deposit per month with a deposit	Ad/Ak	$91.17
Ao	Interest (net of fees)	Data	$40,668
Ap	Gross deposits plus interest	Ad + Ao	$2,914,979

Source: Management information system for individual development accounts (MIS IDA). Means are ratios of averages.

(in fact, 63 percent had already been matched, and the rest may have been matched or withdrawn unmatched after the last month in the data), then the average participant would have accumulated $1,554 through IDAs ($2,886 for savers).

- Average monthly net deposit: The average monthly net deposit (AMND)—defined as net deposits divided by months of participation—was $20.71 for all participants (table 10.3) and $34.07 for savers. Median AMND was $8.25 ($30.38 for savers). With an average match rate of 1.78:1, the average participant accumulated about $58 per month or about $691 per year (for savers, $95 per month or $1,137 per year).
- Matched withdrawals: About 35 percent of participants had made a matched withdrawal as of the last month in the data (line De of

Table 10.2 Unmatched Withdrawals and Excess Deposits in ADD

Line	Item	Formula	Value
Withdrawals (WD) of excess balances			
Ba	WD of excess balances	Data	$698,844
Bb	# of WD of excess balances	Data	1,964
Bc	Average WD of excess balances	Ba/Bb	$356
Bd	# of participants with a WD of excess balances	Data	724
Be	Percentage of participants with a WD of excess balances	$100 \times (Bd/Aa)$	31%
Bf	# of WD of excess balance per participants with a WD of excess balance	Bb/Bd	2.7
Bg	WD of excess balance per participants with a WD of excess balance	Ba/Bd	$965
Excess deposits			
Bh	Excess balances over match cap	Data	$117,967
Bi	# of participants with excess balances	Data	553
Bj	Percentage of participants with excess balances	$100 \times (Bi/Aa)$	24%
Bk	Excess deposit per participants with excess balance	Bh/Bi	$213
Unmatched withdrawals			
Bl	Unmatched WD	Data	$833,636
Bm	# of unmatched WD	Data	6,568
Bn	Average unmatched WD	Bm/Bl	$127
Bo	# of participants with an unmatched WD	Data	1,586
Bp	Percentage of participants with an unmatched WD	$100 \times (Bo/Aa)$	67%
Bq	# of unmatched WD per participants with an unmatched WD	Bm/Bo	4.1
Br	Unmatched WD per participants with an unmatched WD	Bl/Bo	$526

Source: MIS IDA. Means are ratios of averages.

table 10.4). For this group, the average value of matched withdrawals was $974 (line Dg), and the average value of matched withdrawals plus matches was $2,711 (line Dj).

- Matched uses: The largest number (26 percent) of matched withdrawals were for microenterprise, followed by home repair (22 percent), postsecondary education (21.5 percent), home purchase

Table 10.3 Net Deposits in ADD

Line	Item	Formula	Value
Net deposits			
Ca	Net deposits	Ap − (Ba + Bh + Bl)	$1,264,531
Cb	Average match rate on net deposits	Data	1.89
Cc	Net deposits plus match	Ca × (1 + Cb)	$3,657,462
Cd	Net deposits per participant	Ca/Aa	$537.41
Ce	Average monthly net deposit (AMND)	Ca/Ab	$20.71
Cf	# of participants with positive net deposits	Data	1,416
Cg	Percentage of participants with positive net deposits	100 × (Cf/Aa)	60
Ch	Net deposits per participants with positive net deposits	Ca/Cf	$893
Ci	# of participant-months for participants with positive net deposits	Data	43,603
Cj	Average monthly net deposit for participants with positive net deposits	Ca/Ci	$29.00

Source: MIS IDA. Means are ratios of averages.

(20.9 percent), retirement (7 percent), and job training (2 percent). No matched withdrawals went for other uses. Of the 34 percent of savers without a matched withdrawal as of the last month in the data, 55 percent planned for home purchase, 19 percent for micro-enterprise, and 16 percent for education. The remaining 9 percent planned for retirement, home repair, or job training.

- Deposit frequency: On average, participants made deposits in 6 of every 12 months or in 51.6 percent of months (see line Al of table 10.1). Program staff members promoted regular deposits out of the belief that slow and steady wins the saving race, that is, if people set a saving goal and then consume the rest (rather than setting a consumption goal and then saving the rest), then they will make a greater effort to save in difficult months.
- Saving rate: On average, net deposits in IDAs were 1.5 percent of income at enrollment (median 0.5 percent). Across participants, the saving rate decreased as income increased. As discussed later, perhaps the institutional effects of IDAs are stronger than the economic effects of income, and perhaps these institutional effects are strongest for poorer people.

Table 10.4 Matched Withdrawals and Asset Accumulation in ADD

Line	Item	Formula	Value
Matched withdrawals (WD)			
Da	Matched WD	Data	$799,684
Db	# of matched WD	Data	2,154
Dc	Average matched WD	Da/Db	$371
Dd	# of participants with a matched WD	Data	821
De	Percentage of participants with a matched WD	$100 \times (Dd/Aa)$	35%
Df	# of matched WD per participants with a matched WD	Db/Dd	2.6
Dg	Matched WD per participants with a matched WD	Da/Dd	$974
Dk	Average match rate on matched WD	Data	1.78
Dh	Matched WD plus match	Data	$2,226,067
Di	Average matched WD plus match	Dh/Db	$1,033
Dj	Average matched WD plus match per participants with a matched WD	Dh/Dd	$2,711
Matchable balance			
Dl	Matchable balance	Ca – Da	464,847.38
Dm	Average match rate for matchable balance	Data	2.08
Dn	Matchable balance plus match	$Dl \times (1 + Dm)$	$1,431,394

Source: MIS IDA. Means are ratios of averages.

- Utilization: On average, participants used 50 percent of their match eligibility (median 21 percent).
- IDAs and EITC: Each year, net deposits in IDAs spiked in tax season (figure 10.1). Participants likely save a chunk of tax refunds and/or the Earned Income Tax Credit (EITC); some programs in ADD explicitly encourage this. Beverly et al., chapter 9 in this volume; Smeeding, chapter 16 in this volume; and Souleles (1999) support the idea that saving is easier from tax refunds and the EITC than from "regular" income.
- IDAs and deadlines: About 48 percent of participants had annual deadlines; for example, they could make up to $750 of matchable deposits each year for three years. The other 52 percent had "lifetime" deadlines; for example, they could make up to $2,250 of matchable deposits any time in three years. Figure 10.2 reveals two patterns. First, all participants—regardless of the type of deadline—saved more at the start than at the end. Various explanations are

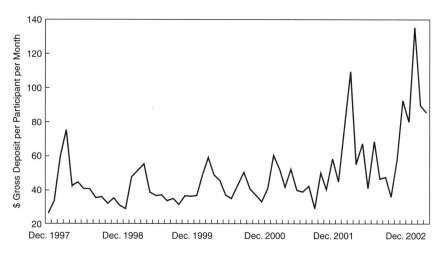

Figure 10.1 Deposits in IDAs spike in tax season. *Source:* MIS IDA and calculations by authors.

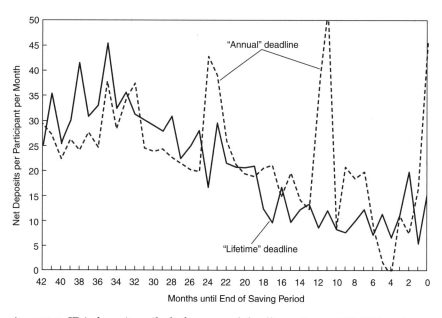

Figure 10.2 IDA deposits spike before annual deadlines. *Source:* MIS IDA and calculations by authors.

possible, including waning enthusiasm, concentration of staff support and financial education at the beginning, and/or shrinking stocks of assets to reshuffle into IDAs. Second, figure 10.2 shows that saving by participants with annual deadlines spiked in the twelfth month of each year. Perhaps annual deadlines help poor people save in IDAs (just as they help nonpoor people save in IRAs) by forcing them to make a use it or lose it decision that cannot be put off.

Questions and Discussion

Can the poor save in IDAs? Participants in ADD saved about $21 per month, made deposits about every other month, and saved about $1 for every $2 that could be matched. With a match rate of 1.78:1, average accumulation in IDAs was about $700 per year.

The possibility that the poor—even the very poor—can save cannot be dismissed. IDAs may have the potential to boost saving and asset accumulation by some poor people.

Did the poor take full advantage of IDAs? On average, participants in ADD left about $470 in matches unused each year. Yet poor savers in IDAs are not so different from nonpoor savers in IRAs. For example, 90 percent of eligible people in a given year do not contribute to IRAs (Bernheim, 1997). Among IRA contributors, one-third save the maximum amount in three straight years; in IDAs in ADD, exactly one-third of savers saved the maximum amount.

Do the poor save more with IDAs than without them? Research using MIS IDA data was not set up to answer this question.

Are IDAs enough to make a difference? For the nonpoor, a few hundred dollars—or even a few thousand dollars—may not seem like much. Participants in ADD do use IDAs, however, to buy assets expected to have high returns and that mark key steps in the life course. Perhaps more important, participants say in qualitative research that IDAs improve their outlooks. Perhaps what matters is not only the amount saved but also the process and the simple existence of a savings account.

For perspective, median liquid assets at enrollment were $125 (outliers make the median more representative than the mean; see Schreiner, Clancy, and Sherraden, 2002). Median illiquid assets (mostly houses and cars) were $2,500; debt was $2,875; and net worth was $360. (Median net worth is not median assets minus median liabilities.) If all net deposits were used in matched withdrawals, the average participant will have accumulated $1,554 in IDAs ($2,886 for savers.) Thus, as a share of assets, IDA accumulations are large, even if all IDA deposits were reshuffled.

Why were unmatched withdrawals so common and so large? The MIS IDA data do not answer this question, but at least two explanations are possible. First, some participants may just barely subsist and have highly variable income and/or expenses. If income drops (or if expenses spike, perhaps due to job loss or illness), then short-term needs may outweigh the long-term opportunity costs of not saving as much as possible in IDAs. Second, some participants may be shortsighted.

Should IDA programs restrict unmatched withdrawals? If, at enrollment, participants worry that they might later succumb when tempted to make withdrawals for consumption, then they might welcome restrictions on unmatched withdrawals. Indeed, Moore et al. (2001) report that some ADD participants seem to appreciate informal restrictions on unmatched withdrawals. Still, recurrent emergencies are a fact of life for the poor. One of the few ways that IDAs might do harm would be to put the cash of the poor out of their reach. Perhaps IDA programs could offer, at enrollment or afterward, the choice (but not the requirement) to put some deposits in an IDA with greater restrictions. Another option is to offer a second account, labeled "For Emergencies," alongside the IDA. This might encourage participants to see IDAs as long-term savings.

Why were there so many low savers? Given the supportive context of IDAs, the number of low savers—like the number of unmatched withdrawals—was surprising. Of course, saving will never be easy for the poor, and some share of low savers is inevitable, but three changes to policy and program design might help. First, permanent access to IDAs would make the issue moot, as everyone would always have an IDA, even if the balance were zero. People could use IDAs when they were ready. Second, some programs in ADD kicked people out for low or infrequent deposits. This freed up match funds for other participants, but if the goal of IDAs is long-term improvement in well-being, then it makes little sense to cut off access precisely to those for whom saving is the most difficult. Not all people will save the same amount in the same length of time, but this does not mean that low savers would not benefit from greater access to subsidized savings. Third, programs could identify factors linked with low savers to channel extra attention to them at the outset of their membership (Schreiner and Sherraden, 2002).

AMONG THE POOR, WHO SAVES IN IDAs?

This section looks at how participants' characteristics were associated with savings outcomes in IDAs. The question of whether IDAs are better suited to some people matters for two reasons. First, IDAs might be universal or targeted (e.g., only to the "working poor"). Second, because IDAs require participants to save, some worry that IDAs may work only for the most advantaged of the poor. ADD suggests that although more advantaged people sometimes save more than others, even relatively disadvantaged people can still save in IDAs.

Comparison with the General U.S. Low-Income Population

Compared with people in households in the U.S. Census Bureau's September 1995 *Survey of Income and Program Participation* with income at or below

200 percent of the family-size adjusted poverty threshold, participants in ADD were better educated, more likely to be employed, and more likely to have a bank account. This probably reflects how programs in ADD targeted the "working poor." Participants are also more likely to be female (80 percent), African American (47 percent), or never married (49 percent, with 86 percent of these women with children). This reflects how programs in ADD targeted the disadvantaged among the "working poor."

Demographic and Socioeconomic Characteristics

Two regressions were used to link a wide range of participant and program characteristics—first, with the likelihood of being a saver (probit regression), and then, for savers, with AMND, that is, the level of average monthly net deposits (ordinary least squares regression). The two steps help control for unobserved factors that might influence AMND (Schreiner, Clancy, and Sherraden, 2002). Because of possible two-way causation between IDA participation and economic characteristics, the regressions use data collected at the time of enrollment. To control for possible two-way causation between programs' characteristics and programs' expectations of participant behavior (as well as other program-level unobserved characteristics), both regressions include programs' fixed effects. The least-squares regression does not control for censoring of desired savings at the match cap.

Missing values were handled with zero-order regression. The probit was significant at $p = 0.01$, and R^2 in the least-squares regression was 0.36. A series of tables report the results from the two regressions that are relevant to this chapter. Full results, including additional tables, are available from the authors on request.

Gender

About 80 percent of participants in ADD were female. Gender was not associated with the likelihood of being a saver or with AMND for savers (table 10.5).

Race/Ethnicity

About 47 percent of participants in ADD were African American, 37 percent Caucasian, 9 percent Hispanic, 3 percent Native American, 2 percent Asian American, and 3 percent "Other." In the probit saver regression, Asian Americans and "other" ethnicities were 17 and 16 percentage points more likely to be savers than Caucasians. Native Americans were 13 percentage points less likely to be savers. Caucasians, African Americans, and Hispanics had about the same likelihood of being savers. In the least-squares AMND regression, the only significant estimate is that African Americans save about $6 less per month than Caucasians.

Of course, these associations are due not to race and/or ethnicity per se, but rather to a constellation of socially produced unobserved factors

Table 10.5 Regression Relationships among Gender, Race/Ethnicity, Education, and Employment for Being a Saver and, for Savers, the Level of Savings

Independent Variable	Probability Saver			AMND for Savers		
	Mean	Δ % pt.	*p*-value	Mean	Δ$	*p*-value
Gender						
Male	0.20			0.22		
Female	0.80	2.9	0.38	0.78	0.09	0.95
Race/ethnicity						
Native American	0.03	−13.3	0.07	0.02	−3.7	0.38
African American	0.47	−2.6	0.45	0.39	−5.9	0.01
Caucasian	0.37			0.43		
Hispanic	0.09	7.9	0.13	0.10	2.6	0.30
Other	0.03	16	0.04	0.03	1.1	0.76
Asian American	0.02	17	0.08	0.03	0.5	0.90
Education						
Did not graduate from high school	0.16			0.13		
Completed high school or earned GED	0.25	−0.1	0.99	0.22	1.18	0.58
Attended college but did not graduate	0.37	5.8	0.13	0.37	0.24	0.91
Graduated from 2-year college	0.04	−0.9	0.90	0.03	−4.5	0.24
Graduated from college (2-year/ 4-year unspecified)	0.11	17	0.01	0.14	1.25	0.65
Graduated from 4-year college	0.07	23	0.01	0.11	2.2	0.48
Employment						
Unemployed	0.05			0.04		
Employed, full-time (>35 hours per week)	0.59	6.0	0.30	0.60	1.8	0.55
Employed, part-time (<35 hours per week)	0.23	7.1	0.23	0.23	4.8	0.13
Not working (homemakers, retired, disabled)	0.04	2.8	0.72	0.05	−2.4	0.54
Student, not working	0.06	−1.4	0.85	0.04	9.0	0.03
Student, also working	0.03	22	0.01	0.03	5.7	0.23

Note: Means taken over only nonmissing observations. AMND = average monthly net deposit.

(sedimented through centuries) that have come to be linked with both saving and race/ethnicity. In a perfect model that controlled for everything, the estimated link between race/ethnicity and savings would be zero.

In the regressions here, observed factors explain about 80 percent of the gap. Even 20 percent, however, is large. Most analyses attribute to discrimination any differences in outcomes correlated with unobserved factors that are correlated with race/ethnicity. This is correct, but it forgets that differences in outcomes correlated with observed factors correlated with race/ethnicity are also due to discrimination. With more data, the correlation between outcomes and unobserved factors would shrink, but not because discrimination decreased. In the end, what matters are inclusive improvements in long-term well-being. This requires policies that shrink the gaps in observed and unobserved factors and, thus, lead to smaller gaps in savings and asset accumulation.

Do IDAs help narrow these gaps? The MIS IDA data do not reveal whether disadvantaged groups increased their savings more than other groups or even whether IDAs increased savings for anyone. It is virtually impossible, however, for IDAs to have worsened the African American to Caucasian wealth ratio. For example, the average Caucasian in ADD participated for 27.5 months, and the average African American participated for 24.4 months. With a match rate of 1.78:1, the worst case is that all IDA deposits from African Americans ($12.94 per month) came from shifted assets and that all deposits from Caucasians ($23.11) came from new savings. Even so, the ratio of net worth for participants in ADD in these two groups would fall from about 5.3:1 at enrollment ($5,486 for Caucasians vs. $1,037 for African Americans) to about 4.5:1 ($7,253 vs. $1,600) at the end of ADD, although, in this example, the absolute gap increases. IDAs do not pretend to be a panacea for racial/ethnic gaps in wealth, but they do seem to have improved equity in at least some ways, and they certainly can improve access to institutionalized saving mechanisms for the poor regardless of race/ethnicity. Still, much more could be done, including within IDA programs.

Education

About 84 percent of ADD participants had completed high school, and 24 percent had some type of college degree. Broadly, participants with a college degree were much more likely to be savers, but education was not linked with AMND.

Employment

Because programs in ADD tended to target the "working poor," most participants were employed; 78 percent worked full-time or part-time. Compared with the unemployed, students who were working were more likely to be savers (by 25 percentage points) and students who were not working saved about $8 more per month. These very large associations matter because educational accounts may be an important policy option.

Receipt of Public Assistance

About 51 percent of participants in ADD received some type of public assistance—AFDC, TANF, food stamps, and/or SSI/SSDI—at or before enrollment. Controlling for other factors in the regressions, the receipt of public assistance was not correlated with savings outcomes (table 10.6). While not conclusive, this bodes well for the possibility that even the very poor can save in IDAs (Zhan, Sherraden, and Schreiner, 2004).

Income

On average, participants in ADD were at 116 percent of the poverty line (median 106 percent). About 88 percent of participants were below 200 percent of poverty. In regressions, income was not strongly linked with being a saver or with AMND. (The two statistically significant coefficients in

Table 10.6 Regression Relationships on Receipt of Public Assistance and Income for Being a Saver and, for Savers, the Level of Savings

	Probability Saver			AMND for Savers		
Independent Variable	Mean	Δ % pt.	*p*-value	Mean	Δ$	*p*-value
Receipt of public assistance						
TANF or AFDC never	0.62			0.64		
TANF or AFDC formerly	0.38	−0.3	0.92	0.36	−1.81	0.21
TANF currently	0.10	−3.8	0.43	0.08	1.74	0.53
No SSI/SSDI	0.89			0.89		
Receives SSI/SSDI	0.11	2.8	0.58	0.11	2.60	0.30
No food stamps	0.83			0.84		
Receives food stamps	0.17	6.07	0.15	0.16	−3.1	0.18
Household income ($ monthly)						
Total income	$1,377			$1,418		
Recurrent income (spline)	$1,154			$1,153		
0 to $800	$666	−0.0071	0.32	$654	0.0037	0.31
$801 to $1,600	$363	0.0001	0.98	$362	−0.0002	0.96
$1,601 or more	$125	0.0030	0.54	$137	0.0059	0.01
Intermittent income	$223	0.0047	0.17	$266	0.0051	0.01

Note: Means taken over only nonmissing observations.

table 10.6 are very small.) Furthermore, across participants, the savings rate fell as income rose; the very poor saved a greater share of income in IDAs than did the less poor. Economic theory (Deaton, 1992) and U.S. data (Wolff, 1998) would not predict this.

What explains this? First, a host of measurement issues tends to depress measured income more for the very poor than for the less poor (Schreiner et al., 2001); this might induce a spurious negative correlation between income and the savings rate. Second, censoring of desired savings at the match cap could also induce a spurious negative correlation. Third, the institutional features of IDAs—matches, targets, deadlines, direct deposit, financial education, and staff support—may have not only overshadowed the economic effect of income but also been strongest for the very poor (Sherraden, Schreiner, and Beverly, 2003). For example, the pull of the savings target may be greater for those furthest away. Likewise, the match is a larger share of total resources for the very poor than for the less poor. Furthermore, the very poor may have more to learn about how or why to save; therefore, in response to a given level of financial education, they may change their behavior more dramatically. Likewise, the very poor may have a greater need for social support. All three factors—measurement noise, censoring, and institutional effects—probably are at work, but the MIS IDA data cannot disentangle them. Still, the broad lesson is that less income did not imply less savings in IDAs.

Assets

ADD participants who had saved in the past—as shown by the presence at enrollment of a checking account, a home, or a car—were much more likely to be savers, although, given that they were savers, they did not save more (table 10.7). Furthermore, the likelihood of being a saver increased (up to a point) with the balance in savings and checking accounts. (Ownership of a passbook account, regardless of balance, was associated with a lower likelihood of being a saver and a decrease in AMND.) MIS IDA does not reveal why past savers had more success: perhaps they had more assets to reshuffle, perhaps they were more comfortable with banks, or perhaps the presence of past savings marked unobserved characteristics that also led to higher IDA savings. In any case, the results do not suggest that people who have not already saved cannot save in IDAs (clearly some can and do), but it does suggest that people who have already saved successfully in other forms tend also to have more success in IDAs.

Debts

Participants with debt, regardless of the kind or amount, were about 7 percentage points less likely to be savers and, if they were savers, they saved

Table 10.7 Regression Results on Assets and Liabilities for Being a Saver
and, for Savers, the Level of Savings

Independent Variable	Probability Saver			AMND for Savers		
	Mean	Δ % pt.	p-value	Mean	Δ$	p-value
Liquid assets						
Possession of a passbook savings account						
No	0.50			0.45		
Yes	0.50	−6.7	0.03	0.55	−3.1	0.06
Balance in passbook savings	$220			$282		
$1 to $700 (spline)	124	0.04	0.01	158	0.01	0.30
$701 to $2,200	76	−0.01	0.10	98	0.00	0.38
$2,201 or more	20	−0.01	0.57	26	0.01	0.43
Possession of a checking account						
No	0.36			0.25		
Yes	0.64	11	0.01	0.75	0.11	0.95
Balance in checking	$213			$283		
$1 to $1,500 (spline)	193	0.01	0.01	253	0.00	0.44
$1,501 or more	20	−0.01	0.47	29	0.00	0.39
Nonliquid assets						
Renter	0.84			0.77		
Home owner	0.16	13	0.02	0.23	3.4	0.17
No car	0.35			0.27		
Car owner	0.65	9.2	0.01	0.73	−0.1	0.98
Value of nonliquid assets	$12,864	0.00	0.40	$18,167	0.00	1.00
Liabilities						
No debt	0.32			0.31		
Some debt	0.68	−6.7	0.03	0.69	−2.3	0.15
Value of liabilities	$9,797	0.00	0.13	$12,987	0.00	0.19

Note: Means taken over only nonmissing observations.

$2.30 less per month. ADD reinforces the commonsense idea that debt inhibits saving.

Other Factors

The regressions controlled for a host of other participant characteristics, which, to conserve space, are not discussed here. Detailed results are available from the authors on request.

HOW DO IDAs WORK?

Links between saving and the institutional structure of IDAs matter for two reasons. First, asset accumulation depends not only on personal tastes but also on the constraints and opportunities afforded by institutions (Sherraden, 1991). Second, policy can affect institutions.

This section looks at five institutional aspects of IDAs. First, the presence of a match, apart from its economic incentives, may signal that saving is worthwhile. Second, people may mentally change the match cap, which is technically a limit, into a goal, so higher match caps might lead to higher savings. Third, an annual deadline may help participants avoid procrastination. Fourth, although economic models often assume that there is no need for learning, financial education may increase knowledge of the techniques and benefits of saving and thus help people change their behavior. Fifth, direct deposit may help people make regular saving automatic and, thus, protect them from being tempted to spend all of their paycheck.

The same two-step regressions discussed in the previous section were used to link the likelihood of being a saver (probit regression) and the level of savings for savers (least-square regression) to match rates, savings targets, deadline types, direct deposit, and financial education.

Match Rates

In ADD, 29 percent of participants had a match rate of 1:1, 52 percent had 2:1, 16 percent 3:1, and 6 percent had from 4:1 to 7:1. In economic theory, higher match rates increase saving, known as the "substitution effect," because consumption becomes more expensive relative to saving. Higher match rates also, however, decrease saving, known as the "income effect," because a lower level of saving is needed to reach a given level of asset accumulation. The net effect is ambiguous. The consensus in studies of 401(k) plans (Schreiner, 2001) is that the presence of a match boosts participation but that higher match rates—at least in excess of 0.25:1 or so—do not increase (and may decrease) contributions.

Regardless of the effects of institutions and economics, the censoring of desired savings at the match cap damps any measured correlation between match rates and savings. Although one-third of savers in ADD were at the match cap, this analysis does not control for censoring.

Institutional effects and substitution effects lead to a positive link between match rates and AMND, but income effects and censoring dampen the link and may turn it negative.

Match Rates and Savers

For the likelihood of being a saver, censoring and income effects are irrelevant. Compared with match rates of 1:1, match rates of 4:1 to 7:1 were strongly linked with a greater likelihood of being a saver (table 10.8). Other

Table 10.8 Regression Results on Institutional Aspects for Being a Saver and, for Savers, the Level of Savings

Independent Variable	Probability Saver			AMND for Savers		
	Mean	Δ % pt.	p-value	Mean	Δ$	p-value
Match rate						
1:1	0.29			0.30		
2:1	0.52	7	0.14	0.49	−9.1	0.01
3:1	0.16	12	0.17	0.17	−8.7	0.07
4:1 to 7:1	0.06	15	0.06	0.06	−12.7	0.01
Match cap						
Monthly savings target	42	0.22	0.04	42	0.64	0.01
Match-cap structure						
Annual deadlines	0.52			0.49		
Lifetime deadlines	0.48	1.4	0.84	0.51	7.6	0.04
Use of direct deposit to IDA account						
No	0.94			0.92		
Yes	0.06	19	0.01	0.08	−1.7	0.51
Hours of general financial education						
Total (spline)	12.4			13.1		
More than zero					1.8	0.78
1 to 10	9.5			9.9	1.0	0.03
11 to 20	2.3			2.7	0.07	0.79
21 or more	0.6			0.6	0.32	0.27

Note: Means taken over only nonmissing observations.

regressions with different baselines—not shown here—show that match rates of 2:1 and 3:1 are also associated with a greater likelihood of being a saver. Because institutional effects and/or substitution effects are the only forces in play, these results make sense, and they also fit experience in 401(k) plans. Higher matches increase the opportunity cost of not saving and so increase the likelihood of saving something.

Match Rates and Savings

In the regression, savers with a match rate of 1:1 saved about $9 more than savers with 2:1 or 3:1 match rates and about $12.70 more than savers with match rates from 4:1 to 7:1 (table 10.8). Apparently, income effects and censoring drowned out substitution effects and institutional effects. For participants with fixed accumulation goals (such as a down payment for a house), a higher match rate allows reaching the goal with less savings.

Savings Targets

Deposits up to the match cap are eligible for matches. The monthly savings target is the match cap divided by the months in which matchable deposits are possible. Calling this a target reflects both that participants may change caps into targets and that many programs in ADD advised participants to try to deposit this amount each month.

The average monthly savings target in ADD was $42, and average AMND was about half that. In the regressions, higher targets were strongly linked both with a greater likelihood of being a saver and, for savers, with higher AMND (table 10.8). The following factors may explain this.

- Institutional effects in which participants change limits into goals. People challenged with a higher limit/goal may save more.
- Desired net deposits are often censored, inducing a spurious positive correlation between savings and match caps.

Deadlines

In theory, deadlines might matter in two opposing ways. First, annual deadlines might help procrastinators to save regularly; in fact, nearly every financial advisor believes that regular saving, as opposed to irregular saving, leads to greater accumulation. Second, "lifetime" deadlines might allow participants to make very large deposits whenever they receive large cash inflows. Still, because people with annual deadlines can have excess deposits in one year carried over and applied to the next year, the advantage of lifetime deadlines would seem small.

Table 10.8 shows, however, that participants in ADD with lifetime deadlines were 1.4 percentage points more likely to be savers and—if they were savers—they saved $7.60 more per month. The reasons for this are unclear.

Direct Deposit

In theory, direct deposit should improve savings outcomes, both because it allows the saver to avoid having to decide each month whether to save and because it reduces transaction costs. The MIS IDA data do not contain information on access (as opposed to use) to direct deposit in ADD. For participants, the use of direct deposit was associated with a greater likelihood of being a saver (a huge effect, 19 percentage points), although not with greater savings.

Financial Education

Besides matches, a key feature of IDAs is required financial education. Evidence from 401(k) plans (Bayer, Bernheim, and Scholz, 1996; Bernheim and Garrett, 1996) suggests that financial education increases the likelihood of participation (akin to being a saver) and that the effects are largest for lower-income employees and for those who saved little before.

In ADD, the broad goals of the general financial education classes were the following:

- Increase awareness of savings as a wise choice through discussion of long-term benefits
- Instill stronger future orientation through exercises in planning and budgeting
- Transfer practical techniques to find cash to save, to deposit it in IDAs, and to leave it in the account
- Communicate IDA rules
- Provide a setting for peer support and for the exchange of experiences

MIS IDA recorded hours attended by each participant (see Schreiner et al., 2001, for discussion of the financial education data in more detail). Average hours required were 12, and the average attendance was 10.4 hours.

Because participants who left ADD had fewer opportunities to attend financial education, the probit regression on the likelihood of being a saver omits hours of financial education. In the least-squares AMND regression, net deposits increased $1 per month per hour of general financial education, up to 10 hours. After that point, more general financial education had no effect. This suggests that some financial education improves saving outcomes. Furthermore, short courses may be just as effective as longer courses.

WHAT DO IDAs COST?

Wise allocation of scarce resources requires some knowledge of costs. All resources have opportunity costs; a dollar used in an IDA is a dollar removed (at least implicitly) from some other use. What matters is not that IDAs have benefits for participants, nor that IDAs have benefits for society as a whole. Rather, what matters is that the social net benefits of the use of resources in IDAs exceed the social net benefits of those resources in their alternative uses.

Cost data in MIS IDA for ADD are spotty and cannot be cross-checked. Furthermore, some programs sometimes failed to record cost data. Thus, this section focuses on some simple estimates at one site where a special cost study was undertaken. Costs are probably higher than in a "typical" IDA program, as this site was one of the first IDA programs and, as such, incurred extra expenses in start-up, policy work, and guidance for other IDA programs. Data collection for ADD itself added extra costs. The main results, according to Schreiner (2004), were the following:

- One month of participation for one participant cost (excluding matches) about $61.

- With net deposits of $20 per month, each dollar saved had a social cost of about $3.
- With an average match rate of 1.5:1, $1 of asset accumulation cost society about $1.82.

These estimates ignore nonfinancial costs as well as benefits of all kinds. They rest on a host of imprecise measurements, heroic assumptions, and back of the envelope guesses. They also ignore many aspects of the bundle of inputs and outputs that is an IDA. Finally, the margin of error is unknown.

Are costs high or low? There is no benchmark to judge (but see Ng, 2001). The ultimate criterion is whether benefits exceed costs, but benefits have not been measured. Furthermore, the possible efficiency of IDA programs is unknown. IDAs are young, and best practices continue to evolve. Still, measures of cost can inform policy even without measures of benefits by setting benchmarks and calling attention to efficiency (Schreiner and Yaron, 2002).

Although average costs did fall through time and even though these rough cost estimates may have upward biases, IDAs are still costly. For example, even if costs fell to $1 per dollar of net deposits, funders—in particular, the federal government, the only possible funder for a permanent, universal IDA policy—might have difficulty supporting IDAs with the current bundle of services and decentralized structure, even if social benefits do turn out to exceed costs.

At the same time, qualitative evidence from ADD suggests that participants place a high value on financial education and close contact with staff. The tension between the desire for intensive services and the cost structures that would allow for wide access may lead in the long term to two tiers of IDA designs, the first with broad access, simple services, and lower costs, complemented by a second tier with targeted access, intensive services, and higher costs (Sherraden, 2000).

SUMMARY AND POLICY DISCUSSION

To escape poverty requires asset accumulation. The United States has many policies that subsidize saving, but they often exclude the poor because they leverage existing wealth, operate via tax breaks, or require debt. IDAs are a new policy proposal meant to help the poor build assets without these requirements. Withdrawals from IDAs are matched if they are used to buy a home, pay for postsecondary education, or finance self-employment. Participants also receive financial education and support from IDA staff.

Summary of Results from ADD

The poor can save in IDAs. The 2,353 participants in ADD saved, on average, $20.71 per month. They made deposits in 6 of 12 months and used half of their match eligibility. Matched at 1.78:1, the average participant accumulated about $58 per month ($700 per year) in IDAs.

Even the very poor can save in IDAs. Participants in ADD were more advantaged than the low-income population in some ways but more disadvantaged others. In some aspects, such as asset ownership, participants who were less poor saved more than participants who were very poor. Gender, income, and receipt of public assistance, however, were not linked with savings outcomes. In fact, the share of income saved in IDAs was greater for the very poor than for the less poor. Part of the explanation may be that the institutional effects of receiving financial education and social support are strongest for the poorest.

Racial/ethnic wealth gaps remain. Members of all racial/ethnic groups saved in IDAs, but there were large gaps among groups. Although IDAs decreased the ratio of Caucasian net worth to African American net worth, the pattern of unequal outcomes is disturbing because it represents lost potential for asset building, particularly for African Americans and Native Americans. Future work should ask why this is and what might be done to improve inclusion.

Institutions matter. The institutional structure of IDAs—including match rates, savings target, deadline, direct deposit, and financial education—is strongly associated with savings outcomes. For example, higher match rates are linked with a greater likelihood of saving something but, given that something is saved, lower levels of savings. The likelihood of saving something also increases with the use of direct deposit. Each additional hour of financial education, up to 10 hours, is linked with a $1 increase in monthly net deposits.

IDAs are costly. IDAs cost a lot because programs provide high levels of personal service. In the long term, two tiers of programs seem likely, one with a universal, permanent, low-cost design, complemented by a second that offers greater services and costs more.

Policy Discussion

This final section discusses broad IDA policy issues, at times with speculations that go beyond the evidence from the MIS IDA data for ADD.

Do IDAs Harm the Poor?

Some worry that access to IDAs will cause the poor additional hardships. After all, saving does mean postponing consumption, so, at least in the short term, people who save also consume less and, all else constant, are worse off. Savers make a short-term sacrifice because they expect that it will improve their long-term well-being. Of course, saving can be overdone, but saving in IDAs is voluntary; no one is forced to participate, and unmatched withdrawals are possible at any time. ADD provides little evidence that matches in IDAs have enticed participants to harm themselves by saving too much. Income and the receipt of public assistance were both unrelated to saving outcomes in ADD, suggesting that even the very poor can save.

How Do Institutions Matter?

Institutional explanations of saving performance are useful because of their potential to lead to policy implications. While ADD shows that institutions matter and the research described in Schreiner et al. (2001) and Beverly and Sherraden (1999) offer bases from which to begin theory development, informing public policy and shaping program design require specific knowledge not only that institutions matter but also how they matter. Do the poor use IDAs because the match provides a high rate of return? Do they use IDAs because of the social and psychological incentives and opportunities through staff and peer support and through the message that assets matter even for the poor? Or do they use IDAs to help commit themselves to save through regular goals and implicit penalties for unmatched withdrawals? Most likely, all these institutional aspects matter, but how much each matters is unknown.

Will IDAs Replace Welfare?

Some worry that IDAs will siphon funds away from cash subsistence support for the poor. Some even worry that floating the idea that the poor can save will open the floodgates to arguments for doing away with cash assistance. Also, various coincidences and misunderstandings have led some lawmakers to see IDAs as welfare rather than asset building (Edwards and Mason, 2003). Of course, a dollar allocated to IDAs is a dollar not allocated elsewhere. Still, there is no evidence that funding IDAs has decreased funding for traditional welfare; indeed, funds for IDAs are a drop in the bucket compared to funds for cash assistance. Furthermore, states that fund IDAs do so only from Temporary Assistance for Needy Families (TANF) funds already earmarked for innovative or rainy day uses. As Sherraden writes, cash assistance is "absolutely essential" (1991, 294). Welfare aims to keep poor people from starving in the short term, while IDAs aim to help people develop in the long term.

How Long Should IDA Programs Last?

Sherraden's (1991) original IDA proposal calls for universal permanent accounts, opened at birth, with greater subsidies for the poor. In this sense, IDAs were never meant to be "programs" with ending dates any more than IRAs or 401(k) plans are. In practice, IDAs have been time limited because advances in the field, funded as demonstrations, have outstripped policy development (Edwards and Mason, 2003). If, however, the goal is to improve the long-term well-being of the poor, then many practices common in demonstrations—such as setting deadlines for matched withdrawals or kicking out low savers—are counterproductive. In contrast, IRAs and 401(k) plans do not kick out participants or suspend their tax benefits if they save small amounts or stop making contributions. A better design would allow IDA participants to save and hold balances for as long as they wish. Some participants would be content to save for years without making a matched withdrawal, sometimes depositing regularly, sometimes not depositing, and sometimes making unmatched withdrawals in emergencies. Ideally, everyone would have an account that would always be available to use, with annual statements—regardless of balance—that would act as gentle reminders of the possibility of saving.

NOTE

We thank the private foundations that fund the American Dream Demonstration (ADD): Ford, Charles Stewart Mott, Joyce, F. B. Heron, John D. and Catherine T. MacArthur, Citigroup, Fannie Mae, Levi Strauss, Ewing Marion Kauffman, Rockefeller, and the Moriah Fund. We also thank the Evaluation Advisory Board: Margaret Clark, Claudia Coulton, Kathryn Edin, John Else, Robert Friedman, Irving Garfinkle, Karen Holden, Laurence Kotlikoff, Robert Plotnick, Salome Raheim, Marguerite Robinson, Clemente Ruíz Durán, and Thomas Shapiro. Robert Friedman, founder and chair of the Corporation for Enterprise Development (CFED), conceived and produced ADD. Brian Grossman, René Bryce-Laporte, and other CFED staff have also supported the evaluation of ADD. Karen Edwards, Suzie Fragale, and Anupama Jacob provided consistently excellent managerial and editorial support. We are especially grateful to the host organizations in ADD and to their individual development account (IDA) staffs.

REFERENCES

Ackerman, B., and A. Alstott. (1999). *The Stakeholder Society*. New Haven, Conn.: Yale University Press.

Bayer, P. J., B. D. Bernheim, and J. K. Scholz. (1996). *The Effects of Financial Education in the Workplace: Evidence from a Survey of Employers*. National Bureau of Economic Research Working Paper No. 5655.

Bernheim, B. D. (1994). "Personal Saving, Information, and Economic Literacy: New Directions for Public Policy." In *Tax Policy for Economic Growth in the 1990s*. Washington, D.C.: American Council for Capital Formation, 53–78.

Bernheim, B. D. (1997). "Rethinking Savings Incentives." In *Fiscal Policy: Lessons from Economic Research*, ed. A. J. Auerbach. Cambridge, Mass.: The MIT Press, 259–311.

Bernheim, B. D., and D. M. Garrett. (1996). *The Determinants and Consequences of Financial Education in the Workplace: Evidence from a Survey of Households*. National Bureau of Economic Research Working Paper No. 5667.

Beverly, S. G., A. M. McBride, and M. Schreiner. (2003). "A Framework of Asset-Accumulation Strategies." *Journal of Family and Economic Issues* 24(2), 143–156.

Beverly, S. G., and M. Sherraden. (1999). "Institutional Determinants of Savings: Implications for Low-Income Households and Public Policy." *Journal of Socio-Economics* 28(4), 457–473.

Conley, D. (1999). *Being Black, Living in the Red: Race, Wealth, and Social Policy in America.* Berkeley: University of California Press.

Deaton, A. (1992). *Understanding Consumption.* Oxford, U.K.: Clarendon Press.

Edwards, K., and L. M. Mason. (2003). *State Policy Trends for Individual Development Accounts in the United States: 1993–2003.* St. Louis, Mo.: Center for Social Development (CSD), Washington University.

Friedman, R. (1988). *The Safety Net as Ladder.* Washington, D.C.: Council of State Policy and Planning Agencies.

Haveman, R. (1988). *Starting Even.* New York: Simon and Schuster.

Johnson, E., J. Hinterlong, and M. Sherraden. (2001). "Strategies for Creating MIS Technology to Improve Social Work Practice and Research." *Journal of Technology for the Human Services* 18(3/4), 5–22.

Lusardi, A. (2000). "Explaining Why So Many Households Do Not Save." Unpublished manuscript. University of Chicago.

Maital, S. (1986). "Prometheus Rebound: On Welfare-Improving Constraints." *Eastern Economic Journal* 12(3), 337–344.

Moore, A., S. Beverly, M. Schreiner, M. Sherraden, M. Lombe, E. Y.-Nei Cho, L. Johnson, and R. Vonderlack. (2001). *Saving, IDA Programs, and Effects of IDAs: A Survey of Participants.* Research report. St. Louis, Mo.: CSD, Washington University.

Ng, G. T. (2001). *Costs of IDAs and Other Capital-Development Programs.* Center for Social Development Working Paper No. 01-8. St. Louis, Mo.: CSD, Washington University.

Oliver, M. L., and T. M. Shapiro. (1995). *Black Wealth/White Wealth.* New York: Routledge.

Schreiner, M. (2001). *Match Rates and Savings: Evidence from Individual Development Accounts.* Center for Social Development Working Paper No. 01-6. St. Louis, Mo.: CSD, Washington University.

Schreiner, M. (2004). Program costs for individual development accounts: Final figures from CAPTC in Tulsa. Research Report. St. Louis, Mo.: CSD, Washington University.

Schreiner, M., M. Clancy, and M. Sherraden. (2002). *Savings Performance in the American Dream Demonstration: Final Report.* St. Louis, Mo.: CSD, Washington University.

Schreiner, M., and M. Sherraden. (2002). *Drop-out from Individual Development Accounts: Prediction and Prevention.* Center for Social Development Working Paper No. 02-2. St. Louis, Mo.: CSD, Washington University.

Schreiner, M., M. Sherraden, M. Clancy, L. Johnson, J. Curley, M. Grinstein-Weiss, M. Zhan, and S. Beverly. (2001). *Savings and Asset Accumulation in Individual Development Accounts.* St. Louis, Mo.: CSD, Washington University.

Schreiner, M., and J. Yaron. (2001). *Development Finance Institutions: Measuring Their Subsidy.* Washington, D.C.: World Bank.

Shapiro, T., and E. N. Wolff. (2001). *Assets for the Poor: The Benefits of Spreading Asset Ownership.* New York: Russell Sage Foundation.

Shefrin, H. M., and R. H. Thaler. (1988). "The Behavioral Life-Cycle Hypothesis." *Economic Journal* 26, 609–643.

Sherraden, M. (1988). "Rethinking Social Welfare: Toward Assets." *Social Policy* 18(3), 37–43.

Sherraden, M. (1991). *Assets and the Poor: A New American Welfare Policy.* Armonk, N.Y.: M. E. Sharpe.

Sherraden, M. (2000). "On Costs and the Future of Individual Development Accounts." St. Louis, Mo.: CSD, Washington University.

Sherraden, M., M. Schreiner, and S. Beverly (2003). "Income and Saving Performance in Individual Development Accounts." *Economic Development Quarterly* 17(1), 95–112.

Souleles, N. S. (1999). "The Response of Household Consumption to Income-Tax Refunds." *American Economic Review* 89(4), 947–958.

Thaler, R. H. (1994). "Psychology and Savings Policies." *American Economic Review* 84(2), 186–192.

U.S. Census Bureau. *Survey of Income and Program Participation.* Available at http://www.sipp.census.gov/sipp. Last accessed December 14, 2004.

Wolff, E. N. (1998). "Recent Trends in the Size Distribution of Household Wealth." *Journal of Economic Perspectives* 12(3), 131–150.

Zhan, M., M. Sherraden, and M. Schreiner. (2004). "Welfare Recipiency and Savings Outcomes in Individual Development Accounts." *Social Work Research* 28(3), 165–181.

11

The Impacts of IDA Programs
on Family Savings and Asset Holdings

Michael A. Stegman and Robert Faris

This chapter supplements the growing body of empirical analysis of the national individual development account (IDA) demonstration known as the American Dream Demonstration (ADD). The subject of the chapter is the financial impacts of ADD on the net savings and asset holdings of program participants. The methodological focus and unique contribution of this research lie in our efforts to answer the important counterfactual question of what ADD participants would have saved had they not joined an IDA program. Because it deals with a hypothesis, we cannot answer this question exclusively from program data and participant interviews. Until results of an IDA experiment become available, we must rely upon statistical analysis using a different counterfactual question.

The research strategy we employ has three steps. First, we use the 1998 national *Survey of Consumer Finances* (SCF) to create a pool of households that closely resemble ADD enrollees. We call this pool the national IDA population (NIP). Next, we estimate a statistical model of the savings behavior of NIP, and apply the parameters of that model to each ADD participant to generate what we refer to as that individual's predicted savings trajectory. A savings trajectory is an estimate of the amount of money a given ADD participant would have saved if she or he had not enrolled in an IDA program, controlling for the duration of the enrollment period. Then we subtract individual savings trajectories from actual ADD balances to determine what we refer to as the savings effects of ADD.

The first section of the chapter addresses the conceptual question of whether bank balances are an adequate proxy for household savings. The second section discusses how we reweighted the 1998 national SCF, which contains a rich array of data on the savings and assets of American families, to conform to the asset profile of the ADD population. This is the first step in modeling the savings behavior of the national IDA population. We discuss the development of our econometric model of family savings in the third section.

Next, we use our model to generate estimates of the savings and asset effects of ADD on different types of families and then employ a fixed effects regression model to quantify the influence of family and program characteristics on participant savings. The next section addresses the issue of fungibility and the impacts that the substitution of IDA savings for non-IDA savings might have on the net savings and asset holdings of ADD enrollees. We then assess the impact of IDAs on unbanked participants and finally present our conclusions.

A MODEL OF SAVINGS OR BANK ACCOUNT BALANCES?

The dependent variable in our savings model, which we use to estimate the financial impacts of ADD, is average annual savings, defined as the combined balance of all bank accounts owned by a household, divided by the age of the primary account in years. Given the low returns on such accounts and the proliferation of higher-yield investment opportunities that span the risk-reward spectrum, some might question our decision to base our savings model on such a restrictive concept of household savings. We decided to use combined account balances for our analysis for two reasons. First, through the provision of matching funds from program sponsors, IDA programs encourage participants to make periodic deposits into special purpose, low-interest savings accounts. The fact is, ADD is a bank account driven program, designed to encourage and reward low-income households for establishing a culture of saving—not an initiative in portfolio diversification. Second, and more important, this is the way most Americans who resemble ADD participants actually save. Nearly two-thirds of the national IDA population—whose makeup we discuss below—hold large proportions of their financial assets in savings and checking accounts. In fact, 40 percent hold all of their financial assets in such accounts, while an additional 22 percent have no financial assets[1] at all. For most of the 38 percent of these IDA-eligibles who do hold financial assets beyond their bank accounts, the value of these assets is less than $2,000. This is also true for ADD participants: 53 percent hold all of their financial assets in bank accounts, 18 percent have no financial assets at all, while just 29 percent own financial assets beyond their account balances. Moreover, the majority of the latter own less than $2,500 in nonbank financial assets.

The national IDA population and ADD participants are also closely matched on their ownership of non-financial assets. Among the total IDA population, 57 percent have no nonfinancial assets at all; 43 percent own productive nonfinancial assets[2] of some kind; and, of that 43 percent, 37 percent claim their cars are their only nonfinancial asset. Among ADD participants, 31 percent have no nonfinancial assets at all, 69 percent own productive nonfinancial assets of some kind, and of that 69 percent, 45 percent have only a car. In short, because bank account balances reflect the vast majority of household savings for both the national IDA population and ADD participants, we base our model of household savings on combined savings and checking account balances.

DEVELOPING A NATIONAL COUNTERPART TO THE ADD POPULATION

Because our impact analysis heavily relies upon our estimates of the savings behavior of what we call the national IDA population, it is very important that this population closely conform to the profile of ADD participants. This is because we use the actual behavior of the IDA population in our statistical procedures to estimate the impacts of ADD on participants' savings and asset holdings.[3] Specifically, our estimating procedure assumes that, in the absence of ADD, IDA holders would save amounts similar to the non-ADD participants who compose our national IDA population, controlling for socioeconomic and other characteristics. As mentioned in the introduction to this chapter, we reweighted the national SCF, using the distribution of assets owned by the ADD population, resulting in a weighted subsample of SCF households that has a nearly identical distribution of assets. Inasmuch as ADD is a program targeted to lower-income, low-wealth individuals with little savings, we could have based our national IDA population on weights, using either the actual distribution of household income and/or asset ownership of the ADD population. We chose to base the new SCF weights on assets because, when applied to the SCF sample, weights based on income did not perform well.[4]

The weights were computed by multiplying the existing SCF weights[5] by a ratio adjustment. This was done as follows: the weighted counts of respondents in the SCF data were grouped into 50 adjustment cells, defined by the asset variable (e.g., $0–$250, $251–$500, and so on). The counts for ADD respondents were also grouped into these categories. For each cell, the ratio adjustment was calculated by

$$postwt_i = \frac{ADD_i}{WTSCF_i} \tag{1}$$

where ADD_i is the count for ADD in that cell and $WTSCF_i$ is the SCF count, using the original SCF weight. The final weight is then defined as follows:

$$fw_i = postwt_i * wt_i \tag{2}$$

where wt_i is the original SCF weight. The final weight gives the SCF data a distribution identical to the ADD data along the discrete asset categories.

The distributions according to a continuous measure of assets are also nearly identical. While closely matched on assets—the national IDA population has median assets of $2,700, compared with $2,600 for ADD participants—the two populations differ in other ways. While the overall median incomes of the two populations are not too divergent—$15,942 for the national IDA population versus $13,176 for ADD participants—African American ADD participants have a much higher median income than one would expect, based upon their asset holdings. Moreover, ADD participants are more likely to be black, single women, and in their thirties and forties than their national IDA counterparts. ADD participants are also substantially less likely to be high school dropouts or over 50 years old (tables of ADD data are available from the authors upon request).[6]

While the national IDA sample is, on the whole, very similar to the population of ADD participants on known dimensions, there exists the possibility of unobserved heterogeneity—that the two differ along unknown dimensions. Because these factors cannot be observed or controlled for, our analysis assumes that there is no significant heterogeneity across the two populations that is not already captured by the many socioeconomic and other variables we include in our model.

ESTIMATING SAVINGS TRAJECTORIES

To reiterate, the question we attempt to answer in this chapter is what would ADD participants have saved had they not joined an IDA program? Not all of the information we need to address this issue is speculative in nature. For instance, using information collected from program management information systems (MIS IDA) across the fourteen ADD sties, we know participants' combined bank account balances at the time of enrollment, the amount of money thus far deposited in their IDA accounts, and their socioeconomic characteristics.

However, because our information on non-IDA bank balance(s) is only collected at the time of enrollment and is not regularly updated, we have no way of knowing whether participants are saving any money outside their IDA accounts during their time in ADD. Nor do we know whether their IDA deposits represent net new savings or merely the transfer of money from non-IDA bank accounts—where their deposits earn no matching funds— into IDA accounts, where every dollar they deposit is matched by at least one additional dollar. While we can simulate the impacts of fungibility on net household savings, which we explain later, in order to proceed with our analysis, we have to assume that during their time in ADD, all net participants' savings are reflected in their ADD balances (that is, they are not making any new deposits to a non-IDA account). We think that this is a reasonable assumption, given participants' low incomes and low preenrollment bank balances, as well as the financial benefits of concentrating all net new savings in IDA accounts that earn substantial matching funds.

We address the issue of how much ADD participants would have saved were they not enrolled in an IDA program by first regressing average annual savings of banked national IDA households on a variety of socioeconomic variables. We then apply the parameter estimates to ADD participants, generating predicted savings of ADD participants. Finally, to estimate the savings effects of ADD, we subtract the predicted savings of each ADD participant from the individual's IDA balance. We describe our estimating technique below.

Because the SCF is a cross-sectional database, we cannot observe savings over time. Instead, we estimate the effects of time on savings. Table 11.1 presents the results of an ordinary least squares (OLS) regression of household demographic and socioeconomic characteristics of the national IDA population on their combined account balances. In order to estimate savings trajectories, our model includes the number of years the household has held its current bank account(s),[7] which we also cause to interact with all of the other independent variables.[8] This model suggests that bank balances tend to increase with time and that this trend is more pronounced among several groups, including Hispanic and African American households, households with children, those with higher incomes and assets, and those with less debt. The rate of growth of account balances is slower among renters and households headed by older people.

Our estimates of higher savings trajectories for African Americans and Hispanics would appear to contradict other research studies, which generally find that minorities are less likely than whites to save and that whites tend to have higher bank balances than either blacks or Hispanics[9] (Carroll and Samwick, 1998; Kennickell, Starr-McCluer, and Surette, 2000). This apparent paradox can first be explained by the fact that our model estimates savings per time period, not total account balances, and second, that univariate statistics are not directly comparable to regression effects: We hold income and other socioeconomic factors constant. In our analysis, it is evident that part of the differences in savings balances between whites and minorities is explained by differences in the age of their respective bank accounts: The average account age for banked whites in the national IDA population is 10.1 years (15.0 for all banked whites), the average for African Americans is 7.4 years (11.3 for all banked African Americans), and for banked Hispanics in the national IDA population it is 6.4 years (8.5 for all banked Hispanics). These findings are important not only because they explain part of the disparity between the savings behavior of minorities and Caucasians, but they also suggest that, despite their lower current balances, African Americans and Hispanics may become more attractive and profitable banking customers over time.

In the fully specified model (that is, considering all of the interaction terms), we estimate that the median household in the national IDA population saves about $70 per year. We estimate that, including the effects of all other factors, the median annual savings of banked African American households is about one-third more ($93) than the overall median; that of whites about 10 percent less ($63); and that of Hispanics ($159) over twice the median (see table 11.2).

When we apply these trajectory coefficients to each ADD participant (table 11.3), we find similar results: The median household saves $69 a year, African American participants save somewhat more ($74), Caucasians

Table 11.1 Ordinary Least Square Regression of Bank Account Balances for Banked Households in the National IDA Population, 1998

Variable	Coefficient	Standard Error
Constant	662.98	(367.30)
Race (Caucasian is reference)		
African/American	−314.12*	(129.39)
Hispanic	−430.12*	(177.44)
Other minority	1732.54***	(230.36)
Household composition (unmarried couple is reference)		
Single female	256.06*	(124.64)
Single male	178.93	(147.59)
Married couple	−404.04**	(134.23)
Education (college graduate is reference)		
High school dropout	−302.00	(159.97)
High school graduate only	−786.49***	(123.37)
Attended college	−567.39***	(129.21)
Other socioeconomic variables		
Age	−85.50***	(13.70)
Age × age	0.93***	(0.14)
Number of children	−137.86**	(48.25)
Income ($ thousands)	47.12***	(4.91)
Income squared ($ millions)	−0.18***	(0.05)
Assets (excludes bank account assets) ($ thousands)	0.05***	(0.00)
Assets squared ($ millions)	0.0004	(0.00)
Debt ($ thousands)	−12.48*	(5.20)
Debt squared ($ millions)	−0.15**	(0.04)
Unemployed	247.68*	(126.17)
Receiving TANF	−12.50	(150.53)
Renter	1471.96***	(173.60)
Years using current bank	116.09**	(37.57)
Years at bank squared	1.60***	(0.29)
Interaction terms		
African American × years owning account	49.20***	(11.08)
Hispanic × years owning account	126.92***	(19.03)
Other × years owning account	3.91	(18.12)
Single female × years owning account	−1.92	(10.72)

(continued)

Table 11.1 (continued)

Variable	Coefficient	Standard Error
Single male × years owning account	14.14	(13.91)
Married couple × years owning account	10.14	(11.07)
High school dropout × years owning account	1.95	(11.81)
High school graduate × years owning account	12.26	(10.64)
Some college × years owning account	1.70	(11.50)
Age × years owning account	−3.62***	(1.22)
Age squared × years owning account	0.017	(0.01)
Number of children × years owning account	16.19***	(4.92)
Income × years owning account ($ thousands)	0.18	(0.24)
Income squared × years owning account ($ millions)	0.003***	(0.00)
Assets × years owning account ($ thousands)	0.0002**	(0.00)
Assets squared × years owning account ($ millions)	−0.0007***	(0.00)
Debt × years owning account ($ thousands)	−3.12***	(0.36)

Source: Federal Reserve Board, 1998. Microdata available at www.federalreserve.gov/pubs/oss/oss2/scfindex.html.
*p < .05, **p < .01, ***p < .001

Table 11.2 Predicted Annual Savings of National IDA Households, 1998

	25%	Median	75%
Overall	$0	$70	$131
Caucasian	$0	$63	$108
African American	$0	$93	$150
Hispanic	$0	$159	$218
Other minority	$0	$65	$110
Single female	$0	$81	$133
Single male	$0	$69	$106
Married couple	$0	$79	$141
Unmarried couple	$0	$50	$123

Source: U.S. Federal Reserve Board, 1998.
Note: N = 2,817. 25% = 25th percentile, 75% = 75th percentile.

Table 11.3 Predicted Annual Savings of ADD Participants, Net of IDA Participation, 2000

	All Participants			Active Participants			Inactive Participants		
	25%	Median	75%	25%	Median	75%	25%	Median	75%
Overall	$0	$69	$145	$9	$74	$156	$0	$46	$104
Caucasian	$6	$54	$115	$7	$55	$127	$0	$42	$76
African American	$0	$74	$148	$0	$81	$158	$0	$20	$110
Hispanic	$0	$170	$296	$51	$201	$311	$0	$111	$178
Other minority	$20	$66	$117	$16	$66	$121	$47	$85	$95
Single female	$1	$69	$142	$15	$73	$154	$0	$50	$106
Single male	$0	$75	$140	$5	$77	$149	$0	$65	$119
Married couple	$13	$84	$178	$13	$86	$183	$6	$71	$143
Unmarried couple	$0	$44	$109	$0	$57	$124	$0	$0	$56

Source: Center for Social Development, American Dream Demonstration, account monitoring data, 2000.
Note: N = 2,154 overall, 1,743 active. 25% = 25th percentile, 75% = 75th percentile.

somewhat less ($54), and Hispanics more than twice as much ($170).[10] Married couples ($84) are estimated to save more than single women ($69) or single men ($75), while unmarried couples save substantially less ($44). Finally, when controlling for their socioeconomic characteristics, the expected annual savings of active ADD participants differs only slightly from those of the whole ADD population.

Because 20 percent of all ADD participants are "inactive," with IDA balances of zero,[11] it is useful to separate results between active and inactive participants. When that is done, we see that the median predicted trajectory for active participants ($74) is roughly one-third larger than that of inactive participants ($46). This disparity remains across all racial/ethnic groups and by household composition (single male or single female/married couple or unmarried couple), although the differences are larger among some groups than others: The predicted trajectory of inactive Hispanics ($111) was just over half that of active Hispanics ($201), and the predicted trajectory of inactive African Americans ($20) is less than one-quarter of that of active African Americans ($81). This lends some support to the model specified in table 11.1, as it suggests that the variables associated with higher savings trajectories are also correlated with active participation in ADD.

To estimate the total amount that ADD participants would have saved had they not joined the program, we multiply the expected annual savings for each participant by the number of years in ADD. Since the average number of years is 1.11, the estimates of total savings are only slightly larger than those presented in table 11.3.

THE SAVINGS AND ASSET EFFECTS OF THE NATIONAL ADD DEMONSTRATION

Before proceeding further, it is useful to place into perspective the modest non-IDA savings estimates we applied to ADD participants above. Looking at combined (savings and checking) account balances in 1998 of all U.S. households by income quartile and race/ethnicity, the median balance for the lowest 20 percent of all banked American households, regardless of race or ethnicity—those with incomes below $13,176—have a median bank account balance of just $610. Given their lower incomes on average, 40 percent of all African American households fall into the bottom quintile of all incomes, and the median bank balance for this group is just $200. Among African Americans in the fourth quintile of all incomes, the median bank balance is $800. This same pattern is repeated for Hispanics. The median account balance for the 25 percent of all Hispanic households whose income places them in the bottom quintile for all households is just $400, and it is $800 for those in the fourth quintile.

The vast majority of ADD participants have incomes that would place them in the bottom 40 percent of all U.S. households, where the combined median bank balance is just $940—$1,100 for whites, $450 for African Americans, and $500 for Hispanics. Given these realities, it is not unreasonable to expect ADD participants to have savings trajectories like those reflected in table 11.2.

Consistent with these patterns, ADD participants' IDA balances, excluding all matching funds, are quite modest. The overall median IDA account balance, excluding inactive participants, is $316, and it is just $181 for blacks. Non-Hispanic whites, Hispanics, and ADD participants of "other" racial and ethnic backgrounds all have median balances that are roughly twice those of African Americans. Single women have a lower median IDA balance ($276) than married couples ($385), and banked participants have a median IDA balance ($361) that is more than twice that of those who were unbanked before they opened their IDA accounts ($151). College graduates and older participants also have higher IDA balances than their less educated or younger counterparts (Center for Social Development, 2000).

These patterns largely track those of monthly IDA contributions and are similar to those found by Mills et al. (2000) in other IDA programs. The median monthly deposit for all active ADD participants is $24, with African Americans' monthly contributions about 25 percent lower ($19). Hispanic and other minorities make greater monthly deposits than whites or African Americans ($34 and $33, respectively). College graduates, married couples, and older participants have higher monthly contributions than others (Center for Social Development, 2000).

Savings Effect

Using the savings trajectories generated from table 11.1, we can assess the actual impacts of ADD on participants' savings, which we call the savings effect of IDAs. This is simply the difference between what ADD participants actually saved and what we estimate they would have saved. The savings effect is calculated as follows:

$$\text{Savings Effect} = \text{IDA Balance} - (\text{Annualized Savings}$$

$$\times \text{Years in ADD}) \qquad (3)$$

where IDA balance is defined as total individual IDA contributions, excluding matching funds. Annualized Savings is derived from table 11.1, and Years in ADD is the number of years the participant has been enrolled in the IDA program, which is obtained from administrative program data.

Table 11.4 displays the predicted savings effects of IDAs by race/ethnicity and household composition. We estimate that the median ADD participant has saved $117 more than he or she would have saved had the individual not been enrolled in an IDA program. The average savings effect is almost two and one-half times greater at $285. This suggests not only that low-income people can save but that one or more of the resources (or all of them) involved in IDA programs—financial education, peer support and encouragement, an accessible and cooperating financial institution, along with financial inducements in the form of matches—provide effective ways of helping people get into the habit of saving. If we exclude inactive participants in our calculation of savings effects, the picture is even brighter. Fully half of all active ADD participants had additional savings of at least $236 over the amount they would have saved absent their IDAs, while the average boost to their overall savings was $368.

While IDAs appear to increase the savings of most participants, the magnitude of the increase varies significantly by race and marital status. At the

Table 11.4 Predicted Savings Effects of IDAs, 2000

	Percent Active Participants	All Participants			Active		
		25%	Median	75%	25%	Median	75%
Overall	80.5%	$0	$117	$467	$31	$236	$544
Caucasian	81.9%	$6	$257	$601	$100	$370	$695
African American	78.9%	−$6	$56	$293	$10	$112	$364
Hispanic	78.0%	−$13	$175	$532	$50	$303	$579
Other minority	86.6%	$8	$328	$676	$68	$403	$710
Single female	79.6%	−$1	$94	$410	$22	$198	$503
Single male	74.9%	−$36	$97	$469	$27	$277	$607
Married couple	84.0%	$0	$214	$592	$63	$313	$687
Unmarried couple	80.9%	$0	$101	$427	$26	$205	$508

Source: Center for Social Development, American Dream Demonstration, account monitoring data, 2000.
Note: N = 2,154 overall; 1,743 active. 25% = 25th percentile, 75% = 75th percentile.

median, African Americans experience dramatically lower savings effects than any racial or ethnic group ($56 overall, $112 for active participants). IDAs make a greater difference to whites ($257 overall, $370 active); Hispanics ($175 overall, $303 active); and other minorities ($328 overall, $403 active). Married couples ($214 overall, $313 active) also enjoyed greater savings effects than nonmarrieds—single women ($94 overall, $198 active); single men ($97 overall, $277 active); and unmarried couples ($101 overall, $205 active).

The importance of these positive estimates is enhanced when we consider that there are compelling reasons for IDA participants to save less than they would have otherwise saved. Because the ADD population is, for the most part, highly income constrained, it is understandable why some number of participants might reduce their "normal" rate of saving because of the availability of matches—after all, at the end of the day, they will still end up with more money in the bank than they would have but for the IDA. Only one-fifth of all ADD participants (20.9 percent) are estimated to have negative savings effects, with an average of – $91. If we exclude inactive participants, less than one-sixth (13 percent) experienced negative savings effects (see table 11.5).

Liquid Asset Effects

IDA programs have two related objectives: to encourage a new savings discipline among participants and simultaneously to help them build long-term assets. Whereas our measure of the savings effect of IDAs attempts to measure the former, the latter is captured in a measure that we call the liquid asset effect of ADD. The liquid asset effect speaks to the question of how much more money IDA holders end up with because of the highly leveraged nature of ADD, which includes substantial matching funds.

Table 11.5 Percent of ADD Participants with Negative Savings Effects, 2000

	Overall (Percent)	Active Participants (Percent)
Overall	20.9%	13.0%
Caucasian	16.6%	6.7%
African American	23.7%	17.7%
Hispanic	24.8%	15.9%
Other minority	19.6%	12.9%
Single female	22.5%	14.1%
Single male	24.6%	17.2%
Married couple	19.1%	10.2%
Unmarried couple	17.1%	12.1%

Source: Center for Social Development, American Dream Demonstration, account monitoring data, 2000.
Note: N = 2,154 overall, 1,743 active.

Specifically, the liquid asset effect (hereafter referred to as "asset effects" or "asset effect") is calculated as:

$$\text{Asset Effects} = [\text{IDA balance} + \text{match funds}]$$
$$- (\text{Annualized Savings} \times \text{Years in ADD}) \qquad (4)$$

Because some programs reward deposits with matches of more than \$2 or \$3 for every dollar an individual deposits from his or her own income, IDA programs produce significant asset effects. Overall, ADD participants enjoyed a median asset effect of \$559 and a mean asset effect of \$1,033 (see table 11.6). Active IDA participants have a much greater median asset effect of \$905 and a mean of \$1,288. This indicates that because of match funds and increased individual contributions, ADD participants have, on average, over \$1,000 more to invest in long-term assets than they would have if they had not actively participated in an IDA program.

Consistent with their lower contributions and IDA balances, black participants' asset effects are generally lower (\$326 overall, \$559 active)—though they are still significantly positive—than those of Caucasians, Hispanics, and other minorities. Married couples seem to enjoy larger asset effects (\$908 overall, \$1,208 active) than unmarried participants.

WHO BENEFITS MOST FROM ADD?

This section explores the relationship between savings effects of IDAs and participant and program characteristics. We use monthly savings effects as

Table 11.6 Liquid Asset Effects of IDAs, 2000

	Percent Active	All Participants			Active Participants		
		25%	Median	75%	25%	Median	75%
Overall ($N = 2,154$)	80.5%	$15	$559	$1,651	$219	$905	$1,871
Caucasian	81.9%	$57	$906	$2,023	$401	$1,191	$2,268
African American	78.9%	$0	$326	$1,154	$140	$559	$1,464
Hispanic	78.0%	$0	$924	$2,041	$579	$1,405	$2,291
Other minority	86.6%	$51	$1,027	$2,032	$346	$1,302	$2,319
Single female	79.6%	$9	$466	$1,514	$187	$803	$1,734
Single male	74.9%	$0	$400	$1,841	$155	$943	$2,213
Married couple	84.0%	$62	$908	$2,054	$386	$1,208	$2,316
Unmarried couple	80.9%	$20	$490	$1,572	$172	$793	$1,833

Source: Center for Social Development, American Dream Demonstration, account monitoring data, 2000.
Note: N = 2,154 overall, 1,743 active. 25% = 25th percentile, 75% = 75th percentile.

our dependent variable in order to capture changes in the rate at which savings effects change over time—either through a learning process through which the IDA holder internalizes a savings culture, or, possibly, as the IDA holder finds it increasingly difficult to save on a regular basis, with a resulting decline in saving over time.

One methodological problem we faced in this analysis was how to address the problem of inactive participants. We cannot employ a Heckman two-step model to control for categorical differences between active and inactive participants, because our dependent variable is incompatible with such a procedure. Inactive participants, who by definition have $0 IDA balances, do not necessarily have $0 savings effects. In fact, many inactive participants have negative savings effects, which means that they would have saved more had they not opened an IDA account and then failed to make any deposits.

Because of the distribution of our dependent variable, we chose to run a probit regression model, using the independent variables presented in table 11.7. We then included the predicted probability of active participation (from the probit) for each ADD participant in the OLS equation. Another methodological issue we address is that of unobserved heterogeneity among IDA programs, which we account for through a set of program dummy variables.

Before discussing our results, it is important to highlight the difference between our dependent variable and the analysis of IDA deposits or account balances, such as that covered by Mark Schreiner, Margaret Clancy, and Michael Sherraden (2002). Rather than focusing on the factors that are associated with greater IDA savings, our analysis speaks to factors that are associated with the relative impacts of ADD on participant savings. For example, it is possible that the receipt of welfare is associated both with smaller IDA contributions (Schreiner, Clancy, and Sherraden, 2002) and larger savings effects: Welfare recipients may contribute less than others to their IDA but, nonetheless, save substantially more than they would have saved had they not enrolled in ADD.

Consistent with our univariate findings, the savings effects of IDA programs vary substantially across racial and ethnic lines. Controlling for a large number of other factors, IDA programs have a more modest effect on the savings behavior of African Americans and Hispanics than of whites or other minorities. On average, the monthly savings effects for African Americans and Hispanics are, respectively, $10 and $8 less than that of whites. This does not imply that minorities are failing or not benefiting from ADD, nor that their IDA programs are failing them. Ignoring, for a moment, the fact that it is possible to achieve asset-building success (which includes matching funds) while saving less of one's own money than would otherwise be the case, the race/ethnicity coefficients in our model do not imply that African Americans and Hispanics have negative savings effects—only that they experience lower savings effects than whites or other minorities.[12]

Table 11.7 OLS Regression of Monthly Savings Effects, 2000

Variable	Coefficient	Standard Error
Constant	−13.11	(11.88)
Ethnicity (Caucasian is reference)		
African American	−9.65***	(2.01)
Hispanic	−7.72*	(3.03)
Other minority	−1.52	(3.04)
Household composition (unmarried couple is reference)		
Single female	0.30	(2.01)
Single male	−0.58	(3.32)
Married couple	0.74	(2.41)
Education (college graduate is reference)		
High school dropout	−5.53*	(2.71)
High school graduate only	−7.69***	(2.37)
Attended college	−4.63*	(2.08)
Other socioeconomic characteristics		
Number of children	−1.16*	(0.54)
Age	−0.02	(0.08)
Income ($ thousands)	0.25**	(0.09)
Assets ($ thousands)	0.08	(0.04)
Debt ($ thousands)	0.05	(0.05)
Unemployed	−1.25	(2.08)
Unbanked	7.07***	(2.20)
Renter	−2.51	(3.53)
Receiving TANF	1.00	(2.67)
Rural	−2.86	(3.16)
Intended use of IDA (home purchase is reference)		
Use for education	−1.13	(2.14)
Use for business	−1.53	(2.29)
Use for other asset	4.35	(3.01)
Other program features		
Months in program	−0.21	(0.16)
Hours of general financial education	1.74***	(0.36)
Hours of financial education squared	−0.05***	(0.01)
Match rate	−0.98	(1.35)
Total contribution limit	0.017***	(0.00)

(continued)

Table 11.7 (continued)

Variable	Coefficient	Standard Error
Total contribution limit squared	−0.000002*	(0.00)
Limit is lifetime, not annual limit	6.32	(3.31)
Predicted probability of active participation	12.98	(8.71)
Fixed effects		
Program 1	16.96**	(6.23)
Program 2	16.55**	(6.10)
Program 3	−9.19	(5.14)
Program 4	8.78	(6.21)
Program 5	−8.04	(6.60)
Program 6	7.33	(4.81)
Program 7	5.20	(11.16)
Program 8	−7.26	(4.34)
Program 9	6.88	(4.95)
Program 10	6.15	(6.89)
Program 11	3.71	(5.79)
Program 12	4.88	(5.25)
Program 13	14.43*	(5.81)
$N = 2{,}001$	Adjusted R square: .16	F score: 9.8***

Source. Center for Social Development, American Dream Demonstration, account monitoring data, 2000.
Note: $*p < .05$, $**p < .01$, $***p < .001$

Education also influences relative impacts of ADD. College graduates enjoy larger monthly savings effects than high school dropouts, high school graduates, or college dropouts. Because the unbanked participants would not otherwise save anything in the absence of ADD, with other conditions being equal, unbanked ADD participants enjoy a $7 per month larger savings effect than banked participants.

In contrast to our univariate analysis, controlling for such characteristics as age, income, and education, an ADD participant's marital status appears to have no bearing on monthly savings effect. Nor does age affect the relative financial impact of individual development accounts—holding other things constant, the young and the old benefit equally from IDAs. This is also true for employment and welfare status, whether a participant lives in an urban or rural location or owns or rents a home.

We also find that IDAs appear to be equally effective in encouraging savings regardless of their intended use. We also find savings effects to be reasonably time insensitive. Controlling for other factors, the average monthly savings effect of a participant who has had an IDA for 18 months is not significantly different from the savings effect of someone who has been in ADD for just a few months.[13] On the other hand, financial education does appear to stimulate a learning process—monthly savings effects increase with additional hours of financial education, although the rate of savings increase gradually tapers off with more education.

The IDA program's total contribution limit, defined as the maximum amount of a participant's IDA deposits over the life of the program that are eligible to receive matching funds, is also positively related to savings effect, although it, too, reflects decreasing returns to scale. The median contribution limit across the 14 ADD programs is $1,500; the minimum is $240. Our model suggests that a person facing the median contribution limit would experience, on average, a monthly savings effect that is $21 greater than someone in a program having a $240 limit.

This is particularly interesting in light of the fact that two years into ADD, individual program contributions limits are a binding constraint on very few participants: Only 8 percent of all ADD participants had met or exceeded their program contribution limits. While it is quite speculative, this suggests that IDA programs with high contribution limits seem to induce more ambitious savings goals and results from their participants. Finally, although match rates are critical to participants' ability to amass significant assets, our model suggests that they are not related to savings effects.[14] This is largely congruent with the findings of Schreiner, Clancy, and Sherraden (2002), and suggests that matching funds are an important inducement to householders to enroll in an IDA program, but the size of the match does not influence how much more or less of his or her own money a household might save.

ARE IDAs FINANCED FROM NON-IDA SAVINGS?

There is a growing literature on whether tax-advantaged retirement plans, such as 401(k)s, result in additions to net wealth (see, e.g., Engen and Gale, 2000). While empirical studies present mixed evidence, Engen and Gale's recent work (2000) suggests that 401(k)s held by groups with low earnings "are more likely to represent an addition to net wealth than 401(k)s held by high-earning groups," because the latter are more likely to finance their retirement plans with reductions in existing assets (Engen and Gale, 2000, 1).

Until now, we have implicitly assumed that all IDA deposits represent additions to household net wealth. This implies that ADD participants do not finance their IDAs by transferring resources from an existing transaction or savings account into their IDA account to take advantage of matching opportunities. In light of the fact that more than 80 percent of ADD participants had a preexisting bank account, it is not unreasonable to expect that some of them are transferring money from low-yielding accounts to their IDAs that yield returns of 100 percent or more.

Although we have no way of knowing the extent to which this kind of shuffling (that is, transferring of funds from one account to another) is going on, we have found (not shown in tables) a small but statistically significant relationship between bank account balances at the start of the program and IDA savings, while other research indicates that at least 12 percent of ADD participants did sell assets in order to increase their IDA savings (Moore et al., 2000). These results, including Engen and Gale's findings that between 71 and 89 percent of 401(k) savings are financed through asset reductions, suggest that some degree of shuffling is also likely to apply to some ADD participants.[15] To the extent that shuffling is taking place, then net IDA deposits overstate net household savings, as reflected in our estimates of the savings effects of IDAs.

Table 11.8 presents the results of an adjustment process that reduces net IDA balances under different assumptions of the degree of shuffling.[16] We simulate the effects of shuffling on ADD balances in 10 percent-increments of participants' bank accounts at the start of the program. Thus, for example, the 10-percent shuffling line in table 11.8 implies that a participant has shifted 10 percent of his or her preexisting bank account balance into her IDA account; the 20-percent line suggests that one-fifth of a participant's IDA balance came from his/her non-IDA account, and so on.

Although our shuffling analysis is hypothetical, it does suggest that even substantial amounts of shuffling still yield relatively large IDA balances. If banked participants transferred half of their existing balances into their IDAs, the median IDA balance for active participants would still be $125, and one-quarter of all active participants would still have over $450 in net new savings.

Table 11.8 Adjusted IDA Balances under Varied Shuffling Assumptions, 2000

	All Participants			Active Participants		
Shuffling Assumptions	25%	Median	75%	25%	Median	75%
No shuffling	$15	$177	$564	$97	$316	$645
10% shuffling	$0	$149	$508	$63	$273	$593
20% shuffling	$0	$115	$464	$36	$221	$536
30% shuffling	$0	$85	$417	$16	$182	$502
40% shuffling	$6	$60	$370	$6	$154	$480
50% shuffling	$0	$40	$336	$0	$125	$454
60% shuffling	$0	$26	$311	$0	$108	$425
70% shuffling	$0	$14	$288	$0	$86	$395
80% shuffling	$0	$6	$271	$0	$61	$369
90% shuffling	$0	$0	$254	$0	$50	$354
100% shuffling	$0	$0	$243	$0	$36	$321

Source: Center for Social Development, American Dream Demonstration, account monitoring data, 2000.
Note: "Shuffling" refers to shifting money from older bank accounts to the new IDA instead of saving new money. $N = 2,310$ overall; 1,867 active.

Table 11.9 repeats this analysis for savings effects. Under moderate shuffling rates, IDAs continue to have a significant positive impacts on most participants. Even assuming 50-percent shuffling—that half of a participant's IDA deposits came from another account—half of all active ADD households would have saved at least $56 more than they would have in the absence of their IDAs. We conclude from this analysis that, in general, IDAs effectively encourage greater savings, even when a significant percentage of IDA deposits are financed through reductions in non-IDA savings.

WHAT ABOUT PREVIOUSLY UNBANKED ADD PARTICIPANTS?

Thus far, we have assumed that some kind of bank account is a precondition to saving, which implies that the 19 percent of previously unbanked ADD participants would have no savings were it not for their IDA. Considering that many low-income households have "mattress cash" or other nonbank liquid assets of one form or another (Edin and Lein, 1997), we should modify our assumption that 100 percent of unbanked ADD IDA balances represent net additions to wealth.

In order to approximate their annual non-IDA savings, we apply the coefficients from our OLS model of banked ADD participants (reported in table 11.2) to all unbanked participants. Treating the unbanked as if they were banked most likely overstates their true non-IDA savings because, though they may not be observable, there are factors that cause otherwise

Table 11.9 Adjusted Savings Effects under Varied Shuffling Assumptions, 2000

	All Participants			Active Participants		
Shuffling Assumptions	25%	Median	75%	25%	Median	75%
No shuffling	$0	$117	$467	$31	$236	$544
10% shuffling	−$19	$81	$398	$10	$182	$477
20% shuffling	−$39	$49	$350	−$8	$141	$441
30% shuffling	−$50	$25	$306	−$27	$111	$394
40% shuffling	−$59	$12	$273	−$41	$81	$367
50% shuffling	−$67	$5	$247	−$52	$56	$333
60% shuffling	−$72	$0	$223	−$59	$40	$313
70% shuffling	−$76	$0	$205	−$68	$26	$292
80% shuffling	−$79	$0	$186	−$72	$19	$265
90% shuffling	−$82	$0	$168	−$76	$12	$252
100% shuffling	−$86	−$2	$152	−$80	$10	$238

Source: Center for Social Development, American Dream Demonstration, account monitoring data, 2000.
Note: N = 2,310 overall; 1,867 active. 25% = 25th percentile, 75% = 75th percentile.

similar households not to have a bank account. This suggests that the true savings trajectories of unbanked ADD participants are no larger than the ones estimated here and that the savings effects we estimate for the unbanked are likely to be understated (as the higher savings trajectory is subtracted from the IDA balance to derive the savings effect).

Table 11.10 presents predicted annual savings trajectories and savings effects of unbanked ADD participants. Based on the net amounts of their IDA accounts, we estimate that, on average, unbanked ADD participants save $135 per year. Reducing estimated savings effects by the non-IDA savings estimates from our model still produces positive savings effects for most unbanked participants.[17] The mean savings effect is $61 for all unbanked participants (median is –$27) and $147 for active unbanked participants (the median is $45). From this we conclude that even if unbanked IDA holders were to have some "mattress savings" that are not identified at the time of enrollment, as existing bank balances are identified for banked applicants, IDAs generate positive net savings for the unbanked as well as the banked.

We also tested these revised savings effects estimates in a multivariate context, using the same model specified in Table 11.7. The coefficient for unbanked switched from significantly positive to mildly negative and statistically insignificant, with no other substantive changes among the other variables. This suggests that IDAs work at least as well for unbanked families as for banked.

CONCLUSION

This research contributes to the growing body of empirical studies of individual savings accounts (IRAs) by attempting to answer the counterfactual question: How much difference does an IDA make to a household's net wealth? We find that IDAs have a small but significant positive impact on net savings. Two years into ADD, the median participant has saved $117 more than he or she otherwise would have saved, while the mean savings

Table 11.10 OLS-Predicted Savings Trajectories and Savings Effects of Unbanked ADD Participants, 2000

Predicted Savings	25%	Median	75%	Mean
Predicted annual savings of unbanked (overall)	$98	$131	$172	$135
Adjusted savings effects, unbanked (overall)	–$95	–$27	$112	$61
Predicted annual savings, unbanked (active)	$97	$131	$172	$135
Adjusted savings effects, unbanked (active)	–$41	$45	$235	$147

Source: Center for Social Development, American Dream Demonstration, account monitoring data, 2000.
Note: N = 446 overall; 299 active. 25% = 25th percentile; 75% = 75th percentile.

effect is a higher $285. Limiting our analysis to active participants with positive IDA balances results in higher savings effects—a median of $236 and an average of $368.

While these net additions to financial assets might seem small in absolute terms, they represent significant relative increases measured against documented bank account balances of low-income U.S. households, the bottom 20 percent of whom have median account balances of just $610. For the 40 percent of black households that fall into the lowest income quintile for all households, median bank account balance is just $200. In short, IDAs may induce net additional savings equal to one-third or more of existing passbook and checking account balances.

Three additional findings are worth repeating here. First, given the important role that IDAs might play in welfare reform, it is encouraging to find that one's welfare status has no bearing on savings effect. This means that IDAs are as effective in helping welfare recipients build assets as they are in helping others save more than they otherwise would. Second, our analysis adds to the accumulating body of empirical research that suggests financial education encourages savings (Bernheim and Garrett, 1996). Finally, while matching funds dramatically leverage individual IDA deposits and help build net wealth, we find no relationship between the match rate and resulting savings effects.

NOTES

1. Financial assets include stocks, bonds, mutual funds, brokerage accounts, bank accounts, pensions and other retirement funds, and cash life insurance.

2. Nonfinancial assets include houses, other residential and nonresidential property, businesses, vehicles, and other miscellaneous assets, including collections and precious metals.

3. Initially, we used an income and asset cutoff to define an ADD–like population, using the Federal Reserve's 1998 *Survey of Consumer Finances* (SCF). Because about 90 percent of all ADD households have incomes of less than 200 percent of poverty level and an equal percentage have assets under $80,000, we chose to include in our national IDA SCF sample population all families who fell within these two parameters. It turned out that the distribution of total assets held by this national sample differed substantially from that characterizing ADD participants— the sample median of $6,750 was over twice that held by ADD households ($2,600)— which required us to redesign our sampling plan.

4. When we weighted the SCF data according to the distribution of income in ADD, the mean of assets was over $95,000 (compared with the ADD mean of $17,000). This is because while virtually all ADD households had both low income and low assets, many SCF households have low income and high assets (and would be given undue influence using an income-based weight), and as such, do not fit the IDA profile. We also explored the use of propensity scores (see Rosenbaum and Rubin, 1983), but this was not feasible, as the method does not work well when applied to two highly heterogeneous populations.

5. The SCF already includes a weight to adjust for the over sampling of wealthy households.

6. Because many SCF households had more assets than the maximum in ADD, the resulting weight for these cases is 0, and so they are not included in the national IDA sample (NIP $n = 2,817$, vs. 4,305 for all SCF).

7. Because the SCF does not include the age of savings accounts, we were forced to exclude a small number of banked households (8 percent) that only owned a savings account. We also had to assume that the age of a checking account also reflects the age of the savings account. Given that over 90 percent of all households with both have them at the same institution, this seems reasonable.

8. See Cohen (1978), and Jaccard, Choi, and Turrisi (1990), for elaboration on interaction effects.

9. Kennickell et al. (2000) finds, for example, that a larger percentage of white families than minorities save (5) and that white families with transaction account(s) have a median balance of $2,600, compared with $1,500 for all banked nonwhites or Hispanics (10).

10. Hispanics and African Americans are estimated to have lower account balances than Caucasians but higher growth rates.

11. This is because they either have never made a deposit or have made unauthorized withdrawals of their previous deposits.

12. In fact, because the vast majority of ADD participants and virtually all active participants experience positive savings effects, we interpret these results in terms of degrees of success.

13. We also tested for nonlinearity, using polynomial terms, but these were insignificant and were dropped.

14. Like Schreiner, Clancy, and Sherraden (2002), we tested the possibility that match rate has a nonlinear influence on savings effect, employing polynomial terms and a set of indicator variables, but found no support for this hypothesis. The polynomial terms were insignificant, as were the indicator variables.

15. The savings of middle-income ($30k–$40k) households were estimated to be largely new, while the authors could not determine whether the savings of low-income households were new or not (Engen and Gale, 2000; see also Engen, Gale, and Scholz, 1994; and Poterba, Venti, and Wise, 1996).

16. We only consider shuffling for banked ADD participants because previously unbanked IDA holders have no accounts from which to transfer deposits. This also implies that all net IDA deposits made by unbanked ADD participants represent net new wealth.

17. We use the same method as before: Subtract the total predicted savings of unbanked participants (net of IDA participation) from their actual IDA balances.

REFERENCES

Bernheim, B. D., and D. M. Garrett. (1996). *The Determinants and Consequences of Financial Education in the Workplace: Evidence from a Survey of Households.* National Bureau of Economic Research (NBER) Working Paper 5667. Cambridge, Mass.: NBER.
Carroll, C., and A. Samwick. (1998). "How Important Is Precautionary Saving?" *The Review of Economics and Statistics* 80(3), 410–419.

Center for Social Development. (2000). *Savings Patterns in IDA Programs.* Research Report. St. Louis, Mo.: Center for Social Development (CSD), Washington University.

Cohen, J. (1978). "Partialed Products Are Interactions; Partialed Powers Are Curve Components." *Psychological Bulletin* 85(4), 858–866.

Edin, K., and L. Lein. (1997). "Work, Welfare, and Single Mothers' Economic Survival Strategies." *American Sociological Review* 62(2), 253–269.

Engen, E. M., and W. G. Gale. (2000). *The Effects of 401(k) Plans on Household Wealth: Differences across Earnings Groups.* National Bureau of Economic Research Working Paper (original draft, May 2000; revised draft, August 2000).

Engen, E. M., W. G. Gale, and J. K. Scholz. (1994). "Do Savings Incentives Work?" *Brookings Papers on Economic Activity,* 1, 85–151.

Federal Reserve Board (FRB). (1998). *Survey of Consumer Finances.* Available at http://www.federalreserve.gov/pubs/oss/oss2/method.html. Last accessed March 5, 2002.

Jaccard, J., K. W. Choi, and R. Turrisi. (1990). "The Detection and Interpretation of Interactive Effects between Continuous Variables in Multiple Regression." *Multivariate Behavioral Research* 25(4), 467–478.

Kennickell, A., M. Starr-McCluer, and B. Surette. (2000). "Recent Changes in US Family Finances: Results from the 1998 Survey of Consumer Finances." *Federal Reserve Bulletin* 86 (January), 1–29.

Mills, G., G. Campos, M. Ciurea, D. DeMarco, N. Michlin, and D. Welch. (2000). *Evaluation of Asset Accumulation Initiatives.* Prepared under contract number 53-8198-4-026 for the U.S. Department of Agriculture, Food and Nutrition Service.

Moore, A., S. Beverly, M. Sherraden, L. Johnson, and M. Schreiner. (2000). "How Do Low-Income Individuals Save, Deposit, and Maintain Financial Assets?" Presented at the Center for Social Development's "Inclusion in Asset Building: Research and Policy Symposium," September 21–23.

Poterba, J., S. Venti, and D. Wise. (1996). "How Retirement Savings Programs Increase Saving." *Journal of Economic Perspectives* 10(4), 91–112.

Rosenbaum, P., and D. Rubin. (1983). "The Central Role of the Propensity Score in Observational Studies for Causal Effects." *Biometrika* 70(1), 41–55.

Schreiner, M., M. Clancy, and M. Sherraden. (2002). *Savings Performance in the American Dream Demonstration: A National Demonstration of Individual Development Accounts.* Research Report. St. Louis, Mo.: Center for Social Development, Washington University. Available at http://gwbweb.wustl.edu/csd/Publications/2002/ADDreport2002.pdf. Last accessed January 3, 2003.

PART IV

TOWARD AN INCLUSIVE ASSET-BUILDING POLICY

The chapters in this part discuss policy design. The authors are analysts and policy innovators who are accomplished in taking existing knowledge and using it to shape large-scale policy designs and proposals. Each of the five chapters helps to inform the design of a large-scale and inclusive asset-based policy.

Robert Friedman and Ray Boshara have been in the forefront of asset-based policy initiatives in Washington, D.C.; they have organized working groups, policy studies, and legislative initiatives. The first individual development account (IDA) bill in the U.S. Congress, which later became the Assets for Independence Act of 1998, was drafted by these authors. The discussion of principles and policy options in the current chapter arose in part from deliberations of the Growing Wealth Working Group, which Friedman and Boshara convened. Their chapter is valuable in laying out fundamental policy design features and rationales, along with policy options that have the potential to move asset-based principles into practice.

Peter Orszag and Robert Greenstein examine retirement pensions in terms of coverage and distribution of public benefits. Though associated with liberal policy positions, the research of Orszag and Greenstein is respected as solid and dependable on both sides of the political aisle. These authors level their analytical attention at the retirement pension system, which can only be described as systematically biased in favor of those who are well-off. Most low-income workers do not have an opportunity to participate in decision making at the workplace, and enormous public benefits are distributed to higher-income workers via tax deferments. Orszag and Greenstein suggest reforms that can make pension policy more inclusive.

Elaine Rideout is a "mother" of the federal Thrift Savings Plan (TSP); she helped to design it while working at the Office of Management and Budget. In terms of inclusion, the TSP is the most successful employer-based, defined contribution policy in the country, reaching a far greater proportion of all workers, including low-income workers, than the typical 401(k) or similar retirement plan. The TSP should be of great interest to anyone who cares about a truly inclusive asset-based policy because it is not merely a savings product but a plan that has the potential of reaching everyone. Market mechanisms by themselves, no matter how great the incentives, will not be able to include the whole population. Ultimately, a savings plan will be required, and the TSP is one model that can be built upon in the future.

Another strategy for inclusive policy is to begin with an account for all children at birth. If each new birth cohort is given an account (as in the new Child Trust Fund in the United Kingdom), then after several generations everyone in the country will have an account. This may seem like a long pathway to inclusive asset-based policy, but children's savings accounts (CSAs) have important advantages. These include (1) the potential to be truly universal, that is, give an account to everyone, in contrast with employment-related policies that leave out many Americans; (2) greater bipartisan support for accounts for children; (3) greater opportunity to be progressive, for example, provide greater subsidies for the poor; and (4) potential for life-long asset accumulation. All things considered, CSAs may be the most promising long-term strategy toward inclusive asset-based policy. This idea has been a longtime interest of Fred Goldberg. In his chapter, he spells out his vision for achieving a universal CSA.

In the final chapter here, Timothy Smeeding links Earned Income Tax Credit (EITC) lump-sum distributions with the potential for saving and asset accumulation. He asks EITC recipients how they use their tax refunds. Consistent with a growing body of work in behavioral economics, Smeeding finds that EITC recipients think of this irregular income as different from other income; they envision the lump sum as having potential for larger or different purposes. Saving might be one such purpose, though little in the current structure of EITC policy would promote or facilitate this. One desirable policy change would be to allow a split in EITC payments so that a portion could be automatically assigned to a savings account.

The analyses, ideas, rationales, and designs presented in this part may be the richest group of asset-based policy proposals yet assembled in one publication. Of course, many other options are possible. None of these authors would say that the policy goal should be one particular design to the exclusion of others. It may be that an inclusive asset-based policy will one day be composed of several of these options or portions of these options, as well as other policy designs that are not described here. In this regard, the reader may want to focus more on policy characteristics that are desirable rather than particular policy strategies.

12

Going to Scale: Principles and Policy Options for an Inclusive Asset-Building Policy

Robert E. Friedman and Ray Boshara

This chapter presents some principles and policy options for achieving larger scale, progressive asset-building policies. This is not a theoretical chapter about policy development, the U.S. Congress, and the administration; rather, it reflects the Corporation for Enterprise Development (CFED)'s direct experience with practitioners, policy makers, and others in forging progressive asset-building policies for individual development accounts (IDAs) and other asset-building tools. Specifically, this chapter discusses principles and dimensions of asset-building policy, summarizes the status of current asset development policies, and offers a set of policy recommendations to reach scale.

From the earliest days of the American republic, when Thomas Jefferson talked of "a nation of small farmers and shopkeepers," there has been an economic correlate of political democracy. Just as we believe that democracy works best if all ideas have access to public debate and consideration, so we believe that the economic marketplace works best if it can harness the ideas and energies of all citizens. Indeed, if we examine our history to identify the policies that have created significant, widely shared, and enduring economic progress, they are democratic investments in the common genius of the American people: universal education, the Homestead Act, and the G.I. Bill.

Of course, the realization of that economic ideal, like that of its political correlate, has been slow and difficult. Gloria Steinem reminds us that at the founding of the Republic, "We the people" meant white male adult landowners. Gradually, excluded groups like African Americans, women, immigrants, nonlandowners, and youth were added. Though we still have a long way to go, the next phase of the civil rights movement, we believe, lies in increasing all U.S. citizens' access to full economic participation.

Our economic history, like our political history, is also the story of opening the ranks of economic actors. For the first hundred years of U.S. history, African Americans were property; they did not own it. For one hundred fifty years, banks lent against only capital and collateral; it was only in the early decades of the twentieth century that they began to lend against wages. Home ownership was brought to the purview of the middle class only when the federal government established the thirty-year mortgage. Though restrictive covenants reduced home ownership opportunities for African Americans by limiting mortgages to new construction in the suburbs, the creation of public markets, workers' rights, small business programs, antidiscrimination laws, universal education, and public libraries opened the economic system to broader participation. When the Great Depression threatened to sideline most of the American people from economic participation, the New Deal, World War II, and the G.I. Bill rescued the middle class and laid the foundation for our postwar growth.

We have finally come to recognize that widespread asset poverty looms as a major barrier to economic participation and productivity. A majority of American households are asset poor at a time when access to the economic mainstream—a down payment on a home, capitalizing a small business, postsecondary education, or a retirement nest egg—requires at least a few thousand dollars. It is becoming increasingly clear that work and income alone will not allow many working families to escape poverty and achieve a modicum of economic independence and security.

Much of the asset disparity of the country is the result of policy (CFED, 2001; Sherraden, 1991, 2000a) and, in Melvin Oliver and Thomas Shapiro's (1995) memorable and well-documented phrase, "the sediment of past discrimination." Today, our nearly $300 billion per year asset-building policy for individuals (Sherraden, 2000a) rewards home ownership, business ownership, savings, investments, and pensions through the tax system in a way that excludes most of the people who already lack assets (and tax liability). Meanwhile, asset acquisition by low-income people has generally been penalized through federal and state governmental policies, ranging from asset limits and benefit reductions in income-support programs to higher effective tax rates on income than capital. We believe that if exclusionary asset policies can be effective in amplifying asset inequality and its myriad psychological, social, and economic effects, then inclusive asset policies can be equally effective in spreading the creation of wealth, which would emphasize the need for an inclusive asset-building system in this country.

The aim of this chapter is to suggest principles and policy options that should guide the development of such a system, both in design and implementation. Our discussion draws primarily from research centered on IDAs.[1] IDAs are one form of asset building, categorized as matched savings accounts that are earmarked for high-return assets (generally, business development, postsecondary education, home ownership, and sometimes retirement investing). Another aspect of IDAs is that they include financial education for account holders. Though other approaches exist, it is the apparent simplicity of IDAs that makes them a well-packaged set of asset-building tools. They also often help support microenterprise and entrepreneurial development, two of the least understood and least appreciated asset-building strategies. Research and policy development over the last twenty-one years have taught us a good deal about the dimensions and techniques of asset building that should guide the development of future practice and policy.

PRINCIPLES AND DIMENSIONS FOR LARGE-SCALE ASSET BUILDING

Dimensions of Asset Building

Twenty-one years of studying what elements are needed for effective economic development policy and programs has only underscored development finance pioneer Belden Daniels's essential insight, "Development is something people do, not something done to them." The effectiveness of IDAs (which are, after all, rather modest injections of cash and training) can only really be explained by the way low-income people use them. Account holders themselves—people who save and earn matching funds for their savings; organize their consumption and reduce their debts; plan and save for their own businesses, education, or homes; and teach their children, spouses, and neighbors about savings and asset building—make the difference.

Many poor and low-income people who are limited not by lack of capacity but by a lack of real and accessible economic opportunity. In this sense, the heart of asset-building policy is the recognition that people themselves are the best assets. As Michael Sherraden (1991) writes of asset building, "The underlying assumption is that the national economic pie is not finite. It can grow with the spirit and ability of the people. Paradoxically, the more people who have a piece of the pie, the faster it will grow."

The related conclusion of a major study CFED undertook a decade ago for the Charles Stewart Mott Foundation was that economic opportunity programs are effective to the extent that they build the confidence, competence, and connections of low-income people (Nothdurft and Dyer, 1990). IDAs are effective precisely because they are able to impact the three c's by applying a fourth: capital. In fashioning asset-building policy, then, it is crucial to keep in mind that asset-building policy is effective to the extent it engages the hearts, minds, and energy of people and helps connect them to the larger world.

That said, we perceive at least five distinct asset-building elements of IDAs that should be considered in designing any asset-building strategy: savings, matching funds, education, investments, and asset accounts. The power of IDAs may thus reside in the fact that this apparently simple tool combines so many positive elements.

Savings

The dynamics of savings is poorly understood by both neoclassical economics and the popular culture as "deferred consumption," defined as the amount remaining after subtracting expenses from revenues. Savings should instead be perceived as the base for economic progress. The poor save in IDA programs, and the very poor at about four times the rate of the less poor (Schreiner et al., 2001), because they recognize that savings determine the price of stability and hope for the future.

Regular savings lie at the heart of IDA programs and, in fact, early practice lessons revolved around how to array match rates, minimum and maximum deposits, personal finance training, and other aspects of IDA programming to compel and reinforce saving habits. We often forget that one of the virtues of money and numbers is that they provide a clear way to mark progress, not always an easy thing to do in the amorphous world of development. At the outset of the American Dream Demonstration (ADD), we expected that IDAs might be considered successful once account holders actually began to use them to purchase assets. Instead, the fundamental psychological shift seems to come as soon as after about six months as account holders, for the first time, experience a measure of economic control when they realize that they have steadily increasing assets. Even if their asset purchase is months or years away, they feel that their goal is attainable when they see their savings multiplied by matching funds. ADD programs also found that requiring training in personal finance before allowing matched savings resulted in high program dropout rates. However, after matched savings started, account holders began to appreciate the value of what they had learned from the training.

It is possible to conceive of an asset-building strategy that does not require savings, but the impact of such a strategy would likely be different and politically more difficult without a clear showing of corresponding effort on the part of account holders. Sherraden (2000b) instructs rightly that we need to look for "the powerful independent variable"—the single intervention that is capable of producing multiple positive effects. The power of savings and asset accumulation, taken together, is such that they produce changes in aspirations, economic and social behavior, and quality of economic investments.

Matching Funds

IDAs match the savings of low-income IDA holders by using funds from private and public sources. Savings alone can help build assets, but without the input of resources from elsewhere, asset disparities and asset poverty are likely to overwhelm bootstrap efforts. A family is not always recognized as a financial institution, but when it comes to asset building, it is an essential one. Asset holding is a multigenerational dynamic funnel through which the assets of one generation are transferred to the next. For example, down payments for houses often come from parents. It will be difficult to create an asset floor for the asset-poor majority in this country without at least beginning to offer low-income and low-wealth people incentives (subsidies) comparable to those now provided through the tax system to mostly the wealthy. By offering matching funds for savings, IDAs link such incentives to saving actions by asset builders.

Education

Account holders typically comment that they join IDA programs for the matching funds, but they stay because of the training. IDA programs generally provide at least ten to twenty hours of financial and investment training. Peer group exchange and asset-specific training in entrepreneurship, home ownership, and effective postsecondary education augment this training. Though this education element is labor intensive and expensive, many account holders and practitioners believe it is as important as other aspects of the program. IDAs underwrite investments that are inherently riskier than retirement savings. This leaves less room for failure for account holders who are already asset poor. Practitioners are, therefore, coming to believe that training activities play a key role in increasing savings levels and regularity of savings by clarifying and underscoring asset goals.

Investments

Seizing on public and private matching funds, some see IDA programs as wealth redistribution programs. In so doing, however, they miss the wealth creation aspects of IDAs—savings, education, and particularly the returns on investments. Though these investments are not without risks, the earmarked uses of most IDAs (business capitalization, home ownership, postsecondary education, and retirement) provide, on average, some of the highest returns on investments in our economy. We also need to recognize not only the magic of entrepreneurship, enterprise, and learning these investments summon from account holders but also the importance of evaluating and monitoring IDAs and other asset-building programs on a return on investment basis.[2]

Accounts

IDAs are structured as accounts in financial institutions owned directly or indirectly by account holders. Asset accounts are becoming a preferred tool of public policy for many reasons (Sherraden, 1996), including the fact that individuals want more control over their lives and that new technology enables us to individualize socioeconomic policy. Opening accounts in financial institutions, thus, begins to connect the marginalized poor to the economic mainstream and its institutions.

THE ASSET-BUILDING SYSTEM

The demonstrated promise of IDAs underscores a broader challenge and opportunity; from the beginning, we knew that if IDAs worked, millions of Americans could take advantage of the asset-building opportunity IDAs represented. A majority of American households are asset poor in that they have less than $1,000 in investable assets (Anderson, 1999; Haveman and Wolff, chapter 4 in this volume). Just under half of all working people take home less than $15,000 in annual wages and nearly three-quarters make under $30,000.[3] The key question is, thus, how do we move from a system of community-based demonstration initiatives, averaging from one hundred to two hundred accounts, to a system providing for millions of accounts? To answer this question, the following five design principles are suggested.

Inclusive and Progressive Asset-Building Incentives

Assets are necessary for people to grow socially and economically. The U.S. government's large asset-building tax policy contains significant subsidies and incentives that currently help the top two quintiles of Americans to accumulate assets (Sherraden, 2000a; Wolff, 2001). The issue is how to extend effective asset-building incentives and access to the asset-poor majority of Americans who cannot take advantage of the current asset-building tax incentives, generally do not work for employers offering pension coverage or matched savings programs like 401(k)s, live in families without assets, and frequently are not served by mainstream financial institutions.

An equitable, productive asset-building system must offer access, facilitation, information, and incentives to low-wealth families (Beverly, 1997; Beverly and Sherraden, 1999); must be progressive, balancing existing incentives; and must provide access to equivalent or larger investments to the asset- and income-poor majority of U.S. citizens.

Large and Real Goals

As noted above, the goal is to bring asset building opportunities to millions of American families. Some 40 million families are working, but their incomes are less than 200 percent of the official poverty measure. At the same time, an inclusive asset-building policy must enable the poor to accumulate a sufficient nest egg—at least a few thousand dollars in a few years—to give them a realistic chance to achieve their asset goals when put together with other programs. Though initial proposals may be relatively small, the aim should be to develop a system on the order of the nearly $300 billion committed to asset building policies for individuals, which currently excludes those who are already asset poor.

Expand Existing Asset-Building Programs

An inclusive policy can find funds in the tax expenditure system, which already underwrites investments of this scale and has been the fastest growing segment of public funding at both the state and federal levels. Indeed, inclusive asset building primarily entails examining how to extend existing policies, such as individual retirement accounts (IRAs), 401(k)s, home mortgage interest deductions, tax breaks for business investments, and postsecondary education, to people and communities not already being reached. Refundable tax credits would be the most direct (albeit the least politically viable) way to accomplish this expansion or inclusion, but it is possible to use tax credits to employers, financial institutions, and private contributors to extend the system as well.

Complement Safety Net Programs

Asset-building policies should complement income-support policies, not substitute for them. Indeed, the two systems are interdependent: we can only take care of those who cannot support themselves in the mainstream economy if we offer those who are capable a reasonable opportunity to succeed. Two critical guidelines emerge from this: First, we must remove the asset-building penalties enmeshed in current safety net programs so that low-income people can begin to move forward economically without being pulled back by counterproductive rules; second, we must work to find explicit ways to develop safety net programs using some of the returns from asset-building policies.

Multi-Sectoral System

While it is possible to imagine a universal savings and investment system, operated almost wholly by the government (not unlike Social Security), it seems that the development of an optimal system will be enhanced by the contributions of different sectors with different strengths. Moreover, the larger the number of stakeholders in the emerging system, the faster it can grow. Therefore, we see the emerging marketplace as one that holds separate and complementary roles for low-income families and the public, private (e.g., corporations and financial institutions), philanthropic, and nonprofit sectors. Indeed, each of these sectors is already involved in IDAs as small demonstration initiatives, and the role of each sector will most likely change as we move to scale.

Specifically, public policy must move from sponsoring thousands of accounts (through general fund appropriations of millions of dollars) to providing billions of dollars of asset-based tax incentives equivalent to those now granted mostly to the wealthy. IDAs, children's savings accounts, employer-based accounts, and other similar matched savings programs should be developed. Financial institutions must move from providing IDAs as a community development tool to providing them as a profitable product—capable of reaping returns from an emerging market of new savers, investors, entrepreneurs, home owners, and skilled employees. They will need to find ways to reduce the cost of managing smaller accounts, by using new technologies and forging new partnerships. Employers will need to see savings matches as a new way to retain and upgrade employees, as well as to supplement wages by harnessing public incentives. Community-based organizations will need to develop larger-scale, lower-cost, and more effective techniques for outreach, recruitment, counseling, training, and monitoring thousands of account holders. The philanthropic sector will need to be galvanized with tax incentives to fund nonprofit operations and matches. And, ultimately, account holders will have to own, drive, and advocate for the system.

Scale and Community

This dream of a universal savings and investment marketplace evokes nightmares for some. Community activists and social service providers who have embraced IDAs as a community program fear that a move to scale—especially one where financial institutions and the tax system are major actors—will drive out nonprofit providers and quality, community-sensitive programming by either directly or indirectly failing to provide an adequate funding stream. The result, they fear, would be a universal system that effectively excludes the poorest, those most in need of training.

On the other hand, financial institutions and businesses fear that overemphasizing the soft programmatic aspects of IDA programs, rather than their essential identity as financial products or services, will permanently undermine the growth of the system and limit the availability of IDAs to a few boutique programs of widely varying quality.

These challenges need not be inevitable. Perhaps we should envision a system where a universal, basic financial product paired with an incentive (or match) are available everywhere—from outlets ranging from on-line services to local check cashiers and automated teller machines (ATMs)—enhanced by capable and interested nonprofit organizations that can take advantage of well-developed programmatic tools (such as personal finance curricula and outreach materials), and financed by philanthropic and government support.

HOW TO GET THERE

This section provides a brief description of the status of federal and state asset-development policies and a set of specific policy options for inclusive asset development policies.

Longtime advocates of IDAs have always seen IDAs as a way of establishing that low-income people can save and accumulate assets. One could say that the next goal should be to move from "pockets of success to universal access." However, it is important to reiterate here that universal access does not mean expanding a new poverty program, but rather, expanding the reach of the asset-building system already in place through tools such as IDAs, children's accounts, and the like. Though there are other development and design challenges, this country has already figured out very effective systems (historically and currently) to foster land ownership, home ownership, business development, retirement savings, and postsecondary education that can be used as starting points. This distinction is of great importance and has large implications for policy design and advocacy when the task at hand becomes, "How do we develop an inclusive asset building policy?"

For example, it means that the key starting point is the tax code, where asset-building expenditures to individuals total, as already noted, nearly $300 billion per year. It also means that advocates of asset policy will not be focused primarily on the traditional domestic poverty committees in Congress or the traditional executive branch departments, such as Health and Human Services, but instead, on agencies such as the Treasury and the tax-writing committees in Congress. In the antipoverty world, this is a very important shift. Certainly, traditional antipoverty advocates have, for example, rightly focused on the regressive nature of the tax code, but rarely have they viewed the tax code itself as a tool for creating wealth for the poor.

Federal IDA Policies

While federal asset-building policy proposals have existed since the early 1990s, only the past two or three years have seen significant progress in moving these proposals through Congress and getting them signed into law.[4] This section presents a summary of the existing resources and policies for IDAs and significant recent and current progressive proposals to build asset wealth.

In general terms, the federal government is supporting or promoting IDAs and similar asset-building tools for low-income families in three ways: (a) inclusion of IDAs in existing programs, (b) federal IDA and related demonstrations, and (c) "getting to scale" proposals.

Inclusion of IDAs in Existing Programs

Starting in 1996, IDAs or IDA-like accounts have been incorporated as an allowable (but not required) use in the following federal programs that promote safety nets, economic development, and financial integration.

Temporary Assistance for Needy Families   In the welfare overhaul of 1996, states were given the option of including IDAs in their Temporary Assistance for Needy Families (TANF) programs. By the year 2002, thirty-four states had done so, but only seventeen had actually used their TANF funds for IDAS. Between 1999 and 2000, those states committed a total of $14 million in TANF funds for IDAs.

Welfare-to-Work Grants   In 1997, Congress made about $3 billion available for the "hardest to serve" people who were moving from welfare to work and allowed grantees to use these funds for IDAs. As of 2000, New York City and three states have secured these funds for IDAs.

Bank Enterprise Award Program   In 1999, the Treasury Department's Bank Enterprise Award Program, which provides competitive grants to financial institutions for community development activities, offered $50 per IDA to help offset the administrative costs of IDAs. In the 2000 program announcement, that amount was increased to $100 per IDA.

Electronic Transfer Accounts   Financial institutions that offer electronic transfer accounts (ETAs)—designed to deliver federal benefits, such as Social Security payments, electronically—are permitted to add a savings product, such as IDAs, to the account. As of November 2000, more than six hundred financial institutions in over nine thousand locations were offering ETAs, although few have been linked to a savings product.

Affordable Housing Program of the Federal Home Loans Banks   A number of Federal Home Loan Banks (FHLBs) around the country offer IDA-like matched savings programs (with up to 3:1 matches) for low-income families who are saving for a down payment on a first home.

Tax Treatment of IDAs   While technically not a funding source, the internal revenue service (IRS) issued a ruling in October 1999 that states the following: for IDAs funded through the Assets for Independence (AFI) Demonstration Program, interest on individual deposits is taxable, but all matching funds (and interest earned thereon) are not taxable. Also, in 2000, it was clarified with the IRS that this ruling could apply to non–AFI-funded IDAs, provided the structure of the IDA and IDA program resemble those funded under AFI.

Federal IDA and Related Demonstrations

Two agencies at the Department of Health and Human Services are running IDA demonstrations, and a "First Accounts" pilot project was recently initiated by the Treasury Department.

The AFI Demonstration Program   Authorized in 1998 by Congress for $25 million per year for five years, the AFI Demonstration Program was appropriated only $10 million in its first two years and then $25 million in each of the three succeeding years. Under AFI, competitive grants are made to community-based organizations to run IDA programs.

First Accounts   A $10 million Treasury Department pilot project, called First Accounts, will support pilot partnerships between financial services providers and community organizations to provide access to low-cost accounts, ATMs and other electronic banking points, and financial literacy education to those who are not recipients of federal benefits and who do not use bank services (the unbanked). Like ETAs, financial institutions can link a savings product to the First Account.

Office of Refugee Resettlement   The Office of Refugee Resettlement (ORR) at the Department of Health and Human Services has thus far awarded approximately $15 million over the past few years in competitive grants for IDAs to nearly thirty community-based organizations serving refugees. The program, while small, has proved to be highly successful, largely because the agency had broad authority to tailor its program to meet the asset needs of refugees. For example, the ORR program allows IDAs to be used not only for the "big three" assets—buying a first home, starting a business, and/or obtaining an education—but also for automobiles neces-sary to secure and keep employment and computers.

"Getting to Scale" Proposals, 1999–2000

Beginning in early 1999, billion and multibillion-dollar, progressive asset-building proposals began to emerge from both sides of the aisle. The fol-lowing policies were proposed:

Savings for Working Families Act   The Savings for Working Families Act (SWFA) was first introduced in April 1999 and then again in early 2000, 2001, 2002, and 2003 and was sponsored by Senators Joseph Lieberman (D-Conn.) and Rick Santorum (R-Pa.) and Representatives Joe Pitts (R-Pa.) and Charles Stenholm (D-Tex.). The bill proposes a 1:1 match and up to $500 per year per person for savings in an IDA; it also provides a full tax credit to financial institutions and others that provide the matching and program funds. The bill—the first multibillion-dollar proposal specifically aimed at expanding IDAs—came very close to being enacted in late 2000. As this book was going to press, a version of the SWFA had passed the Senate and could become law under President George W. Bush during his second term.

1999 and 2000 Budget Resolutions   The 1999 Budget Resolution and the 2000 Budget Resolution stated that Congress should change the Federal tax law to encourage low-income workers and their families to save for a home, starting a business, education, or taking other investments for long-term development. IDAs were specifically mentioned in the 1999 Findings and in the 2000 Resolution. Both of these resolutions sent an important signal, but they did not have the force of law.

Various Proposals for Children   Federal proposals to establish savings accounts for all children have emerged over the last few years on both sides of the aisle in Congress (see Curley and Sherraden, 2000, for a detailed summary), although none of them have become law. For example, former Senator Bob Kerrey (D-Neb.) along with others, long championed "KidSave" accounts (first as part of Roth IRAs and then as grants to be repaid later in life), but the proposal never emerged from the Senate. Also, recent Republican proposals to eliminate the federal estate tax (or death tax) were rhetorically met by counterproposals from some Democrats to preserve the estate tax and use the "saved" revenues to establish and fund accounts for all children.

President Bush's "New Prosperity Initiative"   In April 2000, the then Republican presidential nominee, George W. Bush, pledged to create 1.3 million IDAs. Similar to the SWFA, Bush's proposal was to use tax credits to financial institutions to set up and match IDAs. During his first term as president, Bush included an IDA tax credit in his Budget Blueprint, and it has since been included as part of the Charity, Aid, Recovery and Empowerment (CARE) legislation.

State IDA Policies

As reported by Karen Edwards of the Center for Social Development (CSD) of Washington University, IDA policy activity is flourishing at the state level. Almost half the states[5] in the country preceded the federal government in passing IDA legislation. Thus far, state-supported IDA programs are responsible for over $30 million in IDA program funding. CSD reports that, as of December 2002:

- Thirty-four states have passed IDA legislation.
- Seven states have authorized state supported IDA programs, through administrative rule making.
- Since 1996, thirty-four states included IDAs in welfare reform plans for the possible use of TANF block grant funds.
- At least twenty-two state IDA programs have benefited from the Assets for Independence Act (AFI Act) IDA Program funding.
- Twenty-nine states either have or are developing statewide IDA coalitions or collaboratives.
- IDA programs have been implemented or are being planned at the community and/or state levels in all but three states—Alaska, North Dakota, and Wyoming (Edwards and Rist, 2001).

State appropriated funding streams come from a variety of sources, including direct appropriations from state, county, and city general funds; TANF funds; Welfare-to-Work funds; Community Development Block Grants (CDBG); Community Services Block Grants (CSBG); dedicated tax credits; and leveraged private funds. Funding of IDAs by states appears likely to continue growing.

POLICY PRINCIPLES

In February 2000, the Growing Wealth Working Group—a diverse collection of tax, antipoverty, and asset-building experts convened by CFED and CSD—adopted the following goal, which was meant to help guide the development of asset-building policies: "We seek an asset-building policy that is inclusive, progressive, simple, participant-centered and enduring." Specifically, each term can be characterized as follows:

- *Asset building* refers to financial accumulation and high-return investments.
- *Inclusive* means universal. It includes information, incentives, access, and facilitation to include everyone.
- *Progressive* means more for the poor. It refers to progressive distribution of benefits and adequacy of asset accumulation.
- *Simple* refers to administrative feasibility. To every possible extent, asset-building policy should be easy to understand and administer and fit into existing patterns and resources.
- *Participant-centered* means that account holders have a voice in the policy design and application.
- *Enduring* has two meanings. One is sustainability of asset-building policy, which includes low operating costs, investment efficiency, and profitability. The other is life-long asset accounts for participants.

These policy design principles are meant to apply to a wide range of policies; after all, no blueprint to build assets for low-income persons exists. More than likely, for political, fiscal, and implementational reasons, asset-building policies will be put into place incrementally, probably over the course of a few decades. It is very hard to know how that will happen, given the unpredictability of congressional and presidential elections, the state of the economy, and the longer term performance of early asset-building efforts, such as IDAs.

Also, it is important to note that the larger assets framework, articulated by Sherraden (1991, 2000a, 2000b) and Oliver and Shapiro (1995), is not simply limited to the acquisition of assets, although the policy options listed below are. For many Americans, the issue is also protecting or controlling the assets they have (such as the need for many elderly citizens to guard against risky home equity loans or the inability of Native Americans to deploy the vast assets they own). In addition, the options below do not explicitly address the stark differences in wealth holdings between whites and nonwhites, although most of the policy proposals are likely to benefit nonwhites disproportionately, given relative differences in income. What follow, then, are wide-ranging policy options to create and foster accumulation opportunities; generally, these options are not mutually exclusive.[6]

POLICY OPTIONS

Expand IDAs for the Working Poor

Following the welfare overhaul of 1996 and the focus of most existing IDA programs on the working poor, it is perhaps not surprising that policies to expand IDAs significantly for the working poor have proved to be very popular in Congress.

Currently, the most significant and politically viable proposal to build assets for the working poor is the SWFA, which offers federal tax credits to financial institutions and others to set up, match, and support IDAs. Under this legislation, which is designed to help move IDAs to scale, the tax credits serve as a funnel to pass federal matching funds to the working poor rather than through refundable tax credits to individuals. The tax credit structure, consequently, uses the bank's tax liability instead of the account holder's to deliver the match. A wide range of nonprofit organizations, credit unions, and others are expected to partner with financial institutions to implement the SFWA, which could initially reach hundreds of thousands and eventually millions of people.

Create and Fund Asset Accounts for Children, Starting at Birth

A number of proposals to establish and fund accounts for children have emerged from Congress, academics, and analysts over the last few years, although not all of them are progressive. Beginning asset accumulation at birth through individual accounts for all children holds enormous potential to build an inclusive, universal system; reduce child poverty; provide an important orientation toward the future; expand college attendance, home ownership, and business capitalization rates; better prepare people for retirement; and foster intergenerational transfers of wealth.

This potential is, however, matched by a series of challenges. Children's accounts can be approached in many ways (see Goldberg, chapter 15 in this volume; see also Ackerman and Alstott, 1999; Curley and Sherraden, 2000; Kuttner, 1998; Rowe, 2001); at the same time, many difficult political, ideological, and administrative issues must be resolved. As Fred Goldberg summarizes, three questions must be answered: (a) How are the accounts funded? (b) How are they administered? and (c) What rules govern distributions?

While these issues are difficult to resolve, there are two advantages of phasing in a system of children's savings accounts over time that must be underscored. First, by funding cohorts of children as they are born, the cost of this system is spread out over several years. For example, for approximately $4 billion per year, each newborn child in the United States would receive an account and a $1,000 deposit, the beginning of his or her life-deposit account. And second, after a few decades, as children grow up to be adults, a universal infrastructure with accounts for everyone would be in place. This would make the system much more feasible politically, administratively, and fiscally.

Provide Accounts for Everyone

The federal government could provide a universal infrastructure for asset building by setting up accounts for everyone, even if it made no deposits into the accounts. These accounts would then become the basis or entry point for financial products and a wide range of account-based subsidies, such as IRAs, 401(k)s, or children's savings accounts funded from individual, public, and private sources.[7] Also, if Sherraden (1996) is correct that, at some point in the next ten or twenty years, all of the individual asset accounts are going to merge into one account and system, up-front provision of those accounts could greatly facilitate the integration of the poor into that system.

Foster Financial Integration

Jean Hogarth and Kevin O'Donnell (1998) show that lower-income families with a deposit account are more likely to become home owners; to own a vehicle; to have insurance; to have term savings, such as certificates of deposits; to have IRAs; and to have access to other forms of credit, including major credit cards. They also assert that if reasonable account options are provided, low and moderate income people would use them. This research was, in fact, the rationale behind the recently enacted "First Accounts" pilot, described earlier, as well as one of the goals of the federal Electronic Funds Transfer Act of 1999 (EFT '99), which mandates electronic provision of federal benefits, to enable the unbanked to have an entry point into the financial mainstream to get that "first account."

Realizing the full potential of EFT '99 is precisely the subject of Michael Stegman's book, *Savings for the Poor: The Hidden Benefits of Electronic Banking* (1999). His principal recommendation is a national expansion of IDAs, while his other proposals include greater interagency coordination at the federal level (especially between Treasury and HUD), major financial education campaigns, and specific policy items to help EFT '99 achieve financial integration.

John Caskey (chapter 8 in this volume), a pioneer in research on the unbanked, also offers three important policy recommendations to be carried out in conjunction with private and nonprofit sector efforts to reach the unbanked. First, the government should help fund and evaluate pilot efforts to make affordable banking services more available in low-income communities. Second, the government should remove regulatory barriers that may prevent banks from implementing such pilot efforts. And third, greater Community Reinvestment Act (CRA) weight should be given for the efforts of financial institutions to provide basic financial services to lower-income households.

"Democratize" Retirement Savings Policies and Participate in Social Security Reform Efforts

There are great opportunities and equally great threats in moving asset-development policies forward through reforms to and expansions of retirement policy. While the threats may appear to outweigh the opportunities, these retirement policies are, nonetheless, very likely to be seriously considered and even become law in a second term Bush administration. Therefore, attempts to democratize such policies or ensure that they are inclusive and progressive must be pursued. For purposes of this discussion, retirement policy can be organized into three categories: (a) tax-favored, employer-based pensions, such as 401(k)s, and the federal government's equivalent, the Thrift Savings Plan (TSP); (b) private, voluntary savings accounts, such as IRAs and Roth IRAs; and (c) Social Security. These three sources of retirement savings are often called the "three-legged stool" of a secure retirement.

Employer-Based Accounts

The workplace holds great potential to build assets. Sondra Beverly and Michael Sherraden's (1999) four "institutional determinants of savings"—access, information, incentives, and facilitation—are or can be present in the workplace. Also, stable incomes are more likely in the workplace, making saving more probable. Finally, there are many excellent workplace-based, "defined contribution" systems (which are increasingly replacing "defined benefit" pensions) to build on, such as 401(k)s, 403(b)s, and the federal government's TSP. However, a major challenge here is that not all employees have access to or participate in pension plans and that existing plans disproportionately benefit higher-wage workers. Encouragingly, Peter Orszag and Robert Greenstein (chapter 13 in this volume) report, "[O]ffering low-and moderate-income workers the opportunity to participate in a matched savings program may be particularly important in encouraging a significant share of them to save." In addition to expanding the coverage of 401(k)s and other employer plans, policy makers should consider the plans listed below.

Expand or Learn from the Federal Thrift Savings Plan (TSP)

The plan is a very successful $9 billion per year, matched savings program that is available to 2.4 million federal workers (and better than most employer plans in reaching low-income workers), but it is not available to nonfederal workers.[8]

Establish IDAs or Other Progressively Matched Savings Programs in the Workplace

Once the SWFA IDA tax credit has been established for financial institutions (as the legislation proposes), and once the complex legal, tax, and coordination (with other benefits) issues associated with IDAs in the workplace are sorted out, then IDAs could potentially be established in the workplace by expanding the IDA tax credit to employers.

Private Savings

Adding a refundable or direct deposit component to IRAs would greatly expand their reach and appeal to low-income people. Unfortunately, a series of Congressional proposals would make the system even more regressive by raising deductible contribution limits, as well as in other ways.

Social Security

This chapter cannot do justice to the fierce debate over Social Security reform, in particular whether a portion of it should be privatized. It is clear that some see Social Security reform as the only or best way to build wealth on a large scale for all Americans (as well as the best way to save the Social Security system), while others see Social Security as the most significant safety net program remaining for low- and moderate-income Americans that should not be privatized. What appears likely, however, is that, at some point, given the Republican control of both the White House and Congress, some portion of Social Security will be privatized.

If that is the case, then it seems that advocates of asset development must become a part of the debate to ensure that such accounts are progressive, inclusive, and informed by the experiences of IDAs and other progressive efforts.

Revise Asset Limits in Safety Net Programs and Link Them to Asset-Building Policies

Given that income support policies have traditionally disallowed the accumulation of savings and assets and that lump-sum transfers are potentially a large source of savings, it is particularly important that the issue of assets be addressed in this context, preferably along the following three lines:

1. Asset limits in food stamps, Supplemental Security Income (SSI), Medicare, and (some) TANF programs should be raised, streamlined, and coordinated. The current system is terribly complex— with some asset limits set by the federal government, others set by the federal government yet subject to state interpretation, while others are determined by the states.[9]
2. Explicit asset-building opportunities should be explored and expanded in these safety net programs.
3. Lump-sum payments should be formally linked to asset-building programs such as IDAs.

Expand State-Level Initiatives to Build Savings and Assets

Like the federal government, state governments have many ways to foster asset accumulation and, given the growth of the New Federalism along with decentralization of much social policy, state-level asset-building opportunities seem likely to expand. Furthermore, preliminary analyses of state-level asset budgets by CFED in California and North Carolina show that state tax and other policies encourage asset-building for the non-poor in the same ways that policy does at the federal level. Accordingly, social and economic development policies at the state level should be examined to increase asset-building opportunities for the poor. Finally, rapidly expanding state-sponsored college savings plans (so-called Section 529 plans) hold the potential to foster savings for education among lower-income households, so these should be explored and linked to IDAs where possible (as Vermont did in 2000).

Explore and Expand Alternative Ownership Strategies

The policy recommendations offered thus far are admittedly account based. While not the focus of this chapter, a broader view of ownership does reveal several other possibilities for creating more stakeholders in America.

Jeff Gates, author of *The Ownership Solution* (2000) and *Democracy at Risk* (1998), has articulated several interesting and provocative models for "third-way capitalism" and "peoplizing ownership." While Gates sees great potential in revising tax and energy policy, as well as government contracts, as means to expand ownership, he sees little potential in strategies based on household savings tied to labor. He is most enthusiastic about ways that corporations can "include more stakeholders as shareholders, transforming outsiders into insiders." Another interesting set of ownership initiatives has been articulated by the Capital Ownership Group (COG), which is an "informal 'virtual think tank' of several hundred activists, academics, and other professionals whose mission is to create a coalition that promotes broadened ownership of productive capital."[10]

CONCLUSION

While the above agenda is definitely ambitious, it is important to observe that in just the last few years, a strong academic and political consensus has emerged that progressive asset building is the wisest policy direction to pursue (CFED, 2001). The question appears to be no longer "whether," but "how." This, in our view, is remarkable, in light of our thirty-plus years, combined over a twenty-year span, in the antipoverty and economic development fields. This consensus, which represents and transcends both the political and ideological right and left, surely accounts for part of the success IDA policy has enjoyed in the last few years. (It should be noted that the hard data generated by ADD, showing that poor people can save, deserves a large share of the credit as well). The fact that IDA policy proposals have gone from a few thousand in 1996, to a few million in 1998, to .5 billion of the SWFA in 2001 speaks to the enormous appeal that building assets for all Americans has. A large set of policy and political challenges do remain; however, public policy is, in our view, the sine qua non of a truly just society, built on widespread asset ownership. It is, therefore, imperative that these challenges be identified, addressed, and overcome.

NOTES

1. While the authors take responsibility for the lessons we offer, much of our work is based on research, theories, and policies pioneered by others. Our discussion draws from several sources, among them: (a) the seminal research of Michael Sherraden and CSD, whose work, including *Assets and the Poor* (1991), *Social Security in the 21st Century* (1996), and *Saving Patterns in IDA Programs* (coauthored with Johnson, Clancy, et al., 2000), created the research, theoretical, and policy framework for asset-building policy; (b) the pioneering work of Peter Barnes on common assets, summarized in *Who Owns the Sky?* (2001); (c) the Growing Wealth Working Group, a national brain trust of 50 experts in tax policy, asset building, and development policy convened by CFED and by CSD of Washington University to flesh out large-scale, asset-building principles and policies; (d) the Downpayments on the American Dream Policy Demonstration, also called ADD, which CFED had the good fortune to organize; (e) our thirteen community partners; and (f) 2,400 account holders, who also served as evaluation partners from whom we could learn. ADD is the first large-scale, well-funded, multidimensional test of the efficacy of IDAs as a tool for economic independence. The ADD participants' experiences and feedback have helped us to identify and evaluate the economic and social effects of IDAs, as well as the savings, asset acquisition, and economic literacy they entail. This valuable body of knowledge will inform and impel state and federal policy development. We've also been assisted by the larger IDA field, some 300-plus community programs strong, as well as their financial institutions, policy makers, philanthropic and community partners, and a network of more than one hundred Volunteers in Service To America (VISTA) workers in programs across the country, which were all linked by the IDA Learning Network and national learning conferences that CFED sponsors.

2. Three years ago we created a model for this sort of analysis at CFED. See Friedman, Clones, and Wilson (1997).

3. See Goldberg and Graetz (1998).

4. For an excellent summary of the genesis of federal IDA policy, see Michael Sherraden (2000b). For a detailed description of current and proposed IDA policies, see CFED (2001) and www.idanetwork.org.

5. For further details on state IDA policies, see http://gwbweb.wustl.edu/csd/statepolicy and the *State IDA Policy Resource Guide,* published in 2001 by the Corporation for Enterprise Development and Center for Social Development.

6. For further details on and the status of these proposals, see CFED (2001) and www.idanetwork.org.

7. Such accounts—first called universal savings accounts (USAs) were, in fact, proposed by CFED and CSD (1996) and may have contributed to the development of President Bill Clinton's own retirement—called by 1999 only "USA."

8. See Rideout (chapter 14 in this volume) for an excellent summary of the TSP.

9. See the *Federal IDA Policy Briefing Book* (Rist et al., 2001) for a detailed discussion of asset limits and other asset issues in income support programs.

10. For more information on COG and its policy recommendations, see http://cog.kent.edu/.

REFERENCES

Ackerman, B., and A. Alstott. (1999). *The Stakeholder Society*. New Haven, Conn.: Yale University Press.

Anderson, J. M. (1999). *The Wealth of U.S. Families: Analysis of Recent Census Data*. Chevy Chase, Md.: U.S. Department of Commerce, Bureau of the Census.

Barnes, P. (2001). *Who Owns the Sky?* Washington, D.C.: Island Press.

Beverly, S. (1997). *How Can the Poor Save? Theory and Evidence on Saving in Low-income Households*. St. Louis, Mo.: Center for Social Development (CSD), Washington University.

Beverly, S. G., and Sherraden, M. (1999). "Institutional Determinants of Savings: Implications for Low-Income Households and Public Policy." *Journal of Socio-Economics* 28(4), 457–473.

Corporation for Enterprise Development (CFED). (2001). *Building Assets: A Report on the Asset-Development and IDA Field*. Washington, D.C.: CFED.

Curley, J., and Sherraden, M. (2000). "Policy Lessons from Children's Allowances for Children's Savings Accounts." *Child Welfare* 79(6), 661–687.

Edwards, K., and Rist, C. (2001). *State IDA State Policy Resource Guide*. Washington, D.C.: Center for Social Development and Corporation for Enterprise Development.

Friedman, R., D. Clones, and C. Wilson. (1997). *Return of the Dream: An Economic Analysis of the Probable Returns of a National Investment in Individual Development Accounts*. Washington, D.C.: Corporation for Enterprise Development.

Gates, J. (1998). *Democracy at Risk: Rescuing Main Street from Wall Street*. Cambridge, Mass.: Perseus Books.

Gates, J. (2000). *The Ownership Solution: Toward a Shared Capitalism for the 21st Century*. Reading, Mass.: Perseus Books.

Goldberg, F., and M. Graetz. (1998). "Reforming Social Security: How to Implement a Practical and Workable System of Personal Retirement Accounts." Paper presented at the Conference on Administrative Costs of Individual Accounts, National Bureau of Economic Research, Cambridge, Mass., December 4.

Hogarth, J., and K. O'Donnell. (1998). *If You Build It, Will They Come?* Washington, D.C.: Consumer and Community Affairs, Federal Reserve Board.

Kuttner, R. (1998). "Rampant Bull." *The American Prospect*, 9(39).

Nothdurft, W. E., and B. Dyer. (1990). *Out from Under: Policy Lessons from a Quarter Century of Wars on Poverty*. Washington, D.C.: Council of State Policy and Planning Agencies.

Oliver, M., and T. Shapiro. (1995). *Black Wealth/White Wealth*. New York: Routledge.

Rist, C., et al. (2001). *Federal IDA Policy Briefing Book*. Washington, D.C.: Corporation for Enterprise Development.

Rowe, J. (2001). "Every Baby a Trust Fund Baby." *The American Prospect* 12(1).

Schreiner, M., M. Sherraden, M. Clancy, L. Johnson, J. Curley, M. Grinstein-Weiss, M. Zhan, and S. Beverly. (2001). *Savings and Asset Accumulation in Individual Development Accounts*. St. Louis, Mo.: CSD, Washington University.

Sherraden, M. (1991). *Assets and the Poor. A New American Welfare Policy.* Armonk, N.Y.: M. E. Sharpe.

Sherraden, M. (1996). *Social Security in the 21st Century.* St. Louis, Mo.: CSD, Washington University.

Sherraden, M. (2000a). "Asset-Building Policy and Programs for the Poor" (rev.). Prepared originally for the Ford Foundation conference on Benefits and Mechanisms for Spreading Asset Ownership in the United States, December 10–12, 1998, New York.

Sherraden, M. (2000b). *From Research to Policy: Lessons from Individual Development Accounts.* St. Louis, Mo.: CSD, Washington University.

Sherraden, M., L. Johnson, M. Clancy, S. Beverly, M. Schreiner, M. Zhan, and J. Curley. (2000). *Saving Patterns in IDA Programs.* St. Louis, Mo.: CSD, Washington University.

Stegman, M. (1999). *Savings for the Poor: The Hidden Benefits of Electronic Banking.* Washington, D.C.: The Brookings Institution.

U.S. Congress. (1996). *The Personal Responsibility and Work Opportunity Reconciliation Act.* Washington, D.C.: U.S. Government Printing Office.

U.S. Congress. (1998). *Assets for Independence Act.* Washington, D.C.: U.S. Government Printing Office.

Wolff, E. N. (2001). "The Rich Get Richer . . . and Why the Poor Don't." *The American Prospect* 12(3).

13

Toward Progressive Pensions: A Summary of the U.S. Pension System and Proposals for Reform

Peter Orszag and Robert Greenstein

The three tiers of retirement income and security are Social Security; private savings, accumulated by families and individuals in a variety of forms (e.g., bank accounts and mutual funds); and tax-favored retirement savings.[1] The focus of this chapter is the final tier. Though the government tries to promote pension saving by offering a variety of tax incentives, pension coverage remains unevenly spread, especially among lower-income workers and employees in small businesses. Frustrated by the failure to raise overall coverage rates much above the present 50-percent level and concerned about the implications of inadequate pension coverage of the coming retirement of baby boomers, policy makers included a variety of changes to the pension tax laws as part of the Economic Growth and Tax Relief Reconciliation Act (EGTRRA) of 2001 (Joint Committee on Taxation, 2001).

The purpose of this chapter is to review the shortcomings of the current pension system in the United States for lower-income workers and to evaluate different proposals for reform. Our conclusion is that the approach embodied in the 2001 EGTRRA legislation is fundamentally flawed and that changing the defaults in 401(k)-type plans and expanding a progressive matched savings program represents a much more promising mechanism for boosting retirement security among lower-income workers.

This chapter has six sections.[2] The first section summarizes the shortcomings in the current pension system; section two examines the principal causes of unequal coverage and accumulation rates, documented in the first section; section three discusses the benefits of progressivity in pension reform; section four examines a progressive set of policy changes to raise pension coverage and accumulation rates for lower- and moderate-income workers; section five examines the 2001 legislation and explains why it may endanger pension security among many lower-income workers; and the final section summarizes the main findings of the chapter.

OVERVIEW OF SHORTCOMINGS IN CURRENT PENSION SYSTEM

Governments across the world provide tax incentives for private pensions, which reflects a belief that unless the government provides tax preferences, individuals would not save sufficiently for their retirement. Keeping this in view, policy makers who have examined the current system in the United States often note three substantial problems: (a) only about half of American workers are covered by an employer-provided pension at any given point in time; (b) pension coverage and contribution rates vary significantly across types of workers and, in particular, are skewed toward higher earners; and (c) the amounts being accumulated by workers covered by pensions may not be sufficient to finance expected consumption levels during retirement. This section examines each of these three shortcomings in turn.

Overall Coverage Rates

Data from the Current Population Survey, as reported in Department of Labor publications, suggest that the percentage of full-time, private-sector wage and salary workers covered by a pension has fluctuated only narrowly since 1972, between 48 and 51 percent (see table 13.1).[3] Four brief points are worth noting about these figures:

1. They apply to individual workers at any given point in time. Roughly two-thirds of households have individuals who are covered by a pension at some point during their careers.[4]
2. The distribution of coverage rates between defined benefit and defined contribution plans[5] has shifted substantially toward defined contribution plans over the past three decades.[6]

Table 13.1 Retirement Plan Coverage Rates for Full-Time, Private-Sector Workers

Year	All	Male	Female
1972	48%	54%	38%
1979	50%	55%	40%
1983	48%	52%	42%
1988	48%	51%	44%
1993	50%	51%	48%
1995	48%	49%	48%
1997	50%	51%	48%
1999	51%	52%	49%

Source: U.S. Department of Labor, 1997, table 3.1, for 1972–1993; and U.S. Department of Labor, Pension and Welfare Benefits Administration, 2000, for 1995–1999.
Note: "Covered" means that the employee participated in any type of employment-based pension plan, including defined benefit plans, 401(k)-type plans, deferred profit sharing plans, and stock plans.

3. The coverage rate presented in table 13.1 is based on household survey data from the Current Population Survey. Employer-based surveys suggest somewhat higher coverage rates.[7]

4. Although the overall coverage rate has remained roughly 50 percent, the coverage rate for most age categories has declined.[8] The overall coverage rate has remained roughly constant despite the decline in most age-specific coverage rates because of changing demographics of the workforce (toward older workers, who have higher coverage rates than younger workers).[9]

In summary, table 13.1 illustrates the first concern regarding the pension system: *coverage rates have remained at only about 50 percent over the past three decades.*

Inequality in Pension Coverage and Accumulation Rates

The second policy concern is that pension coverage rates vary substantially by characteristics of the employee. For example, in 1999, only 14 percent of part-time workers were covered by a pension, relative to 51 percent of full-time workers; only 18 percent of workers with less than a high school degree were covered by a pension, relative to 62 percent of workers with a college degree or more; and only 6 percent of workers earning less than $10,000 per year were covered by a pension, relative to 76 percent of workers earning more than $50,000 per year. Other data also indicate that coverage rates are much lower in small businesses than in larger firms. For example, in 1993, only 13 percent of full-time workers in firms with fewer than 10 employees and 25 percent of those in firms with between 10 to 24 employees enjoyed pension coverage. But 73 percent of those in firms with one thousand or more employees enjoyed such coverage.[10]

Apart from rates of pension coverage, contribution rates (contributions as percentage of income) in defined contribution plans also vary across workers, resulting in another source of inequality. For example, low-income workers typically contribute a smaller percentage of their pay to 401(k)-type pension plans than higher-income workers. Among workers ranging from 18 to 64 years of age with a 401(k) plan in 1992, the average employee contribution rate (excluding employer matches) was 3.7 percent of pay for those with household income less than $25,000 and 7.9 percent of pay for those with household income exceeding $75,000.[11]

The inequality in pension contributions manifests itself in various indicators. For example, (a) higher-income workers enjoy more access to pension coverage than lower-income workers do; (b) covered higher-income workers also make larger contributions to pensions than lower-income-covered workers; and (c) because higher-income workers pay taxes at higher marginal tax rates, they receive a larger tax break for each dollar of contribution they make than their lower-earning colleagues do.

Data on the distribution of tax benefits from current pension and individual retirement account (IRA) provisions from the Tax Policy Center show that two-thirds of the tax benefits of current tax preferences for pensions accrue to those whose family incomes place them in the top one-fifth of the income scale. The people in the bottom 40 percent of the income distribution enjoy only 3.1 percent of the total tax benefit, relative to the 7.8 percent enjoyed by those in the top 1 percent of the income distribution.[12]

The inequality in pension contributions is also reflected in inequality in *pension wealth* (the accumulated value in a pension). In 1995, for example, the top 10 percent of the wealth distribution accounted for 62.3 percent of the total pension wealth.[13] More broadly, researchers have demonstrated substantial inequality in overall financial wealth (including assets outside pension funds) upon retirement.[14]

CAUSES OF UNEQUAL COVERAGE AND CONTRIBUTION RATES

Pension Coverage

The U.S. General Accounting Office (GAO)[15] has found that 85 percent of the labor force that worked but lacked pension coverage shared four important characteristics: (a) low incomes, (b) part-time jobs, (c) employment in small firms, and (d) membership in relatively young age groups.

Another way of exploring the coverage issue is to examine whether the noncovered workers are working in firms that do not provide pension coverage or are instead working in firms that offer pension plans—but for some reason do not participate in the plan. We adopt this perspective on coverage in this section.

Table 13.2 shows that in 1999, 58.5 percent of all private-sector workers (including part-time and full-time workers) were employed in firms that sponsored pension plans. Among these workers, 75 percent were covered by the plan, and 25 percent were not. In total, 56 percent of the private workforce was not covered by a pension (the somewhat lower figures in table 13.1 apply to full-time private-sector workers). The 56 percent consists of the 14.5 percent (0.25×0.585) of the workforce employed by firms with pension plans but not covered by them, plus the 41.5 percent of the workforce employed by firms without pensions. Low overall coverage rates thus arise because many workers are employed by firms that do not offer pensions (roughly three-quarters of the noncovered population) and because some workers are employed in firms offering pensions, but they are not covered by them.

Workers in Firms without Pension Plans

The absence of pension plans in many firms, especially small businesses, reflects many factors. One of the most commonly identified factors is the

Table 13.2 Pension Coverage of Private-Sector Wage and Salary Workers, 1999

Pension Coverage	Number of Workers (in Thousands)	% of Workers
Covered by a pension		
In firm sponsoring pension plan	57,437	58.5%
Covered by the plan	43,078	43.9%
Not covered by the plan	14,359	14.6%
In firm without pension plan (or "don't know")	40,795	41.5%
Total	98,232	100%
Not covered		
In firm with plan but not covered	14,359	26.0%
In firm without plan	40,795	74.0%
Total	55,154	100%

Source: U.S. Department of Labor, Pension and Welfare Benefits Administration, 2000, and authors' calculations.

complexity of the pension tax law. It is important to note, however, that much of the complexity in the tax code comes from complicated provisions biased toward higher earners. For example, if tax-preferred status were reserved for plans that covered a firm's entire workforce and contributed the same percentage of pay to each worker, the rules would not have to be complicated.[16]

Surveys of small businesses suggest that complexity and administrative costs are not the most important factors in discouraging them from offering pension plans. (The availability of simplified pension plans that are exempt from most of the particularly complicated tax rules reinforces this point.) table 13.3, taken from a recent survey conducted by the Employee Benefits Research Institute (EBRI, 2000) highlights that many firms do not offer pension plans because workers prefer other forms of compensation or because the nature of the firm or industry (e.g., its financial health and/or corporate attitude) makes it difficult to adopt pension plans.

Table 13.3 suggests that many of the most important reasons for firms not creating such plans are not particularly amenable to policy interventions. Policy makers may, therefore, be forced to consider other mechanisms for promoting retirement savings, outside of (or on top of) the employer-based system. Also note that only 3 percent of respondents listed inadequate benefits for business owners as the most important factor for not offering a plan. The 2001 legislation, which is examined in more detail in section six below, is predicated on the questionable argument that inadequate benefits for business owners is a critical factor that dissuades firms from creating pension plans.

Table 13.3 Reasons for Not Offering a Retirement Plan

Reasons	Percent of Respondents Identifying as Most Important Factor for Not Offering Plan
Employees prefer wages and/or other benefits	21%
Workers are seasonal, part-time, or high turnover	18%
Revenue is too uncertain	13%
Business is too new	11%
Costs too much to set up and administer	9%
Required company contributions are too expensive	8%
Too many government regulations	3%
Vesting requirements cause too much money to go to short-term employees	3%
Benefits for the owner are too small	3%
Owner has own deferred compensation arrangement	2%
Do not know where to go for information on starting a plan	1%
Other reasons	6%
Total (with rounding)	100%

Source: EBRI, 2000.

Noncovered Workers in Firms with Pension Plans

Workers who do not participate in a pension plan that their employer sponsors represent about one-quarter of all workers not covered by a plan. These workers comprise two subgroups: (a) those who are excluded from their employers' plans and (b) those who are eligible to participate but choose not to participate. Although the Internal Revenue Code stipulates a series of coverage conditions that must be met by "qualified pension plans," these rules allow qualified plans to exclude some lower-income workers and tilt contributions toward higher earners.

For example, firms are allowed to exclude employees under age 21 or those with less than one year of service with the firm from participation in a pension plan. One year of service is generally defined as 1,000 hours during a 12-month period. Thus, part-time and seasonal workers who do not work 1,000 or more hours for a single employer *never* qualify to participate in a pension plan. Table 13.4 shows that more than half of those excluded from employer-sponsored plans either do not meet the age and/or years of service requirements (36 percent) or do not work enough hours (19 percent) to qualify for participation in the plan. A firm is also allowed to exclude some portion of the remaining rank-and-file workers from the plan.[17] Table 13.4 indicates that 6 percent of noncov-

Table 13.4 Reasons for Noncoverage of Private-Sector Wage and Salary Workers Employed by Firms Sponsoring Pension Plans, 1999

Reason	Percent of Workers Identifying Reason
Do not meet age and/or service requirements	36%
Do not work enough hours	19%
Choose not to contribute	26%
Type of job not covered under plan	6%
Other or do not know	12%
Total	100%

Source: U.S. Department of Labor, Pension and Welfare Benefits Administration, 2000, table 13.

ered workers in firms with pension plans were not covered because their type of job was not eligible for the pension coverage. Table 13.4 also indicates that roughly one-quarter of noncovered workers in firms sponsoring pension plans choose not to participate, highlighting that some workers—disproportionate numbers of younger workers and those with low incomes or short tenures[18]—choose not to save even if offered a tax-preferred mechanism for doing so.

Other parts of the tax laws also allow higher-income workers to contribute (or receive) a higher percentage of their compensation in pension benefits than lower-income workers—as long as the differential does not exceed certain thresholds. For example, the "permitted disparity" rules allow integration of the employer's pension plan with Social Security.[19] This allows the firm to provide higher contributions to high-income workers without violating the nondiscrimination rules that normally apply.[20] In 401(k) plans, the contribution rates of higher-income executives are allowed to exceed those of rank-and-file workers, as long as the differential does not exceed certain bounds.

In summary, in both defined benefit and defined contribution plans, significant disparities are permitted in the generosity of the pension relative to income. Firms are often able to take advantage of the rules to skew benefits substantially toward higher earners.[21]

BENEFITS OF PROGRESSIVITY IN PENSION POLICY

Given the gaps in the current system, our thesis is that sound pension policy reform entails directing more of the pension tax incentives to middle- and lower-income workers who currently are saving little, if anything, in pensions. This emphasis on workers with low pension coverage is warranted for several reasons, including national saving and equity.

National Saving

One of the nation's economic imperatives is to raise the national saving rate to prepare for the retirement of the baby boom generation. Tax incentives intended to boost pension saving will raise national saving[22]—if they increase private saving by more than the cost to the government of providing the incentive. To raise private saving, the incentives must not simply cause individuals to shift assets into the tax-preferred pensions but must generate *additional* contributions. Since those with modest or low incomes are less likely to have other assets to shift into tax-preferred pensions, *focusing pension tax preferences on moderate- and lower-income workers increases the likelihood that lost tax revenue will reflect additional contributions rather than shifts in assets.*[23]

Progressivity and Fairness

As noted above, two-thirds of the benefits from existing tax preferences for pensions accrue to those in the top one-fifth of the income scale. Although "fairness" is partially in the eye of the beholder, we believe that any additional preferences should be less skewed. Higher-income workers are also less likely to be in danger of living in poverty in older age. This is another reason it makes sense to focus attention on lower-income workers in fashioning new tax-favored pension initiatives.

Any progressive pension reforms should be judged primarily in terms of how much additional coverage for moderate- and low-income workers they deliver and at what cost in terms of lost revenue.

PROPOSALS FOR EXPANDING PENSION SECURITY

A progressive set of reforms should center on three factors that have generally been shown to boost pension participation, especially among lower- and moderate-income workers: (a) some sort of progressive government matching contribution for employee contributions, (b) ease of savings, and (c) financial education in the workplace about the benefits of saving.[24]

Progressive Government Matching Contributions

One propitious approach to bolstering retirement income security among lower- and moderate-income workers would involve a progressive government matching formula—one that provides relatively larger matches to lower-income workers than higher-income workers. Data on participation rates in 401(k) plans among lower- and moderate-income workers suggest that such a progressive matching approach may be highly beneficial. In particular, a surprisingly large share of lower- and moderate-income workers participate in a 401(k) plan if offered the chance.

In other words, the *conditional participation rate* (that is, the participation rate among those workers who are offered the opportunity to save through a 401(k) plan) is surprisingly high, even for lower-income workers. To be sure, those offered the opportunity to participate in a 401(k) plan may be different in terms of their propensity to save from the rest of the population.[25] Our interpretation of the evidence still is that *offering low- and moderate-income workers the opportunity to participate in a matched saving program may be particularly important in encouraging a significant share of them to save.*[26] The evidence from 401(k) plans, furthermore, suggests that once someone starts to save, he or she continues to do so: Participation is persistent.[27]

Thus, a progressive government matching formula could be particularly beneficial for at least two (potentially related) reasons:

1. The tax treatment of pension contributions naturally creates an implicit *regressive* government matching formula. For every $1 that a taxpayer in the 35-percent marginal tax bracket contributes to a tax-preferred pension, for example, the taxpayer receives a tax benefit of 35 cents. A taxpayer in the 15-percent marginal tax bracket, however, receives only a 15-cent tax benefit for the same $1 contribution. To offset the regressivity of the implicit match provided by the tax code, the explicit government match should be *progressive*.

2. Although the conditional participation rate for lower-income workers who are offered 401(k) plans is higher than many analysts may have suspected, it is substantially lower than that for higher-income workers. To encourage higher rates of participation among lower-income workers, therefore, a more aggressive matching formula may be required.

Ease of Savings

Evidence suggests that participation rates are significantly affected if workers are to choose between automatic enrollment (unless they object) or affirmative indication of participation in a pension plan. In particular, participation is significantly higher if workers are enrolled in a savings plan unless they specifically opt out of the plan, relative to the participation rate if workers are *not* enrolled in the plan unless they specifically opt in.

For example, one recent study examined 401(k) savings behavior of employees in a large U.S. corporation before and after changes to the 401(k) plan. Before the plan change, the employees had to elect to participate in the 401(k); after the change, employees were automatically enrolled unless they specifically requested to opt out. Given that none of the economic features of the plan changed, the purely "rational" model of economic behavior would suggest that the change would have had no effect on 401(k) savings behavior. Contrary to the predictions of the model, however, the study found that 401(k) participation increased dramatically once automatic enrollment went into effect. The authors conclude that their results suggest "changes in savings behavior can be motivated simply by the 'power of suggestion.' "[28]

Financial Education

Enhancing financial education appears to be extremely effective in bolstering private retirement saving and elective pension contributions. As just one example of the education gap, a 1998 EBRI survey concluded that only 45 percent of workers have even attempted to figure out how much they will need to save for their retirement. Other surveys have also found that many American workers lack financial knowledge.[29]

The evidence suggests that the impact of employer-provided financial education on lower-income workers is greater than on higher-income workers. Higher-income workers tend to be more financially sophisticated to begin with and, therefore, the employer-provided education does not benefit them as much as lower-income workers. Expanded financial education campaigns and more encouragement to firms to provide financial education in the workplace may prove to be beneficial in raising retirement security for lower- and moderate-income workers.

THE ECONOMIC GROWTH AND TAX RELIEF RECONCILIATION ACT OF 2001

Description of Pension Provisions

The EGTRRA of 2001 included a series of important changes to the pension and IRA laws. Unfortunately, most of the changes violate the principles delineated above for sound pension reform. For example, the retirement saving provisions in EGTRRA are disproportionately aimed at higher earners; therefore, they are unlikely to raise national saving and will exacerbate the inequities in the income distribution of tax subsidies for retirement saving. Indeed, analysis by the Institute for Taxation and Economic Policy found that roughly 75 percent of the pension and IRA tax reductions would accrue to the 20 percent of Americans with the highest incomes.

To be sure, the legislation includes several helpful reforms in the pension laws. For example, it simplifies the rules on rolling over account balances from one type of retirement account to another, which, in turn, streamlines the system and may increase pension portability for some workers. The legislation also included a progressive matched savings tax credit, described further below.

The major pension and IRA provisions, however, involve various changes that allow larger contributions by high-income workers and do little, if anything, to simplify the system. The theory behind this approach is that liberalizing the rules for higher-income executives will lead more businesses to adopt pension plans and thereby help their middle- and lower-income

employees. The survey evidence presented above, however, raises questions about whether such a theory has any significant empirical support.
Among the most expensive retirement saving provisions in EGTRRA are
the following:

- *Increased Dollar Limits for Employee Contributions to 401(k) Plans.* In
  2001, workers were allowed to deposit a maximum of $10,500 in a
  401(k) account. EGTRRA raises the maximum to $15,000 by 2006
  (and by an additional $5,000 for those age 50 and over). However,
  the change generally affects only those at the top end of the income
  distribution. In 1996, for example, only 5.5 percent of participants
  in 401(k) plans made the maximum allowable contribution. Those
  constrained by the previous cap are disproportionately high-income
  employees: the average compensation among those making the
  maximum contribution, according to Treasury Department data,
  was approximately $130,000. Increasing the limit to $15,000 disproportionately benefits those at or near the top of the compensation scale.
- *Increased Maximum Employer-Employee Contributions.* The limit on
  deposits to a 401(k) account applies to employee contributions. The
  previous tax law also required that *combined* employer-employee
  contributions to 401(k)s and other defined contribution pension
  plans were not to exceed $35,000, or 25 percent of gross pay,
  whichever was lower. EGTRRA raises the maximum combined
  employer-employee contribution to $40,000, which again benefits
  primarily highly paid workers (the ones whose earnings are high
  enough to accommodate annual pension contributions of $35,000
  or more). EGTRRA also eliminated the requirement that such contributions should not exceed 25 percent of gross pay.
- *Expansions of Individual Retirement Accounts.* EGTRRA more than
  doubles the amount that a taxpayer and spouse can contribute each
  year to an IRA. Under prior law, a taxpayer and spouse could each
  contribute $2,000; EGTRRA raises the maximum contribution to
  $5,000 by 2008. An additional $1,000, as of 2006, can be contributed
  by taxpayers who are 50 years old and older. Thus, the total
  amount a couple can contribute will rise from $4,000 to $10,000,
  and the maximum an elderly couple can contribute will rise to
  $12,000. The proposed change will likely have little effect on fam-
  ilies and individuals who either made no IRA contributions under
  prior law or who deposited less than the $2,000 IRA limit. A
  Treasury study (Carroll, 2000) concluded that only 4 percent of all
  taxpayers who were eligible for conventional IRAs in 1995 made
  the maximum allowable $2,000 contribution.[30] The Treasury paper
  concluded: "Taxpayers who do not contribute at the $2,000 maxi-
  mum would be unlikely to increase their IRA contributions if the
  contribution limits were increased whether directly or indirectly
  through a backloaded [Roth] IRA" (14).[31]

- *Increased Maximum Considered Compensation.* Prior to EGTRRA, tax-favored pension benefits were based on compensation up to a maximum compensation level of $170,000. For example, if a firm contributed 5 percent of wages to a defined contribution pension plan, the maximum contribution was $8,500 (5 percent of $170,000). EGTRRA raised the maximum compensation level from $170,000 to $200,000. This change benefits only those paid more than $170,000 per year, the highest-paid 1 percent of workers.
- *Increase in Benefit Payable under a Defined Benefit Pension Plan.* Under prior law, the maximum allowable annual payment from a defined benefit pension plan was $135,000. EGTRRA increases the $135,000 limit to $160,000. This increase benefits only those at the very top of the income distribution, whose salaries are large enough to yield annual pension payments of more than $135,000. In addition, EGTRRA raises the amounts that can be paid from a defined benefit pension plan for early retirees by an even larger proportion, which allows plans to incorporate even larger early retirement subsidies than allowable under prior law.
- *Relaxed Top-Heavy Protections.* A special set of rules apply to pension plans that, while meeting the general nondiscrimination rules, deliver most of their benefits to company executives and owners. The "top-heavy" protections, as these safeguards are known, apply to plans in which 60 percent or more of the pension benefits accrue to such key employees. If the top-heavy rules are triggered, firms must undertake additional steps, such as accelerated vesting and certain minimum contributions or benefits, to help rank-and-file workers. EGTRRA weakened the top-heavy rules by redefining who qualifies as a "key" employee, and by selectively counting and not counting certain pension contributions in evaluating the top-heavy criteria. On the one hand, some of these changes simplify the rules, which is consistent with one of our principles for reform. But a report from the GAO found that the top-heavy rules generally do not involve substantial administrative costs.[32] In any case, weakening the rules may cause greater inequality in pension benefits.
- *Roth 401(k).* EGTRRA creates a "Roth" 401(k) modeled after the Roth IRA. Under a Roth 401(k), contributions can be made on an after-tax basis, would accumulate tax-free, and then can be withdrawn without tax. (Under a traditional 401(k), the contributions are exempt from tax but the withdrawals are not.) The introduction of the Roth 401(k) further complicates the retirement saving system and allows more retirement saving to be undertaken on a tax-preferred basis than a traditional 401(k).[33]

Most of these provisions were drawn from earlier pension legislation sponsored by Representatives Robert Portman (R-Oh.) and Benjamin Cardin (D-Md.). In analyzing the effects of that legislation, Norman Stein (1999) concluded, "Although there are good things in the Portman-Cardin bill, some of its major provisions would not contribute enough to good retirement policy to justify their substantial price tags, and other of its provisions would harm more people than they would help. It would be ironic and deeply unfortunate if this well-intentioned but flawed legislation is enacted, for it may well be remembered as the Retirement Insecurity and Pension Reduction Act of 1999. I fear that this possibility, an illustration of the law of unintended consequence, is all too real" (1–2).

The Saver's Credit

The EGTRRA legislation creates a tax credit of up to 50 percent of the contributions (up to $2,000 in contributions) made to IRAs and 401(k) plans by low- and moderate-income workers. The tax credit is progressive, beginning at 50 percent of the amounts (up to $2,000) deposited by the lowest-income families and phasing down to zero (0) percent. Married couples with incomes over $50,000 and single taxpayers with incomes over $25,000 are ineligible for the credit.

Several crucial details of the credit, however, result in its being of very limited value. It provides little or no benefit to the vast majority of lower-income workers and only a very small benefit to others:

1. Because the tax credit is not refundable, it provides *no* additional saving incentive to the vast numbers of families who otherwise qualify on paper for the 50-percent credit rate based on their annual income (under $30,000 for married couples and $15,000 for singles with no children).[34] These people are excluded from the credit because they have no income tax liability against which the credit could be applied.
2. For families with somewhat higher incomes, the fact that the credit is not refundable poses much less of a problem. But for these families, the credit is of little value, as it provides such a small incentive for saving. For example, a married couple earning $45,000 per year receives only a $200 tax credit for depositing $2,000 into a retirement account. This small credit represents a very low matching rate and, therefore, provides little incentive to participate.

The credit for lower- and middle-income savers, designed to address concerns about the regressivity of the pension provisions, could thus be substantially improved. Most low-income families, especially ones with children, do not qualify for it because it is not refundable: Of the 60 million tax units with incomes in the qualifying range to benefit from the 50-percent tax credit if they made a 401(k) or IRA contribution, only 10 million would actually benefit.[35] Furthermore, the credit ostensibly sunsets in 2006. A better designed credit is essential to evaluate appropriately the benefits of the general approach.

In summary, the pension and IRA provisions in EGTRRA score very poorly on our proposed criteria for reforming the retirement saving system. They do little to raise national saving and may even reduce it, and they further tilt the distribution of retirement saving tax subsidies toward higher earners.

CONCLUSIONS

From the above discussion, we arrive at the following conclusions: (a) pension reforms should be directed primarily at expanding pension coverage among moderate and lower-income workers, both to build national saving and to strengthen retirement security; (b) most of the pension benefits in the 2001 tax legislation would accrue instead to higher-income workers who already enjoy high rates of pension coverage; and (c) a much more promising approach to bolstering retirement security would include providing some sort of progressive government matching contribution for employee contributions, making it easier to save and providing financial education in the workplace about the benefits of saving.

The benefits of such a progressive approach to retirement security include a much higher likelihood of adding to national saving, reducing elderly poverty, and improving the distribution of retirement tax subsidies. For both efficiency and equity reasons, this type of progressive package is, thus, much more attractive than the pension provisions in the 2001 tax legislation.

NOTES

Much of this chapter draws upon joint work with Mark Iwry and William Gale, but the views expressed here represent those of the authors alone.

1. Private and government pensions accounted for 18 percent of the total income of the elderly in 1996. Social Security Administration (1999), 6.

2. Many of the themes of this chapter are also underscored in Gale and Orszag (2003).

3. The General Accounting Office reports an improvement in pension coverage rates between 1988 and 1998. See General Accounting Office (2000a). Its figures, however, reflect only two points in time. They also include all workers, not just full-time workers. Between 1988 and 1998, the share of part-time workers in the workforce fell slightly, and the share of full-time workers rose. In 1988, part-time workers represented 17.5 percent of employment; in 1998, they represented 16.9 percent.

4. According to data from the Health and Retirement Survey (http://www.bls.census.gov/cps/cpsmain.htm), which provides information on the income and wealth holdings of people born between 1931 and 1941 and, therefore, currently in their peak retirement years, 65.6 percent of households had positive pension wealth. See Gustman and colleagues (2000).

5. A defined benefit plan provides a payment in retirement that depends only on the worker's wage and years of service; thus, it defines the benefit that will be received. A defined contribution plan, on the other hand, defines the contribution

that the firm will make, but the retirement benefit that can be financed from that contribution depends on the rate of return earned before retirement. Defined benefit plans, therefore, assign accrual risk (the risk that funds set aside today will not accumulate at the expected rate of return) to the firm. Given a worker's earnings history, retirement benefits are certain. Defined contribution plans, on the other hand, assign accrual risk to the individual worker; even conditional on an earnings history, retirement benefits depend on the efficacy with which contributions were financially managed.

6. See Gale, Papke, and VanDerhei (1999).

7. The Current Population Survey is a monthly survey of roughly 50,000 households conducted by the Census Bureau for the Bureau of Labor Statistics. Pension coverage rates are higher in the Employee Benefits Survey (roughly 60 percent, relative to 50 percent in the Current Population Survey), an establishment-based survey conducted by the Bureau of Labor Statistics (http://www.bls.gov/ncs/ebs/home.htm). For a discussion of the results from these two surveys, see Herz, Meisenheimer, and Weinstein (2000).

8. For example, the coverage rate for those aged 16 to 24 fell from 27 percent in 1979 to 21 percent in 1993, the coverage rate for those aged 30 to 34 fell from 56 percent in 1979 to 50 percent in 1993, and the coverage rate for those aged 50 to 54 fell from 65 percent in 1979 to 61 percent in 1993. The coverage rates for those aged 40 to 44 and 45 to 49 both increased. Those are the only age categories to experience an increase in coverage rates between 1979 and 1993. See U.S. Department of Labor (1997), table 3-1.

9. The figures in table 13.1 also do not reflect workers who make contributions to individual retirement accounts (IRAs), which were initially designed to assist those who were not covered by an employer-provided plan. But Carroll (2000) found that only 7 percent of the taxpayers eligible for conventional IRAs in 1995 contributed to an IRA in that year (with at least one-fifth of these participants also covered by an employer-provided plan). Thus, including IRAs in the analysis would not substantially affect the overall coverage rate.

10. U.S. Department of Labor, Social Security Administration, Small Business Administration, and Pension Benefit Guaranty Corporation (1994), table B9.

11. General Accounting Office (1996), table II.4.

12. Burman et al. (2004).

13. Mishel, Bernstein, and Schmitt (1999), table 5.4. It is worth noting that pension wealth is somewhat more evenly distributed than other forms of financial wealth. At the very top of the wealth distribution, the differences between pensions and other forms of wealth become particularly pronounced: The top 1 percent of the wealth distribution in 1995 held 51.4 percent of stocks and mutual funds and 65.9 percent of bonds, but only 17.7 percent of pension funds. "Pension wealth" excludes the present value of Social Security benefits.

14. See, for example, Venti and Wise (1998); and Lusardi (2000). Venti and Wise note that substantial inequality in wealth holdings exists even at the same lifetime earnings levels and conclude that, "In the United States it is not only households with low incomes that save little. A significant proportion of high-income households also save very little; and not all low-income households are nonsavers. Indeed a substantial proportion of low-income households save a great deal" (191). Lusardi relates saving behavior to financial planning and notes that approximately one-third of Americans who are close to retirement have done little or no retirement planning.

15. General Accounting Office (2000a).

16. Some rules would have to allow for employees who leave the firm early in the year and other complexities. For further discussion of a reform along these lines, see Halperin and Munnell (1999). (The Halperin and Munnell proposal, it should be noted, includes many other elements in addition to the simplification described here.)

17. See Orszag and Stein (2001) for further discussion of the relevant rules.

18. General Accounting Office (2000a), 17.

19. Approximately 50 percent of workers covered by defined benefit plans in medium and large firms are in an integrated plan (Slusher [1998]). In defined contribution plans, Social Security integration is much less common.

20. The maximum permitted disparity between the contribution rate above the Social Security maximum taxable earnings ($76,200 in 2000) and below it is 5.7 percentage points. In other words, a firm can contribute 10 percent of pay to the defined contribution plan for an individual's earnings below $76,200 and 15.7 percent of pay for any earnings above $76,200 without violating the nondiscrimination rules.

21. For a discussion of how some firms are able to satisfy the nondiscrimination rules, while still directing 90 percent or more of their contributions to executives, see Orszag (2000) and Orszag and Stein (2001).

22. National saving is the sum of public saving and private saving. All else being equal, every dollar of lost revenue reduces public saving by one dollar. Consequently, for national saving to increase, private saving must increase by more than $1 in response to each dollar in lost revenue. If the revenue loss is fully offset through other fiscal measures, then the net impact on national saving is simply the change in private saving. In this case, public saving would be unchanged.

23. Economists continue to debate the impact on private saving from existing pension incentives. Most economists agree, however, that whatever the overall effect, focusing incentives on those with fewer opportunities to shift assets from taxable to nontaxable forms is likely to produce a larger increase in private saving for any given reduction in government revenue. For a discussion of the impact of existing tax preferences, see Engen, Gale, and Scholz (1996), and Poterba, Venti, and Wise (1995).

24. See also the related suggestions in Gale and Orszag (2003).

25. This issue is the subject of heated debate. See, for example, Poterba, Venti, and Wise (1995). For an opposing view, see Engen, Gale, and Scholz (1996).

26. The relatively low level of participation in IRAs, relative to the conditional 401(k) participation rate, may highlight four important factors in encouraging saving: a positive matching rate; financial education in the workplace; and peer effects and the role of the nondiscrimination rules, which tie maximum contribution rates for higher-income workers to those undertaken by lower-income workers. The evidence on the impact of higher matching contributions in 401(k) plans is actually somewhat mixed, although the presence of a match does appear to raise contributions.

27. See, for example, Papke, Petersen, and Poterba (1996).

28. Madrian and Shea (2000).

29. Levitt (1998).

30. Carroll (2000).

31. Carroll (2000, 7). It is only the very small minority of eligible taxpayers contributing the maximum $2,000 to an IRA who are likely to benefit from raising the maximum contribution amount on Roth IRAs above $2,000. A large share of such

taxpayers are likely to be higher earners who are not covered by an employer-provided pension and are, therefore, eligible for making contributions to conventional IRAs regardless of their income. (The income limits on eligibility do not apply to those who are not covered by an employer-provided pension.) In addition, an increase in the IRA contribution limits (to $5,000) is likely to work to the detriment of some low- and middle-income workers by inducing some small businesses not to offer an employer-sponsored pension plan.

32. General Accounting Office (2000b).

33. For example, $15,000—deposited into a conventional 401(k) plan today, accumulated at a 5-percent real tax-free rate of return over 20 years and then taxed at a 31-percent rate upon withdrawal—will yield $27,461.63 in after-tax income in 20 years. But $15,000 of after-tax dollars put into a Roth 401(k) today, accumulated at a 5-percent real tax-free rate of return over 20 years, and then distributed tax free will yield $39,799.46 in after-tax income in 20 years. For the equivalent deposit in a traditional 401(k) plan today to obtain the same $39,799.46 of after-tax income in 20 years, the original deposit would have to be $21,937.13, an amount that exceeds the permitted limits on 401(k) plans.

34. For example, a married couple with two children in 2003 started owing income tax at an adjusted gross income (AGI) slightly higher than the $30,000 threshold for the 50-percent credit rate. Furthermore, the income threshold is not indexed to inflation, meaning that fewer and fewer families can even potentially benefit from the nonrefundable credit over time.

35. Results from the Urban Institute-Brookings Institution Tax Policy Center model suggest that 21.1 million joint filers, 12.4 million head-of-household filers, and 26.6 million single filers qualify for the 50-percent credit based on income. Of these 60 million filers, only 10 million would receive any benefit from the credit if they made an IRA or 401(k) contribution. Only 64,000, or 0.1 percent, of those qualified on the basis of income would receive the maximum credit if they made the maximum allowable contribution. See also Orszag and colleagues (2000) and Gale, Iwry, and Orszag (2004) for further discussion.

REFERENCES

Burman, L. E., W. G. Gale, M. Hall, and P. R. Orszag. (2004). "Distributional Effects of Defined Contribution Plans and Individual Retirement Arrangements." *National Tax Journal* 57(3), 671–702.

Carroll, R. (2000). *IRAs and the Tax Reform Act of 1997*. Washington, D.C.: Office of Tax Analysis, Department of the Treasury, January.

Employee Benefit Research Institute (EBRI). (1998). "Retirement Confidence Survey." Available at http://www.ebri.org/rcs/1998.

Employee Benefit Research Institute. (2000). "The 2000 Small Employer Retirement Survey: Summary of Findings." Available at http://www.ebri.org.

Engen, E., W. Gale, and J. K. Scholz. (1996). *Personal Retirement Saving Programs and Asset Accumulation: Reconciling the Evidence*. NBER Working Paper 5599, May.

Gale, W., J. M. Iwry, and P. R. Orszag. (2004). "Improving the Saver's Credit." Policy Brief No. 135, July. Washington, D.C.: Brookings Institution.

Gale, W., and P. Orszag. (2003). "Private Pensions." *Agenda for the Nation*. Washington, D.C.: The Brookings Institution.

Gale, W., L. Papke, and J. VanDerhei. (1999). "Understanding the Shift from Defined Benefit to Defined Contribution Plans." A paper prepared for the Conference on ERISA after 25 Years: A Framework for Evaluating Pension Reform, The Brookings Institution, September.

General Accounting Office (GAO). (1996). "401(k) Pension Plans: Many Take Advantage of Opportunities to Ensure Adequate Retirement Income." GAO/HEHS-96-176.

General Accounting Office. (2000a). "Pension Plans: Characteristics of Persons in the Labor Force without Pension Coverage." GAO/HEHS-00-131, August.

General Accounting Office. (2000b). "Private Pensions: 'Top-Heavy' Rules for Owner-Dominated Plans." GAO/HEHS-00-141, August.

Gustman, A., O. Mitchell, A. Samwick, and T. Stenmeier. (2000). "Pension and Social Security Wealth in the Health and Retirement Study." In *Wealth, Work, and Health: Innovations in Measurement in the Social Sciences,* eds. J. P. Smith and R. J. Willis. Ann Arbor: University of Michigan Press, 47–68.

Halperin, D., and A. Munnell. (1999). "How the Pension System Should Be Reformed." Presented at The Brookings Institution conference, ERISA after 25 Years, September.

Herz, D. E., J. R., Meisenheimer, and H. G. Weinstein. (2000). "Health and Retirement Benefits: Data from Two BLS Surveys." *Monthly Labor Review* (March), 3–20.

Joint Committee on Taxation. (2001). Summary of Provisions Contained in the Conference Agreement for HR 1836, the Economic Growth and Tax Relief Reconciliation Act of 2001. May 26. Available at http://www.house.gov/jct/x-50-01.pdf.

Levitt, A. (1998). "The SEC Perspective on Investing Social Security in the Stock Market." Speech by the SEC Chairman at the John F. Kennedy School of Government, October 19.

Lusardi, A. (2000). "Explaining Why So Many Households Do Not Save." Unpublished working paper. University of Chicago, Irving B. Harris Graduate School of Public Policy Studies, January.

Madrian, B., and D. F. Shea. (2000). *The Power of Suggestion: Inertia in 401(k) Participation and Savings Behavior.* NBER Working Paper No. 7682, May.

Mishel, L., J. Bernstein, and J. Schmitt. (1999). *The State of Working America 1998–1999.* Washington, D.C.: Economic Policy Institute.

Orszag, P. R. (2000). *How the Cross-Testing Pension Loophole Harms Low- and Moderate-Income Workers.* Washington, D.C.: Center on Budget and Policy Priorities, March.

Orszag, P. R., R. Greenstein, I. Lav, and J. Sly. (2000). *The Tax Credit for Low- and Middle-Income Savers in the Senate Finance Committee Pension Bill: Would Lower Income Families Really Benefit?* Washington, D.C.: Center on Budget and Policy Priorities, September. Available at http://www.cbpp.org/9-13-00tax.htm. Last accessed December 15, 2004.

Orszag, P. R., and N. Stein. (2001). "Cross-Tested Defined Contribution Plans: A Response to Professor Zelinsky." *Buffalo Law Review* 49 (Spring/Summer), 628–674.

Papke, L., M. Petersen, and J. Poterba. (1996). "Did 401(k)s Replace Other Employer-Provided Pensions?" In *Advances in the Economics of Aging,* ed. D. Wise. Chicago: University of Chicago Press, 219–240.

Poterba, J., S. Venti, and D. Wise. (1995). "Do 401(k) Contributions Crowd Out Other Personal Saving?" *Journal of Public Economics* 58, 1–32.

Slusher, C. (1998). "Pension Integration and Social Security Reform." *Social Security Bulletin* 61(3), 20–27.

Social Security Administration. (1999). *Fast Facts and Figures about Social Security.* Washington, D.C.: Office of Research, Evaluation, and Statistics, Social Security Administration.

Stein, N. (1999). Testimony before the Subcommittee on Oversight, House Ways and Means Committee, March 23.

U.S. Department of Labor. (1997). *Report on the American Workforce 1997.* Washington, D.C.: Author.

U.S. Department of Labor, Pension and Welfare Benefits Administration. (2000). "Coverage Status of Workers under Employer Provided Plans." Available at http://www.dol.gov/dol/pwba/public/programs/opr/CWS-Survey/hilites.html.

U.S. Department of Labor, Social Security Administration, Small Business Administration, and Pension Benefit Guaranty Corporation. (1994). *Pension and Health Benefits of American Workers.* Washington, D.C.: Author. Available at www.dol.gov/ebsa/programs/opr/bluebook/cover.htm.

Venti, S. F., and D. A. Wise. (1998). "The Cause of Wealth Dispersion at Retirement: Choice or Chance?" *American Economic Review* (May), 185–191.

14

The Thrift Savings Plan Experience: Implications for a Universal Asset Account Initiative

Elaine C. Rideout

Public policies that promote asset accumulation are catching on in the United States. The leading asset-based policy approach, individual development account (IDA) programs, are now established at the federal level, via the Assets for Independence Act (AFIA), and in at least thirty-four states. The accounts are established for low-income savers who are provided with matching contributions, as well as financial education and counseling. There are currently over five hundred community IDA programs in operation with over ten thousand working poor participants, and over thirty thousand AFIA-funded accounts matured in 2003–2004 (CSD, 2000; Department of Health and Human Services, 2003). Proponents of the asset-building movement in the United States are grappling with a number of issues in an effort to make these policies universally available. A number of these issues are very similar to those faced by the nation's now widespread capital accumulation movement, which essentially began in 1981 when the Internal Revenue Service (IRS) released rules for the establishment and implementation of 401(k) retirement savings plans. Specifically, the development and establishment of the government's own 401(k)-style thrift savings plan (TSP) for federal employees in the mid-1980s offers asset builders a case-study-in-scale. Today, section 401(k) is probably the best-known part of the U.S. code, and the TSP has become the largest 401(k) in the country.

Much can be learned from the process of innovation that led to the successful establishment of the TSP. The three-year effort that culminated in the TSP privatization of a portion of the federal civil service pension resolved a number of issues and concerns that are relevant today in the context of asset-building policy expansion, as well as to reformers advocating individual Social Security accounts. The following issues, highlighted here, will be discussed in greater detail in this chapter:

- *Conventional wisdom:* Conventional wisdom holds that "poor people don't save." How effective are savings and asset-building tools for populations that are least able to save, and what measures are necessary to secure equal access and proportional participation across income levels?
- *Funding:* A sustainable funding stream is essential to the success of asset-building policy. The approach requires an enormous up-front investment of capital, while the payoff is long term. It is often challenging to achieve long-term funding when budgets are annually debated and the long run is usually thought of as five years. Reformers of the old civil service pension, the precursor to the TSP, which was funded on a "pay-as-you-go" basis like Social Security is now, found forward financing of individual TSP accounts to be a particularly difficult challenge.
- *Central versus decentralized administration:* How should asset-building programs be administered? Should they be employer-based? If so, how would the system accommodate self-employed and non-working savers? Should investments and account management be centrally managed, or should they be decentralized, as individual retirement accounts (IRAs) currently are? How do policy makers ensure that all savers receive consistent, comprehensive information that will allow them to make well-informed investment decisions? How do they ensure that excessive management fees do not undermine essential returns?
- *Government interference in the private marketplace:* If the government is managing investments, it must be done without compromising the independence of American private enterprise.
- *Risk:* How can policy designers mitigate investment risk? How do they help ensure that savings invested in the financial markets will not be mismanaged or even destroyed? How do they make sure investors make prudent investment choices?

All these issues were discussed, in a highly charged partisan environment, over three years of federal pension reform deliberations. Today, the pension system that resulted is anything but controversial. For employees at all income levels, the TSP is among the most popular of all federal benefits. Its success holds much promise for replication by asset-building reformers. This chapter explores how the founders of the TSP resolved the issues raised above and applies the lessons learned to identifying optimal strategies for the development of a large-scale, comprehensive, national asset-building policy.

BACKGROUND: THE CAPITAL ACCUMULATION MOVEMENT

While the objective of the asset-building movement is the immediate accumulation of nonfinancial capital assets, the capital accumulation movement arose to facilitate financial capital accumulation for retirement security. The capital accumulation movement took off in 1981, when the IRS released the rules and regulations for the establishment of 401(k) plans. The 401(k) plan essentially clarified the pretax status of earlier cash or deferred arrangement (CODA) profit sharing plans—either in cash or company stock. Profit sharing in the United States was born in 1797 in a glass factory in Pennsylvania. Congress passed legislation permitting tax-favored treatment of the plans in 1921. When the stock market crashed in 1929, an estimated 70 percent of all profit sharing plans were ended. Companies did not begin to reinstate them widely until the 1940s. As a result of the bankruptcy of Studebaker in 1963, the largest in U.S. history at that time, and the collapse of its pension plan, the Employee Retirement Income Security Act (ERISA) was enacted in 1974 to help preserve the pensions of corporate employees even in the event of bankruptcy. But ERISA was unclear about the status of existing profit sharing arrangements, which prompted the passage of Section 401(k) of the Internal Revenue Code in 1978 (Profit Sharing/401(k) Council, 2000).

Since then, the nation's employers have moved away from traditional defined benefit plans to participant-directed, defined contribution plans, the primary vehicles for capital accumulation today. Traditional defined benefit plans guarantee that workers will receive certain benefits at retirement, while defined contribution plans provide workers with certain contributions to their retirement funds. Under traditional defined benefit plans, employers are held responsible for producing returns that would be adequate to pay for the specific benefits promised in accordance with individual wage and service criteria. In defined contribution plans, however, employees typically make investment choices, and the value of their final benefits depends on how successfully they invest their account balances. The investment risk is, thus, borne by the employee instead of by the employer. Defined contribution plans continue to displace traditional defined benefit employee pensions and include IRAs; CODA profit sharing plans; KEOGH plans; and section 401(k), 403(b), and 457 retirement savings plans. Two other developments that hastened this movement are government regulation and market competition.

Government Regulation

Many employers and employer organizations blame the government for unwittingly hastening the demise of the traditional defined benefit corporate pension. The Profit Sharing/401(k) Council of America attributes much of the decline of defined benefit pension plans to overly zealous oversight and the onerous regulatory burdens imposed by the Department of Labor (Profit Sharing/401(k) Council, 2000).

U.S. lawmakers' attempts to boost anemic U.S. savings rates and the surging stock markets of the 1990s also fueled the capital accumulation movement. As defined contribution plans became popular with employees, employers found it easier to eliminate or cut back on expensive and unwieldy defined benefit plans if they could offer employees a savings, profit sharing, or stock ownership plan instead.

Market Competition

The forces of global competition, impressive track records of institutional investors, and government rules that allow corporations to capture excess contributions to boost corporate balance sheets have all contributed to the number of defined benefit to defined contribution plan conversions. Many corporations have found that converting from defined benefit programs, with their dynamic and thus less predictable actuarial financing burdens, to defined savings plans, with their static cost predictability, has benefits in addition to increased cash flows and more accurate budget projections. As market returns swelled over the last decade, many pension funds became either fully funded or overfunded. The excess funds of overfunded defined benefit plans were frequently diverted to invest in new plant and equipment, to help finance company stock buybacks, or simply to enhance the bottom line.

While the financial incentives to control costs and reclaim excess plan assets are often appealing to managers, the marketplace has also changed to favor the capital accumulation movement. A mobile workforce places a high premium on portable benefits, and traditional defined benefits are not portable. To remain competitive globally, U.S. businesses are cutting back on workers and paring benefits, frequently by employing part-time workers, short-term project workers, temporary workers, and independent contractors. They are also instituting profit sharing, performance-based pay, and other productivity-enhancing policies, and substituting equity for cash compensation.

In 1999, corporate 401(k) plans covered 55 million participants. A majority of U.S. employers (87 percent of companies with over one hundred employees) offer the plans as a way to save for retirement. For small companies, 42 percent of all employees participate in a plan (Profit Sharing/401(k) Council, 2000). At year-end of 2003, according to the Investment Company Institute in Washington, D.C., workers had approximately $3.6 trillion invested in 401(k) plans, IRAs, and other capital accumulation plans. These plans have become so important to workers that companies today need to offer the plans to attract and retain quality employees.

The overwhelming success and popularity of personal asset accounts like the 401(k) plan extend to the federal TSP, which has become the largest 401(k) retirement savings and investment vehicle in the country.

THE THRIFT SAVINGS PLAN

The TSP (also known as the Plan), currently with over \$140 billion in assets under management, was inaugurated in 1987, shortly after the enactment of the Federal Employee Retirement Savings Act (FERSA) of 1986 (Rideout and Cavanaugh, 1989). The Plan is a federal employee benefit, with 3.3 million participants enrolled, including members of Congress, congressional staff, and civilian and military personnel. The Plan allows federal workers to supplement their federal defined benefit pensions with their own savings. Employees make voluntary contributions via payroll deductions, and their employing agencies match a portion of their savings. Contributions and earnings are tax deferred until they are withdrawn at retirement. Active participants may borrow against their account balances for certain purposes, including buying a home, education, and medical expenses. They may also make limited emergency withdrawals.

Accounts are participant directed; that is, participants choose how to invest their fund balances. Currently, participants may choose from five investment funds: a government securities investment (G) fund, a common stock index investment (C) fund, a fixed income index investment (F) fund, a small cap stock index investment (S) fund, and an international stock index investment (I) fund.

The Federal Retirement Thrift Investment Board (FRTIB), a small, independent federal agency, governed by a five-member, bipartisan board of directors and a chief operating officer (CEO) appointed by the board, administers the TSP. The FRTIB is unique among federal agencies in that its board and executive director serve as fiduciaries. They are required by law to act prudently and solely in the interest of TSP participants and beneficiaries. Because all funds held in trust by the Plan belong to participants and not the government, this management structure was established to ensure that the Plan would be free of political interference. To ensure the fiduciary accountability envisioned by ERISA and reinforced for the TSP in FERSA, the FRTIB is an independent government entity and is exempt from most of the normal terms and conditions placed on agencies of the executive branch of government. Its operating expenses are not subject to budget review, for example. While the FRTIB is independent of executive or congressional interference, it is subject to alternative forms of strict oversight, including that of a fourteen-member Employee Thrift Advisory Council that represents federal employee unions and other employee organizations, a fiduciary compliance audit by the Department of Labor, and oversight audits by a private accounting firm and the General Accounting Office.

The FRTIB serves participants primarily on a wholesale, as opposed to a retail level, establishing policy and regulation and primarily serving policy makers and agency administrators, and, less often, individual Plan participants. It relies on an extensive network of agency personnel offices to educate employees about their options under the Plan. The employing agencies' personnel, payroll, and other administrative officers are responsible for employee counseling, Plan enrollments, and the accurate and timely transmission of participant data to the Plan's record keeper, currently a private information technology (IT) contractor. The Plan contracts with the Department of Agriculture's National Finance Center to manage the Plan's Service Office to serve agency staff as well as separated, retired, and other Plan participants directly, processing everything from address changes to investment allocations and reallocations, disbursements, court orders, IRA rollovers, and so on.

THE ASSET-BUILDING MOVEMENT

The tools for capital accumulation, like the TSP and other 401(k)s, are well established. Analogous tools for asset accumulation, such as IDAs, are only beginning to be widely recognized. Both IDAs and 401(k)s usually include a matched savings component, but while 401(k)s are matched by employers, IDA savings are matched by governments, employers, and charitable organizations. The chief difference between IDAs and 401(k)s is that IDAs lack the pretax benefit of 401(k)s, but allow for preretirement withdrawals for asset-building purposes. Like the TSP and most capital accumulation plans, IDAs require the active involvement of participants who are equal players in the process. The participants must save money out of their own paychecks, manage their own investments, and decide what degree of investment risk they are willing to take. Both types of account holders typically receive financial education and counseling.

Governments, private foundations, nonprofit service providers, and private financial institutions support IDA programs administratively. The Corporation for Enterprise Development (CFED) has conducted evaluations of participation in IDA programs and has concluded that IDA programs return five times the cost of their initial investment in the form of new businesses, new jobs, increased earnings, higher tax receipts, and reduced welfare expenditures (Boshara, 1999).

In addition to IDAs supported by CFED's American Dream Demonstration (ADD) initiative and the federal AFIA, other self-directed savings tools that facilitate asset building are beginning to emerge. The Federal Home Loan Banks' (FHLBanks) Affordable Housing Program, a set-aside program, and the Department of Housing and Urban Development's (HUD) Family Self-Sufficiency and HOME Investment Partnerships programs are examples. Under current tax law, employers may choose to match flexible spending accounts (FSAs) used for IDA-type purposes. Employers have even implemented reverse IDAs financed through 401(k) programs. The Town of Cary, North Carolina, for example, projects forward an employee's 401(k) account balances and advances up to 90 percent of that amount for the down payment on a home. In another example, a Baltimore web design firm augments employees' savings efforts with a $15,000 down payment on inner-city homes that are within walking or biking distance from the firm.

LESSONS

The evolution of the capital accumulation movement, especially the TSP, provides asset-building practitioners and policy advocates a good example of a savings innovation taken quickly and successfully to scale and may offer valuable insights for asset-building reformers as they attempt to do the same.

Conventional Wisdom the Biggest Obstacle

For TSP advocates, as for today's IDA proponents, the biggest obstacle was the conventional wisdom, "Poor people don't save." One solution to this dilemma identified by the FERSA framers was a front-loaded government match of employee savings. All new employees under the Plan receive an up-front contribution equal to 1 percent of their salaries. Employee contributions up to 5 percent of salary are then matched on a graduated scale from 100 percent to 50 percent. While all low-income FERSA employees (those earning between $10,000 to $19,999 annually) have TSP accounts, over 50 percent are also active savers, via payroll deductions. Since only approximately 22 percent of these workers saved at the inception of the program, it is likely that the match, plus FRTIB's personalized education and service efforts, have helped to encourage active participation at the lowest income levels. Many of the lowest-paid federal employees are new hires. FRTIB statistics show that in 1998, 78 percent of the youngest federal workers (aged 20–29) participated in the Plan. Participation in this group has increased each succeeding year since the inception of the Plan (*Analysis*, 2000).

The success of the TSP in attracting workers at the lowest income levels is likely due to a combination of factors beyond matching contributions. These include the automatic enrollment and up-front contribution, retail education that targets each participant, the convenience of tax-deferred saving via payroll deductions, and favorable investment returns/low costs. Of particular relevance to asset builders, the TSP experience suggests that IDAs with similar features could attract even higher participation rates, given the shorter-term preretirement nature of asset purchase goals. Early results from a number of IDA experiments seem to be bearing this out.

Resolving Funding Obstacles

Resolving funding obstacles was critical to the development of the TSP. Because the Civil Service Retirement System (CSRS) was funded on a pay-as-you-go basis, like Social Security, incoming payroll tax withholdings were used to pay the monthly benefit checks going out to retirees. But unlike Social Security, the CSRS at that time was a mature system because the number of employees entering the pipeline roughly matched the out-flowing population. FERSA reformers had to find a way to forward fund the new TSP matching and tax benefits without increasing the payroll tax. Eventually, they agreed that the new TSP employee contributions would have to be made on top of existing payroll taxes instead of any of these taxes being diverted to TSP and away from the base pension benefit. The cost of employer matching contributions was partly paid for with savings realized by cutting some of the program's defined benefits and by raising the retire-ment age. New G-Fund employee investments marginally enhanced the government's ability to manage the national debt internally.

Central versus Decentralized Administration

Like asset-building reformers, framers of the TSP also wrestled with the issue of central versus decentralized administration. The question was whether the TSP should be centrally managed or modeled after a voucher system, where funds are transferred to IRA managers or local financial ser-vice providers. Ultimately, the sizable economy of scale advantages of a single, central provider (the FRTIB) won out. A central provider can ensure the production of uniform disclosure documentation, manage investment education material distribution, spread management costs over a larger contributor base, and, by narrowing investment choices, reduce transac-tion costs.

TSP administrative expenses have been lower than anticipated by the framers of the Plan. According to the FRTIB, expenses are down to approximately .06 percent (60 cents per $1,000 balance). This compares very favorably with the .26 percent to .49 percent fees charged by Teachers Insurance and Annuity Association–College Retirement Equities Fund (TIAA-CREF), the large New York-based pension plan for educators, for its no-load mutual funds, which are now open to all investors. In contrast, active portfolio managers typically charge approximately 2 percent per year for services, including investment research, trading commissions, and management costs.

Administrative costs of the TSP are offset by profits made on securities lending by the investment managers. The massive scale of the Plan further lowers costs because TSP fund managers are able to cross-trade with other large institutional investors. Cross trading minimizes market impact costs, that is, the impact of other traders moving market prices in reaction to large block trades. As electronic trading networks expand, very large institu-tional investors will be able to cross-trade anonymously more efficiently, thus boosting liquidity and eliminating transaction costs. Anonymity allows institutional investors to sell large blocks of stock with little market impact repercussions because buyers do not vanish as word leaks out that "smart money" is selling (Alpert, 1999).

The centralized management model also avoids the risk of unscrupulous brokers duping participants out of their savings. British "personal pension" reforms, which occurred at approximately the same time as the FERSA, blew up into a national scandal when it became apparent that private service providers persuaded many participants to leave the public system and forfeit employers' matching contributions. Participants were then sold high-risk, high-expense investment schemes that inevitably left them much worse off than they were before the reforms were enacted.

A centralized system does restrict a participant's choices among investment products. The framers of TSP considered the advantages of reduced risk and capital preservation to be well worth this sacrifice. For asset builders, the decision is not so clear-cut, given the low cost of some of today's more innovative financial products. For example, new index securities, exchange traded funds (ETFs), and real estate investment trusts (REITs) allow retail investors to "buy" the performance of markets or a given industry or sector of the market. Investors who buy U.S. Treasury bonds directly from the government under the Treasury Direct program pay nothing in investment costs. Thanks to the size and track record of the financial services industry in general, more large funds are beginning to waive minimum balance requirements, a practice exclusive to TSP- and TIAA-CREF-size funds until recently.

For asset-building investors, capital preservation is very important because of the relatively short duration of these investments that are cashed out long before retirement. For this reason, it would be hard to find a better investment alternative than the TSP's centrally managed G-Fund. The Fund earned a no-risk 6.2 percent compounded annual rate of return (after expenses) from 1993 to 2002 (*Thrift Savings Plan Highlights*, 2004). To match that, an IDA participant would have to find a Federal Deposit Insurance Corporation (FDIC)-insured, short-term certificate of deposit (CD) that paid substantially more, given bank management fees.

Asset-building policy makers might consider a plan that offers two basic options: (a) a centrally managed, G-Fund-type default option for asset-building investors without local access to high-return, low-fee investment opportunities, and (b) a decentralized option offering a broader menu of passive fund choices for longer term investors. The government could issue criteria that would help limit investor choices to specific categories of private funds, just as the FRTIB selects TSP investment funds in accordance with prudent risk, return, and diversification criteria. Financial service providers whose products meet the criteria could compete to become "certified" providers of IDA-type products. Private scorecards, similar to Morningstar's five-star rating system, could serve this effort as well.

While the advantages of a single provider of financial and investment education material are impressive, it is equally important that advice and support be available at the retail level. This is especially important in a low-income IDA-context, but the one-on-one support that is best suited for this population would be extremely expensive to administer for larger populations and could, if not carefully designed, significantly shrink asset holders' investment gains. For this reason, program designers should consider identifying a separate funding stream to support this expense. One way to do this would be to maintain funding levels of local social service agencies even while welfare rolls shrink. Another would be to provide tax breaks to local financial institutions willing to provide these educational services. Arguably, financial education in general is an issue requiring the attention of policy makers. Surveys show that 60–90 percent of all U.S. employers provide some sort of financial education to workers. According to a study cited by the Conference Board of New York, employers receive $3 in participant contributions for each dollar spent on financial education (Mayer, 1999).

Investing Public Funds in the Private Marketplace

The prospect of investing public funds in the private marketplace often sparks fears that the government will soon be meddling in corporate boardrooms. The framers of the TSP grappled at length with this issue and ultimately resolved it to the satisfaction of both political parties with several measures, including a proxy voting prohibition mechanism. In addition, Plan investment choices are limited to passive stock and bond investments. Passive fund managers do not try to outperform the stock market; instead, they simply aim to match a broad market's performance. Because TSP Fund managers invest in index funds that replicate broad market performance, they are not tied to the fortunes of any one particular company. The FRTIB selects the index fund that best fits the FERSA statute and the needs of participants and beneficiaries. It contracts with a private, commingled index fund provider that best meets certain standards in areas such as tax-exempt assets under management, personnel and years of experience, tracking and trading performance, custodial service, fiduciary record, and fees.

Risk

Passive investing also mitigates risk. Risk is always a major concern for savings plan participants because they alone suffer the consequences of bad investment choices. The framers of the TSP and the FRTIB fund administrators, in addition to nearly eliminating fees, have minimized risk and optimized returns through a number of strategies. The Plan's G-Fund, for example, invests in short-term, nonmarketable U.S. Treasury Securities issued specially to the Plan. The yield is established by statute as the average of market rates of return on U.S. Treasury marketable securities with four or more years to maturity, which is the same rate allocated by the U.S. Treasury to the Social Security and civil service retirement trust funds. The G-Fund is invested, however, in securities with a one-day maturity, thus, it avoids the interest-rate risks typically associated with government bonds.

TSP investment risk is also managed through investment diversification. Asset allocation techniques help diversify investment portfolios, and sophisticated derivative hedging tools are used by professional fund managers to mitigate risk. Through established investment policy objectives, the Plan provides investment vehicles that allow TSP investors to diversify their portfolios by dividing their assets among the Plan's investment funds. Currently, the Plan offers the risk-free, short-term G-Fund; equities (Standard & Poor's [S&P] 500 index); intermediate and long-term debt securities (the Lehman Brothers U.S. Aggregate [LBA] bond index); small-cap stocks (the Wilshire 4500 stock index); and an overseas stock index (the Europe, Australasia, Far East [EAFE] stock index).

One of the most significant achievements of TSP has probably been the unequivocal demonstration that there is a fiscally prudent and socially appropriate occasion for the controlled investment of tax dollars in the private market economy. When it comes to maximizing participant choice while minimizing participant risk and optimizing participant returns, the FRTIB's track record proves that it can be done ethically and well.

POLITICS OF REFORM

The political environment in 1986 was crucial to achieving the bipartisan support that lead to the enactment of the FERSA pension reform and the TSP. Several factors ultimately favored a fairly drastic overhaul of the civil service pension program, instead of a band-aid approach to keep an existing program financially afloat.

In the early 1980s, the CSRS faced twin threats: a solvency crisis with rapidly escalating unfunded liabilities and an identity crisis. The federal government had conducted an analysis of its employee compensation package against those of comparably sized private employers. The CSRS pension, which had been designed for a workforce of predominantly male workers locked into thirty-year careers with the federal civil service, was found to be hopelessly outdated in comparison with modern corporate pension plans. Today, a new generation of workers is beginning to question the structure of Social Security in much the same way.

The opportunity to modernize the CSRS arrived with coincidental legislation that brought new federal workers into the Social Security program to help shore up its solvency. But while the legislation covered new federal employees under Social Security, it did not remove them from the civil service program. In order to avoid this double jeopardy, where new employees' paychecks could be docked for both Social Security and civil service payroll taxes, a new civil service pension benefit had to be developed that more closely resembled a modern corporate pension supplemented by Social Security. Self-imposed congressional deadlines to prevent double jeopardy provided momentum and helped bring discipline to the process. While both parties favored reform, their reform goals were different. Republican backers and the Reagan administration wanted privatization, accrual financing, and benefit cuts that would reduce the mounting liabilities of the expensive CSRS pension. Democrats, backed by federal employee unions, did not want to cut program benefits or costs, but they wanted to enhance program portability in recognition of a modern workforce that included women, short-term workers, and younger workers who benefited little from the old CSRS.

Because of the large number of legislative policy priorities that converge with the asset builders' agenda, today's political climate offers a similar opportunity. Current issues that lend themselves to asset-building legislation include earnings and wealth gap concerns; low savings rates; and reform of the welfare, tax, and pension/Social Security systems. These last three reform agendas are especially promising, given the near term likelihood of a legislative policy vehicle.

Earnings/Wealth Gaps

The wealth divide has grown to the point where the assets of the top 1 percent exceed those of the lower 95 percent of all Americans. According to the Congressional Budget Office, during the 1990s, the highest-paid one-fifth of the population enjoyed inflation-adjusted wage gains of 15 percent, while the poorest 20 percent actually saw their real wages decline. The booming stock market and equity compensation schemes of the 1990s exacerbated the historical gap by disproportionately rewarding wealthy investors, while the lowest quadrant, with no assets to put at risk, received no benefit from the 1990s stock run-up. According to the Federal Reserve's 2003 *Consumer Finances Report,* the difference in median net wealth between the 10 percent of families with the highest incomes and the 20 percent with the lowest incomes jumped 70 percent from 1998 through 2001 (Hagenbaugh, 2003).

Savings Rates

U.S. savings patterns have fallen to an all-time low. Since World War II, the U.S. savings rate has fallen from an average of 7.7 percent of gross domestic product (GDP) in 1945 to a rate of −0.9 percent in 2001, the lowest rate recorded since the Commerce Department began keeping monthly savings records in 1959. Policy makers will now be looking even harder for policy strategies to boost America's anemic savings rate. Incentivizing investment and savings not only improves productivity but promotes sustained economic growth.

Social Services/Welfare Reform

With the advent of welfare reform, government social policies at the macro and grassroots levels have been moving toward an inclusive, participatory structure. Inclusive government systems do not impose government solutions upon beneficiaries but empower them to become active participants in the process. In the old entitlement-dominated world of Aid for Dependent Children (AFDC), indigent beneficiaries were recipients of some level of subsistence support; they had no control over the process other than to manipulate the system to maximize individual benefit levels (e.g., by remaining unmarried or getting divorced). The system, while well meaning, established a culture of dependency even for those who had no mental or physical disabilities. Participant stakeholder programs, in contrast, are not externally imposed. They are typically risk sharing programs, in which the participant shares with the government, and sometimes with other partners, some responsibility and risk. With the successful passage and implementation of Temporary Assistance for Needy Families (TANF), additional participant-centric social policies have, and will continue to emerge. Both the IDA and TSP programs share a "participant stakeholder" programmatic structure. Other examples include the school choice and charter schools movement, medical and unemployment savings accounts, HUD's rent banking programs, the Appalachian Regional Commission's Appalachian Community Learning Program (ACLP), and the "New Markets" initiative.

Social Security Reform

With Social Security and Medicare underfunded by approximately $18 trillion and costs continuing to escalate as the working population ages, reform is already an urgent priority. Provisions that incorporate participant choice via self-directed Social Security accounts (preferably matched at low-wage levels) will emphasize individual strengths and harness individual and entrepreneurial energies. If a funding mechanism can be agreed upon, a progressive new system of self-directed Social Security asset accounts will share in and grow with gains in U.S. microeconomic and macroeconomic productivity. While the government's administrative role in a partially privatized Social Security system may be smaller, it will still perform the important function of ensuring the accountability and integrity of the system as a whole.

Tax Reform

IRAs and 401(k)s came into being via legislation amending the tax code. A similar approach is available to proponents of asset-building policy. There is a plan with widespread bipartisan support in Congress for a tax incentive for financial institutions to match the savings of low-income savers. In addition, there is widespread congressional and Bush administration support for IRA expansion legislation. Such reforms could include tax credit provisions to promote the matching of low-income savings. While similar proposals in the past have targeted retirement savings, liberal loan and cash-out provisions could make it similarly effective for near term asset building.

Other Pension Reform

In December 2001, in a possibly precedent setting move, the Railroad Retirement and Survivors Improvement Act of 2001 was signed into law, supported by both the railroad industry and the rail unions. The plan allows for the investment of Plan funds in nongovernmental equity and debt assets. The fund's investments are monitored by an independent board similar to the FRTIB, and employee payroll withholdings and employer contributions are adjusted to ensure actuarial balance in accordance with plan investment performance (U.S. Railroad Retirement Board, 2003). The Railroad Retirement Act defined benefit/contribution hybrid proposal closely parallels some recent developments in the pension reform/conversion activity of large corporate pension providers. A highly visible example of this approach is IBM's cancellation of a long-standing and generous traditional pension plan in favor of a controversial cash balance alternative. Cash balance benefit plans are a hybrid combination, in that they convert the value of the pension an employee has earned to date into an actuarial present value. The employer then manages the account so that it accrues a fixed amount of interest that can increase by a factor that is determined by seniority. This latter provision, in which the account is essentially guaranteed a rate of return and the employer retains some investment risk, is another way to address the "risk of return" issue associated with participant-directed accounts and will be an option addressed in the discussions of personal asset accounts and Social Security reform.

POLICY VEHICLES

Given that the political and policy agenda items mentioned earlier are aligned closely with the parallel objectives of asset-building policy advocates, a number of legislative vehicles are obvious candidates for the institutionalization of asset-building policies and tools on a large-scale, sustainable basis. The following three legislative vehicles appear closest in shared objectives among the potential allied policy initiatives.

Social Services/Welfare Reform

Just as the TSP helped lead the way toward a new kind of retirement security, asset- and wealth-building approaches offer potential for a new kind of social order. Wealth-building tools have systemic potential via national legislation to further welfare reform objectives and those of other social service programs. Matched savings programs would encourage low-paid employees to remain in the workforce long enough to advance in the workplace. Likewise, the disincentive for not working would be greater. Over time, low-wage participants would gain not only a down payment for a home, an education, or a business but would also have a wage history that would allow them to procure a mortgage and leverage additional debt. Subsequently, asset acquisition will increase their ability to finance a child's college education, thus ensuring that the next generation will be able to build upon the foundation of their parents' achievements.

One option for funding a universal social services asset-building initiative for the working poor would be at the federal appropriation level, like the AFIA. Savings accumulating in state TANF programs could help finance matches and/or administrative expenditures. The savings in state unemployment funds may also provide an appropriate funding source. While an IDA-like program for the working poor/former welfare recipients could be managed centrally at the federal level, it could also be effectively administered through existing local social service offices. The social service offices could provide "retail" client services, ensuring that recipients receive financial materials and counseling and referring them to eligible financial service providers.

If, as CFED has shown, IDA investments yield over $5 for each dollar invested, earmarking federal funds for this effort will more than pay off in the long run. The expenses of self-sufficiency promoting programs could be largely offset by savings realized from conventional dependency-oriented programs, which, as low-income families come off the welfare rolls, will shrink to serve only those individuals who are physically or mentally incapable of sustaining themselves.

Tax Reform

In general, tax credit approaches that create incentives for retirement savings are ineffectual at lower income levels. According to the Heritage Foundation, most individuals earning less than $21,000 or married couples earning less than $30,000 annually pay no federal income taxes as a result of the Earned Income Tax Credit (EITC). Tax credits are of little value to the working poor who do not pay income taxes (approaching 40 percent of all households) and those who pay much more in payroll—Federal Insurance Contributions Act (FICA)—taxes than in income taxes.

The largest levy that 75 percent of all American families now pay is not the progressive income tax but the regressive payroll tax. While income tax burdens for most Americans are lower than at any time in the past forty years, the payroll tax has increased from 3 percent in 1960 to

7.65 percent today. Payroll taxes accounted for 33 percent of total federal revenues in 2000, up from 12 percent in 1960. The regressive payroll tax is based on a flat rate that applies only to wages and largely exempts wages above $87,000. In addition to the 7.65 percent deducted from workers' wages, employers pay an additional 7.65 percent that workers essentially absorb because wages are depressed accordingly. Self-employed workers and independent contractors pay the entire 15.3 percent themselves (Halstead, 2000).

Generally, tax credits, unless otherwise stated, are nonrefundable. This means a tax filer must have a tax liability to get the money back. Other than a reduction in the payroll tax, the only tax approach that would effectively reward the savings of lower-income people would be a refundable credit. With a refundable credit, no tax liability would be required, and the credit could be claimed on top of an EITC credit.

One way to build a nationwide, tax-based asset-building strategy would be a refundable credit provision. Low-wage workers would be encouraged to save a percentage of their EITC refund via automatic deduction. This amount along with the matching credit would then be directly deposited by the government into a centrally managed, tax-deferred TSP-style fund or forwarded to the qualified financial service provider designated by the participant. Participants would receive the needed investment information and counseling, make investment allocation choices, and receive quarterly statements as their funds grew each year. And, unlike the retirement savings credits proposed by federal policy makers thus far, these funds would be made available for the purchase of assets such as a home, tuition for education, or a business. This IDA policy option would help to offset the current regressivity of the overall tax burden at the lowest levels.

An alternative 401(k)-style approach would award tax credits to employers who offered IDA-type benefits to their employees. Unfortunately, relying solely on an employer-based tax strategy would suffer two disadvantages: (a) many employers would consider it onerous to administer yet another government program for their employees, and (b) it would not provide universal coverage because not all workers have an employer. Business advocates, in response to President Bill Clinton's $33-billion universal savings account (USA) proposal, recommended that, rather than ask the business community to administer a "complex new program" that would involve maintaining individual accounts with separate accounting of employee, company, and any federally provided benefits, policy makers should offer savings tax benefits directly to low-income families (Profit Sharing/401(k) Council, 2000).

Social Security

A solvency crisis led to the privatization and reform of the federal pension system—and a similar crisis threatening Social Security may lead to a similar result. The inclusion of personal asset accounts in the discussions of Social Security reform offers a tremendous opportunity for the asset-building movement.

The crisis in Social Security is driven by demographic projections, which foresee an 80-percent increase in the number of Americans over the age of 65 over the next twenty-five years. Social Security actuaries (SSA) project that, by 2030, there will be only two workers supporting each retiree, as opposed to nearly four workers to one beneficiary today. If the actuaries are right, massive, accruing, Social Security and Medicare unfunded liabilities could approach 4.5 percent of GDP by 2030. The smaller pool of workers, forced to shoulder the burden of the enormous baby boomer generation's Social Security checks and health costs, will be hit hard by tax increases and/or new federal borrowing to pay for it.

Census Bureau projections contradict SSAs. The Bureau predicts that increased immigration—up to 13 percent of the population by 2050—could offset baby boomer retirements. But because the relaxation of immigration regulations is so controversial and because the consequences are so dire if the SSA actuaries are correct, most people agree that the issue must be resolved sooner rather than later.

Some of the politicians' nascent interest in discussing changes to the untouchable "third rail" of American politics can be attributed to polling data. An April 1999 GOP poll found that 79 percent of voters favored individual ability to invest a portion of their Social Security payroll taxes in personal retirement accounts. Even 55 percent of those over the age of 65 liked the idea.

The primary argument for not investing participant-directed Social Security accounts in the private sector is, of course, the destruction of trillions of dollars in assets following the recent stock market meltdown and the demise of some of the markets' most high-flying performers, including Long Term Capital Management (LTCM), WorldCom, and Enron. Fundamentally, the free market prices U.S. stocks; they reflect what rational investors are willing to pay for (unadulterated) company earnings. As earnings rise, stock markets rise and vice versa. While no one can predict future market performance, experts have calculated the return on the average taxpayer's Social Security contributions to be around 2 percent. Risk-averse investors who would prefer the status quo are essentially betting that the American economy, the most productive in the world, will not grow any faster than 2 percent over the long haul. Even the most conservative mix of stocks and bonds yields at least 5 percent over time. For today's younger workers, a market-based return would be a clear improvement over the status quo.

The Social Security reform effort, with its payroll withholding mechanisms already in place, would make an ideal vehicle for empowering the poor to build assets. At low-wage levels, to help offset the regressive payroll tax, any personal Social Security account should be matched, and limited preretirement withdrawals should be allowed.

Because of Social Security's pay-as-you-go financing, any privatization of Social Security will be expensive. Just as with FERSA and the TSP, self-directed Social Security account funding and any low-wealth matching provisions would have to be set aside now and, thus, would not be available to pay for current benefits. While budget surpluses are the preferred way to finance forward-funded Social Security reforms, earmarking tax receivables (for example, the taxes collected when the baby boomers cash in their tax-deferred retirement accounts) may make the higher up-front costs of reform more politically palatable. Because of this increased near term expense, there is great political risk in broadening matching benefits beyond the low-income population. The high costs of any such middle-class entitlement add-ons, without offsetting Social Security benefit reductions to pay for them, could jeopardize the chances for establishing the asset-building framework for the working poor. Taxing or reducing the Social Security benefit checks of wealthy Americans, could, for example, help pay for benefit enhancements such as an IDA component for low earners.

As with civil service retirement reform, with full actuarial funding, the Ponzi-like financing of dynamic government Social Security entitlements under static tax and spend schemes will become a thing of the past. Furthermore, self-directed asset accounts, because they belong to individuals, will be safe from politicians and bureaucrats borrowing from them to pay for more immediate budget priorities.

A long phase-in and voluntary conversion provisions will be key components of any transition from the current Social Security system to a reformed asset-promoting system, as was the case with the CSRS-FERSA transition. Current and near term retirees must be guaranteed current benefit levels. New hires would be automatically covered under the new Plan, and those in the middle would have the option to cash out and invest their accrued Social Security benefit under the rules of the new plan.

To the degree that personal investment accounts become the backbone of a new Social Security system, the defined benefit component of Social Security could become necessary only for those whose savings are insufficient to keep them out of poverty, those who are chronically unemployed or physically or mentally disabled, or those who have somehow lost their savings due to conditions beyond their control. Eventually, the defined benefit portion of Social Security would then convert to a safety net benefit likely comparable in size and nature to the benefits offered today, as most workers could rely on the aggregate of their matched accounts, additional savings, and any employer-provided pensions for their retirement security.

CONCLUSION

In the traditional world of pensions, retirement security was said to rest on a three-legged stool of Social Security, employer-provided retirement benefits, and personal savings. But today's world looks very different. Too many people have neither savings nor assets. Employer-provided defined benefit pensions are disappearing. All employers do not universally offer defined contribution plans. Self-employed, temporary, part-time, and contract workers typically earn no company pension benefits. Today, one-third of Social Security recipients do not have the assets provided by the other two legs of the stool—Social Security has become their only barrier against poverty.

Now Social Security is also threatened. Young workers perceive that Social Security, while sustaining their grandparents, will not be there for them. Changes must be made now in recognition of this new reality and the changing world of work.

For the information age worker, numerous job and career changes will become a fact of working life. A new workforce culture, centered on the individual, is emerging to supersede old hierarchal and social structures. Productivity, instead of the rigid rules of the past, will become crucial to personal and institutional advancement. Stock options, profit sharing, and incentive-based pay are already beginning to replace earlier forms of compensation, even for union workers (Strickberger, 2000).

Political realignments follow fundamental economic change. Public policies structured less for beneficiaries and more for engaged participants that embody personal choice and shared risk characteristics may be a better fit for a new century of technologically empowered individuals in a globally competitive, information based world.

Just as the capital accumulation movement shifted the responsibility for retirement security from corporations to individuals; the asset-building movement will strategically shift government poverty eradication efforts to actively engaged participant stakeholders. Asset builders have a number of natural allies in their efforts to grow a national agenda. Allied reform constituencies include those attempting to redress imbalances in the areas of earnings and wealth, savings rates, social welfare reforms, and tax and pension reforms. The confluence of these agendas is fortuitous and suggests that individual, participant-centric policies; asset building; and low-wage savings and investment accounts are poised to enter American civic life on a national scale.

Asset builders can learn much from the successful creation of the world's largest savings program, the TSP. Poor people can and will save, but the government must make it easier for them to do so. According to Bureau of Labor statistics (n.d.), U.S. households do not even begin to save until household income reaches $40,000 per year. The working poor will need matching contributions, financial literacy education, and personal assistance to achieve their goals.

There are a number of approaches policy makers could take to achieve the establishment of a national-scale asset-building initiative. They could modify or offset regressive payroll and sales taxes. They could divert welfare dollars to this effort. They could offer a refundable tax credit match to EITC recipients who choose to save a percentage of their tax refund, by depositing both their savings and the match into a tax-deferred, TSP-style account. They could incorporate low-income, asset-building policy into Social Security privatization.

Financing a universal asset-building system for low-income Americans will require a dedicated revenue stream. Investing today in a national low-wealth, asset-building plan will pay off in the near term by infusing new savings and investments into the economy. In the medium term, cost reductions in other social service programs or the earmarking of tax-deferred receivables could pay for the plan. In the long run, as the poor move into the middle and upper classes, new tax revenues will compensate for investments made today.

Personal asset accumulation accounts may call for central government administration, under the condition of rigorous fiduciary accountability and independent governance. Existing Social Security and EITC administrative infrastructure may make this the logical approach. On the other hand, asset accounts for low-income savers who are current or former clients of the social welfare system could be serviced via retail social service offices. Accounts created via private employers, the tax code, or existing IRA or 401(k) mechanisms might best operate on a decentralized basis, with qualified financial service providers competing for IDA business. Alternatively, a combination model might rely on local private service providers for retail-level activities, while account and investment management could be administered centrally.

The problem of government influence in the private marketplace can be resolved, as the TSP has shown, through well-designed governance and investment policies. The decision to invest passively in index funds instead of actively picking stocks not only helps mitigate risk but also helps ensure that there will be no government interference in private capital markets.

Investment risk can be managed, as with private insurers, by "the law of large numbers"—managing many small risks by pooling individual exposures in large portfolios. One way the TSP has been able to reduce market risk and optimize returns is the popular G-Fund, which, as currently managed, guarantees a return that exceeds inflation. In addition, market risk can be reduced via passive investment strategies, such as low-fee index funds, that outperform most actively managed funds in most years.

Americans, through their 401(k) plans and IRAs, have already become accustomed to investing for retirement in the stock market. According to the Federal Reserve's 2003 *Consumer Finances Report*, 52 percent of U.S. families owned stocks in 2001, up from 49 percent in 1998. While there are short-term fluctuations in market-based returns, younger Americans, if given the option, would see higher returns from the stock market in the long term than the 2 percent currently offered by Social Security.

Three policy vehicles currently offer the greatest potential for the successful consummation of the asset-building agenda: social welfare reform, tax reform, and Social Security reform. It is now widely recognized that traditional, centrally planned social welfare approaches have failed to live up to their promise. The forces of individual initiative and the private marketplace must be pressed into service if the objectives of equality, equal opportunity, and a decent living standard for all are to be achieved. The role of government must shift from social engineer and bureaucratic administrator to principal partner, ensuring fiscal accountability, equal opportunity and access, and compliance with established rules and responsibilities.

Universal adoption of asset-based, stakeholder-oriented social policies will further the demise of the massive social welfare bureaucracies of the twentieth century. A bipartisan effort to revamp entitlement programs along the lines of participant choice and empowerment balances Republican values of individual freedom and a smaller, less intrusive government with Democratic objectives of equality and communal welfare.

Social welfare, tax, and pension policy in the twenty-first century must rely less on externally imposed redistribution strategies. Instead, the objective should be inclusive access to the dynamos of capitalist growth: education, capital, and physical resources. Asset building will be an important part of this movement, a movement away from cyclical dependency toward economic self-sufficiency for all Americans.

REFERENCES

Alpert, B. (1999). "Wall Street Revolution." *Barron's,* July 26.

Analysis of 1998 Thrift Savings Plan Participant Demographics. (2000). Washington, D.C.: The Federal Retirement Thrift Investment Board, May.

Boshara, R. (1999). *Overview of IDA Policy and Practice.* Washington, D.C.: The Corporation for Enterprise Development, September 1.

Bureau of Labor. (n.d.). Consumer expenditures statistics/reports. Available at http://bls.gov/cex.

Center for Social Development (CSD), Washington University. (2000). Home page. Available at http://gwbweb.wustl.edu/csd/asset/idas.htm. Last accessed August 2004.

Department of Health and Human Services, Administration for Children and Families. (2003). Home page. Available at http://www.acf.dhhs.gov/programs/ocs/demo/ida/background.html. Last accessed July 2004.

Federal Reserve. (n.d.). Reports to the Congress. Available at http://www.federalreserve.gov/boarddocs/rptcongress.

Hagenbaugh, B. (2003). "Nation's Wealth Disparity Widens." *USA Today,* January 23.

Halstead, T. (2000). "Want to Cut a Tax, Think Payroll." *The Washington Post;* reprinted in *The Raleigh News & Observer,* April 30.

The Investment Company Institute. (n.d.). Home page and related links. Available at http://www.investmentcompanyinstitute.org/funds/abt/faqs_401(k).html#TopofPage. Last accessed January 2005.

Mayer, G. (1999). "Workers Want Not Only Financial Plan but Planning, Too." Knight-Ridder Newspapers; reprinted in *The Raleigh News & Observer,* December 5.

Profit Sharing/401(k) Council of America. (2000). Home page and related links. August. Available at http://www.psca.org/presmar.html, http://www.psca. org/pp6.html, http://www.psca.org/smalrele.html, http://www.psca.org/ usapress.html. (Pages correspond, respectively, with mentions in text.) Last accessed August 2004.

Rideout, E., and F. Cavanaugh. (1989). Statement by Francis X. Cavanaugh, Executive Director, Federal Retirement Thrift Investment Board before the Subcommittee on Compensation and Employee Benefits of the House Committee on Post Office and Civil Service, July 25.

Strickberger, D. (2000). "Work America." *The Wall Street Journal*, September 15.

Thrift Savings Plan Highlights. (2004). Washington, D.C.: The Federal Retirement Thrift Investment Board, October.

U.S. Railroad Retirement Board. (2003). Home page. Available at http://www. rrb.gov/opa/pr/pr0113.html. Last accessed June 2004.

15

The Universal Piggy Bank: Designing and Implementing a System of Savings Accounts for Children

Fred Goldberg

This chapter identifies the primary design issues that must be addressed in a broad-based system of tax-preferred savings accounts for children (or children's savings accounts–CSAs) and summarizes a method for implementing whatever system is adopted.[1] The three design questions are the following:

1. How should CSAs be funded?
2. What rules should govern distributions from CSAs?
3. How should CSAs be administered and invested?

The most challenging design issues relate to funding and distribution rules. With respect to funding, the choices are (a) a universal system funded through a 100-percent refundable tax credit (or direct government outlay) automatically provided to all eligible children, (b) a voluntary system funded through voluntary contributions encouraged by tax incentives, or (c) a hybrid system with both universal and voluntary features. Within the context of a voluntary system, a further fundamental design issue is the type(s) of tax incentives used to encourage contributions, for example, refundable or nonrefundable tax credits, tax deductible contributions, or elimination of taxes on accumulated earnings. In addition, under a voluntary system tax credit, deduction and contribution limits must be determined, and eligibility requirements must be established (e.g., the amount that could be contributed, the amount of credit or deduction associated with contributions, and whether benefits are phased out for upper-income taxpayers).

With respect to distributions, the primary issue is under what circumstances distributions are permitted. The basic choices are that (a) CSA funds can be used only to meet retirement needs, with unused funds distributed on the death of the beneficiary; (b) CSA funds can also be withdrawn for specified needs (e.g., disability or health care) and/or investment purposes (e.g., education, a home, a vehicle, or a business); (c) CSA funds can be withdrawn for any purpose; or (d) a hybrid system can be used, with different portions of the funds subject to different distribution rules. There are also the questions of whether and to what extent assets should be protected from creditor claims and whether and to what extent CSA assets should be considered in means-tested programs and financial aid determinations.

The primary implementation question is whether CSA investment funds should be sponsored only by the private sector or whether the government should also sponsor a limited number of "no frills" CSA investment funds. Either of these approaches could be readily implemented by building on existing public and private systems, principally, the Thrift Savings Plan (TSP), maintained for employees of the federal government, the Internal Revenue Service (IRS), and investment funds maintained by the private sector. The choice would depend largely on whether a universal or voluntary system is adopted because, as a practical matter, a universal system would likely require a limited number of government-sponsored funds in addition to funds maintained by the private sector. Particularly in the context of a universal system, there is also the question of whether and to what extent the government should encourage or assume responsibility for promoting financial literacy.

OVERVIEW

Two noteworthy trends in public policy during the 1990s were widespread concern over income-based policies to assist the poor and growing interest in policies to encourage wealth creation and savings.[2] The former culminated in bipartisan support for welfare reform legislation that was enacted in 1996 and is reflected in the continuing, widely held view that those reforms have been successful. The latter is manifested by the frequent enactment and proposed enactment of tax-favored savings programs. Building on individual retirement accounts (IRAs) that were started during the 1970s, we now have Roth IRAs, SIMPLE IRAs, Coverdell education savings accounts, section 529 plans, Archer medical savings accounts, and individual development accounts. The Clinton administration proposed universal savings accounts; in 2003, the Bush administration proposed lifetime savings accounts, retirement savings accounts, and employee retirement savings accounts; and, since 1995, there have been recurring proposals to establish some form of broad-based children's savings accounts. The purpose of this chapter is to explore the primary design and implementation issues that would need to be addressed in connection with a policy of broad-based, tax-favored savings accounts for children.

The CSA concept is that some or all children would have access to savings accounts established for their benefit, funded in whole or in part through tax

credits and/or other tax incentives. CSAs pose three main design and implementation questions: (a) how should CSAs be funded, (b) what rules should
govern distributions from CSAs, and (c) how should CSAs be administered
and invested?

The next section addresses questions related to the funding of CSAs. With
respect to funding, the primary issue is how federal tax incentives should be
structured. The fundamental choice is whether to establish (a) a universal
system funded through a 100-percent refundable tax credit (or direct government outlay) that is automatically credited to the account of each eligible
child, (b) a voluntary system funded through voluntary contributions
encouraged by tax incentives, or (c) a hybrid system with both universal and
voluntary features. Within the context of a voluntary system, the primary
design issues are (a) the types of tax incentives (refundable or nonrefundable
tax credits, tax-deductible contributions, or deferral or elimination of taxes
on accumulated earnings); (b) limitations on those incentives (maximum
credit or contribution amounts); and (c) the question of whether those incentives are means-tested (i.e., phased out for upper-income taxpayers).

After the discussion of funding, the chapter addresses questions
related to rules governing distributions. With respect to distributions, the
primary issue is under what circumstances distributions should be permitted. The basic choices are that (a) CSA funds can be used only to meet
retirement needs, with unused funds distributed on the death of the beneficiary; (b) CSA funds can also be withdrawn for specified investment
purposes (e.g., education, a home, a vehicle, or a business) and/or for
specified needs (e.g., unemployment, disability, or health care); (c) CSA
funds can be withdrawn for any purpose; or (d) CSA funds can be seg-
mented with different distribution rules applied to each segment.

It is important to emphasize that the design and distribution issues are
fundamental policy questions of great importance. The views on all sides are
strongly held and reflect core principles that are not easily compromised.

Unlike the design and distribution issues, implementation is relatively
easy. The next section addresses questions related to the administering and
investment of CSAs. By building on existing administrative structures, primarily, the IRS and investment funds maintained by the private sector, and
by applying lessons learned from various retirement programs, mainly, the
federal government's TSP and private sector experience with various tax-
based savings incentives, CSAs can be implemented in ways that (a) are easy
to understand and administer; (b) minimize administrative costs; (c) meet
reasonable expectations for simplicity, security, control, and independence;
and (d) can accommodate a wide range of policy choices (including those
listed above), as well as changes in those choices over time. The primary
implementation question is whether CSA investment funds should be sponsored only by the private sector or whether the government should also
sponsor a limited number of basic (no frills) CSA investment funds. Either
of these approaches could be readily implemented, and the choice would
likely depend on how the design issues listed above are resolved.

The chapter concludes by outlining political compromises that Congress is likely to make with respect to CSAs and recommending a course of action that, while politically challenging, has the greatest potential for making CSAs an enduring and successful program.

FUNDING CSAS

Universal, Voluntary, or Hybrid System

The threshold design question is whether CSAs should be a universal, voluntary, or hybrid system. A universal system reflects the judgment that all eligible children should participate. A voluntary system reflects the judgment that parents and others, including extended family members, are ultimately responsible for making such decisions.[3] A hybrid system would contain elements of both a universal and a voluntary system. A universal system would entail a 100-percent refundable tax credit (or direct government outlay) in the amount of the intended benefit that would be provided all eligible children. For example, if the program were structured as a $1,000 per child tax credit, all eligible children would have their CSAs funded through a $1,000 refundable tax credit in a universal system, whereas in a voluntary system, eligible taxpayers could elect to fund CSAs for their children. Unlike universal CSAs, various tax incentives would be necessary to encourage the funding of voluntary CSAs. These incentives could replicate current law. For example, contributions could be tax deductible, and earnings could be tax deferred (like traditional IRAs); contributions could be nondeductible, but earnings and distributions could be tax exempt (as for Roth IRAs and Coverdell education savings accounts); or contributions could be encouraged through matching credits (e.g., saver's credit).

Some of the primary arguments advanced by proponents of a universal system include the following:

1. CSAs are in the nature of a public good that should be provided for all eligible children.
2. Universal CSAs would create a savings platform that would remove barriers to additional, voluntary savings by children and families. In contrast, a purely voluntary system of CSAs would do nothing to remove the structural barriers to saving and would result in limited participation by those children and families who would benefit most from new savings.
3. Universal CSAs that could be used only to meet retirement needs would amount to pre-funding the government's existing obligations to provide retirement income and health care benefits to the elderly. They are a prudent and practical way of addressing the actuarial shortfalls in the Social Security and Medicare trust funds and the future demands on general revenue that will be imposed

by both Medicare and Medicaid. In this regard, it is worth noting that incentives to encourage annuitization and to exclude CSA assets from means-tested programs such as Medicaid, are important considerations.

4. Universal CSAs are a prudent tax cut because they would increase long-term savings and promote economic growth.
5. A universal system is easier to administer and understand.

On the other hand, the arguments advanced by those who support a voluntary system but oppose a universal system include the following:[4]

1. While tax incentives to encourage savings for children may be appropriate, parents, extended family members, and others should decide what is in the best interests of children.
2. Universal CSAs would become yet another unfunded federal entitlement program.
3. Whatever the initial design, political pressures would ultimately cause Congress to permit CSAs to be used for almost any purpose,[5] undermining the long-term policy goals of the program and reinforcing the unfunded entitlement characterization.
4. A voluntary system, supported by strong tax incentives, would have better chances of enactment compared with a universal system. Those who argue for a universal system are sacrificing "good" policy in the futile pursuit of a "better" policy.

Beyond these questions of ideology, politics, and political philosophy, there is the practical question of which taxpayers would choose to participate in a voluntary system. Participation levels would depend on a variety of factors, including how the program were structured and marketed. It is worth noting, however, that patterns of asset ownership and participation in other voluntary savings programs (such as IRAs, 401(k) plans, and medical savings accounts) suggest that participation in voluntary CSAs may be limited, especially among low- and middle-income families. For example, the percentage of families with any type of tax-favored retirement account varies considerably with family income: around 10 percent for families with incomes of less than $15,000; around 30 percent for families with incomes between $15,000 and $30,000; around 50 percent for families with incomes between $30,000 and $50,000; around 75 percent for families with incomes between $50,000 and $100,000; and around 90 percent for families with incomes over $100,000.

In response, it has been suggested (persuasively, in my view) that participation rates are strongly affected by design features. For example, incentives based on tax deductions are of little or no benefit to low- and lower-middle-income families, while after-tax contributions whose earnings are tax exempt provide some benefit, and refundable credits can provide substantial incentives for such families to save. Likewise, restrictions on distributions are a substantial deterrent to contributions by low- and lower-middle-income families, and income phaseouts are a barrier to widespread marketing by financial institutions.

Other barriers that would need to be addressed to increase participation by low- and middle-income families in voluntary CSAs include the implied tax on savings imposed by government and private sector means-tested programs (such as Medicaid, Head Start, Pell grants, and means-tested scholarship programs offered by public and private educational institutions); the fact that many low- and lower-middle-income families are unbanked and have few if any dealings with mainstream financial institutions; the absence of strong support among advocacy groups on behalf of low- and lower-middle-income families for asset-based policies; and the bewildering complexity of the tax law's current patchwork of savings incentives.

The Case for Refundable Credits

Refundable tax credits are a necessary element of any universal system absent a direct government outlay.[6] In a voluntary system, however, three different types of tax incentives can be provided: up-front tax deductions, with accumulated earnings subject to tax; after-tax (nondeductible) funding with no tax on accumulated earnings; or some form of matching tax credits.[7] In the context of tax credits, the question arises whether the credits are available only to offset tax liability or whether those credits are "refundable" and received regardless of whether the person contributing to the account owes any taxes. If the credit were not refundable, a number of issues would have to be resolved—for example, would tax liability include both income and payroll taxes; would tax liability be determined before or after application of other provisions (e.g., child care tax credits and earned income tax credits); and how would the credit be apportioned if the contributing taxpayers were making contributions on behalf of more than one child?

Proponents of a universal, refundable credit CSA system argue that the purpose behind CSAs is to provide wealth creation opportunities for all children and, therefore, CSAs should not be dependent on the earnings and tax liability of the child's parents. They argue, further, that a child's well-being should not depend on the willingness of his or her parents (or others) to provide funding for a CSA. Proponents of a voluntary, refundable credit CSA system argue that parents' incentives to provide for their children should not be constrained by their family income and tax liability. Opponents of refundable credits argue that refundable credits are disguised welfare payments—the government is taking from those who pay taxes and giving to those who do not. Additionally, it is argued that experience with the Earned Income Tax Credit demonstrates that refundable tax credit programs are subject to widespread fraud.

Unfortunately, the debate over refundability has been couched in rhetorical terms that are not particularly helpful. From the traditional perspective of tax policy and tax administration, the case for refundable credits is compelling, particularly in the context of a one-time or short-duration credit (e.g., credits for contributions to accounts for children under the age of 18). While a detailed discussion of the refundability issue is beyond the scope of this chapter, a brief summary of the key arguments follows.

Annual Tax Filing and Carryover Rules

Administrative considerations require that taxpayers file their returns and pay their taxes each year. While there is no practical alternative, the annual accounting period results in numerous distortions. The tax law tries to rectify a number of these distortions, primarily through carry forward and carry back provisions. For example, businesses can use their tax losses to offset a prior or future year's income, can use their alternative minimum tax liability as a credit against future year regular tax liability, and can carry back or forward their capital losses and their unused research and development (R&D) and foreign tax credits. Individuals can carry their capital losses and unused passive losses forward for an unlimited time, and both corporations and individuals can carry forward their unused charitable contribution deductions. All of these provisions are appropriate on tax policy grounds, as they simply mitigate the arbitrary impact of our annual accounting system.[8]

Annual Tax Filing and CSAs

The arbitrary impact of the annual accounting period is especially prevalent in the context of CSAs. In situations where families' incomes and personal circumstances fluctuate above and below the income levels triggering tax liability, they will move in and out of eligibility for nonrefundable CSA credits.[9] This fluctuation may occur for myriad reasons: a young family with several children may not yet be earning sufficient family income (around $35,000) to trigger tax liability; a family may be temporarily not subject to tax as the result of unemployment or disabling illness; or a family may be temporarily not subject to tax because one or both family members take time off to care for their children. In each of these circumstances, absent a refundable credit, the family and its children are arbitrarily penalized by the annual accounting period. For example, assume that $40,000 of family income is required to take full advantage of a nonrefundable, one-time child credit of $1,000. If Family A has a child in Year 1 while Family B has a child in Year 2, and both families have $30,000 of income in Year 1 and $40,000 of income in Year 2, Family B would get the credit while Family A would not get the credit. This result is, of course, indefensible as a matter of common sense and on grounds of tax neutrality.[10]

The Carryover Alternative

One way of dealing with the arbitrary impact of the annual accounting period would be to permit families to carry back and carry over their ability to claim the credit. The problem with a carryover regime, however, especially in the context of CSAs, is that it would be quite complex. Among the many questions that would have to be addressed are (a) the appropriate carryover period(s), (b) provisions (if any) to address lost earnings on CSAs that are not funded currently, (c) the impact of changes in dependent status and marital status, and (d) rules governing allocations of the credit among children born to the same parents at different times. A refundable credit avoids these difficult issues, while not raising the compliance issues that some associate with refundable credits.[11] Moreover, it seems reasonable to conclude, based on available data and as a matter of shared confidence in economic opportunity and upward mobility, that most families will pay sufficient income tax to cover the CSA credit over their working lives.

The Case for No Phaseouts

At the other end of the spectrum, there is debate over phaseouts: Should participation in CSAs be phased out for families with incomes above a certain amount? Once again, the argument is characterized by far more heat than light. Those who support phaseouts argue that the rich do not need tax subsidies to provide for their children and that the tax expenditures that would subsidize upper-income taxpayers in the absence of a phaseout could be better spent on other programs. Those who oppose phaseouts argue that a child's access to assets should not depend on the willingness of his or her parents (or others) to fund a savings program; it is unfair to penalize children (and their families) because their parents pay a lot in taxes; from a policy perspective, there is great virtue in a universal program that is open to all, regardless of income—especially a program that focuses on children; and that phaseouts create needless tax complexity.

The same basic tax policy and tax administration considerations help inform this debate as well. The annual tax accounting period creates the same potential distortions at the high end as it does at the low end. As noted above, family income may fluctuate from year to year for many reasons. For example, assume that a one-time child credit phases out for families with $50,000 of income. If Family C has a child in Year 1 while Family D has a child in Year 2, and both families have $40,000 of income in Year 1 and $50,000 of income in Year 2, Family C would get the credit while Family D would not get the credit. As with nonrefundable credits, this result is also indefensible as a matter of common sense and on grounds of tax neutrality.[12] In this context, however, two additional practical considerations come into play and argue strongly for no phaseouts.

Selling a Policy

Hard evidence and anecdotal information demonstrate that marketing efforts by financial intermediaries—and therefore participation rates by eligible taxpayers—decline in the context of phaseout rules. As a practical matter, participation in a voluntary system by those who "need" to participate will increase significantly if financial institutions can market the voluntary system to all families, not just those with incomes below some threshold. Indeed, it seems likely that, within limits, financial institutions would more aggressively market a system with lower contribution limits, refundable credits, and no phaseouts relative to a system with higher contribution limits, no refundable credits, and phaseouts.

Self-Inflicted Wounds

Advocates for low- and lower-middle-income families are most vociferous in demanding phaseouts as a matter of "fairness." Setting aside the fact that this fairness claim is specious on policy and administrative grounds, the more important point is that it has been counterproductive. In effect, policy makers at both ends of the political spectrum have reached a tacit agreement—where tax favored savings are concerned, no refundable credits at the bottom in exchange for phaseouts at the top. This is a terrible bargain from the standpoint of low- and lower-middle-income families. These families would benefit enormously from a trade: Eliminate phaseouts in exchange for refundable credits and a lower contribution limit.

Other Funding Issues

Contribution Limits

Any CSA system is certain to have contribution limits. Thus, for example, limits under 2004 law range from $2,000 for the saver's credit[13] to $3,000 for regular and Roth IRAs (with "catch up" contributions to IRAs for persons aged 50 and older);[14] to $40,000 for employer-sponsored defined contribution plans such as 401(k) plans;[15] to $55,000 for section 529 plans.[16] This issue is critically important for a number of reasons. As discussed below, contribution limits can have a major impact on the revenue costs of the program. In addition, however, contribution limits raise several additional issues.

Administrative Costs

All accounts, regardless of size, incur significant fixed administrative costs. Low contribution limits may discourage participation by financial intermediaries and eligible taxpayers (other than in a universal system with refundable credits, where participation is not an issue).

Participation at Maximum Contribution Limits

As a practical matter, relatively few taxpayers are able or willing to take full advantage of high contribution limits. For example, a Treasury Department study found that only 4 percent of taxpayers eligible for IRAs in 1995 saved up to the $2,000 contribution limit.[17]

Competition with Other Tax Preferred Savings Programs

High contribution limits may conflict or be perceived as conflicting with other tax-favored savings programs. For example, it has been argued that high regular or Roth IRA limits would undermine employer-sponsored plans.

Target Savings

It has been suggested that a program's policy objectives should have some impact on contribution limits. For example, contribution limits might take account of housing or postsecondary education costs or amounts necessary to fund an annuity sufficient to cover deductibles or supplemental health insurance costs.

Transition Issues

Transition rules raise important and challenging issues in the context of CSAs. This is most evident in the context of a universal system that provides a one-time, refundable credit for newborn children. When the program is enacted, should children under a designated age also be eligible? Once again, this issue has significant revenue implications: In the United States, about 4 million children are born each year, and there are currently about 48 million children under age 12 and 72 million children under age 18. While this paints the issue in its starkest form, similar questions arise in the context of a voluntary system. In particular, can parents (or third parties) make "catch-up" contributions for older children to reflect amounts that could have been contributed if the program had been in place when they were born?

Eligible Contributors and Voluntary Additional Contributions

Another design issue: Who would be permitted to make contributions to CSAs? For example, under current law, only the worker is permitted to make contributions to regular and Roth IRAs owned by the worker or his or her spouse; workers and their employers may make contributions to qualified plans (e.g., 401(k) plans); and anyone, including the beneficiary, is permitted to make contributions to section 529 plans. In the CSA context, the additional question is whether and to what extent contributors would be eligible for the applicable tax incentives. For example, in the context of a voluntary system with a nonrefundable credit and an income phaseout, with no tax on accumulated earnings, the rule might limit the credit amount on a per child basis (e.g., the per child CSA credit might be limited to $1,000 per year), while anyone would be permitted to make after-tax contributions with earnings on those contributions not subject to tax. Likewise, the law might establish different maximum contribution amounts for different classes of contributors (e.g., immediate family members might have a higher maximum than extended family members and third parties).

Two related issues arise in the context of a universal system, defined as a system in which CSAs are funded for all eligible children through refundable credits or other government outlays—namely, whether voluntary additional contributions would be permitted and, if so, subject to what rules and restrictions. For example, immediate family members might be permitted to make after-tax contributions up to some maximum amount (with accumulated earnings not subject to tax). Or extended family members (and third parties) might also have the opportunity to make limited, after-tax contributions.

Rules relating to eligible contributors and voluntary additional contributions are connected in important ways to other CSA design issues. For example, expanding the class of eligible contributors and permitting voluntary additional contributions might help mitigate the impact of a nonrefundable system, presumably, with a limit on the aggregate amount that could be contributed on behalf of any individual beneficiary. In addition, the rules governing distributions from additional contributions could differ from the rules governing base contributions to a CSA. It is important to emphasize, however, that additional design features will increase complexity for taxpayers, financial intermediaries, and the IRS; these added elements may also increase the number of tax compliance and enforcement issues.

It should also be noted that other tax-favored savings provisions could be integrated with CSAs, including Coverdell education savings accounts, traditional and Roth IRAs, and small saver and individual development accounts. Particularly in a universal system with refundable credits and no phaseouts, CSAs would serve as a platform for these other programs, facilitating participation and permitting meaningful simplification of the existing rules.

Revenue Impact

The revenue impact of CSAs will be heavily influenced by the program design. Thus, for example, a universal system providing all children with $1,000 at birth and $500 each year for five years (that is, a refundable credit with no phaseouts) would likely cause the government to lose around $100 billion in revenue over ten years.[18] Transition rules that would cover a cohort of children born before the effective date would add a significant one-time cost. Interestingly, if benefits were phased out for families with incomes in excess of $100,000, the revenue loss would be reduced by about 5 percent, while eliminating the refundability feature would reduce the revenue cost by almost 50 percent. Depending upon its structure, a voluntary system would likely result in a far smaller revenue loss.

FUNDING MECHANISMS

Traditional Structure

There are several potential mechanisms for contributing to CSAs. Most likely in the context of a voluntary system encouraged by tax incentives, funding would be accomplished in the same way as in other tax-favored savings programs that are not employer based. If the system relied on deductions or credits, a participating taxpayer would simply contribute to the account through a participating financial institution and claim the appropriate tax benefit—in much the same way that traditional IRAs and retirement vehicles eligible for the small saver's credit are funded under current law. If the system were structured around after-tax (nondeductible) contributions and nontaxable distributions, a participating taxpayer would simply contribute to the account through a participating financial institution in much the same way that Roth IRAs and section 529 plans are funded under current law.

Direct Funding by IRS

While the current methods of funding tax-favored accounts provide a useful framework for the funding of CSAs, there is at least one alternative approach that should be explored in the context of a universal or voluntary system relying on tax credits. In a credit-based system, funding could run directly from the IRS/FMS (Financial Management Service, a bureau of the Department of the Treasury) to the financial institution sponsoring the beneficiary's CSA. The eligible taxpayer or other person claiming the credit on behalf of the beneficiary would simply provide instructions regarding the account, including where the credit should be wired.[19] As evidenced by the growing number of electronically filed tax returns and the number of refunds issued by wire transfer to taxpayer accounts, the technology to implement this system is already available and widely used.[20]

A primary virtue of this approach is that it addresses compliance issues that have been raised in the context of refundable credits. These concerns are twofold. First, whether justified or not, there is a general perception that many taxpayers claim refundable credits to which they are not entitled.[21] Second, to the extent that there are compliance problems with refundable credits, the IRS has difficulty enforcing compliance and recouping credits that should not have been claimed because the amounts at issue are small and the affected taxpayers are not likely to have the resources to repay erroneously claimed credits. Each of these compliance issues is largely avoided in the context of a refundable credit, wired directly to a child's account, where the income of the child's parents and the residency of the child are immaterial. By requiring that participating financial institutes retain those funds for some period of time and by imposing appropriate information reporting requirements, the IRS would be in a position to verify that the refund was properly issued and to recoup those funds if the refund were issued in error.[22]

Claiming Refundable Credits

If CSAs include a refundable credit feature, it is necessary to provide for parents, as well as others who are entitled to claim eligible children as dependents, who are not required to file tax returns because their incomes are below the applicable filing thresholds. The easiest way to address this issue would be to permit these persons to file some type of CSA credit form with an IRS Service Center during the tax return filing season. Depending on the funding mechanism, the IRS would issue the credit to the taxpayer who claimed the credit or wire those funds directly to the CSA account.

In the context of a refundable credit, it is also necessary to provide for children who cannot be claimed as dependents on an income tax return (e.g., children living in orphanages and state foster care facilities). Perhaps the most straightforward approach would be to permit the person or organization with guardianship or custodial responsibility to file a CSA credit form in the same manner as parents not required to file tax returns.

DISTRIBUTIONS FROM CSAS

Permitted Uses of CSA Funds

Along with the structure of federal tax incentives, rules governing the permitted use of CSA funds present the most controversial design issue. Brief summaries of four different approaches to the issue of use of funds and the primary policy arguments in favor of each follow.

Restrict Use to Retirement Needs

One approach would be to limit use of CSA funds to meet retirement needs, supplementing Social Security and Medicare/Medicaid benefits. The case for this approach is strongest in the context of a universal system with refundable credits and no phaseouts, where the CSA account is used as an administrative platform for other savings programs (e.g., regular and Roth IRAs, section 529 plans, saver's credit accounts, and IDAs). The primary policy argument in favor of this approach is that CSAs would provide a permanent platform or infrastructure for lifetime savings. A second policy argument in favor of this approach is that CSAs would pre-fund a portion of all individuals' retirement needs, thereby reducing some of the pressure on Social Security and Medicare/Medicaid. Finally, retirement only CSAs would promote intergenerational transfers of assets among low- and lower-middle-income families if the account holder died before retirement.

Permit Limited Preretirement Uses

A second approach would be to permit use of CSA funds for specified pre-retirement purposes. In general, these uses fall in one of two categories: investment and need. Within the investment category, suggested uses include human capital (education and job training), capital assets (a first-time home), and income-related (a car for transportation to work or seed money to start a business). Within the needs category, suggested uses include unemployment, health care, and disability. The case for this approach is strongest in a universal system or in a voluntary system with significant tax incentives (such as tax credits). The two primary policy arguments in favor of this approach are (a) that the government's subsidy, in the form of significant tax incentives, gives it a legitimate stake in restricting uses to activities that are in the nature of quasipublic goods and (b) that the society at large would benefit from these types of permitted investments (e.g., education, home ownership, and/or microenterprise) and from pre-funding "needs" that it would otherwise be forced to cover on a pay-as-you go basis (e.g., disability, health care, and/or supplemental unemployment income).

Simply recognizing that the government's stake in the program merits restrictions on distributions does not help determine what restrictions are appropriate. This question must be resolved by reference to the program's goals, taking into account issues such as the capacity of beneficiaries to make informed decisions, for example, considering at what age beneficiaries should be permitted to access funds and for what purposes, and the possibility that need-based objectives may conflict with investment-based objectives (e.g., permitted withdrawals to supplement unemployment income may conflict with the goal of accumulating assets for a first-time home purchase).

No Restrictions on Use

A third alternative would be to impose no restrictions on use, other than a restriction on use of funds prior to the time the beneficiary reached majority or some other age. The case for this approach is strongest in a voluntary system with relatively limited tax incentives, for instance, in a system of after-tax (nondeductible) contributions with no tax on accumulated earnings. The primary policy arguments in favor of no restrictions are that any material restrictions on use may discourage participation by low- and lower-middle-income families—and that, in any case, individuals know best how to make use of their savings.

A Hybrid System

A fourth alternative would be a hybrid system that would segment CSA funds and impose different restrictions on each segment. For example, the goal of a permanent savings platform could be accomplished if individuals were precluded from reducing their account balance below some floor.[23] The government's interest in restricting uses to the extent of tax subsidies, especially in the form of tax credits, could be achieved by restricting the use of funds reflecting those benefits, including earnings. There may be no restrictions on the use of voluntary contributions, especially if the amount of those contributions is limited and they are made with after-tax dollars.

PRESERVATION OF ASSETS

Another issue relates to the preservation of CSA assets. For example, it may be appropriate to provide that CSA assets are not subject to the claims of creditors. The case for this approach is most compelling when there are significant restrictions on the use of CSA funds, especially when there are substantial tax incentives, for example, significant tax credits. Less apparent but equally important are rules to preclude "penalty taxes" on CSA funds. These implied taxes are levied by government and the private sector in the form of means-tested programs. Thus, for example, a beneficiary's access to Medicaid or student loans may be affected by his or her CSA assets. Likewise, CSA assets might affect access to or the amount of scholarship money or student aid. These penalty taxes are a widespread and powerful deterrent to savings by low-, lower-middle, and middle-income families. At least in circumstances of significant restrictions on use, these penalty taxes cannot be justified on policy grounds and should be curtailed when possible.

INVESTING AND ADMINISTERING CSA FUNDS

Private Sector Investment Vehicles

While there are restrictions on the types of permitted investments in existing tax-preferred savings vehicles, taxpayers participating in such programs have generally been free to select the private sector financial institution where they maintain their savings.[24] In part, this reflects the efficient, diverse, and generally well-regulated nature of our capital markets; in part, it reflects a judgment that individuals should be free, within limits, to make their own investment choices. As a practical matter, it is virtually certain that a voluntary system would rely on the same investment framework.[25] In a universal system, however, it is likely that some form of government-sponsored CSA investment funds would be given serious consideration as a backstop for investment through private sector financial institutions.

Government-Sponsored Funds

It is estimated that more than 25 percent of all families have no dealings with the financial sector (that is, they are unbanked), and more than 40 percent of all families have no savings in the form of financial assets. Under these circumstances, the primary argument in favor of government-sponsored funds (GSFs) is that they are a practical necessity—they provide the only realistic way of introducing many of the participants in a universal system to the world of savings and investment activity. The question is whether GSFs can be designed and administered in ways that are accessible to individuals who have little or no familiarity with financial institutions and capital markets, do not interfere or compete with the private sector, and can be administered efficiently and inexpensively.

Design and Implementation of GSFs

The design and implementation of GSFs has received a great deal of attention in the context of Social Security private accounts. In general, GSFs would be modeled on the TSP that manages $100 billion in retirement savings for more than three million active and retired federal government workers. The TSP allows participants to choose from among a limited number of investment alternatives and provides limited account services (such as relatively limited access to account and other information, limited investment alternatives, and limited ability to change investment choices) that reduce administrative costs. The investment of TSP assets and much of its administration is contracted out to private sector financial institutions (privatized) under competitive bidding procedures.

From an investment standpoint, much of the TSP experience would be directly applicable to GSFs. It appears likely that GSFs could be designed and efficiently administered in ways that would be responsive to participants' needs. There are, however, two key differences, funding and use of funds. The TSP is a traditional, employer-sponsored retirement program, where the contribution process is administered by the employer and the distribution rules are relatively straightforward. In contrast, CSAs are not employer based, and, as noted above, CSA assets are potentially subject to many uses in addition to retirement.

For the most part, funding issues could be easily addressed by building on the IRS/FMS infrastructure. As noted above, it would be possible (if not preferable) in a universal system for the IRS/FMS to fund CSAs through direct wire transfers to financial institutions designated by participants. In that context, GSFs would simply be an alternative designated recipient of CSA funds.

If CSA assets can only be used for retirement, then distributions from GSFs could be handled in much the same way as distributions from the TSP. If, however, other uses were permitted (education, first-time home purchase, health care, and/or supplemental unemployment income), the distribution issues would become far more challenging. As the administration of complex distribution rules would likely require an elaborate administrative system (ranging from account maintenance and compliance/certification procedures to the transfer of withdrawn funds), it seems unlikely that the federal government should or would play such a role.

Government-Sponsored Funds as Temporary Investment Vehicles

For a whole host of reasons, ranging from concerns over market distortions and unfair competition to practical political considerations, GSFs should not interfere or compete in any material way with private sector financial institutions. The best way to achieve this result is to view GSFs as temporary investment vehicles. Thus, for example, it would make sense to minimize the barriers to transferring funds from GSF accounts to private sector accounts; severely restrict access to GSF accounts for purposes other than rolling over GSF funds to private sector accounts (e.g., only on the death or retirement of the beneficiary); provide that CSAs can be used as a platform for other tax-favored savings only if they are maintained with private sector financial institutions; and, perhaps, require that funds be transferred from GSF accounts to private sector accounts when they reach some specified balance (e.g., $5,000). In addition to minimizing the potential adverse impact of GSFs on private sector financial institutions, treating GSFs as temporary investment vehicles would have other benefits. From the government's perspective, it would not be required to administer complex rules governing multiple uses of CSA funds and would not be required to administer CSAs as a platform for other tax-favored savings. From the perspective of the so-called unbanked and those who have no financial assets, GSFs might serve as a "way station," facilitating the transition to direct dealings with private sector financial institutions. From the perspective of financial institutions, GSFs would lessen their need to administer high-cost, low-deposit accounts.

CONCLUSIONS

Before CSAs can gain political momentum, general agreement must first be reached among their supporters on three fundamental policy issues: (a) a universal, voluntary, or hybrid system, (b) the design of tax incentives if there is a voluntary or hybrid system, and (c) rules governing distributions.

Experience suggests that the political process would opt for a voluntary system with a compromise that denies tax incentives to upper and upper-middle-income taxpayers and rejects refundable credits that would be of most benefit to low- and lower-middle-income families. This chapter concludes that there is no compelling justification for either of these limitations in the context of CSAs intended to promote long-term savings. Experience further suggests that the compromise would permit use of funds for post-secondary education costs, first-time home purchases, hardship, and retirement. This chapter concludes that the justification for these restrictions depends on the scope of incentives provided by the government. Thus, for example, there is little justification for material restrictions on voluntary contributions associated with few tax benefits, while there may be a compelling case for restrictions on use of funds associated with significant tax benefits.

In contrast, the most politically difficult model but the one with the greatest potential for significant impact would be a universal system with the following features:

1. Refundable credits that are not phased out
2. A voluntary add-on system permitting limited additional contributions with after-tax dollars and no tax on accumulated earnings
3. Accounts administered primarily but not exclusively by the private sector with limited duration, no-frills investment funds modeled along the lines of the government's TSP
4. A requirement that some (or all) of the credit and earnings on the credit not be withdrawn prior to permanent disability, death, or retirement—thereby assuring a universal and permanent savings platform
5. Substantial restrictions on withdrawal on any credit (plus earnings) not covered by #4 above
6. Limited (or no) restrictions on withdrawals of voluntary contributions and earnings on those contributions

The intermediate case would be a voluntary system with the following features:

1. After-tax (that is, nondeductible) contributions encouraged by a combination of no tax on accumulated earnings and a phased-out, refundable matching credit for low- and lower-middle-income taxpayers
2. No income limits on participation
3. Tiered restrictions on withdrawals (e.g., a minimum investment period for credit-eligible contributions, including associated credit and accumulated earnings)
4. Some minimum balance that could not be withdrawn prior to disability, retirement, or death, thereby assuring a permanent savings platform
5. No withdrawals except for postsecondary education or first-time home purchases prior to a designated minimum age
6. Accounts administered solely by the private sector

NOTES

1. Aspects of the administrative structure and certain data described here are based on Goldberg and Graetz, *Reforming Social Security: A Practical and Workable System of Personal Retirement Accounts* (1998).

2. Tax incentives for retirement savings by individuals have been in the law for more than twenty-five years (the first IRA legislation was enacted in 1974), and employer-sponsored retirement plans have been favored by the tax law for many decades.

3. At various times, we refer for convenience to "parents" in describing persons who establish or fund CSAs for the benefit of children. We recognize that the situation is more complex, as 4 percent of all children live with someone other than a "parent" (e.g., a grandparent, other relative, or foster parents) or have their own household. See Federal Interagency Forum on Child and Family Statistics (2000). Throughout this chapter, we try to note when special rules may be necessary or desirable for these children.

4. It is, of course, worth noting that CSAs in any form would continue to be opposed by those who would prefer to use federal revenues to pay down the deficit, to cut taxes in some other way, or to spend money elsewhere.

5. For example, under current law, IRA and 401(k) funds can be withdrawn or borrowed without penalty for various purposes and can be withdrawn for any purpose on payment of a 10 percent penalty.

6. It may also be advisable for a universal system not to tax earnings accumulated in CSA accounts, given that taxing accumulated earnings would substantially complicate the filings of many low- and middle-income families.

7. Under any of these structures, decisions would have to be made regarding persons permitted to make contributions (e.g., parent, immediate or extended family members, and community organizations), the maximum amount of permitted contributions, and whether that amount would be determined by reference to the beneficiary or the contributor. In addition, the match percentage in a credit system would have to be determined.

8. Prior to its repeal in 1987, income averaging permitted taxpayers to reduce the impact of progressive rates on year to year fluctuations in their incomes. While justified by some on grounds of "simplification," it was primarily a way to raise revenue in the context of substantial rate reductions. Income averaging was and remains sound tax policy.

9. It should also be noted that deductions can be viewed as credit equivalents. For example, a $1,000 deduction for a taxpayer in the 15-percent bracket is the equivalent of a $150 credit; a $1,000 deduction for a taxpayer in the 35-percent bracket is the equivalent of a $350 credit.

10. These results are particularly harsh in the context of a universal or voluntary system with one-time or short-duration credits that are not refundable.

11. The IRS would have the time to verify eligibility and recoup erroneously issued credits from CSA assets.

12. Variations in the cost of living create an additional inequity in the context of phaseouts. Taking from the example in the text, assume that Big City income of $50,000 is equivalent to Small Town income of $40,000. A family making $50,000 in Big City does not get the credit, while the "identical" family making $40,000 in Small Town does get the credit.

13. Internal Revenue Code (I.R.C.) Section 25B (2003). The highest match rate is 50 percent, resulting in a maximum credit of $1,000.

14. I.R.C. Sections 219(b); and 408A(c)(2) (2003).

15. I.R.C. Section 415(c) (2003).

16. I.R.C. Sections 529(c)(2); and 2503(b) (2003).

17. See Orszag (2002), citing Carroll, *IRAs and the Tax Reform Act of 1997* (January 2000).

18. This is the funding proposed by Senators Breaux, Grassley, Gregg, Kerrey, Lieberman, Robb, Thomas, and Thompson in 1999 and 2000, and by former Senators Kerrey and Moynihan in 1998. Neither of these proposals provided for refundable credits, and both proposals were phased out for upper-income families.

19. Note that in the context of a universal system with refundable credits and no phaseouts, no tax return information would be required to verify eligibility. Thus, a designated person (e.g., the custodial parent) could claim the credit on behalf an eligible beneficiary on some type of CSA credit form filed with the IRS or some other federal government agency without the need to claim the credit on that person's tax return.

20. A second alternative would rely on the funding mechanism in recent individual development account proposals. Under this approach, the participating financial institution would fund the credit amount for each CSA and claim a credit on its tax return equal to the aggregate credits that it funds plus an allowance for administrative costs. The primary virtues of this approach are (a) parties with no tax liability can participate without the need for refundable credits payable to or on behalf of those participants; (b) it may encourage participation by financial institutions because they can recoup a portion of their administrative costs; and (c) participation by those institutions is likely to result in a more efficient system with broader participation by low- and lower-middle-income taxpayers.

21. There is some evidence that the extent of noncompliance is overstated and that the rates of noncompliance for refundable credits are no greater than other forms of noncompliance. See Liebman (1998).

22. Of course, the compliance issues would be far less in the context of a universal system with refundable credits and no phaseouts.

23. In this regard, it is worth noting that other countries with broad-based private retirement accounts restrict withdrawals when account balances fall below some level.

24. The one exception is section 529, where each state has effectively conferred a monopoly on a single financial institution responsible for administering its "state" plan.

25. While further investment restrictions in the form of diversification requirements might be considered, especially in a voluntary system with significant tax incentives (e.g., refundable credits), where funds could only be used for retirement, it seems unlikely that these restrictions would be enacted (unless, perhaps, CSAs were established as a partial substitute for Social Security).

REFERENCES

Federal Interagency Forum on Child and Family Statistics. (2000). *America's Children 2000*. Available at http://www.childstats.gov.

Goldberg, F., and M. Graetz. (1998). *Reforming Social Security: A Practical and Workable System of Personal Retirement Accounts*. National Bureau of Economic Research Working Paper No. 6970, December.

Liebman, J. B. (1998). "The Impact of the Earned Income Tax Credit on Incentives and Income Distribution" *Tax Policy and the Economy* 12(39), 83–119.

Orszag, P. R. (2002). *The Retirement Savings Components of Last Year's Tax Bill*. Online document. Available at http://www.cbpp.org/9-18-02tax.pdf. Center on Budget and Policy Priorities, September 18, 2002.

16

The EITC and USAs/IDAs: Maybe a Marriage Made in Heaven?

Timothy M. Smeeding

This chapter addresses the possibility of linking the savings desires of the low-income population to two or more policy instruments: the Earned Income Tax Credit (EITC) and a set of proposed policy instruments that subsidize savings behavior for low-income households through the tax code and other mechanisms, which we call universal savings accounts/individual development accounts (USAs/IDAs). The evidence presented here suggests both motive and desire for low-income families to save. The EITC offers low-income families a clear-cut opportunity to accumulate assets and to build positive net worth. The USA/IDA legislation hopes to build on this motivation and to assist financially and logistically to meet these goals. We call this interaction "asset-based transfer policy." However, a number of important questions need to be addressed before we can determine if this marriage of policies between the EITC and USAs/IDAs is indeed a heavenly one. In particular, further consideration of the design of USA/IDA-type asset accumulation policies and their congruency with the savings desires of low-income beneficiaries, particularly those who benefit from the EITC, seems a good next step. The potential is there, but the case is not yet strong for such a linkage.

THE CASE FOR ASSET-BASED TRANSFER POLICY

> *The poor are just like the rest of us, except they don't have as much money.*
> —HAROLD WATTS, 1970

The motives that underlie the desire to save and accumulate assets are not very well understood. Economic theories about saving, such as the "life-cycle hypothesis," are not well borne out by empirical evidence. Rates of saving differ substantially across nations with similar levels of economic development (e.g., high in Japan and Germany, compared to the United States), suggesting that cultural as well as economic factors determine savings. One influential economist argues that the United States is a nation driven by "luxury fever," which pushes our consumption desires beyond our savings capacity (Frank, 1999). In fact, the evidence is that both net worth and nonhousing/household debt have grown in America over the past two decades (Wolff, 2000).

It should, perhaps, come as no surprise that the public policy tenor toward the poor has changed from one of penalizing asset accumulation and saving (though liquid asset tests to determine eligibility for "means"-tested programs targeted at the poor are still enforced) to one of encouraging asset building. There is recent qualitative and quantitative evidence that the poor do indeed desire to accumulate assets and to save for specific purposes (Beverly, Tescher, and Marzahl, 2000; Edin, 2001; Romich and Weisner, 2000; Sherraden, 1991; Smeeding, Ross Phillips, and O'Connor, 2000).

However, desire and action are often two different realities (Shefrin and Thaler, 1992; Thaler, 1990). Motives, goals, and aspirations of savers, particularly low-income savers, may differ from those of policy makers and policy analysts. Hence, the congruence and interactions of two or more sets of policy instruments may be difficult to predict ex ante. It is with these hesitations in mind that we begin.

Our study reviews some recent evidence on desired savings among EITC beneficiaries, as well as some of the difficulties of designing an effective asset-building policy for this population. We first review the EITC and the evidence on savings desires among a sample of more than 800 recipients surveyed in Chicago in 1998. Then we delve into the possible rationales for savings and some of the new policies for promoting asset accumulation among the poor. This leads us to some suggestions for making a more complete assessment of the design, feasibility, and effectiveness of an asset-based transfer policy for low-income families and the policy's interaction with the EITC.

THE EITC AND ASSET ACCUMULATION

The largest U.S. cash income support program for low-income families is the EITC. In 1998, the EITC was expected to cost the federal government $30.5 billion, according to the Council of Economic Advisers (1998).[1] More than 19.7 million taxpaying units benefited from the EITC in 1998; roughly 80 percent of total benefits were returned to claimants in the form of an Internal Revenue Service (IRS) tax refund check. Though state EITCs were not studied, because Illinois (the sample site) did not have a state EITC program in 1998, ten states had their own Earned Income Credit program at that time (Johnson and Lazere, 1999). These state-level tax instruments supplement the federal EITC, adding both to the impact and the total outlays for the EITC (Greenstein and Shapiro, 1998).

Despite its enormity, very little is known about the impact of the EITC on the families who receive it. Unlike other income-transfer programs, the EITC is received by almost all client families (99 percent of recipients) as an annual lump-sum tax refund check, paid sometime in the spring of the year after earnings are received. Moreover, the EITC is administered by the IRS via the personal income tax system, thus permitting eligible clients to self select for benefits without a formal review and certification of eligibility (Liebman, 1998). For these reasons, the EITC is likely to have very different effects from a benefit received monthly over the year in which the qualifying income is earned, or a benefit administered by the social welfare programs. As a result, the EITC offers an opportunity to observe behavioral response to a lump-sum transfer and its disposition for purchases and, particularly, for savings.

EITC BACKGROUND

The EITC was enacted in 1975 to provide refundable tax credits to low-income workers and, originally, to refund some fraction of their Social Security taxes (Eissa and Hoynes, 1999). It was significantly expanded in the Tax Reform Act (TRA) of 1986 and the Omnibus Budget Reconciliation Acts (OBRA) of 1990 and 1993. By 1999, a maximum federal refundable tax credit of $3,816 was available to low-income households with two children and earned income between $9,540 and $12,460.[2] Participation rates in the EITC were estimated to be about 85 percent in 1990 (Scholz, 1990, 1994) but they have increased since that time and also as the maximum benefit and income ceiling have increased and eligibility standards have been broadened.[3]

The most significant changes in the EITC in the 1990s took place in benefit generosity to families with two children. The 1993 OBRA expanded the maximum credit for families with two children from $1,511 in 1993 to $3,816 in 1999 and to higher amounts in subsequent years. The result was a 40-percent earnings subsidy for low-earnings families with two children in 1999, compared with a 19.5-percent subsidy in 1993. The EITC now helps families with two children and incomes of up to $34,458 (in tax year 2004), compared with incomes up to $23,050 in 1993. Because of this growth, the EITC benefits a wide range of families, from those who might be cycling on and off welfare (more accurately, Temporary Assistance for Needy Families, or TANF), to those with near median incomes. Examining this broad range of beneficiaries, we would expect to find different types of effects for different types of recipients. In fact, these differences may be quite important for asset-building policies, as different subgroups of EITC recipients may have vastly different reasons for saving.

Among lower-income families, EITC is not counted as TANF income in most states (Meyer and Rosenbaum, 1999), nor is it counted toward food stamps or Medicaid eligibility in the month that it is received. The EITC, therefore, offers a powerful work incentive for low-income earners with children, for example, the TANF population. One recent econometric study (Meyer and Rosenbaum, 1999) concludes that the EITC has been the foremost driving force that explains increased hours worked by former welfare mothers over the 1993–1996 period (see also Blank, Card, and Robbins, 1999; Council of Economic Advisers, 1998). Of course, as with all targeted income supplement programs, benefits must, at some point, be phased out. The federal EITC for families with two or more children in 1999 declined at a rate of 21.06 percent per dollar earned from $12,460 to $30,580. Nada Eissa and Hilary Williamson Hoynes (1999) find that the phaseout reduces work effort by married women by a noticeable amount. Thus, higher-earning families in the "phaseout" region of the EITC respond differently than do lower earnings units in the "phase-in" or "plateau" ranges.

If we count benefits as additional income in the year that the benefits accrue, the EITC also has a powerful antipoverty effect because it is the largest single program that removes children from poverty. Among the working poor, some 30 percent of children who would otherwise be poor (based on household earnings and other sources of income) are lifted from poverty by the EITC (Greenstein and Shapiro, 1998).

In sum, recent studies have shown that the EITC increases work efforts of low-income families by supplementing earnings, thus raising net incomes and reducing poverty. However, these studies treat the EITC as an income subsidy and, for the most part, ignore its "lump-sum" delivery mechanism and its effect on savings.

ECONOMIC AND BEHAVIORAL EFFECTS

Because of its unique administration and "lumpy" character, the EITC offers a rare opportunity to examine the direct economic impact of the program on recipients. The lumpy nature of the EITC arises from several forces. A full 99 percent of recipients receive a lump-sum amount when they file their income taxes in the following year (Scholz, 1994) and not as a flow during the year.[4] There are several possible explanations for this lump-sum occurrence, including (a) employers' unwillingness to participate in the program; (b) employees' unwillingness to inform the employer of their participation in the EITC due to stigma effects or fears of lower pre-tax wages; and (c) employees' desire for the forced savings aspects of the EITC. There is some evidence that recipients prefer the forced savings aspects of the EITC (Olson and Davis, 1994; Romich and Weisner, 2000). While the forced savings theory supports a possible link between EITC lump-sum refunds and targeted savings vehicles, the relative impacts of these factors and perhaps others have yet to be examined.

Regardless of the reason for the type of benefit receipt, the lumpy nature of the EITC benefit and its recent rapid increases in benefit generosity create a rare and different opportunity to study the effects of the program on household finances—both on expenditure patterns and on asset behavior (that is, debt, credit, and savings).[5] In fact, until recently (see Beverly, Tescher, and Marzahl, 2000; Beverly et al., 2001; Smeeding, Ross Phillips, and O'Connor, 2000), very little had been written on the effects of the EITC on household financial behavior or how households use EITC benefits, despite the fact that benefits received can be as high as 50-percent of the previous year's income, for example, in states with high state supplements (DeParle, 1999).

CHICAGO STUDY OF EITC USAGE

The data in Timothy Smeeding and colleagues' (2000) work were drawn from a sample of 7,000 low-income Chicago area taxpayers who utilized the free tax preparation services provided by the Center for Law and Human Services (CLHS) in the winter and spring of 1998. The CLHS has ten centers in the Chicago metropolitan area where low-income taxpayers can receive free assistance from professionally qualified volunteers in preparing their tax returns. From January through April 1998, we interviewed low-income taxpayers in general and EITC beneficiaries in particular at these sites. More than 90 percent of taxpayers interviewed were willing to discuss their refunds. This produced a sample of 826 tax returns, which CLHS calculated would generate data on both a federal tax refund and the EITC as part of that refund. About one-quarter (208) of these families also completed a follow-up phone interview six weeks after filing to verify their receipt of the EITC and to answer again the same questions posed to them earlier on their use of the EITC.[6]

USES OF THE EITC

The purpose of this study was to examine two important types of usage for the EITC: making ends meet and improving social mobility. Respondents were given several categories of future purchases: goods or services, paying off existing bills, or saving the refund for future anticipated or unanticipated needs. While several other bundles of categories of uses could be created, we initially selected these two particular categories.

Significantly, the EITC is targeted on low-income working families with children; more than one-half of those in our sample received one or more means-tested transfers in 1997–1998. Our data suggest that our sample head of household population was largely made up of former welfare mothers, who, in 1998, found formal jobs or increased their hours of work at existing jobs and were trying to make ends meet. These mothers, most of whom were much less attached to the labor force in earlier times, may have had unmet consumption needs or may have used the EITC mainly to spread their consumption over the year.

Recent studies show that typical household expenses make up over 100-percent of welfare clients' incomes, the rest being made up from borrowing or from unreported earnings (Edin and Lein, 1997). Among these types of households, Kathryn Edin and Laura Lein have shown that the move from informal unreported work to formal work adds to expenses (such as child care and transportation), which reduces or negates the positive impact of higher earned income and may leave the households in no better economic circumstances than when they were on welfare. More recently, Pamela Loprest (1999) reports similar findings. Among welfare mothers, Edin (2001) found that living day to day (or month to month) was the typical way of life and that formal asset building, saving, or even formal contacts with financial institutions (that is, using banks or credit cards) were rare events. Edin found that, despite their poor economic circumstances, many interviewees were aware of and interested in accumulating assets and/or using earned income to improve their social mobility (Edin, 2001). Among recipients just struggling to make ends meet, the EITC could be seen as a way to buy durables, pay off outstanding bills, and meet other urgent consumption needs. To the extent that the EITC helps meet current consumption needs, it may not be different from other types of income subsidies, child care subsidies, and similar benefits (such as food stamps) in terms of its impact on recipients.

While the majority of Edin's samples were "credit constrained" and had little leverage to borrow money, many still expressed a strong interest in having access to credit and accumulating savings for durable purchases (Edin, 2001). Many of them, however, also realized that saving EITC benefits in formal settings, such as bank accounts, would negatively affect their eligibility for welfare benefits, leading most low-income, former welfare recipients to avoid banks. Because of these and other cultural factors, many low-income families may be credit constrained, in that they either lack access to formal credit markets or, having access, their credit records (or lack thereof) are not deemed creditworthy enough for them to obtain a bank loan. For populations similar to these, and in particular among those who are struggling to move from welfare to something better, the EITC with its lump-sum payment presents an opportunity to make extraordinary types of purchases that they might not otherwise be able to make or to save for "big ticket" items such as homes, cars, or college.

The literature on assets and the poor (e.g., Bird, Hagstrom, and Wild, 1999; Edin, 2001; Oliver and Shapiro, 1995; Shapiro and Wolff, 2001; Sherraden, 1991) suggests that even low-income families are willing to make sacrifices, by postponing current consumption to improve their long-term economic well-being, when presented with appropriate incentives and opportunities to save. Because of its large size relative to current income, the EITC presents an opportunity for otherwise credit constrained, low-income families to move beyond current consumption and to use the EITC for what Thomas Shapiro and Edward Wolff (2001) refer to as "asset-building" or "improving social mobility." These terms were used to describe several types of asset-enhancing uses of the EITC for improving longer term economic mobility and well-being. Many of these uses are consistent with both Edin's (2001) findings and those found by Sara Rimer (1995) and Jennifer Romich and Thomas Weisner (2000) in their more limited set of interviews and also have been verified by other studies (see Beverly, Tescher, and Marzahl, 2000; Beverly et al., 2001). In fact, we find some evidence for each of the savings motives given below.

Moving and Housing

Recent studies indicate that significant numbers of low-income, central city residents would move to safer neighborhoods if they could afford to do so. Recent studies, based on the Moving to Opportunity (MTO) experiment, verify that low-income, central city residents who participate in MTO overwhelmingly (70 to 75 percent of movers) choose to move away from violence and crime when given the chance (Ludwig, Duncan, and Hirschfield, 2001). Chicago has a number of dangerous inner city neighborhoods, including those in which we sampled our interviewees (see also Sampson, Earls, and Raudenbusch, 1997). Because moving a household requires both direct moving expenses and the demonstrated ability to pay the first and last months' rent, the EITC can provide such an opportunity. Alternatively, residents who have growing stakes in their neighborhoods could use the EITC to repair or improve their homes. In fact, a small fraction of our sample were home owners who were paying off mortgages, and many of them claimed this as a priority use of the EITC. The desire to own their own homes may also have had an important longer term effect on asset accumulation among EITC clients.

Automobiles and Transportation

Increasingly, studies of welfare to work are finding that owning or having access to a reliable means of transportation is a key to reducing the time costs of work-related travel, thus enabling a job seeker to expand the area of job search to obtain higher wages and improve economic well-being. The EITC also provides opportunities to purchase, upgrade, or repair a car, make a down payment on a better car, or pay for car insurance. Because lack of transportation is a serious impediment to searching for a job, maintaining employment, and job mobility, the EITC may provide a critical bridge to a higher level of economic well-being via a dependable source of transportation (Ong, 2002). Sandra Danziger and colleagues (2000) find that 47 percent of their sample of low-income welfare recipients do not own or have access to a car, but for those who do, the marginal effects of car ownership on earnings are equivalent to the marginal effects of completing high school in terms of higher future earnings. Edin (2001) also reports that individuals can use cars to begin self-employment as informal taxi drivers, pickup and delivery agents, or to drive as "junkers." Hence, being able to purchase a car or a truck, insure a car, repair a car, and/or pay off a car loan increases work opportunities and enhances job performance—individuals with cars can apply for more types of and better paying jobs, are more likely to be punctual, and are less likely to miss work due to lack of transportation.

Human Capital

The EITC also presents a source of funds for human capital investment both for tuition and as an alternative to student loans or to pay off former student loans, either for the recipients or their children.[7] In effect, a $1,000 to $2,000 EITC is a good substitute for a tuition voucher to a parochial or private school in communities where public schools are inadequate (Rimer, 1995). Recipients can also use EITC benefits to improve their children's early learning by improving the quality of their child care or for other for child-related, learning enhancing expenses. The EITC can also pay the recipient's tuition at a local community college or trade school (Romich and Weisner, 2000).

Saving

Another important use of the EITC, which improves social mobility, is saving for specified purposes (Thaler, 1990). Movement from welfare or government safety nets to self-protection via precautionary savings is an important indicator of upward social mobility. Making regular car payments and paying off bank loans, medical bills, and credit card bills are all uses of the EITC that help establish or improve a credit history. Repaying informal loans or sharing EITC refunds with family members is also indicative of social capital building and maintenance of nongovernmental means of support in case of emergencies. In fact, a growing number of U.S. policy makers feel that saving is a worthy activity that should be subsidized for low-income Americans in the same way that tax deductions for IRAs, 401(k)s, and pensions subsidize savings for others (Boshara, 2005; Seidman, 2001). If the EITC effectively subsidizes savings as well as work, it has a double benefit for society, as detailed more fully below.

CLASSIFICATIONS OF BUNDLES

Smeeding, Katherin Ross Phillips, and Michael O'Connor (2000) separated their EITC categories of use into two corresponding "bundles." In their sample, payment of regular bills (rent, utilities, food, groceries, clothing, personal expenses), and purchases of clothing were classified as expenses for "making ends meet" (first bundle). Purchases of household appliances or household furniture, as well as other personal or regular household expenses, were also categorized in the first bundle. Using the EITC to "improve social mobility" (second bundle) included all forms of debt repayment, savings, and other expenditures that were easily identified as increasing chances for improved mobility, including all forms of work-related expenses. These uses included payment of credit card, automobile, and personal debt. They also included human capital building (tuition payments and medical bills), expenses for cars (purchases, repairs, insurance), moving expenses, and home improvements, as discussed above. Sharing money with family members was also classified as an equity expense (in the second bundle), in that it builds social capital and maintains informal credit links.

RESULTS

Here we review the results of the Chicago study with a particular eye toward asset accumulation and desired savings behavior. A more complete set of results for all recipients is found in Smeeding, Ross Phillips, and O'Connor (2000).

Priorities

First, respondents were asked to list up to three priority uses of the EITC benefit. Of the 826 respondents, 617 or 74.7 percent had at least one "first" priority use for the EITC, while 40 percent also had a second priority, and 12 percent a third priority use as well. These priorities are summarized in figure 16.1. They indicate that bill paying was the single highest priority

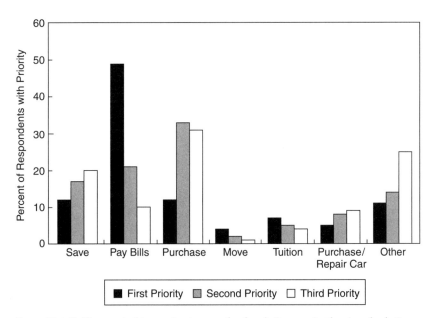

Figure 16.1 Self-reported important uses of refund. *Source:* Author's calculations, based on Smeeding, Ross Phillips, and O'Connor (2000).

use of the EITC for almost one-half of all beneficiaries, with purchases being the leading second use. Across all three priority levels, between 75 and 80 percent of respondents would use the EITC to pay a bill or make a purchase of some commodity. Clearly, the EITC helps make ends meet; this result was fully expected.

However, almost one-half of all respondents (49 percent) also stated that they would save some or all of their EITC checks (figure 16.1). Purposes for saving were mixed. Less than 40 percent claimed they were saving to pay off current or future bills, while more than 80 percent were saving for at least one equity building purpose, such as purchasing a car, home, or education for themselves or their children. Sondra Beverly and colleagues (2001) reported similar findings, with only 21 percent of their EITC savings plan participants stating that precautionary savings were their first priority use for savings.

Smeeding, Ross Phillips, and O'Connor (2000) also identified three specific key uses of the EITC that enhance social mobility: moving, paying tuition, or purchasing or repairing a car. Each of these uses is summarized in figure 16.1. While moving seems to be an all-or-nothing decision (with only 3 percent listing it as a secondary or tertiary preference, compared to 4 percent who list it as a primary preference), paying tuition or purchasing/repairing a car are more evenly spread across the preference scale. Altogether, 16 percent of the sample stated they would use the EITC to pay tuition, while 22 percent would make a car-related use of the refund. These uses suggest that the EITC also plays a large role in improving social mobility, a finding that the authors did not expect. All other priority uses of the EITC are summarized in the final columns and amount to only 11 percent of primary priorities and 14 percent of secondary priorities. The separately identified categories, upon which we focus below, seem to be driving the results.

Specific Uses

Combining priority uses across all respondents, so that all persons stating each use (as a first, second, or third priority) are represented, and when the priorities were bundled, as suggested in the previous section of the chapter, researchers Smeeding, Ross Phillips, and O'Connor (2000) arrived at the best overall snapshot of EITC use (see table 16.1). Several important patterns are evident in this table.

More than one-half of all beneficiaries had a social mobility-related use for the EITC. This use increased with income and benefit level, peaking for those with the maximum benefit (panel B). Moving, transportation, and saving all peaked in the plateau range and declined slightly in the phaseout range. Tuition expenses increased slightly as incomes rose.

Making ends meet was an important use of the EITC for almost one-half of the sample (panel C). Utilities and rent were higher priorities than food and clothes.

Table 16.1 Important Uses of the Refund within EITC Range

Panel	Category	Percent of Respondents within EITC Range			
		Phase-In	Plateau	Phaseout	Overall
A	Households receiving EITC	46.0	15.5	38.5	100.0
B	Any improving social mobility use	46.1	65.6	59.8	54.4
	Move	3.7	10.2	3.5	4.6
	Car/transportation	10.8	24.2	13.8	14.0
	Save	22.4	34.4	32.1	28.0
	Tuition/school	7.1	10.9	11.3	9.3
C	Any "making ends meet" use	50.8	46.1	45.9	48.2
	Utilities	32.9	37.5	31.1	32.9
	Rent	29.5	32.0	30.2	30.1
	Food	16.6	15.6	21.7	18.4
	Clothes	22.1	14.8	17.6	19.3
D	Plans for EITC				
	None	24.2	10.2	17.6	19.5
	Improving social mobility only	25.0	43.8	36.5	32.3
	Making ends meet only	29.7	24.2	22.6	26.2
	Both	21.1	21.9	23.3	22.0
Total N		380	128	318	826

Source: Author's calculations, based on Smeeding, Ross Phillips, and O'Connor, 2000. Totals may not add due to rounding.

As expected, the lowest-income households in the phase-in range had higher immediate needs than those in the phaseout range. Utilities and rent dominated food and clothes as consumption needs for this group.

Less than 20 percent of the sample had no plans for the EITC, with those in the phase-in range most likely not to state a use (panel D). Both this data and anecdotal evidence (DeParle, 1999) suggest that these were likely to be lower-income individuals who did not expect a refund.

If we were to prioritize usage according to our designated bundles of uses, we would find that, while those who would make both types of use are evenly spread across the range of refunds at 21 to 23 percent of respondents, about one-third would make social mobility uses only, while one-quarter would use the EITC check only to make ends meet. Both bundles follow predictable patterns across the EITC range, with those in the phase-in region having "making ends meet" as the higher priority, while those at the plateau or in the phaseout ranges placing a higher priority on uses that improve longer run social mobility. Thus, there are some suggestions that the determinants of EITC usage vary in predictable ways.

Access to Credit

If we are to study savings behavior among EITC beneficiaries, it is important to understand how EITC recipients relate to financial institutions. The ability to protect assets until they are needed seems important to long-term mobility. Low-income respondents who use check-cashing services and who have no formal relationship to financial markets (i.e., no checking or savings accounts, credit cards, loans, or mortgages) are less likely to be able to keep a large EITC refund intact for future needs. In general, they will also be less likely to benefit from federal asset-building policies.

In fact, access to financial and credit markets differs markedly across the income ranges of beneficiaries in the Smeeding, Ross Phillips, and O'Connor (2000) study (see table 16.2). Only 40 percent of those in the phase-in range had one or more of the types of financial affiliations listed above (in the text and in the table). Only 24 percent had a checking account. In contrast, almost 73 percent of those in the phaseout region had some contact with financial markets. Checking and savings accounts, credit card usage, and bank loans all increased across the EITC range. In contrast, use of a check-cashing service declined steadily across the income ranges, with 58 percent of those in the phase-in range and 44 percent of the plateau group using such services. Many of our respondents did, however, indicate that they wanted to open a checking or savings account with their EITC checks upon receipt.[8] Preliminary comparisons indicate that these

Table 16.2 Access to Financial and Credit Markets by EITC Range

Assets and Formal Credit	Percent of Respondents within EITC Range			
	Phase-In	Plateau	Phaseout	Overall
Percent with different forms				
Checking account	24.0	36.7	49.7	35.8
Savings account	16.1	28.9	42.1	28.1
Credit card	16.6	27.4	37.7	26.4
Bank loan	1.8	2.3	5.0	3.2
Mortgage	3.7	2.3	10.1	5.9
Any of the above	40.0	59.4	72.6	55.6
Percent using a check-cashing service for their EITC				
	57.8	44.3	34.2	44.3

Source: Author's calculations, based on Smeeding, Ross Phillips, and O'Connor, 2000.

breakdowns of choices are similar to those found by other researchers who have accessed national samples to investigate use of credit cards and checking and savings accounts among low-income populations (see Bird, Hagstrom, and Wild, 1999; Carney and Gale, 1999). John Caskey (chapter 8 in this volume) and Jeanne Hogarth and Jinkook Lee (2000) report that approximately 10 million households nationwide are "unbanked," largely minority renters with no savings and with younger household heads. Clearly, bringing banking services to this population, many of whom receive the EITC, will be a crucial future task for those promoting asset-building policies.

DISCUSSION

Altogether, the findings of Smeeding, Ross Phillips, and O'Connor (2000) suggest that knowledge of the EITC is high, that the large majority of people who receive the EITC expect it, and that most of those people have at least one use related to building social mobility for the EITC. Yet many recipients have few or no formal ties to financial markets, and many rely on informal services to cash their refund checks. Thus, while the EITC offers some hope as a vehicle for tax-financed asset accumulation policy, we have not yet achieved that goal. Furthermore, as others have suggested, additional subsidies for tax-funded savings, which EITC participants favor, are liable to be needed.

This study was the initial exploration of the ways in which families used our largest targeted income-transfer program, the EITC. As far as we know, it is the only such study to date, though others have urged similar studies (e.g., Hotz and Scholz, 2001). The EITC is unique because of its tax admin-istered nature and its lumpy, annual nature. This lumpiness may provide a key vehicle to overcome a short-term liquidity crisis and to provide recip-ients with opportunities to move beyond support of current consumption to meet more strategic longer term goals. It may also provide a vehicle for asset-building policies. While debt payment and consumption spreading behavior were expected, more than one-half of EITC recipients used their refunds to improve their prospects for social mobility. The large majority of EITC recipients were aware of the program and were able to articulate several specific uses for their refund, including investments in higher cur-rent and future earnings such as schooling, transportation, and moving.

SAVINGS POLICY IMPLICATIONS

If we wish to encourage social mobility uses for the EITC, Smeeding, Ross Phillips, and O'Connor (2000) found that these uses were positively related to having formal contact with financial institutions. As the federal govern-ment increasingly moves toward electronic benefit transfer (EBT) over the next several years, formal relations with banks and the financial literacy that is required should be encouraged by policy makers (Stegman, 1999). Opening a checking account offers a safe means of storing the EITC until individuals can sort out priority uses. In turn, checking and savings accounts offer opportunities for precautionary savings and longer-term asset building. Public policies that permit or encourage asset accumulation for low-income households are obviously important here and could further strengthen ties with formal financial institutions.

Legislation to create special subsidized savings accounts for unique purposes, such as home ownership, postsecondary tuition, or retirement, has recently appeared on the policy agenda (Boshara, 2005). As USAs and IDAs are currently in the experimental stage, if we believe that asset accumulation is an important part of upward social mobility, only those with formal ties to financial intermediaries will be able to take advantage of these efforts. It may be useful in some cases to offer outright subsidies to EITC beneficiaries to open savings accounts for specified purposes (see Seidman, 2001), thus providing them incentives to open bank accounts and to save for specific goals.

The EITC helps meet current consumption needs but also offers avenues for upward social mobility. The findings of the Chicago study suggest that increased incentives for savings, greater access to credit markets, and federal programs to match low-income savings for specified purposes (such as home purchases or schooling) could lead to greater savings and work effort by the low-income, low-wage population and, hence, to greater levels of self-insurance and self-sufficiency. The importance of the EITC for promoting savings-based policy cannot be understated. Without the EITC, almost one-half of its recipients could not have met their first priority use for the EITC, while the large majority of the rest could meet their primary need only to a lesser extent or with some delay. Hence, the EITC provides an important source of support for working poor families. As such, the EITC appears to be our most effective federal program for leading low-income families on a path toward true economic independence. The question we must investigate further is how the EITC interacts with other recent legislative actions, existing programs, and new proposals to promote asset accumulation among low-income populations.

LINKING THE EITC AND SAVINGS: PROMISES AND PITFALLS

Can the EITC and USAs/IDAs interact to provide a significant, combined effect on the asset position of low-income households? If the EITC is good policy and USAs/IDAs are good policy, then perhaps the two should co-exist. The interaction between the two programs should be positive, even if small at first. Yet it is not completely clear that USA/IDA policy should be tied to the EITC. If the USA/IDA design can help EITC recipients meet their needs while achieving its goals, the combined effect might be large, and the two together might make for better policy. At this time, we can only speculate about this interaction.

First, it is evident that asset accumulation policy for low-income families is liable to be a complicated venture (Shefrin and Thaler, 1992; Thaler, 1990). For instance, Smeeding, Ross Phillips, and O'Connor (2000) found that about one-quarter of their sample have credit cards and, of these, 80 percent had credit card debt averaging about $2,400. Yet only 18 percent of these respondents listed paying off credit card debt as a priority use for the EITC refund they received. Clearly, promotion of financial literacy is another consideration for asset accumulation policy.

Joseph Hotz and J. Karl Scholz (2001) suggest that further research of this type in a dynamic context is sorely needed. Most families who receive the EITC in one year receive it in the next. Indeed, more than one-third of the Smeeding, Ross Phillips, and O'Connor (2000) sample stated that they received the EITC last year. The dynamics of the EITC may, therefore, help families to move to economic independence. Of course, changes in employment, marriage and cohabitation, divorce or separation, family living arrangements, and various other factors could also affect transition. Following a sample of recipients over time would shed additional light on these topics and identify more clearly the pathways from dependency on means-tested transfers to economic independence, the use of savings, and the potential for the EITC as a basis for asset-building policy. However, absent such evidence, we must build our analyses on the data that we have now.

The Promise

Clearly, there is potential for the EITC to be linked to asset-building policy (Beverly et al., 2001; Seidman, 2001). Before leaving office, President Clinton proposed legislation to expand the federal EITC further with an even larger benefit for families of three or more children. The list of states offering some added EITC benefit is growing, with Illinois now beginning such a policy. Research undertaken by Robert Cherry and Max Sawicky (2000) proposes combining the EITC with refundable child tax credits, thus strengthening the structure of tax credits for low-income households and removing some of the labor supply disincentives in the current program. Moreover, there has been no increase in the fraction of households selecting the early payment option for the EITC, suggesting that lump-sum transfers at a fixed time will grow even larger in future years. Hence, the argument for linking the EITC to savings-based policy is becoming increasingly persuasive.

What are the savings goals of low-income households in the peak EITC benefit ranges of roughly $9,500 to $12,500? The evidence shown above suggests that their primary goals are the desire to become economically independent, to avoid returning to welfare, to accumulate human capital via more and better education for their children and themselves, and to accumulate durables (including cars and home ownership).

The recent proposals for subsidized savings accounts and other asset-based policies clearly intend to build assets among the poor. Because the tax code is used to subsidize savings and asset accumulation for high-income households, why not use it for low-income units as well? As mentioned earlier, these proposals come in two basic varieties: savings for retirement, such as Clinton's universal savings accounts (USAs), and individual development accounts (IDAs), which subsidize savings for other purposes. We cannot be sure of the success of such policies because no one has attempted to carry out such an asset-building policy on a large scale. And while the EITC evidence in the Chicago study, as well as the Beverly et al. (2001) study, suggest that low income families have the desire to save, one must question how successful the EITC and targeted savings linkage might be.

Potential Pitfalls

First, we need to better understand the motives for saving among the poor and their linkage with legislated purposes for saving via USAs/IDAs. The EITC population is largely a low-income group. According to IRS data for 1996, of the 19.5 million filers who claimed the EITC, 7.8 million claimed one child, while 8.0 million claimed two or more children (U.S. Internal Revenue Service, 1999). Over 97 percent of the total cost of the credit for tax year 1996 ($28.2 billion) went to the 82 percent of filers who claimed one or more eligible children. National samples from 1997 also divide EITC beneficiaries into two major groups: (a) about 70 percent are single parents filing as heads of households or single persons, and (b) almost 30 percent are low earning two-parent households (U.S. Congress, 1998, table 13-13, 871). Other IRS data suggest that 18 percent of filers in 1996 were single filers without children (U.S. Internal Revenue Service, 1999). Assuming the same fraction of single filers in 1997 as in 1996, this means that 52 percent of national filers were single-parent heads of households in 1997. In contrast, almost one-half of all recipients are in the phaseout range (above $12,400 in 1999), with most of these in two-parent households.

Hence, the largest EITC credits go to young families with children, most of them single parents. In the income ranges where the EITC is the highest ($12,000–$15,000 annual gross earned income), families are more likely to be struggling to escape poverty than to achieve secure middle-class status. At higher income ranges, the EITC subsidy quickly shrinks, as the program phases out (at 21 percent) and as federal income tax liability grows (at 15 percent). Thus, most recipients of the EITC in the $20,000–$25,000 and above income range receive either small tax refunds or pay lower taxes and receive no April tax filing bonus. While people in this group are more likely to participate in a USA/IDA plan, their impetus from the EITC refund is liable to be small.

Therefore, it seems that the families most able to finance long-term savings do not get a large EITC bonus. At the same time, those closest to welfare and those with the least stable familial situations (low income, single parents) are liable to receive the greatest EITC bonuses. Thus, much of the attraction of using the EITC is usually contrasted with the savings intentions of truly low-income mothers with young children who receive the bulk of large EITC payments.

DESIGNING USAs/IDAs FOR EITC BENEFICIARIES

If EITC-linked savings policies are aimed at lower-income households because of the EITC structure, we must, therefore, ask what drives their savings intentions. While there are few studies of these motives, there is some evidence of the desires of EITC recipients for different types of savings (Beverly and Sherraden, 1999; Beverly et al., 2001; Hogarth and O'Donnell, 1999). Clearly, low-income households have a desire for precautionary savings. Short-term liquidity is important for expected and unexpected future bills, particularly for those just leaving welfare. Further, low-income households save for specific goals: to buy a first or better car, to purchase a first home, and to invest in a new business (see also Davis and Lemieux, 2000). Many also save to pay for education for themselves or their children. Finally, after all of these priorities are met, low-income families may choose to save for retirement.

It seems that this list of savings priorities is judicious and sensible, especially for single parents. However, few large EITC beneficiaries will save for retirement. Thus, while EITC-based savings incentives may be useful for some types of savings plans, such as IDAs, they are liable to be less useful as vehicles for add-on retirement savings accounts, such as USAs. Not only do savings needs differ among those with and without children, but once children have grown to age 18 and retirement savings become a priority, the maximum value of the EITC drops precipitously. Proposals for retirement savings plans, like the USA program, seem to recognize this dilemma by allowing withdrawals for college tuition, a first home, or catastrophic medical expenses, as well as for retirement. This is not to say that matched pension accounts are not a good idea (as demonstrated by Orszag and Greenstein, 2000), but that retirement savings accounts do not seem to match well with the savings needs of younger EITC recipients who have young children and receive large, lump-sum amounts.

Additionally, plans that tie up personal savings for specified periods in order to receive subsidies preempt the use of these savings for short-term needs. While a large fraction of EITC recipients may elect to participate in an IDA-type program, the time and use limitations may clash with their short-term needs for emergency bill paying or durables purchases, due to job loss, car breakdown, or related costly "emergencies." There is a long literature on low-income women's tendencies to cycle on and off welfare, and the immediate use of savings may be to avoid cycling back to welfare. However, subsidized IDAs are not designed for such uses.

The Beverly et al. (2001) study found that only 20 percent of the beneficiaries of the EITC took advantage of the opportunity to open a bank account under the ShoreBank "Extra Credit Savings Program" (ESCP). Moreover, 61 percent of these were unbanked, meaning that the ESCP was their only banking account. Most recipients decided to open accounts because banking costs were low and because they offered a safe harbor for their EITC checks. However, by the end of the year, most recipients had severely depleted their accounts for bills and other needs, so that the median closing balance was only $13.00. Hence, the needs of EITC recipients were greater than their abilities to save for long-term goals.[9] Additional studies like this one, drawn from larger samples in multiple areas, can help us to better understand whether EITC recipients can maintain their IDA-like accounts throughout the current year.

LINKAGES BETWEEN LOW-INCOME FAMILIES AND ASSET-BUILDING POLICIES

Low-income families need and want to build assets. Financial institutions offer a safe place to keep assets and to monitor their growth. They also provide an institution for maintaining the fidelity and public accountability required of an USA/IDA type program. Linkages to the EITC may provide both an opportunity and a natural linkage to savings. Indeed, EITC recipients may well find that financial institutions, which offer safety features, and public programs, which subsidize asset accumulation (with a large match for participation), offer attractive uses for part of their EITC refunds. However, such programs are liable to be complex to understand and manage unless participants have considerable and consistent one-on-one guidance. In this next section of the chapter, some of the most important considerations for an EITC-based savings incentive policy are suggested.

Untaxing Assets

Before we even begin to encourage savings by the poor, we need to stop discouraging asset accumulation in means-tested benefit programs. The recent literature finds strong evidence that social insurance in general and means-tested programs in particular discourage savings (see Gruber and Yelowitz, 1997; Hubbard, Skinner, and Zeldes, 1995; Neumark and Powers, 1998; Powers, 1998). The fact that so few lower-income clients have checking or savings accounts could be attributed to the asset tests associated with welfare and Medicaid receipt, which discourage saving and opening bank accounts. In most states, the EITC is not counted toward TANF for benefit determination; however, it is counted toward asset limits after two months for both Medicaid and Supplemental Security Income (SSI). While many states have eased liquid asset tests for TANF clients, food stamp asset limits for most families remain relatively low ($2,000 for liquid assets), thereby penalizing savers who fear losing their jobs and having to reapply for aid. Low limits on the maximum value of a car to qualify for food stamps are liable to have similar effects on eligibility, even when the literature clearly suggests that automobile ownership is a key positive determinant of earnings levels. However, while food stamp asset limits are relatively low, the EITC is exempt from counting against food stamp asset limits for 12 months after receipt, a much longer period than in the cases of SSI or Medicaid. The negative effects of participation in means-tested programs on savings and equity building deserve further investigation.

Policies to limit eligibility to clients whose automobiles are worth less than $4,650 should be reevaluated in states that are keeping this food stamp option, while Medicaid, SSI, and TANF might mimic food stamps by exempting savings from the EITC from asset tests for 12 months, instead of two. In turn, food stamp liquid asset limits of $2,000 could be increased to allow for some asset accumulation among otherwise eligible households.

While many USA/IDA-type savings accounts are explicitly excluded from consideration by these programs, it seems wise to change the program rules themselves if we are to build assets more generally and to promote long-term economic independence. Asset transfers should be seen as a way to transform societies, not as a method to meet emergency needs. Raising asset limits in means-tested programs would allow households the opportunity to build flexible, unsubsidized, precautionary savings balances, which might be the first step toward participation in longer term USA/IDA-like savings schemes.

Financial Literacy

The widespread usage of expensive check-cashing outlets; the popularity of short-term loans from tax refund vendors, such as H&R Block, at 200-percent interest rates; and the persistence of credit card borrowing at 19 to 25 percent interest rates (while "saving" at 1 to 2 percent interest in bank checking and savings accounts) all suggest that the need for financial literacy among low-income households in general, and EITC beneficiaries in particular, is great. While a few pilot programs have begun to educate the welfare-to-work population on financial literacy, a longer term and more general education policy is needed. Financial literacy is a good investment in the type of forward-looking society that would adopt tax-based savings incentives in a meaningful way.

Financial Institutions

One must also question the willingness and cost to financial institutions for maintaining and monitoring USA/IDA and EITC schemes. From a financial perspective, these accounts are liable to be high cost and low revenue, particularly if banks are required to enforce withdrawal policies for specific purposes. While long-term saving arrangements at fairly low rates of interest offer banks a chance to benefit from time-tied savings plans like IDAs and USAs, the costs of administering these accounts is high because of their relatively small size and because of the chance of early withdrawal. DeWayne Davis and Jeff Lemieux's research (2000) reports that the average savings of participants in the American Dream (IDA) Demonstration Project was $286, and the average total account balance (with subsidies) was $845. Many participants also make in-person monthly deposits and withdrawals, consistent with the Beverly et al. (2001) study. Hence, these are fairly high maintenance accounts. And banks like the ShoreBank in Chicago, which are willing to absorb these costs and to offer low-cost asset-building accounts, are liable to attract low-income families as clients for this reason alone, even without an IDA matching scheme.

Moreover, if USA/IDA withdrawal policies are to be enforced, banks must monitor use of withdrawals and obtain "proof" of legitimate usage of funds (e.g., to purchase a home or to start a business). Despite the recent implementation of electronic benefit transfer (EBT) in all but two states as of July 2004, the for-profit banking community, in particular, and low-income friendly credit unions and community-oriented banks, to a greater extent, will incur real costs in administering USA/IDA plans and in bringing the "unbanked" into the financial world. These costs have to be taken into account by policy makers (e.g., by including payments to financial intermediaries to offset the costs of administering and monitoring USAs/IDAs).

CONCLUSION

The evidence presented here suggests both motive and desire for low-income families to save. The EITC and its lump-sum nature offer a natural opportunity for beneficiaries to use part of their refunds for targeted asset-building. However, a number of important questions need be addressed before we can determine if this marriage of policies between the EITC and USA/IDA is indeed heavenly. In particular, the availability of low-cost, asset-bearing accounts seems to attract a substantial proportion of EITC claimants, but not for long periods of time. If longer term asset accumulation is to be linked to the EITC, it seems that further consideration of the design of USA/IDA-type asset accumulation policies and their congruency with the savings desires of low-income beneficiaries seems a good next step. The potential is there, but the case is not yet strong for such a linkage.

NOTES

The author would like to thank the Center for Social Development at the George Warren School of Social Work and Michael Sherraden for comments and support in preparing this paper. Useful comments were also received from Sondra Beverly, Dave Marzahl, and Jennifer Tescher. An earlier version of this paper was published by the *Georgetown Public Policy Review* (Fall 2002). All errors of fact and fiction are the responsibility of the author.

1. Food stamps, TANF, and Supplemental Security Income (SSI) were all budgetarily smaller programs in terms of total costs for 1998 (Council of Economic Advisers, 1998).

2. The EITC is also available to single persons but at a much lower level. In contrast with the treatment of families who have children, the level of EITC benefit for single filers has not changed in real terms since it was introduced in 1994.

3. While higher benefits and word-of-mouth promotion might have increased participation in the EITC since 1990, other factors worked in the opposite direction. In 1991, the IRS began requiring a new form, Schedule EIC, in order to claim EITC. Previously, the IRS would calculate and issue the credit based on information in the form 1040. The participation rate might, therefore, have dropped somewhat in the early 1990s. Our interviews showed that over 20 percent of EITC recipients were not expecting a refund. Many of these individuals would not have filed at all but for the CLHS tax program and others like it. See O'Connor (1999b) for a more detailed analysis. In fact, low-income earners in Milwaukee who were involved in the New Hope Experiment seem to understand the relationship between work and the size of the tax refund as being linear, i.e., "more work, more money" (Romich and Weisner, 2000).

4. This "flow" option has several limitations. First of all, the EITC can be taken as a transfer during the year. If employees fill in a W-5 withholding form and submit it to their employers, they can receive up to 60 percent of the maximum allowable amount of the EITC, scaled to their monthly or weekly checks. The maximum amount of refunds in 1998 was $26 per week (O'Connor, 1999a).

5. Ideally, one would like to separate the economic effects of the EITC, using a counterfactual group to parse out behavioral effects with a comparison group of some type. Because the EITC is a national program open to all low-income, low-wage taxpayers, there is no natural control group. One could examine year-to-year changes in outlays using, for instance, the Consumer Expenditure Survey (CEX; U.S. Department of Labor, n.d.); e.g., Barrow and McGranahan (2000). However, the CEX does not collect tax data and is not designed for assessing the effects of the EITC in respondents. Further, nonparticipants of the EITC are likely to be a nonrepresentative and biased group. As a substitute, Smeeding, Ross Phillips, and O'Connor (2000) devised the questions regarding ability to make spending or saving decisions if the tax refund was not given. These are reported on below.

6. Smeeding, Ross Phillips, and O'Connor (2000) rely on the 826 questionnaires filled out at the time of the tax filing. The 208 call-back interviews provided verification of intended usage of these refunds. Call-backs were limited to those with refunds of $1,000 or more, and we obtained a 50-percent response rate. About 90 percent of the call-backs received the refund amount calculated by the CLHS. Differences were due to federal inquiries regarding legitimacy of the returns or lower refunds due to school loans or child support payments that were outstanding. Among this 90 percent, there was a high (85 percent) correspondence between intended use of refund (sample used here) and actual usage (once the check arrived), with no systematic change in the distribution of tax return usage by type of use. Call-back interviewees were remarkably consistent in their preferences for EITC usage in the phone interview compared with the face-to-face interview.

7. In fact, in other call-back interviews, we found a small number of EITC returns (less than 3 percent) that were reduced by the Internal Revenue Service because of money still owed on guaranteed student loans.

8. This finding helped inspire the recent Beverly et al. (2001) study.

9. While 81 percent of the EITC participants in the Beverly et al. (2001) study who would have participated in their ShoreBank ECSP accounts did not do so, most who did participate were "unbanked." It could be that a large number of nonparticipants did not take advantage of the EITC savings plan because they realized that it

would not be possible to tie up their EITC checks long enough to collect the up to $100 bonus promised at year's end for participants. Title IV of the 2002 Farm Bill (HR 2646), the "Food Stamp Reauthorization Act of 2002," section 4107, permits states to set their own value limits on vehicles (http://www.fns.usda.gov/cga/2002_Farm_Bill/food_stamps.html). The Food Stamp Program's Web site lists the 2004 vehicle policies of each state: 24 states exclude all vehicles, 15 exclude at least one vehicle, and 8 exempt an amount higher than the program's standard auto exemption of $4,650 (U.S. Department of Agriculture, 2004).

REFERENCES

Barrow, L., and L. McGranahan. (2000). *The Earned Income Credit and Durable Goods Purchases.* JCPR Working Paper No. 144. Chicago: Joint Center for Poverty Research.

Beverly, S., J. Tescher, and D. Marzahl. (2000). *Low Cost Bank Accounts and the EITC: How Financial Institutions Can Reach the Unbanked and Facilitate Savings.* Working Paper No. 00-19. St. Louis, Mo.: Washington University, Center for Social Development, September 21–23.

Beverly, S., J. Tescher, J. Romich, and D. Marzahl. (2001). "Linking Tax Refunds and Low-Cost Bank Accounts: Findings from the Extra Credit Savings Program." Presented to the Association for Public Policy and Management Annual Research Conference, Washington, D.C., November.

Beverly, S. G., and M. Sherraden. (1999). "Institutional Determinants of Saving: Implications for Low-Income Households and Public Policy." *Journal of Socio-Economics* 28(4), 457–473.

Bird, E., P. Hagstrom, and R. Wild. (1999). "Credit Card Debts of the Poor: High and Rising." *Journal of Policy Analysis and Management* 18(1), 125–133.

Blank, R., D. Card, and P. Robbins. (1999). *Financial Incentives for Increasing Work and Income among Low-Income Families.* NBER Working Paper No. 6998. Cambridge, Mass.: National Bureau of Economic Research, March.

Boshara, R. (2005). *Individual Development Accounts and Public Policies to Build Savings and Assets for the Poor.* Washington, D.C.: Brookings Institution.

Carney, S., and W. Gale. (1999). *Asset Accumulation among Low-Income Households.* Economic Studies Paper. Washington, D.C.: The Brookings Institution.

Cherry, R., and M. B. Sawicky. (2000). *Giving Tax Credit Where Credit Is Due: A "Universal Unified Child Credit" That Expands the EITC and Cuts Taxes for Working Families.* Briefing Paper No. 91. Washington, D.C.: Economic Policy Institute, April.

Council of Economic Advisers. (1998). *Good News for Low Income Families: Expansions in the Earned Income Tax Credit and the Minimum Wage. A Report.* Washington, D.C.: Council of Economic Advisers, December.

Danziger, S., M. Corcoran, S. Danziger, C. Heflin, A. Kalil, J. Levine, D. Rosen, K. Seefeldt, K. Siefert, and R. Tolman. (2000). "Barriers to Employment of Welfare Recipients." In R. Cherry and W. M. Rogers III, *Prosperity for All? The Economic Boom and African Americans.* New York: Russell Sage Foundation, 245–278.

Davis, D., and J. Lemieux. (2000). *Individual Development Accounts: How Are They Working?* Briefing. Washington, D.C.: Progressive Policy Institute, August 22.

DeParle, J. (1999). "Life after Welfare—First Filers: On a Once Forlorn Avenue, Tax Preparers Now Flourish." *New York Times,* March 21, 1, 20.

Edin, K. (2001). "More than Money: The Role of Assets in the Hopes and Dreams of the Poor." Chapter 6 in T. M. Shapiro and E. N. Wolff, *Asset Building Among the Poor.* New York: Russell Sage Foundation, 206–231.

Edin, K., and L. Lein. (1997). *Making Ends Meet: How Single Mothers Survive Welfare and Low-Wage Work.* New York: Russell Sage Foundation.

Eissa, N., and H. W. Hoynes. (1999). *The Earned Income Tax Credit and Labor Supply: Married Couples.* Economics Department Working Paper No. E99–267. Berkeley: University of California, April.

Frank, R. H. (1999). *Luxury Fever: Why Money Fails to Satisfy in an Era of Success.* New York: Free Press.

Greenstein, R., and I. Shapiro. (1998). *New Research Findings on the Effects of the Earned Income Tax Credit.* Working Paper No. 98-022. Washington, D.C.: Center on Budget and Policy Priorities, March.

Gruber, J., and A. Yelowitz. (1997). *Public Health Insurance and Private Savings.* NBER Working Paper No. 6041. Cambridge, Mass.: National Bureau of Economic Research.

Hogarth, J. M., and J. Lee. (2000). *Use of Financial Services and the Poor.* Working Paper No. 00-13. St. Louis, Mo.: Washington University Center for Social Development, September.

Hogarth, J. M., and K. H. O'Donnell. (1999). "Banking Relationships of Lower-Income Families and the Governmental Trend toward Electronic Payment." *Federal Reserve Bulletin* (July), 459–473.

Hotz, J., and J. K. Scholz. (2001). *The Earned Income Tax Credit.* NBER Working Paper 8078. Cambridge, Mass.: National Bureau of Economic Research, January.

Hubbard, R. G., J. Skinner, and S. P. Zeldes. (1995). "Precautionary Savings and Social Insurance." *Journal of Political Economy* 103(2), 360–399.

Johnson, N., and E. Lazere. (1999). "State Earned Income Tax Credits." *Poverty Research News* III(1), article no. 7.

Liebman, J. B. (1998). "The EITC Compliance Problem." *Poverty Research News* II(3), article no. 3.

Loprest, P. (1999). "How Families That Left Welfare Are Doing: A National Picture." *New Federalism, National Survey of America's Families,* No. B-1. Washington, D.C.: Urban Institute, August.

Ludwig, J., G. Duncan, and P. Hirschfield. (2001). "Urban Poverty and Juvenile Crime: Evidence from a Randomized Housing-Mobility Experiment." *Quarterly Journal of Economics* 166(2), 655–679.

Meyer, B., and D. Rosenbaum. (1999). *Welfare, the Earned Income Tax Credit, and the Labor Supply of Single Mothers.* NBER Working Paper 7363. Cambridge, Mass.: National Bureau of Economic Research, September.

Neumark, D., and E. Powers. (1998). "The Effect of Means-Tested Income Support for the Elderly on Pre-Retirement Saving: Evidence from the SSI Program in the U.S." *Journal of Public Economics* 68(2), 181–206.

O'Connor, M. (1999a). "Comment on Advanced Payment Option." Unpublished manuscript. Chicago, Ill.: Center for Urban Research and Learning, Loyola University.

O'Connor, M. (1999b). "Impact of EITC Expansion on Participation Rates." Unpublished manuscript. Chicago, Ill.: Center for Urban Research and Learning, Loyola University.

Oliver, M. L., and T. M. Shapiro. (1995). *Black Wealth, White Wealth: A New Perspective on Racial Inequality.* New York: Routledge.

Olson, L. M., and A. Davis. (1994). *The Earned Income Tax Credit: Views from the Street Level.* Working Paper Series No. WP-94-1. Evanston, Ill.: Center for Urban Affairs (renamed Institute for Policy Research), Northwestern University.

Ong, P. (2002). "Car Ownership and Welfare-to-Work." *Journal of Policy Analysis and Management* 21(2), 239–252.

Orszag, P., and R. Greenstein. (2000). "Toward Progressive Pensions: A Summary of the U.S. Pension System and Proposals for Reform." Policy Report. St. Louis, Mo.: Washington University, Center for Social Development, September.

Powers, E. T. (1998). "Does Means-Tested Welfare Discourage Savings? Evidence from a Change in AFDC Policy in the United States." *Journal of Public Economics* 68(1), 33–53.

Rimer, S. (1995). "Cutting Tax Credit Means Much to Those with Little." *New York Times,* October 16, 1.

Romich, J., and T. Weisner. (2000). "How Families View and Use the EITC: Advance Payment versus Lump Sum Delivery Source." *National Tax Journal* 53(4, part 2), 1245–1265.

Sampson, R. J., F. Earls, and S. W. Raudenbusch. (1997). "Neighborhoods and Violent Crime: A Multilevel Study of Collective Efficacy." *Science* 277(5328), 918–924.

Scholz, J. K. (1990). *The Participation Rate of the Earned Income Tax Credit.* Working Paper. Madison: Institute for Research on Poverty, University of Wisconsin-Madison.

Scholz, J. K. (1994). "The Earned Income Tax Credit: Participation, Compliance, and Antipoverty Effectiveness." *National Tax Journal* 47(1), 63–87.

Seidman, L. (2001). "Assets and the Tax Code." In T. M. Shapiro and E. N. Wolff, *Assets for the Poor: The Benefits of Spreading Asset Ownership.* New York: Russell Sage Foundation, 324–356.

Shapiro, T., and E. N. Wolff. (2001). "Introduction." In T. M. Shapiro and E. N. Wolff, *Assets for the Poor: The Benefits of Spreading Asset Ownership.* New York: Russell Sage Foundation.

Shefrin, H. M., and R. H. Thaler. (1992). "Mental Accounting, Saving, and Self-Control." In *Choice Over Time,* eds. G. Loewenstein and J. Elster. New York: Russell Sage Foundation, 287–330.

Sherraden, M. W. (1991). *Assets and the Poor: A New Welfare Policy.* Armonk, N.Y.: M. E. Sharpe.

Smeeding, T. M., K. Ross Phillips, and M. O'Connor. (2000). "The EITC: Expectation, Knowledge, Use, and Economic and Social Mobility." *National Tax Journal* 53(4, part 2), 1187–1209.

Stegman, M. A. (1999). *Savings for the Poor: The Hidden Benefits of Electronic Banking.* Washington, D.C.: The Brookings Institution Press.

Thaler, R. H. (1990). "Saving, Fungibility, and Mental Accounts." *Journal of Economic Perspectives* 4(1), 193–205.

U.S. Congress. (1998, 2004). *Green Book: Background Materials and Data on Programs within the Jurisdiction of the Committee on Ways and Means.* U.S. House of

Representatives, The Committee on Ways and Means, WMCP 105-7 and 108-6. Washington, D.C.: Government Printing Office.

U.S. Department of Agriculture. Food and Nutrition Service. (2004). "Food Stamp Program: State Options Report." Available at http://www.fns.usda.gov/fsp/rules/Memo/Support/State_Options/fourth/.

U.S. Department of Labor. Bureau of Labor Statistics. (n.d.). Consumer Expenditure Survey home page. Available at http://www.bls.goc/cex/home.htm. Last accessed December 22, 2004.

U.S. Internal Revenue Service. (1999). "1996 Individual Income Tax Returns: A Collection of 17 Tables, Plus the Introduction and Changes in Law, Description of the Sample, and Explanation of Terms Sections." IRS Publication 1304 (Rev. 3-99). Washington, D.C.: Government Printing Office.

Watts, H. (1970). "Comments on the Findings from the New Jersey Negative Income Tax Experiment." Speech delivered at press conference, Institute for Research on Poverty, University of Wisconsin, Madison, October.

Wolff, E. N. (2000). *Recent Trends in Wealth Ownership: 1983–1998.* Jerome Levy Economics Institute Working Paper No. 300. Annandale-on-Hudson, N.Y.: Bard College, May.

PART V

ASSESSMENT AND
DIRECTIONS

The purpose of this final part is to assess the overall content of the book and directions for both policy and research. Jared Bernstein begins with critical questions on asset-based policy. Bernstein articulately represents an income-based policy perspective. He asks whether it is a priority for the poor to save, whether asset-based policies would create large enough accumulations to matter, and whether funding for asset-based policies might be in competition with funding for income-based policies. Bernstein's chapter is placed toward the end of the book as a critique, to balance more positive views presented in some of the chapters. A careful reader may leave the book with no definitive answers but with important questions to consider in the future.

In the next chapter, scholars from the Center for Social Development (CSD), Edward Scanlon, Deborah Adams, Sondra Beverly, Mark Schreiner, and myself, assess the status of theory and research in two important areas: how savings and assets develop and the effects of asset holding. The institutional approach to saving theory that is being developed at CSD, if and when it is definitively supported by empirical evidence, may have the potential to guide public policy. The concepts of access, incentives, information, facilitation, and expectations have direct policy relevance. Turning to effects of asset holding, theoretical work in this area is rudimentary, consisting mostly of general propositions. If this is to become an influential body of knowledge, theory will have to be specified and tested. One promising direction is cognitive psychological theory; it may be that asset holding changes the way people think, which, in turn, has largely positive results. Looking at the body of empirical evidence, there is reason to think that holding assets leads to positive outcomes, including more options in life, greater material well-being, and more personal satisfaction. However, most existing research is not highly rigorous, and alternative explanations are not always ruled out. Because this knowledge represents the primary rationale for asset-based policy, a large research agenda lies ahead.

The book concludes with an assessment of the various studies, commentary on key issues raised, and thoughts for the future. In brief, the future looks promising for asset-based policy, but there is no guarantee that the poor will be included.

17

Critical Questions in Asset-Based Policy

Jared Bernstein

Scholars of asset building for the poor, such as Michael Sherraden, the editor of this volume, present a compelling case. They argue convincingly that to advocate exclusively for increasing the consumption opportunities for the poor and to ignore asset building is to miss a deeper understanding of poverty's causes and cures.

And yet, despite the fact that there is considerable activity in the policy area around asset building, this theme often gets short shrift in the policy debate regarding the poor. Most popular discussions about working poverty seem to focus on jobs, wages, and incomes. When most advocates for low-income families tick off their policy solutions, individual development accounts (IDAs), for example, are either unmentioned or an afterthought. Why is that?

In this brief chapter, I offer some thoughts on this question, from a left-leaning perspective. The first thread of the argument points out the primacy of paid employment in the current poverty debate. Welfare reform in tandem with a tight labor market and surpluses in the federal budget provide a unique and timely opportunity to advocate for policies that improve the quality of jobs in the low-wage labor market, raise after-tax earnings, and subsidize work-related supports. In this policy climate, asset-based policy has less immediate political currency.

The next section examines two other reasons why asset-based policies too often get short shrift: the immediacy and magnitude problems. To better understand the immediacy point, I explore poverty's determinants through a common decomposition technique and examine the extent to which savings plays a determinant role. My sense from this exercise and from the literature is that most of the poor's immediate economic problems call for income or consumption-based solutions. Of course, if the poor had the assets of the better off, many of these immediate problems would not develop, which leads to the question of whether IDAs held by the poor can generate large enough savings to be as transformational as we want them to be.

Finally, I briefly examine the political economy of asset-based policies for the poor. These are highly redistributive policies, and if they are large enough to make a difference, they are likely to invoke the same government dependency critique that was potently wielded against welfare benefits. In my view, that is a perfectly fine battle to have. Certainly, assets have been systematically distributed away from African American families, for example, throughout our history. But I argue that progressive policy advocates should avoid depending exclusively on redistribution through the tax system to lift the economic fortunes of the poor. The primary methods of distribution, or market outcomes, should also be fair game.

THE PRIMACY OF WORK

The contemporary debate over reducing poverty focuses almost exclusively on work in the private sector, not on savings or asset formation. This is not a new state of affairs. For the past few decades, two related themes have dominated the debate over poverty policy. In fact, it is probably fair to say that these two themes have dominated the debates since the English Poor Laws and the Speenhamland Act.[1] First, there is the issue of whether the able-bodied should be required to work. Second, the question arises as to whether government programs to alleviate poverty worsen the problem by inculcating dependency and other behaviors viewed unfavorably by the tax-paying public.

Regarding the first point, at least from the perspective of safety net policy, the debate appears to have been settled in favor of work. Things were leaning this way when the Family Support Act was enacted in the late 1980s, but the passage of welfare reform in 1996 sealed the deal: The solution to poverty for most able-bodied poor persons was determined to be employment, and this has come to mean employment in the private sector. In former President Bill Clinton's original formulation, those who made good faith efforts to find jobs but failed to do so under the time limits were guaranteed some type of employment, usually "workfare," where they could work off their welfare grant through community service. While plans like this exist in some localities, the thrust has clearly been toward private sector employment.

As is now well known, the poor have responded both to this policy thrust and to the tight labor market by working more than ever before. In fact, the employment rates of low-income single mothers have reached historical highs (see, e.g., Bernstein, 2000). In our book, *The State of Working America, 2000–01* (Mishel, Bernstein, and Schmitt, 2001), we show that the share of poor, mother-only families with any positive hours of work went from 50 percent in both 1979 and 1989 to 65 percent in 1998. These families' average annual hours (pooling across the family) went from about 550 in those earlier time periods to 808 in 1998, close to a 50-percent increase.[2]

Those leaving the welfare rolls have seen their earnings increase along with others in the low-wage sector but not by much. The "leaver studies" typically find former welfare recipients in fairly rocky, low-wage careers, with intermittent periods of work, hourly wages in the $7 per hour range, and little wage mobility.

I stress these findings not to rehash what at this point is pretty widely accepted by most analysts but to point out that this is where I think the current policy battle is—and should be—drawn. The theme among conservatives is that caseloads are down, and employment rates are up: end of story. The counter-theme among progressives is that the goal of welfare reform was not to transform the welfare poor into the working poor; it was to lift the living standards of former recipients significantly, and that has not happened.

If Congress wants the poor to move from welfare to work, then they have a responsibility to ensure that those who are responding to the call can at least leave poverty, and better yet, raise their incomes to levels suggested by the family budget literature. This research finds that in order to meet their basic consumption needs, working families need incomes that are closer to twice the poverty level.[3]

These facts have led to a policy environment that is more conducive to a set of "make-work-pay" policies than might have been expected, given the general theme of fiscal restraint that has dominated recent policy debates. For example, a more generous Earned Income Tax Credit (EITC) and a higher minimum wage are two work-related policies that may be enacted in the near future. Similarly, the expansion of work supports in the form of subsidies for child care, health care, transportation, and so on, have political currency right now. Such ideas are correctly and convincingly cast in the framework noted above: Congress and state legislators have an obligation to make sure that those playing by the new rules are meeting their consumption needs. And these policies go beyond helping the poor—they also reach the near-poor (i.e., families with incomes up to twice their poverty threshold). Of course, poor families also need to meet their needs regarding savings or asset-building, but this line of argument connects less directly to the current work-centered debate.

This is, admittedly, a narrow and time-sensitive view of the current debate. Those promoting asset development take the longer view, a view that is consonant with the whole theme of saving for the future. My only point here is that I sense a significant political opening to push for policies that (a) smooth the path from welfare to work by subsidizing work supports, such as child care and transportation; (b) raise workers' pretax wages; and (c) raise posttax income.

It should be emphasized that work-based policies are by no means the only game in town. Welfare reform allows states to establish IDA programs with Temporary Assistance for Needy Families (TANF) funds and discount IDA assets when determining TANF eligibility. There are also pilot programs in over thirty states, most of which target the working poor. But these programs are smaller and reach many fewer people than the work-based programs mentioned thus far (e.g., the EITC, the minimum wage, and subsidized work supports). I would also argue that they do not have the same political resonance in the current debate. I would not, however, argue that they are any less important, as they ultimately represent an important and overlooked aspect of the economic lives of the poor.

THE ECONOMIC CONSTRAINTS FACING THE POOR: THE IMMEDIACY PROBLEM AND THE MAGNITUDE PROBLEM

In an earlier life, I was a social worker in East Harlem and worked with poor, minority families. As you can imagine, people came to my office with all sorts of problems, but I cannot remember any clients ever complaining about their lack of assets.

This was not, of course, because they did not need savings. In fact, as the work of Sherraden and others has emphasized, access to savings could clearly have solved some problems, such as the abused partner who does not have sufficient resources to move out. Yet for these economically constrained and highly stressed families, assets were an unthinkable luxury.

To my discredit, I did not think of them either. My colleagues and I were simply firefighters, trying to extinguish the flames of hunger, homelessness, lack of health care, abuse, and so on, before they consumed our clients. Due to the immediacy of the poor's income constraints we were—and I suspect most still are—focused exclusively on providing consumption, not savings, opportunities.

Of course, while frontline social workers and progressive policy wonks may ultimately serve the same clients, they clearly have different time horizons. However, as many IDA advocates underscore, most policy analysts continue to focus on consumption or income-oriented solutions. Certainly part of the reason for this is our consciousness about the determinants of poverty today.

It seems axiomatic to assert that the most immediate determinant of poverty is lack of income. But a recent article on asset building for the poor stated, "For the vast majority of households, the pathway out of poverty is not through consumption but through saving and accumulation."[4] It is important to clarify this apparent contradiction.

Those for whom this quote resonates would probably argue that only by significantly increasing their earnings' capacity can the poor lastingly climb out of poverty. And, to do so does not mean a one-dollar increase in the minimum wage or a program that, by providing better child care, enables one to work an extra few hours per week at a $7-per-hour job. It means being able to finance a college education, relocating to a better neighborhood, maybe even starting a new enterprise. Such arguments certainly make sense, but can we learn anything from the literature on poverty's determinants to assess the validity of this reasoning?

One way to frame this research is in terms of micro and macro factors. At the micro level, the most important events associated with lifting families out of poverty tend to be earnings or transfer gains and family structure changes. At the macro level, the strength of real economic growth and the distribution of that growth are the key determinants.

A typical analysis of poverty's determinants takes the form of table 17.1, from Mishel, Bernstein, and Schmitt (2001). (This table decomposes changes in the rate of poverty, but it could easily be applied to levels as well). Each entry in the table represents the contribution to the change in the family poverty rate due to the named factor. For example, over the full twenty-nine-year period covered by the table, educational upgrading by family heads lowered poverty by 3.9 percentage points, while "family structure" (the shift to family types more vulnerable to poverty, such as single-parent families) added 3.1 points. On the macro side, economic growth lowered poverty by 4.3 percentage points, but inequality's growth, particularly in the 1980s and 1990s, more than offset this effect.

Perhaps more convincing research on poverty's determinants comes out of longitudinal studies that follow families over time.[5] These studies also find that family structure changes, such as marriage or a child leaving home, and earnings gains are most highly associated with exits from poverty.

It is not obvious what one learns from these studies about the lack of assets as a poverty determinant, but such information is, to some extent, embedded in the results. For example, the race result in table 17.1 is, of course, driven by the fact that minorities have higher than average poverty rates, and their share of the population has increased over time. But it is not ordained from above (or below) that minorities should have higher poverty rates than whites. It is, in large part, a legacy of discrimination, a factor that clearly has had devastating effects on the ability of minorities to build assets.

Table 17.1 The Impact of Demographic and Education Changes on Family Poverty Rates

	1969–1979	1979–1989	1989–1998	1969–1998
Actual change	−0.5	1.2	−0.1	0.5
Total demographic effect	0.5	−0.3	−0.4	−0.2
Race	0.3	0.4	0.3	1.0
Education	−1.6	−1.2	−1.0	−3.9
Family structure	1.9	0.7	0.5	3.1
Interaction	−0.2	−0.1	−0.1	−0.4
Economic change	−1.0	1.4	0.3	0.8
Growth	−1.5	−1.3	−1.5	−4.3
Inequality	0.5	2.7	1.8	5.1

Source: Mishel, Bernstein, and Schmitt, 2001.

Perhaps it is most elucidating to look at the "big ticket items"—the largest entries—in table 17.1 and to evaluate them in terms of assets. On the poverty reducing side, these are the education levels of family heads and the overall growth in the economy. Leading to higher poverty are the growth of income inequality and family structure or the increase in single-parent families.

Other than education, none of these factors seem *directly* related to asset building (though, as in the case of race, connections can be made). Building human capital through education is, of course, a major goal of such programs, and, in this sense, it is clear that the lack of human capital is an asset that has historically been in terribly short supply among the poor.

Nevertheless, as table 17.1 shows, we have made progress on this front. Over the 29-year period covered by the table, family poverty rates were lower by 4 percentage points, thanks to the educational upgrading (and thus, higher earnings) of family heads (Mishel, Bernstein, and Schmitt, 2001). This is the result of a long-term trend, a huge national investment of hundreds of billions of dollars in building human capital.

Two points emerge from this analysis. First, from the perspective of immediacy, asset building cannot quickly put out the flames of poverty and economic despair. That task lies with income- and consumption-related policies. Once the flames are extinguished, assets can help ensure that the fire does not reignite.

Second, once we relax the immediacy criterion, the role of asset building becomes clear. A low-skilled person with savings can become more highly skilled. An impoverished family with unstable housing can move to a better home in a better neighborhood, something that appears to be associated with better outcomes in the longer term.[6]

These laudable uses of assets raise the magnitude problem, that is, given their income constraints, even with generous matches, how likely is it that the poor can save enough for these large investments? Many advocates of IDAs to whom I have spoken are quite candid about these limitations. It is common for them to stress that the income constraints facing the poor and the cap on most IDAs make it unlikely that a poor family will get very far toward meeting the costs of college education, home ownership, or starting a business. One recent study found that IDAs were leading to saving in the neighborhood of $20 monthly, which, with an average two-to-one match could lead to about $700 per year of savings.[7] This is by no means trivial, but it is unlikely to foot the bill for the kinds of investments that can change the economic trajectory of a poor family. This estimate is also an upper bound. According to another recent study, it is not even clear if IDAs, as currently implemented, are leading to increased savings, compared to the savings that would have occurred in the absence of the program.[8]

Thus, IDA policies will have to become much more generous if they are going to be truly "transformative." Yet, if they are going to reach such magnitudes, will they run afoul of the second historical theme noted above—

inculcating dependency? Will taxpayers support this high level of re-distribution? I turn to these questions in a final section.

THE POLITICAL ECONOMY OF ASSET DEVELOPMENT

As articulated in this volume, there are good sociopolitical reasons to support asset-based policies for the poor. Pride of ownership, a sense of future opportunity, the ability to accumulate human capital, or to save for a big-ticket necessity—all of these are part of middle-class and upward consciousness and lead to a sense of economic security that I suspect is absent for many poor families.

But there are some important political and economic connections that asset-based policies fail to make. First, wage-based policies unify the working class in a way that asset-based policies do not. In fact, it is worth noting that many right-wing advocates support IDAs because they think such policies will connect low-income persons with more of an "ownership" consciousness and less working-class solidarity. On the other hand, one of the potential outcomes of welfare reform is the unification of the poor and the broader working class in a way that previously did not exist. To the extent that poor people who previously had sporadic experience in the labor market move toward full-time, full-year work, their political consciousness may converge with those higher up the wage scale (but still below the median). They will potentially become more familiar with and concerned about the variety of economic trends that have negatively affected the working class, from wage inequality to macro policy. They are also becoming targets for unions that focus on organizing the low-wage labor market, such as the Service Employees International Union.

One can imagine a working-class coalition of workers coming off welfare—unionists, immigrants, living- and minimum-wage advocates, and other groups of traditionally low-wage workers (such as minorities). In the current type of political climate, the first call for such a coalition, I suspect, would be for their "fair share" of economic growth through higher wage rates. That is, their initial target is likely to be the primary, not the secondary, distribution of wages or incomes, the latter being the target of the asset-based approach.

This raises the important point that asset-based policies for the poor are purely redistributive (the same can be said for the EITC). Most progressives are, of course, very comfortable with this aspect of the policy, but my view is that it is a mistake to depend exclusively on redistribution through the tax system, as opposed to policies like wage mandates or collective bargaining, which redistribute the gains of productivity growth through the primary system of distribution or market outcomes.

Progressive social policy has become too complacent about accepting market outcomes. With the exception of the minimum wage, which does not get a lot of support from even progressive policy analysts, today's strategy might be characterized as, "Let the market do its thing; we'll fix it with the fisc." This view seems to maintain that if inflation-adjusted low wages start to fall again, as they have for most of the past twenty years, we'll get them to raise the EITC again, or we'll push for higher matches in our asset plans.

There are two reasons why this strategy is problematic, at least for the foreseeable future. First, to push consistently for ever more redistribution risks raising the dependency critique, which was wielded so potently during the welfare reform debate. Second, to accept market outcomes uncritically unnecessarily limits both the debate and its potential outcome. We should reject the neoclassical notion that any intervention in the primary distribution leads to suboptimal outcomes. This is not always the case regarding economic aggregates, for example, the gross domestic product (GDP), productivity, and job growth, and it is much less so regarding distributional outcomes. While some interventions could wreak havoc—a $15-hour minimum wage would surely lead to job losses—others could improve living standards of low-wage workers without negatively affecting market outcomes or, at least, would affect them such that the benefits outweighed the costs. As former Labor Secretary F. Ray Marshall, of the Carter administration (1977–1981), liked to say, "Sometimes the free hand is all thumbs."

Expounding on my current favorites, in terms of policies that affect pretax wages, is beyond the scope of this chapter. However, the list would include minimum wages, unions, and full employment policies. But the point here is that asset-based policies that are purely redistributive cannot be the only part of the puzzle.

CONCLUSION

Nobody, of course, thinks assets are the only answer to all the poor's problems. I'm sure most progressive advocates feel as I do, that asset building is one leg of the stool. We should avoid the either/or trap, one that those of us who focus exclusively on wages, income, and short-term consumption fall into too often.

Asset-based policies for the poor obviously deserve our attention, focus, and support. We should continue to evaluate them and expand the ones that seem most effective. At the same time, we should recognize their limits. The contemporary policy debate focuses primarily on the labor market, and this offers a unique political opening to push for measures to improve the performance of the low-wage labor market. Also, the immediacy of consumption deficits among the poor continues to militate for the primacy of the income-based approach.

This does not imply a secondary role for asset building—it just states that you need to put out the fire before you start building the new house— and raises the point that for IDAs to realize their stated goals, they will need to be more generous. This suggests a bold redistributive agenda, one that is worth supporting but one that will engender strong political opposition from conservative forces. Thus, as progressives, we cannot simply accept market outcomes and dedicate ourselves to repairing the damage in the secondary distribution. We also need to alter the power dynamics of the current economy so that the fruits of economic growth are more fairly divided.

NOTES

1. These are both early examples of national social policy directed at regulating the poor (Poor Laws, circa 1600; Speenhamland Act, circa 1800).
2. This calculation includes those with zero hours in each time period. Omitting those mother-only families with no hours in the paid labor market, we find that average annual hours of work went from 1,020 in 1979 to 1,237 in 1998 (Mishel, Bernstein, and Schmitt, 2001).
3. See, for example, Bernstein, Brocht, and Spade-Aguilar (2000).
4. Boshara, Scanlon, and Page-Adams (2000), 11.
5. See, for example, Organization for Economic Co-operation and Development (2001).
6. See Rosenbaum and DeLuca (2000).
7. See Center for Social Development (2002).
8. See Stegman and Faris, chapter 11 in this volume.

REFERENCES

Bernstein, J. (2000). "Things I Think We Know So Far About Welfare Reform and the Low-Wage Labor Market." Paper prepared for the conference "Work, Welfare, and Politics," University of Oregon, Eugene, February.

Bernstein, J., C. Brocht, and M. Spade-Aguilar. (2000). *How Much is Enough? Basic Family Budgets for Working Families.* Washington, D.C.: Economic Policy Institute.

Boshara, R., E. Scanlon, and D. Page-Adams. (2000). "Why Assets, Asset-Building, and IDAs for the Poor." Washington, D.C.: The Community Action Digest, National Association of Community Action Agencies, Spring.

Center for Social Development. (2002). *Savings and Asset Accumulation in Individual Development Accounts.* St. Louis, Mo.: Center for Social Development, Washington University.

Mishel, L., J. Bernstein, and J. Schmitt. (2001). *The State of Working America, 2000–01.* Ithaca, N.Y.: Cornell University Press.

Organization for Economic Co-operation and Development (OECD). (2001). "When Money Is Tight: Poverty Dynamics in OECD Countries." *Employment Outlook 2001.*

Rosenbaum, J. E., and S. DeLuca. (2000). "Is Housing Mobility the Key to Welfare Reform?" Washington, D.C.: Center on Urban and Metropolitan Policy, The Brookings Institution, September.

18

Inclusion in Asset Building:
Directions for Theory and Research

Michael Sherraden, Edward Scanlon, Deborah Adams,
Sondra G. Beverly, and Mark Schreiner

Our assignment in this chapter is to stand back and ask which directions for theory and research may be productive for increasing understanding of inclusion of the poor in asset building and for policy application. We begin with what we do *not* address very much in this chapter. The two biggest areas are policy analysis questions and political analysis questions. Regarding policy analysis, several measurement, policy content, and policy impact questions will be critical. Some of the key questions are about definition and measurement: How are assets defined and measured? What is asset poverty? Chapter 4 in this volume, by Robert Haveman and Edward Wolff, makes important contributions toward measurement and assessment of asset poverty. All such measures contain theoretical assumptions, which the authors are careful to note. In the future, new theoretical assumptions about asset poverty may lead to different types of measures. For example, it might be useful to develop measures of moving assets through time (Schreiner, 2004).

Policy content questions also matter. For example, what are the advantages and disadvantages of promoting saving for home ownership versus saving for postsecondary education? Does this differ by income level? By race? We know little about these policy trade-offs. Turning to impact questions, to what extent does public policy increase asset accumulation and for whom? Most important, do policies that are designed to increase asset accumulation in fact do so, or are assets shifted, as appears to be the case in many studies of 401(k)s? Chapter 11 in this volume, by Michael Stegman and Robert Faris, finds that saving in individual development accounts (IDAs) may not represent new savings. Mark Schreiner and his colleagues, in chapter 10, find evidence that IDA deposits come from both new and shifted assets, but their data do not permit estimates of proportions. Experimental data from the American Dream Demonstration (ADD) and other experimental studies may shed more light on these important questions.

Regarding political analysis, there is an active discussion of whether asset-based policy is liberal or conservative, neoliberal or neoconservative. At different times, it has been identified with each of these categories, but it does not seem to fit very comfortably in any of them. For example, IDA policy is typically bipartisan; both former President Bill Clinton and President George W. Bush have been supporters. Perhaps a new current and new political consensus in social policy is emerging. James Midgley's (1999) analysis, which places asset-based policies in a productivist or *social investment* framework, may turn out to be the most useful for interpretation. This might be understood as the policy side of Amartya Sen's (1985, 1993, 1999) focus on well-being as the *development of capabilities.*

Looking at policy and political issues together, we may be at the beginning of an extended debate on the definition of well-being as it informs social policy and perhaps eventually a change in policy content. If this is the case, a very interesting question is whether ideas are driving policy change or whether ideas are formulated to explain policy change that is already happening. Looking back at the welfare state of the twentieth century, it seems clear that the idea of well-being as consumption was hugely influential, and we suspect that the same will be true of ideas going forward. Together, policy analysis and political questions are of great importance. We give them short shrift at the moment only because we cannot cover everything, and our first interest is the basic social science questions that underlie this area of inquiry.

Two questions are most fundamental in thinking about asset-based policy strategies: (a) How do savings and asset accumulation occur? (b) What are the effects of asset accumulation? The first question is necessary for interpreting patterns of asset holding, assessing effects of existing public policies, and designing future policies, particularly those that might include the poor. The second question can potentially build a body of knowledge linking assets to well-being, and in so doing, has the potential to provide a rationale for asset-based policy. Our focus on these two questions emphasizes the social science foundation that will be fundamental to build this area of scholarship, and, at present, theory and research in these areas are not well developed.

HOW DO SAVING AND ASSET ACCUMULATION OCCUR?

Policy for asset accumulation cannot be effectively designed in the absence of specified theory and empirical evidence on how saving and asset accumulation occur.[1] There is a large but inconclusive body of work on saving theory and research (Beverly, 1997; Carney and Gale, 2001). Neoclassical theories represent the core of the discussion. The two most well-known are the life cycle hypothesis (Modigliani and Brumberg, 1954) and the permanent income hypothesis (Friedman, 1957). These theories assume that individuals and households are focused on expected future income and long-term consumption patterns. In recent years, some economists have proposed additions to the life cycle hypothesis and the permanent income hypothesis, the so-called buffer-stock models of saving (see Carroll, 1997; Carroll and Samwick, 1997; Ziliak, 1999). These models emphasize a precautionary motive for saving, particularly for younger households and for households facing greater income uncertainty. Overall, economic theories suppose that people are forward looking and concerned about consumption patterns, that preferences are fixed, and that people are knowledgeable and rational.

Variations on the standard economic theories include a wide range of behavioral, psychological, and sociological theories. Behavioral theories emphasize financial management strategies and self-imposed incentives and constraints (e.g., Shefrin and Thaler, 1988). Although behavioral theories are partly rooted in economics, they modify conventional economic models in two ways. First, behavioral theories do not assume that income or wealth is fungible. Instead, Hersh Shefrin and Richard Thaler's work (1988) proposes that individuals use systems of mental accounts and that the propensity to spend varies across accounts. For example, individuals may code resources as current income, current assets, or future income. They are expected to spend almost all resources coded as current income, very little future income, and some (but not all) current assets. Second, behavioral theories do not assume that individuals have perfect knowledge or behave in perfectly rational ways. Instead, these theories emphasize that individuals sometimes have trouble resisting temptations to spend. Therefore, individuals may benefit from creating their own behavioral incentives and constraints (Shefrin and Thaler, 1988). These rules may be external, although individuals may voluntarily place themselves under restrictions, for example, a Christmas Club savings account, or the rules may be self-imposed ("rules-of-thumb"), such as avoiding borrowing or restricting borrowing to specific purchases. With these rules in mind, household saving is seen at least in part as "the result of the successful and sophisticated imposition of welfare-improving, self-imposed constraints on spending" (Maital and Maital, 1994, 7). Behavioral theories imply that saving and asset accumulation are likely to increase when mechanisms of contractual saving (see Katona, 1975, 230–233) or precommitment constraints are available. These mechanisms make it difficult to choose current pleasure at the expense of future pleasure (Maital, 1986; Maital and Maital, 1994; Shefrin and Thaler, 1988). A common precommitment constraint is payroll deduction. When pension plan contributions, for example, are deducted from an individual's paycheck, temptations to spend that money are virtually eliminated, and the participant no longer has to make, on a monthly or biweekly basis, a conscious decision to postpone consumption. A person's "willingness" to save is, in effect, predetermined, and transaction costs are minimized. Variations on precommitment constraints include over-withholding of income tax (Neumark, 1995) and even mortgage-financed home purchases (Maital and Maital, 1994). Mortgage-financed home purchases facilitate saving because mortgage payments are a contractual obligation and because the part of each payment that goes toward principal increases the buyer's home equity. In fact, there is evidence that the desire for a precommitment mechanism is as strong a motivation for mortgage-financed home purchases as the incentive created by the tax deductibility of interest payments (Maital and Maital, 1994).

Psychological and sociological theories assume that consumer preferences are not fixed but that they change with economic and social stimuli (Cohen, 1994; Duesenberry, 1949; Katona, 1975). In fact, psychological and sociological theories of saving explicitly seek to explain saving-related preferences, aspirations, and expectations. The most well-known economic psychologist, George Katona (1975), has noted that saving is a function of two sets of factors, ability to save and willingness to save. As in standard economic theory, the emphasis on ability to save acknowledges that some individuals, because of limited economic resources or special consumption needs, find it more difficult to defer consumption than others. At the same time, those individuals who can postpone consumption still must *choose* to do so, a decision that requires some degree of willpower (in contrast to standard economic theory, where choice is not required because people figure out the optimal plan and then implement it). Psychological theory focuses primarily on this choice. Other psychological and sociological propositions consider the effects of families (Cohen, 1994), peers (Duesenberry, 1949), and past saving experiences (Furnham, 1985; Katona, 1975) on consumption patterns, saving-related beliefs, and aspirations for saving.

Turning to empirical evidence, life cycle and permanent income models have mixed support, but they especially fail to explain patterns of asset accumulations in low-income households, which are typically low or negative. Among the other theories, very few behavioral, psychological, or sociological propositions have been rigorously tested. Overall, evidence is mixed and incomplete; no single perspective is clearly supported at this time.

Can Low-Income People Save?

Individuals may save in different ways and accumulate different types of assets. For example, they may store tangible goods, they may invest in human capital, or they may loan money or in-kind resources to social network members. In this book, we have looked mostly at financial assets. Discussions of saving in policy and practice often assume that very poor people cannot save because their incomes are too low. Do theory and evidence support this assumption?

Economic theory predicts that the absolute amount of savings will increase with income. This is because people with more income have more resources available to save. Theory also predicts that savings relative to income, the savings rate, will increase with income. This occurs because people with more income also tend to consume more. As they consume more, the marginal benefit from additional consumption decreases. The current cost of saving, in terms of foregone benefits from consumption, is lower for people who consume more, and this increases savings. Empirical evidence indicates that higher-income households save a larger portion of their incomes and accumulate greater wealth than lower-income households. In fact, most low-income households have very low or negative saving rates and very limited or negative asset accumulation (Bernheim and Scholz, 1993; Bunting, 1991; Carney and Gale, 2001; Hubbard, Skinner, and Zeldes, 1994; Wolff, 2001).

Like any given theory, however, this ignores some important issues. For example, the level and rate of savings also depend on expected variation in income and subsistence requirements. The poor face greater risks, and this may increase their saving, both absolutely and relative to their income, as specified in buffer shock theory. Also, the poor may save at higher rates but also dissave at higher rates, so net savings may be zero or negative, even though saving (moving money through time) has, in fact, occurred.

Will Low-Income People Oversave?

By definition, saving postpones consumption. In the short term, people who save consume less and are worse off in this sense, all else constant, than nonsavers. Savers make the short-term sacrifice because they expect it to improve long-term well-being. For very poor people close to subsistence, increased saving might reduce consumption to the point of harm. For example, it would be harmful if a family saved so much that they could not buy enough food for the healthy development of their children. Likewise, it would be harmful if a family saved but did not go to the doctor to set a broken arm or to get antibiotics for a severe infection.

An important question is whether saving by low-income households, for example in IDAs, might reduce short-term consumption so much that the poor suffer hardship. Amanda Moore and colleagues (2001) look for this possibility in surveys and in-depth interviews with IDA participants. For the most part, participants in IDAs report positive effects. For example, 93 percent of respondents in a cross-sectional survey agree or strongly agree that because of IDAs they feel more confident about the future; 84 percent, more economically secure; and 85 percent, more in control of life. However, these authors also present survey evidence that hardship may be caused by IDA saving; about 17 percent of respondents say that one of their savings strategies is to postpone doctor or dental visits, and 8 percent agree or strongly agree that because of IDAs they have to give up food or necessities. Overall, we do not see evidence of extensive hardship caused by IDA saving, but there appears to be some degree of hardship in some households. Of course, it is also possible that saving in 401(k)s causes hardship in some households, though to our knowledge no one has yet studied this possibility.

In this regard, it is important to note that participation in both 401(k)s and IDAs and the level of savings (up to a cap) are voluntary; participants decide whether they want to save and how much to save. The role of choice is fundamental. As a policy principle, if the rich have subsidies like tax benefits to increase assets, then it is a matter of fairness that the poor also have subsidies, and then everyone can make choices. In our view, it is an injustice for public policy to provide differential incentives for saving, giving greater incentives to the wealthy, and particularly questionable if the rationale is to protect the poor from their own saving.

The Role of Institutions

Each of the theories described above calls attention to institutional characteristics that are expected to affect saving and asset accumulation. Neoclassical economic theories emphasize the role of institutions that affect the economic costs and benefits of saving, such as markets and public policies. Psychological and sociological theories consider institutions that affect an individual's understanding or perceptions of economic costs and benefits, that change noneconomic costs and benefits, and/or that shape preferences, for example, peers and family members. Behavioral theories highlight the role of institutions that allow individuals to modify the costs and benefits of saving by creating their own incentives and constraints, such as payroll deduction, saving clubs, and the option to overwithhold income taxes. By integrating these theoretical perspectives, while emphasizing the role of institutions, scholars may be able to develop a theory that more fully explains saving and asset accumulation in the general population and in the low-income population.

An institutional perspective suggests that external factors other than income and preferences may influence saving behavior and that low savings and asset accumulation by poor people might be explained in part by limited institutional saving opportunities. From this perspective, "asset accumulations are primarily the result of institutionalized mechanisms involving explicit connections, rules, incentives, and subsidies" (Sherraden, 1991, 116). These types of asset accumulation occur in the United States primarily through housing- and retirement-related tax benefits, including deductions for home mortgage interest and property taxes, deferment and exclusion of capital gains on sales of principal residences, exclusions for employment-sponsored pension contributions and earnings, deferments for individual retirement accounts (IRAs) and Keogh Plans, and employer contributions to employee pension plans. Because these mechanisms receive preferential tax treatment, individuals who have access and greater incentives are more likely to participate. For example, people with higher marginal tax rates are more likely to participate in tax-deferred savings programs (Joulfaian and Richardson, 2001). The poor do not have the same access or receive the same incentives from institutions that promote and subsidize asset accumulation (Howard, 1997; Seidman, 2001; Sherraden,

1991, 2001). For example, the poor are less likely to have jobs with pension benefits; even if they do, they receive few or no subsidies because they have low or zero marginal tax rates, and the tax benefits are not refundable.

Institutional perspectives are not new (see Gordon, 1980; Neale, 1987), but they are not well specified. If we are making any contribution in this volume, it is in taking a small step toward specifying what "institutions" for saving consist of in practical application. Below, we often use the example of IDAs to discuss these issues. We have previously identified four major institutional constructs: (a) access, (b) information, (c) incentives, and (d) facilitation (Beverly and Sherraden, 1999). The first three are commonly discussed, and we have offered the fourth term, "facilitation," to describe institutional arrangements where depositing is actually done for the participant, as in automatic payroll deduction. Facilitation is a key feature of most contractual saving systems. Based on qualitative research on IDAs, we suggest another institutional variable that may be important in explaining saving performance: (e) expectations (Sherraden et al., 2005). In IDAs, for example, expectations are embodied in the monthly saving target and the social pressure of staff and peers to meet this target. Many IDA participants say that they are trying to save the expected amount each month, and, thus, expectations may cause very low-income people to save more than would otherwise be anticipated.

Turning to empirical evidence, the broad pattern is that accumulation of assets in the typical U.S. household occurs largely via home ownership and retirement pension accounts (Wolff, 2001), which are institutionalized and subsidized. If future social security benefits are counted as assets, then this is an even more consistent pattern and brings in poor households because the poor often hold a larger share of their net worth in social security entitlements (Burkhauser and Weathers, 2001). This overall pattern is strongly suggestive of institutional influences on asset accumulation. Next, we turn to each of the five institutional variables listed above.

Access

There is little evidence from economic analyses regarding the effects of access on saving and asset accumulation, largely because it is difficult to disentangle the effects of access from the effects of unobserved individual characteristics. For example, if workers consider the availability of pension plans when they evaluate job offers, then those who work for firms that offer pension plans may value retirement saving more than the average individual. This would create a positive association between access and saving, even if access has no independent effect. However, some researchers (Cagan, 1965; Carroll and Summers, 1987) have concluded that the very availability of institutionalized saving opportunities promotes saving by calling attention to the need for and benefits of saving.

As a historical and sociological matter, there are clear instances that illustrate access is different for different people. The major example in U.S.

history is the Homestead Act, the long-term impact of which is discussed by Trina Shanks in chapter 2 of this volume. Differential access to asset accumulation by race is an important theme in Melvin Oliver and Thomas Shapiro (1995), Shapiro (2004), and Shapiro and Heather Beth Johnson in chapter 6. Sociological thinking is also useful in thinking about access to pension plans. If half the population does not have access to a pension plan in the workplace, it is not fully informative to interpret this outcome as resulting from individual characteristics and individual choices.

Information

More research is also needed to evaluate the effects of financial information, which is typically provided through some type of financial education. However, some evidence suggests that education positively affects saving behavior. One study finds that more frequent corporate-sponsored retirement seminars were associated with both higher participation and higher levels of contributions to 401(k) plans (Bayer, Bernheim, and Scholz, 1996). Douglas Bernheim and Daniel Garrett (1996) report that participation rates were 12 percentage points higher for companies that offered financial education, and in firms that offered financial education, participation rates were 20 percentage points higher for employees who chose to attend. Education increased new savings of all types as a percentage of income by 1.7 percentage points, which is a large effect. In all cases, effects were greatest for people who saved little before they received education. One study reports that financial education for teens increases savings rates when they become adults (Bernheim, Garrett, and Maki, 2001). Mark Schreiner and colleagues, chapter 10, and Margaret Clancy, Michal Grinstein-Weiss, and Schreiner (2001) consider financial education in IDA programs. They find that, controlling for all other factors, up to twelve hours of general financial education is associated with strong increases in net savings amounts ($1.20 per month for each of the first six hours and $0.56 per month for each of hours seven to twelve); however, after twelve hours of education, there is no clear pattern.

Incentives

The net effect of incentives (rates of return) on saving is a subject of debate. Neoclassical economic theory does not predict that an increase in the rate of return will necessarily increase saving. There are two key issues. First, changes in the rate of return on savings may simply result in the "reshuffling" of the form of assets, with no new saving. Second, for net savers, an increase in the after-tax rate of return has two contradictory effects. Individuals may choose to save more because the price of current consumption increases relative to the price of future consumption (the substitution effect). On the other hand, with higher rates of return, individuals can save less and still enjoy the same amount of future consumption (the income effect). Empirical evidence regarding the effect of incentives on saving is mixed (see Engen, Gale, and Scholz, 1996; Hubbard and Skinner, 1996; and Poterba, Venti, and Wise, 1996, for reviews), though several studies suggest that individuals save less in the face of saving disincentives (Feldstein, 1995; Hubbard, Skinner, and Zeldes, 1995; Powers, 1998). It is also important to note that reshuffling is less likely for low-income households because they are less likely to have savings and other assets to reshuffle. Empirical analysis simulating the effects of private pension plans suggests that pensions do not offset personal saving among lower-income, less-educated workers (Bernheim and Scholz, 1993). This volume's chapter 10 (Schreiner et al.) finds that higher match rates in IDA programs are associated with fewer unmatched withdrawals and are positively associated with staying in the program, but they are not associated with net savings. This latter finding is consistent with data from 401(k)s, where savings amounts do not increase with match rates beyond a very low level, around 0.25:1 (Basset, Fleming, and Rodrigues, 1998; Kusko, Poterba, and Wilcox, 1994).

Facilitation

Direct tests of the proposition that facilitation promotes saving are rare, but anecdotal evidence regarding the effectiveness of direct deposit and payroll deduction is strongly suggestive. Also, the fact that home equity, which accumulates from contractual saving, is the primary form of wealth for most Americans (Davern and Fisher, 2001) provides important indirect evidence. One recent study provides strong, direct evidence that facilitation affects saving behavior. Brigitte Madrian and Dennis Shea (2000) studied 401(k) participation and contribution rates in a company that began automatically enrolling employees in their 401(k) plan. Before the change, employees had to sign up to participate in the 401(k) plan. After the change, employees actively had to opt out of the plan. Although none of the economic features of the plan changed, participation was significantly higher under automatic enrollment. Participants were also quite likely to stay with the default contribution rate and the default fund allocation. Other evidence on the importance of facilitation is the common practice of using the income tax withholding system as a kind of saving plan. Millions of households withhold more than the taxes they owe, planning for a lump-sum refund, despite the strong economic disincentive (the cost of foregone earnings on the money) for saving through this mechanism. In IDA research (Schreiner et al., chapter 10) only 6 percent of participants used direct deposit (the number of those who had an option to use direct deposit but chose not to do so is unknown), and this study finds no significant relationship between direct deposit and net savings amounts. This small percentage of direct deposit users may not provide a good test of this question. Results do suggests that direct deposit kept people saving, and qualitative data point to positive effects of direct deposit (Sherraden et al., 2005).

Expectations

The area of expectations in the institutional sense described above is largely unresearched. This construct has emerged in our research on IDAs. Looking first at quantitative data, the match cap (amount that can be saved and matched) is strongly associated both with being a "saver" and with average net deposits per month among the "savers" (see chapter 10). Controlling for many other program characteristics and personal characteristics, each dollar of increased match cap is associated with 64 cents of increased average monthly net deposits. What could account for this large effect? Qualitative interviews with IDA participants in ADD indicate that they viewed the match cap as an expected savings amount and that staff members and peers often encouraged them to do so. Some IDA participants stated directly that they were trying to fulfill these expectations (Sherraden et al., 2005). A large body of social-psychological research confirms that people tend to do what others expect them to do. However, more research is needed on expectations regarding institutions and economic behavior, especially if IDAs or similar subsidized savings strategies are to operate as intensive programs based in community organizations.

Unobserved Institutional Effects

A noteworthy but much less specific finding regarding institutional effects on savings performance is in the effects of unobserved factors correlated with a given program. For example, in data from the American Dream Demonstration of IDAs, although the regression includes a wide range of characteristics, it cannot control for everything. As a second-best response, it controls for possible links between net savings amounts and unobserved factors correlated with a given program or site. Unobserved factors include program characteristics, such as the strictness of rule enforcement; participant characteristics, such as future orientation; and characteristics beyond programs or participants, such as the local economy. As discussed in chapter 10 (Schreiner et al.), these estimates suggest that unobserved factors correlated with savings performance differ systematically across programs and sites. We do not know the omitted factors nor how much each one matters, but the size of the effects leaves open the possibility that IDA programs vary in unobserved ways that affect savings performance, for example, perhaps in the level of commitment (not just hours or salaries) of staff, or the quality (not only quantity) of financial education.

Summary

The overall theoretical perspective underlying savings policies and programs for the poor, for example in IDAs, is that institutional factors are important in determining saving behavior. If the five institutional constructs discussed above (and perhaps others) do in fact affect saving, then it is important to point out that low-income households typically have limited access to these saving features (Bernheim and Garrett, 1996; Beverly and Sherraden, 1999; Caskey, 1994).

On Theoretical Development

The above discussion of an institutional perspective is preliminary. At this stage, it is not a well-specified theory, but only a list of likely constructs. These constructs and hypothesized relationships are useful steps in knowledge building, especially for practical application in programs and policy, but they do not yet represent a coherent theory.

A key theoretical issue lies in how the origins of institutions are viewed. Douglass North (1990), a major theorist in the New Institutional Economics, begins by seeing institutions as coming from inside people's heads, that is, resulting from human thought patterns. Hence, for the past few years, North has been focusing on cognitive science and how it might help explain the rise of institutions. The reasoning is that institutions can only be the product of what people have done in the past and are expressions of individual cognition, somehow accumulated and expressed as a set of rules now called an institution. In a departure from strict neoclassical models, North's work recognizes limited rationality, imperfect information, changing preferences, and costly decision making. Chapter 5 in this volume, by Ngina Chiteji and Darrick Hamilton, provides examples of constraints congruent with North's theories. Schreiner et al. (2001) offers a similar perspective. Economics is about constrained choice (Becker, 1993), and a theory of institutions is an expansion of economic theory, not something that stands in contrast to it.

A different perspective begins with social structure (class, race, and other segmentations) that operates through informal social arrangements (family upbringing, neighborhood interactions, friendship groups) and formal institutions (schools, banks, real estate companies, the Rotary Club, public policies and programs, and so on). This is a more sociological view, where the emphasis is on structures that prohibit or limit choices. For illustrations of this view, see chapter 6, by Shapiro and Johnson. In a sociological sense, institutions are a reality above and beyond individuals or any aggregation of individuals, and searching for individual level explanations may not be useful.

To overstate, one view sees a reality, at least for social science purposes, composed of individual actors making choices, and the other view sees a reality where social structures are dominant and decisions of individual actors may have little to do with outcomes. James Duesenberry once observed that economics is about how people make choices, and sociology is about how people do not have any choices that they can make. Both of these viewpoints are extreme, and neither by itself is sufficient. We, in fact, hold both perspectives. The fact that economists have worked out better models and empirical methods than sociologists is not an argument for the economic view over the sociological one. In focusing on individual choices, economists may have picked the easier questions, the low-hanging intellectual fruit. We can hope that one day sociologists will develop models that are equally as robust and predictive.

A more applied side of the sociological view is that, at least to some extent, institutions can be purposefully created, for example, as in public policy. From this perspective, there is little need to find cognitive origins of institutions. The focus is on the content of the institutions and how these might be purposefully put into place.

For applied purposes, it is more useful to focus on formal institutions for two reasons. First, if all informal and formal social structures are called institutions, the term becomes so broad and encompassing as to become almost meaningless, which unfortunately is the case in much of the discussion of institutions in both sociology and economics. Second, formal institutions are more easily defined and identified and probably more amenable to change than are informal institutions. For example, one can set out to change a law with at least some sense of what to do and what success would be, but it is much harder to know how to change a cultural norm, and harder to know whether or not this has been accomplished.

Therefore, from an applied standpoint, the view of institutions as coming from the human mind may not be of much practical significance. There is no way to get a handle on it, except in the most abstract theoretical sense. A more accessible view of institutions is to focus on their particular characteristics and how these can be created, altered, or eliminated through purposeful planning and action. In our view, something like the list of constructs above is a more likely pathway toward a theory of institutions that can be applied in public policy and other formal settings.

The institutional constructs we have suggested—access, information, incentives, facilitation, and expectations—may not be the full list or the right list and surely can be improved upon. Other important questions include the following: Which are the more important of these constructs and in what circumstances? How are these constructs interrelated? Is there a logical story that can connect these constructs into a coherent theory that explains saving and asset accumulation? If so, to what extent can this theory be generalized to help explain other phenomena? For example, would the same theory explain not just saving and asset accumulation but also acquisition of human capital? Might it be used to explain participation in sports, religion, or the arts? Ideally, a theory of institutions would be developed that had wide applicability across settings. Toward this larger goal we have as yet barely taken a step.

WHAT ARE THE EFFECTS OF ASSET HOLDING?

Some observers would say it is obvious that assets are good for people; indeed, this is an almost bedrock social philosophy in America.[2] Americans tend to hold the Jeffersonian perspective that small property owning, especially land and homes, is a foundation for democracy, civic engagement, and economic development. However, this basic outlook has, somewhat surprisingly, not been the source of an extensive body of social science research. When we ask the simple question, what are the effects of asset holding, we do not have a definitive body of empirical work with which to answer it.

However, the idea that asset holding promotes beneficial outcomes at neighborhood, household, and individual levels is gaining ground in policy and academic discussions. Social scientists are increasingly including wealth and asset variables in their studies and are doing so in more theoretically careful ways. However, there is a long way to go. One major challenge is to differentiate asset *holding* from asset *use* (Schreiner et al., 2001), which almost no research has done so far.

We turn now to an overview of effects of asset holding on neighborhoods, families, and children. First, we present findings regarding effects on neighborhoods, followed by findings regarding effects on families and children.

Home Ownership's Effects on Neighborhoods

Home ownership has played a central role in American social life and, compared to other types of assets, has been studied more extensively. The study of home ownership, however, is complicated by the fact that owner occupiers are more likely to reside in more prosperous, stable neighborhoods and to live in households with greater assets and income compared with the neighborhoods and households of those who do not own homes. Thus, the effects of home ownership have to be disentangled from these other social variables.

Most research in this area concerns the impact of home ownership on neighborhood stability and functioning. Discussions of neighborhood impacts generally contend that home ownership affects neighborhoods by (a) increasing property maintenance, (b) decreasing residential mobility, (c) increasing residents' social and civic involvement, and (d) enhancing property values (Rohe and Stewart, 1996; Scanlon, 1998).

Property Maintenance

A consistent finding is that home owners are more likely than renters or landlords to maintain and repair housing (Rohe and Stewart, 1996). Theoretically, this has been explained by the basic economic perspective that home owners are attempting to protect and enhance their investments (Butler, 1985; Saunders, 1990) or are demonstrating improved future orientation (Sherraden, 1991). Several studies find that home owners are more likely to engage in housing upkeep (Galster, 1983, 1987; Mayer, 1981), although these factors may be lessened by longer length of residence and concern about racial change in the neighborhood (Varady, 1986).

Residential Mobility

Home ownership is one of the strongest predictors of residential permanence. Controlling for family size, marital status, age, race, and income, home owners tend to stay in one location longer than renters. Causality, however, is open to question in most studies; it is not clear whether reduced mobility leads to home ownership, or home ownership leads to reduced mobility. Residential mobility is not a trivial matter. Residential impermanence appears to have many negative impacts on psychosocial functioning, particularly for youth. A large and growing literature suggests that residential instability is strongly associated with academic and behavioral problems among youth (Kerbow, 1996; Tucker, Marx, and Long, 1998).

An analysis of 1980 and 1990 census data indicates that home ownership is a significant predictor of residential permanence (Rohe and Stewart, 1996). This study estimates that a 10-percent increase in owner-occupied units in a tract would be associated with a 3.6 percent increase in households that stay in their homes five or more years. Another study of 1,476 households finds that renters and central city dwellers are more likely to change residence (Butler and Kaiser, 1971). Researchers have found that those who move are more likely to be young, single, and renters (Forrest, 1987; Pickvance, 1973) A study of 167 households in two metropolitan areas reveals that home owning is negatively associated with residential turnover (McHugh, 1985). William Rohe and Leslie Stewart's (1996) review of ten studies on residential mobility finds only one (Varady, 1986) suggesting that owners are more likely than nonowners to move, and these are residents of neighborhoods in rapid racial transition.

Residential stability is not invariably positive. Richard Burkhauser, Barbara Butrica, and Michael Wasylenko (1995) raise a cautionary note, warning that elderly home owners are three times more likely than young home owners to remain in crime-ridden, distressed communities, raising a potential concern about negative effects of home owning on residential permanence. From a neoclassical economic perspective, an owner can sell and move just as easily as a renter. However, psychologically, people may not want to realize a loss on the value of their property, and transaction costs for moving are higher for owners than for renters.

Also, causality is unclear. Rohe and Stewart (1996) note that lower-income people are less likely to move, suggesting that lower housing values, rather than home ownership, may prevent moving. Indeed, proponents of programs designed to move urban residents to less distressed neighborhoods argue that the initial adjustment difficulties after moving lessen and that program participants eventually have more positive psychosocial outcomes than nonmovers (Pettit, McClanahan, and Hanratty, 1999; Rosenbaum and Popkin, 1991).

Social and Civic Involvement

Home owners are often thought to be more involved civically; some theorists suggest that such involvement will result from an increased sense of stakeholding and efforts to protect property values (Saunders, 1990; Sherraden, 1991). Empirical findings indicate that home owners are somewhat more involved in neighborhood associations and local politics but are not necessarily better neighbors or more involved politically beyond local levels (Rohe and Basolo, 1997; Rohe and Stegman, 1994b). The proportion of home owners on a block is found to increase local civic involvement (Perkins et al., 1990). Other studies confirm this, finding home owners to be more involved in neighborhood civic organizations and to vote locally (Baum and Kingston, 1984; Cox, 1982; Ditkovsky and van Vliet, 1984; Guest and Oropesa, 1986; Rossi and Weber, 1996; Steinberger, 1981). The finding that home owners are more likely to express irritation with transportation noise (Midema and Vos, 1999) may indicate a greater concern about effects on property values or higher levels of commitment to a particular neighborhood. Recent research provides evidence that the greater civic involvement of home owners occurs because of their higher levels of residential stability (DiPasquale and Glaser, 1999). This finding is supported by research indicating that distressed inner city buildings managed by tenant owners have higher levels of social capital (Saegert and Winkel, 1998).

Findings regarding neighboring behaviors are contradictory. Studies of fifty localities in Northern California report that home owners are more likely than renters to be involved in neighboring behaviors (Baum and Kingston, 1984; Fischer et al., 1977). A study of home owners in Rochester, New York, also finds positive correlations between home owning and neighboring. On the other hand, Peter Rossi and Eleanor Weber's (1996) analysis of several data sets finds fewer ties among home owners to their neighbors. This finding is supported by a study of residents of British towns showing that home owners were less likely to be involved with neighbors (Saunders, 1990). Other studies of national U.S. samples report that home owners and renters are not different in terms of likelihood to be involved with neighbors (Fischer, 1982; Kingston and Fries, 1994).

Property Values

Economic studies indicate that home ownership is a good investment for households in the United States. Between 1960 and 1989, the median priced home increased in value by a total of 41 percent, and even the lowest priced homes increased by almost 30 percent (U.S. Department of Housing and Urban Development, 1995). A study of 1980 and 1990 census data finds that home ownership has modest effects on neighborhood property values (such as an increase of tract level home ownership rates increased the property value of a single-family home by $800), but these effects are not as great as the effects of initial housing values, citywide value changes, or changes in tract level income (Rohe and Stewart, 1996). A study of housing affordability, using the Annual Housing Survey, concurred that home ownership is a positive investment, finding that homes occupied by owners as opposed to renters, across the price distribution, increased in value on average (Gyourko and Linneman, 1993).

However, for minority and low-income home owners, these gains are not as great. One study found that for the period 1967–1988, housing values increased by $52,000 for whites and by $31,000 for African Americans (Oliver and Shapiro, 1995). This finding has been confirmed by other research, which has noted differences in housing wealth accumulation by race (Long and Caudill, 1992). These findings indicate that residential segregation and poor neighborhood conditions can lower housing values and decrease wealth accumulation for the poor and minorities. One study demonstrates that even controlling for wealth differences, minorities are much more likely to own homes in central city locations (Gyourko, Linneman, and Wachter, 1999). Although minority owner occupation increased during the 1990s, an examination of home purchases indicates that African Americans in Chicago increasingly purchased homes in segregated or soon to be segregated neighborhoods (Immergluck, 1998). A recent analysis of Australian home owners finds that while both low- and high-income owner-occupiers experience property value increases over time, the effects are far greater for upper-income owners (Burbidge, 2000).

Can home ownership programs, targeted to distressed neighborhoods, reinvigorate property values and raise the local tax base? Little research on this topic exists, and results are not very clear. One study suggests that home ownership programs demonstrate modest impacts on neighborhood property values (Lee, Culhane, and Wachter, 1999). George Galster's (1998) econometric modeling of urban opportunity structures suggests that targeted home ownership programs have only trivial effects on per capita public expenditures. Further research should attempt to clarify the neighborhood economic impacts of geographically concentrated, low-income home ownership programs.

Asset Effects on Families

Some of the research in this area addresses the effects of home ownership on families, while other studies focus on assets in the form of savings, net worth, or small business ownership. Financial and property assets appear to have effects on (a) marriage and marital stability, (b) family health, and (c) economic security.

Marriage and Marital Stability

Assets have been shown to affect both entry into first marriage and marital stability. In a study of the transition to first marriage using data from the National Longitudinal Survey of Youth, investigators find that assets in the form of home ownership significantly accelerate marital entry for both white and African American men (Lloyd and South, 1996). This asset effect remains even when studies control for other personal resources and marriage market characteristics.

Turning to marital stability, married couples with property and financial assets are less likely to divorce than couples without assets. Controlling for a number of other social and economic factors, home ownership has a negative effect on marital dissolution (South and Spitze, 1986). In a study using Panel Study of Income Dynamics (PSID) data from a sample of 575 married couples, one study reports that property and financial assets are negatively associated with marital disruption for African American couples (Hampton, 1982). Other research finds that financial assets also have significant negative effects on marital dissolution among a representative sample of married women in the United States (Galligan and Bahr, 1978). In this study, the effect of net worth on marital stability is strong when controlling for income, race/ethnicity, and education. These findings are consistent with earlier theoretical and empirical work by several scholars on the significance of assets in explaining marital stability (Cherlin, 1977; Cutright, 1971).

An Australian study finds that owning a home outright (that is, not owing on a mortgage loan) reduces the risk of marital dissolution (Bracher et al., 1993). The effect of home ownership on marital stability is significant when studies control for a number of other social and economic factors. The researchers note that home ownership may increase stability by increasing the rewards within marriage or by creating financial or emotional disincentives to divorce. Or it may be that certain unobserved characteristics make people better spouses and also increase home ownership.

A similar caution in interpretation is noted by Deborah Page-Adams (1995), whose findings suggest that home ownership has an effect on marital stability through its negative association with conflict and violence between spouses. It may be that home owning makes couples reticent to put their marriages and their marital homes at risk by arguing to the point of using violence. Alternately, serious marital conflicts and physical violence may preclude home ownership for many couples.

In any case, a negative relationship between assets and marital violence has also been found in a random sample study of married women in the United States (Petersen, 1980) and in a control group study of rural married women in a developing county (Schuler and Hashemi, 1994). The results are consistent with findings from a study using ethnographic data that wealth and property ownership patterns in marriage are causally related to domestic violence (Levinson, 1989). Given the strong association between domestic violence and marital dissolution in the United States, such a relationship between assets and violence could have important implications for predicting marital stability.

Family Health

Studies from the United States and Europe indicate a positive relationship between asset holding and physical health. In a review of health research, researchers note that assets are related to lower mortality and that these effects are partially independent of other socioeconomic resources (Joshi and Macran, 1991). This is consistent with findings from the Office of Population Censuses and Surveys Longitudinal Study in England showing positive, independent effects of assets on men and women's physical health (Goldblatt, 1990; Moser, Pugh, and Goldblatt, 1990). It could be that holding assets makes people feel better, live better, and, therefore, stay healthier. However, it could also be that that ill health reduces assets, due to lost income and higher medical costs. More research is needed to determine which of these two patterns is the more explanatory.

Several studies have shown a positive relationship between home ownership and health. For example, a study in the Netherlands controls for occupation, education, and employment status and finds that male home owners report fewer chronic conditions and better general health and that female home owners perceive themselves to be in better general health than those without homes (Stronks et al., 1997). In other research, controlling for income and education, home ownership is modestly but significantly associated with women's health in the United States (Hahn, 1993). Further, home ownership helps to explain the generally positive relationship between marriage and physical health for women. Again, it could be that home owning is only a proxy for unobserved factors, such as planning and prudence, that explain both home owning and positive health outcomes.

In research from England, asset holding is a better predictor of lung cancer mortality for married women than occupational measures of socioeconomic status (Pugh et al., 1991). For example, married women who live in owner occupied housing with access to a car are two and one-half times less likely to die from lung cancer as those living in rented housing without access to a car. This study also finds that there are substantial differences in the percentage of women who smoke based on occupational status, but much larger differences based on home ownership. Fifty-seven percent of women who rent are smokers, compared with 31 percent of women who own homes. Turning to smoking uptake and cessation, ". . . among women in rented accommodation, the rate of uptake was 23 percent while the cessation rate was 12 percent; among owner occupiers, these percentages were reversed (12 percent and 24 percent respectively)" (Pugh et al., 1991, 1106–1107). This difference in smoking rates is confirmed in other research (Kendig, Browning, and Teshuva, 1998). The direction of causality is in question in the above studies. But controlling for causality through longitudinal data and simultaneous equations, Gautam Yadama and Michael Sherraden (1996) find that assets in the form of savings have a positive effect on prudence, as measured in part by smoking habits.

Turning to research on older family members, one study reports that financial assets are positively related to health among U.S. adults, when controlling for the effects of income and education (Robert and House, 1996). While assets and health are always positively related, the relationship of assets on health is particularly strong for older adults between the ages of 65 and 84. A study of relatively frail older adults controls for income and education and finds that home ownership is negatively associated with nursing home admission and positively associated with successful nursing home exit back to the community (Greene and Ondrich, 1990). In this study, neither income nor education was significantly related to the likelihood of either nursing home admission or discharge when controlling for the effects of home ownership. An interesting study in Singapore and Taiwan finds that elderly family members have greater input in family decisions when they are home owners (Williams, Mehta, and Lin, 1999).

While this review has focused on research from the United States and Europe, findings of positive relationships between assets and health are consistent with results of studies from developing countries that link assets to increased childhood immunization (Amin and Li, 1997); improved nutritional status of women and children (Quanine, 1989); reduced risk of blinding malnutrition among children (Cohen et al., 1985); and decreased infant and child mortality (Amin and Li, 1997; Lee and Amin, 1981). As noted at the beginning of this section, however, not much is known about whether the effects are due to asset ownership or asset use.

Further, findings of assets' effects on physical health parallel those from studies that demonstrate relationships between assets and positive mental health outcomes for family members, including reduced stress (Berger, Powell, and Cook, 1988); increased life satisfaction (Potter and Coshall, 1987; Rohe and Stegman, 1994a; Rossi and Weber, 1996); and reduced neurosis (Rodgers, 1991). But again, the direction of causality is not well established.

Economic Security

In a review article on the effects of asset holding, Page-Adams and Sherraden (1996) note that assets appear to increase the economic security of families on public assistance (Raheim and Alter, 1995) and female-headed families (Cheng, 1995), as well as other families in the United States and in other countries (Krumm and Kelly, 1989; Massey and Basem, 1992; Sherraden et al., 1995). Here we look at additional studies linking assets to economic security for families in the United States.

Four of the studies in this review that address family economic security use home ownership as the measure of assets. While Rossi and Weber (1996) find limited differences between home owners and renters, one important difference between the two groups has to do with asset holding. Controlling for age and socioeconomic status, home owners have about $6,000 more in savings and about $5,000 more invested in mutual funds than renters. Home owners are more likely to carry debt on credit cards, installment purchases, and personal bank loans but are less likely to have unpaid educational loans and overdue bills than renters. Among older adults in both rural and urban areas, controlling for other social and economic factors, home ownership is positively associated with household income (Miller and Montalto, 1998). Thus, assets may have positive economic effects, but there is also a strong likelihood that unobserved factors, to some extent, explain both the above outcomes and home ownership.

Other studies addressing home ownership also control for a number of social and economic factors and find, for example, that home owning reduces the length of joblessness for unemployed workers (Goss and Phillips, 1997) and increases high school graduation and college entry rates among African American youth (Kane, 1994). The latter findings are consistent with those of Richard Green and Michelle White (1997), who find that children of home owners are less likely to drop out of school or to have children before the age of 18 than are children of renters.

Home owners may also be less likely to experience a subjective sense of economic strain or hardship. A study of 193 laid-off autoworkers reports that home ownership, controlling for income and education, significantly reduced subjects' perceived economic strain (Page-Adams and Vosler, 1996). Another study finds that older households have lower levels of hardship and attribute this to higher levels of home ownership and medical coverage (Mirowsky and Ross, 1999). Recent studies have also indicated that indebted home owners are less likely than similarly indebted renters to declare bankruptcy (Domowitz and Sartain, 1999) and less likely to engage in risky investments (Frantantoni, 1998).

Home ownership may play a role in wealth accumulation for U.S. households. In 1995, median net worth for home owners was $78,000, while for renters it was $2,300. For minority home owners, home equity represents almost three-quarters of their median net worth of $48,300, compared with a median net worth of $500 for minority renters (U.S. Department of Housing and Urban Development, 1995). A secondary analysis of a survey of 11,257 U.S. households from 1987 through 1989 finds that home equity accounted for 43.3 percent of white household wealth and 62.5 percent of African American household wealth (Oliver and Shapiro, 1995). Related to the first part of this chapter, equity accumulation in housing is institutionalized through public policies, such as the mortgage interest tax deduction and banking practices such as automatic mortgage payments. Thus, housing equity appears to matter—without it, many U.S. households' assets might be greatly reduced.

In studies using asset measures other than home ownership, wealth is positively associated with financial transfers to adult children and parents in their older years (McGarry and Schoeni, 1995); the economic well-being of women after marital disruption (Cho, 1999); and the ability of single mothers to maintain their families above the federal poverty level (Rocha, 1997). Rocha controls for age, education, number of weeks worked during the past year, and a number of other socioeconomic factors and finds that single mothers with money in a savings account are significantly more likely to have incomes above the poverty line than those without savings. Neither home ownership nor child support payments were strongly associated with living above the poverty level for female-headed families in this study.

In a cross-sectional survey, participants in IDA programs have reported that they feel more economically secure (84 percent), are more likely to make educational plans for themselves (59 percent), and are more likely to plan for retirement (57 percent) because of their asset accounts. Other findings from this study with implications for economic security are proportion of savers who report that they are more likely to increase their work hours (41 percent) or to increase their income in other ways (61 percent) because of their participation in an IDA program (Moore et al., 2001).

While this review has focused on research from the United States and other "developed" countries, findings of positive asset effects on family economic security are consistent with results of studies from developing countries, especially those linking the mother's assets to enhanced material conditions of families (Noponen, 1992; Quanine, 1989; Schuler and Hashemi, 1994). Again, however, much of the research does not clearly establish directionality or rule out alternative explanations.

Asset Effects on Children

The most compelling reason to focus on assets may be intergenerational (Sherraden, 1991; Oliver and Shapiro, 1995). For example, focusing on home purchase, Seymore Spilerman (2004) argues for the importance of considering wealth or family assets over income as determinants of life chances. Dalton Conley (1999) provides evidence that, controlling for several other factors, assets are important for educational attainment.

Home Ownership

Impacts of home ownership on neighborhood and personal well-being have been studied extensively. Scholars argue that home ownership produces beneficial outcomes through enhanced social status (Perin, 1977; Rakoff, 1977); behavioral changes designed to protect investments (Butler, 1985; Saunders, 1978, 1990); and changes in cognitive schema that result when people accumulate assets (Sherraden, 1991). Theoretical and empirical studies have examined claims that home ownership promotes family and personal well-being (Page-Adams, 1995; Rohe and Stegman, 1994a), including intergenerational impacts of home owning.

Children appear to benefit from living in households where parents are home owners. Green and White (1997), in an impressive analysis of four large, national, longitudinal data sets, find that, controlling for education and income, 17–18-year-old children of home owners are less likely than the children of renters to drop out of school and to have children out of wedlock. Other research has also correlated home owning with school attainment (Essen, Fogelman and Head, 1977). These are promising findings, particularly in light of the research results, noted above, that savings and investment income correlate with educational outcomes.

The stability associated with home owning may also provide an explanation of the correlation between housing tenure and educational outcomes (Scanlon, 1997; Scanlon and Adams, chapter 7 in this volume). One commentary on Green and White's findings provides evidence that home ownership's effects on child well-being operate through increased residential stability (Aaronson, 2000). Further evidence of complex relationships between home ownership and residential stability for children can be found in research on the effects of marital disruption. For example, children who live with their mothers following a marital dissolution are more likely to experience residential mobility if their parents owned, rather than rented, homes before the divorce. However, upon the remarriage of their mothers, these children are more likely to move to wealthier neighborhoods than children of divorced parents who were renters (South, Crowder, and Trent, 1998).

For adult children, parental home ownership is related to positive economic outcomes. An analysis of the Netherlands Family Survey finds that parents who are home owners provide more financial help to their adult children (Mulder and Smits, 1999). John Henretta (1984) finds that parental home owning is predictive of adult children's likelihood to own homes, even controlling for income and parental gifts. Further, parental home ownership has an even stronger effect on the likelihood of home owning for adult children in the Netherlands and in Germany than it does in the United States, while other measures of parental socioeconomic status are not predictive of housing tenure (Mulder and Wagner, 1998).

Home owning is associated with enhanced well-being among adults, and this may have benefits for children. For example, controlling for some other social and economic factors, home owners appear to have higher levels of life satisfaction (Potter and Coshall, 1987; Rohe and Stegman, 1994a; Rossi and Weber, 1996); physical and emotional well-being (Greene and Ondrich, 1990; Page-Adams and Vosler, 1996; Pugh et al., 1991; Rodgers, 1991; Vitt, 1994); and future orientation and self-efficacy (Clark, 1997) than renters. It would seem likely that children benefit from living in homes with parents who are healthier and more satisfied with their lives.

Savings and Financial Assets

Household financial wealth and investment income are emerging as variables for study in the well-being of children. Turning first to educational outcomes, Susan Mayer (1997) reports that investment income and inherited wealth have a positive relationship with educational test scores and educational attainment. Similarly, an evaluation of PSID data demonstrates that income from assets (which can be taken as a proxy measure for the assets themselves) is positively related to children's educational attainment (Hill and Duncan, 1987).

A study of intergenerational poverty reveals that the absence of parental assets helps explain the likelihood that adult daughters in female-headed

families will remain in poverty. Further, the effects of parental asset holding on poverty among adult daughters and their children is significant
when controlling for education and socioeconomic status (Cheng, 1995).
Rukmalie Jayakody (1998) suggests that wealth, rather than income, helps
to explain differences between white and African American families in
intergenerational financial assistance.

In a study of factors associated with teenagers' savings and consumption patterns, parental savings, particularly for college, are predictive of
teen savings behavior (Pritchard, Myers, and Cassidy, 1989). In a related
finding, Moore and her colleagues (2001) report that 60 percent of participants in IDA programs say that because they are saving, they are more
likely to make educational plans for their children.

SUMMARY

Altogether, the research summarized above suggests a pattern of associations between asset holding and multiple outcomes that are typically
thought to be positive. This notable pattern should be of interest to those
concerned with finding effective ways of promoting individual, family,
and neighborhood well-being and development. However, it is important
to temper this observation with the caveat that not much of the above
research is longitudinal, and less is experimental. Thus, the direction of
causality is often open to question, and results of many of these studies
could be spurious, that is, due to some unobserved third variable that
explains both assets and the indicated effect(s). While the patterns are suggestive, they are not definitive, and more rigorous research is needed, particularly experimental studies.

Toward Theoretical Specification

Regarding steps toward theory, Sherraden (1991) offered the preliminary
propositions that assets lead to the following: (a) greater future orientation,
(b) development of other assets, (c) improved household stability,
(d) greater focus and specialization, (e) a foundation for risk taking,
(f) increased personal efficacy, (g) increased social status and influence,
(h) increased political participation, and (i) enhanced welfare of offspring.
Together, these theorized outcomes would improve well-being along multiple dimensions, including the eventual reduction of income poverty. The
research summarized above supports a number of these propositions.

These propositions might turn out to be a useful beginning, but they are
not a coherent theory of effects of asset holding. More remains to be done
to elaborate the mechanisms by which the holding of different assets
results in various outcomes (Scanlon, 2001). Sherraden (1991) suggests that
assets alter cognitive schemata that structure an individual's expectations
and understanding of self and the world. The theory chapter in Schreiner

et al. (2001) is an effort to specify a model whereby asset holding, even in the absence of use, can lead to positive effects; it is more specific about how asset holding might alter cognitive schemata. Perhaps this cognitive mechanism can explain many of the theorized outcomes above, but to date little research has been implemented to test this interpretation. One study by Min Zhan and Sherraden (2003) finds that, among single mothers, assets are associated with higher expectations for children's educational attainment, and these expectations are, in turn, associated with higher educational attainment.

Also, theory and future research should begin to pinpoint the circumstances under which asset holding is likely to provide benefits for different populations, so that asset-based policy and community development strategies can be designed to maximize the likelihood of positive impacts. This is especially so for race, which—as illustrated in the studies in this volume (Haveman and Wolff, chapter 4; Shanks, chapter 2; Chiteji and Hamilton, chapter 5; Shapiro and Johnson, chapter 6; and Schreiner et al., chapter 10)—is often related to asset distribution and accumulation.

Three major alternative explanations should be examined in further studies related to assets: (a) that it is income and not assets that cause the above effects, (b) that the above positive outcomes cause assets to accumulate rather than the other way around, and/or (c) that unobserved factors cause both asset holding and other positive outcomes. In fact, many of the above studies do control for income and a number of other likely variables, and they still find assets to be predictive. In most cases, both income and assets are predictive, that is, they have independent effects on well-being as it is measured in the various studies (which is not to say that causality is established). Regarding the possible reverse explanation, that positive attitudes and behaviors cause people to be able to accumulate assets, Yadama and Sherraden (1996) use PSID longitudinal data with simultaneous equations and find that positive attitudes and behaviors indeed explain asset accumulation, but asset accumulation also explains positive attitudes and behaviors. These results may indicate a mutually reinforcing cycle of improvements between assets and positive attitudes and behaviors. Regarding possible spurious relationships, this remains likely, at least to some extent. Unmeasured personality characteristics are likely to affect both asset accumulation and other measures of well-being. Future research should attempt to identify and control for these.

Altogether, much remains to be done in both theoretical specification and empirical verification regarding the role of asset holding and well-being. But the gathering body of evidence is highly suggestive. Theory and research on effects of asset holding raises a question about the singular definition of well-being as consumption. In doing so, this area of inquiry may contribute to a broader view of well-being as capabilities or capacity (Sen, 1985, 1993, 1999). If future research supports this interpretation, the development and holding of financial and tangible assets could be part of this larger view.

NOTES

1. The section on how saving and asset accumulation occur is based on previous and ongoing work. The review of theory draws on Beverly and Sherraden (1999). The discussions of whether the poor can save or might oversave draws on Schreiner et al. (2001). Discussion of the role of institutions and saving by the poor was initiated by Sherraden (1991); detailed in Beverly and Sherraden (1999); extended in Schreiner et al. (2001); and again in Sherraden, Schreiner, and Beverly (2003). The section on theoretical development is based on e-mail exchanges between Sherraden and Schreiner. This is continuing work, likely to be revised in the future.

2. The section on effects of asset holding draws on research summaries by Scanlon and Page-Adams (2001) and Page-Adams et al. (2001).

REFERENCES

Aaronson, D. (2000). "A Note on the Benefits of Homeownership." *Journal of Urban Economics* 47(3), 356–369.

Amin, R., and Y. Li. (1997). "NGO-Promoted Women's Credit Program, Immunization Coverage, and Child Mortality in Rural Bangladesh." *Women and Health* 25(1), 71–87.

Basset, W. F., M. J. Fleming, and A. P. Rodrigues. (1998). "How Workers Use 401(k) Plans: The Participation, Contribution, and Withdrawal Decisions." *National Tax Journal* 51(2), 263–289.

Baum, T., and P. Kingston. (1984). "Homeownership and Social Attachment." *Sociological Perspectives* 27, 159–180.

Bayer, P. J., B. D. Bernheim, and J. K. Scholz. (1996). *The Effects of Financial Education in the Workplace: Evidence from a Survey of Employers.* Working Paper No. 5655. Cambridge, Mass.: National Bureau of Economic Research (NBER).

Becker, G. S. (1993). "Nobel Lecture: The Economic Way of Looking at Behavior." *Journal of Political Economy* 101(31), 385–409.

Berger, P., J. Powell, and A. Cook. (1988). "The Relation of Economic Factors to Perceived Stress in Mobile Families." *Lifestyles* 9, 297–313.

Bernheim, B. D., and D. M. Garrett. (1996). *The Determinants and Consequences of Financial Education in the Workplace: Evidence from a Survey of Households.* Working Paper No. 5667. Cambridge, Mass.: National Bureau of Economic Research.

Bernheim, B. D., D. M. Garrett, and D. M. Maki. (2001). "Education and Saving: The Long-Term Effects of High School Financial Curriculum Mandates." *Journal of Public Economics* 80(3), 435–465.

Bernheim, B. D., and J. K. Scholz. (1993). "Private Saving and Public Policy." *Tax Policy and the Economy* 7, 73–110.

Beverly, S. G. (1997). *How Can the Poor Save? Theory and Evidence on Saving in Low-income Households.* Working Paper No. 97-3. St. Louis, Mo.: Center for Social Development, Washington University.

Beverly, S. G., and M. Sherraden. (1999). "Institutional Determinants of Saving: Implications for Low-Income Households and Public Policy." *Journal of Socio-economics* 28, 457–473.

Bracher, M., G. Santow, S. Morgan, and J. Trussell. (1993). "Marriage Dissolution in Australia: Models and Explanations." *Population Studies* 47(3), 403–425.

Bunting, D. (1991). "Savings and the Distribution of Income." *Journal of Post Keynesian Economics* 14(1), 3–22.

Burbidge, A. (2000). "Capital Gains, Homeownership and Economic Inequality." *Housing Studies* 15(2), 259–280.

Burkhauser, R., B. Butrica, and M. Wasylenko. (1995). "Mobility Patterns of Older Homeowners: Are Older Homeowners Trapped in Distressed Neighborhoods?" *Research on Aging* 17(4), 363–384.

Burkhauser, R. V., and R. R. Weathers II. (2001). "Access to Wealth among Older Workers in the 1990s and How It Is Distributed: Data from the Health and Retirement Study." In *Assets for the Poor: The Benefits and Mechanisms of Spreading Asset Ownership,* eds. T. M. Shapiro and E. N. Wolff. New York: Russell Sage Foundation, 74–131.

Butler, E., and E. Kaiser. (1971). "Prediction of Residential Movement and Spatial Allocation." *Urban Affairs Quarterly* 6(4), 477–494.

Butler, S. (1985). *Privatizing Federal Spending.* New York: Universe Books.

Cagan, P. (1965). *The Effect of Pension Plans on Aggregate Savings: Evidence from a Sample Survey.* Occasional Paper No. 95. New York: National Bureau of Economic Research.

Carney, S., and W. Gale. (2001). "Asset Accumulation among Low-Income Households." In *Assets for the Poor: The Benefits of Spreading Asset Ownership,* eds. T. M. Shapiro and E. N. Wolff. New York: Russell Sage Foundation, 165–205.

Carroll, C. D. (1997). "Buffer-Stock Saving and the Life Cycle/Permanent Income Hypothesis." *Quarterly Journal of Economics* 12(1), 1–55.

Carroll, C. D., and A. A. Samwick. (1997). "The Nature of Precautionary Wealth." *Journal of Monetary Economics* 40(1), 41–71.

Carroll, C. D., and L. H. Summers. (1987). "Why Have Private Savings Rates in the United States and Canada Diverged?" *Journal of Monetary Economics* 20, 249–279.

Caskey, J. P. (1994). *Fringe Banking: Check-Cashing Outlets, Pawnshops, and the Poor.* New York: Russell Sage Foundation.

Cheng, L. (1995). "Asset Holding and Intergenerational Poverty Vulnerability in Female-Headed Families." Paper presented at the Seventh International Conference of The Society for the Advancement of Socio-Economics, April 7–9, Washington, D.C.

Cherlin, A. (1977). *Social and Economic Determinants of Marital Separation.* Doctoral dissertation. University of California.

Cho, E. (1999). *The Effects of Assets on the Economic Well-Being of Women after Marital Disruption.* Working Paper No. 99-6. St. Louis, Mo.: Center for Social Development, Washington University.

Clancy, M., M. Grinstein-Weiss, and M. Schreiner. (2001). *Financial Education and Savings Outcomes in Individual Development Accounts.* Working Paper No. 01-2. St. Louis, Mo.: Washington University, Center for Social Development.

Clark, H. (1997). "A Structural Equation Model of the Effects of Homeownership on Self-Efficacy, Self-Esteem, Political Involvement, and Community Involvement in African-Americans." Doctoral dissertation. School of Social Work, University of Texas at Arlington.

Cohen, N., M. A. Jalil, H. Rahman, M. A. Matin, J. Sprague, J. Islam, J. Davison, E. Leemhuis De Regt, and M. Mitra. (1985). "Landholding, Wealth and Risk of Blinding Malnutrition in Rural Bangladeshi Households." *Social Science Medicine* 21(11), 1269–1272.

Cohen, S. (1994). "Consumer Socialization: Children's Saving and Spending." *Childhood Education* 70(4), 244–246.

Conley, D. (1999). *Being Black, Living in the Red: Race, Wealth, and Social Policy in America*. Berkeley: University of California Press.

Cox, K. (1982). "Housing Tenure and Neighborhood Activism." *Urban Affairs Quarterly* 18(1), 107–129.

Cutright, P. (1971). "Income and Family Events: Marital Stability." *Journal of Marriage and the Family* 33, 291–306.

Davern, M. E., and P. J. Fisher. (2001). *Household Net Worth and Asset Ownership: 1995*. U.S. Census Bureau Current Population Reports, P70–71. Washington, D.C.: U.S. Government Printing Office.

DiPasquale, D., and E. Glaser. (1999). "Incentives and Social Capital: Are Homeowners Better Citizens?" *Journal of Urban Economics* 45(2), 354–384.

Ditkovsky, O., and W. van Vliet. (1984). "Housing Tenure and Community Participation." *Ekistics* 307, 345–348.

Domowitz, I., and R. Sartain. (1999). "Determinants of the Consumer Bankruptcy Decision." *Journal of Finance* 54(1), 403–420.

Duesenberry, J. S. (1949). *Income, Saving and the Theory of Consumer Behavior*. Cambridge, Mass.: Harvard University Press.

Engen, E. M., W. Gale, and J. Scholz. (1996). "The Illusory Effects of Saving Incentives on Saving." *Journal of Economic Perspectives* 10(4), 113–138.

Essen, J., K. Fogelman, and J. Head. (1977). "Childhood Housing Experiences and School Attainment." *Child Care, Health and Development* 4, 41–58.

Feldstein, M. (1995). "College Scholarship Rules and Private Saving." *American Economic Review* 85(3), 552–566.

Fischer, C. (1982). *To Dwell among Friends: Personal Networks in Town and Country*. Chicago: University of Chicago Press.

Fischer, C., R. Jackson, C. Stueve, K. Gerson, and L. Jones. (1977). *Networks and Places: Social Relations in the Urban Setting*. New York: Free Press.

Forrest, R. (1987). "Spatial Mobility, Tenure Mobility, and Emerging Social Divisions in the UK Housing Market." *Environment and Planning* A(19), 1611–1630.

Frantantoni, M. (1998). "Homeownership and Investment in Risky Assets." *Journal of Urban Economics* 44(1), 27–42.

Friedman, M. (1957). *A Theory of the Consumption Function*. National Bureau of Economic Research General Series No. 63. Princeton, N.J.: Princeton University Press.

Furnham, A. (1985). "Why Do People Save? Attitudes to, and Habits of, Saving Money in Britain." *Journal of Applied Social Psychology* 15(4), 354–373.

Galligan, R. J., and S. J. Bahr. (1978). "Economic Well-Being and Marital Stability: Implications for Income Maintenance Programs." *Journal of Marriage and the Family*, 283–290.

Galster, G. (1983). "Empirical Evidence on Cross-tenure Differences and Community Satisfaction." *Journal of Social Issues* 28(3), 107–119.

Galster, G. (1987). *Homeownership and Neighborhood Reinvestment*. Durham, N.C.: Duke University Press.

Galster, G. (1998). *An Econometric Model of the Urban Opportunity Structure: Cumulative Causation among City Markets, Social Problems, and Underserved Areas*. Washington, D.C.: Fannie Mae Foundation.

Goldblatt, P. (1990). "Mortality and Alternative Social Classifications." In *Longitudinal Study: Mortality and Social Organization,* ed. P. Goldblatt. OPCS, Series LS, No. 6. London: HMSO.

Gordon, W. (1980). *Institutional Economics: The Changing System.* Austin: University of Texas Press.

Goss, E., and J. Phillips. (1997). "The Effect of State Economic Development Spending on State Income and Employment Growth." *Economic Development Quarterly* 11, 88–96.

Green, R. K., and M. J. White. (1997). "Measuring the Benefits of Home Owning: Effects on Children." *Journal of Urban Economics* 41, 441–461.

Greene, V., and J. Ondrich. (1990). "Risk Factors for Nursing Home Admissions and Exits: A Discrete Time Hazard Function Approach." *Journals of Gerontology* 45(6), S250–S258.

Guest, A., and R. Oropesa. (1986). "Informal Social Ties and Political Activity in the Metropolis." *Urban Affairs Quarterly* 21(4), 550–574.

Gyourko, J., and P. Linneman. (1993). "Comparing Apartment and Office Investments." *Real Estate Review* 23(2), 17–23.

Gyourko, J., P. Linneman, and S. Wachter. (1999). "Analyzing the Relationships among Race, Wealth, and Home Ownership in America." *Journal of Urban Economics* 8(2), 63–89.

Hahn, B. (1993). "Marital Status and Women's Health: The Effect of Economic Marital Acquisitions." *Journal of Marriage and the Family* 55(2), 495–504.

Hampton, R. L. (1982). "Family Life Cycle, Economic Well-being and Marital Disruption in Black Families." *California Sociologist* 5, 16–32.

Henretta, J. C. (1984). "Parental Status and Child's Homeownership." *American Sociological Review* 49, 131–140.

Hill, M. S., and G. J. Duncan. (1987). "Parental Family Income and the Socioeconomic Attainment of Children." *Social Science Research* 6, 39–73.

Howard, C. (1997). *The Hidden Welfare State: Tax Expenditures and Social Policy in the United States.* Princeton, N.J.: Princeton University Press.

Hubbard, R. G., J. Skinner, and S. P. Zeldes. (1994). "The Importance of Precautionary Motives in Explaining Individual and Aggregate Saving." *Carnegie-Rochester Conference Series on Public Policy* 40, 59–125.

Hubbard, R. G., J. Skinner, and S. P. Zeldes. (1995). "Precautionary Saving and Social Insurance." *Journal of Political Economy* 103(2), 360–399.

Hubbard, R. G., and J. S. Skinner. (1996). "Assessing the Effectiveness of Saving Incentives." *Journal of Economic Perspectives* 10(4), 73–90.

Immergluck, D. (1998). "Progress Confined: Increases in Black Home Buying and the Persistence of Residential Segregation." *Journal of Urban Affairs* 20(4), 443–457.

Jayakody, R. (1998). "Race Differences in Intergenerational Financial Assistance: The Needs of Children and the Resources of Parents." *Journal of Family Issues* 19(5), 508–534.

Joshi, H., and S. Macran. (1991). "Work, Gender, and Health." *Work, Employment and Society* 5, 451–469.

Joulfaian, D., and D. Richardson. (2001). "Who Takes Advantage of Tax-deferred Savings Programs? Evidence from Federal Income Tax Data." *National Tax Journal* 54(3), 669–688.

Kane, T. J. (1994). "College Entry by Blacks since 1970: The Role of College Costs, Family Background, and the Returns to Education." *Journal of Political Economy* 102, 878–907.

Katona, G. (1975). *Psychological Economics*. New York: Elsevier.

Kendig, H., C. Browning, and K. Teshuva. (1998). "Health Actions and Social Class among Older Australians." *Australian and New Zealand Journal of Public Health* 22(7), 808–813.

Kerbow, D. (1996). "Patterns of Urban School Mobility and Local School Reform." *Journal of Education for Students Placed at Risk* 2, 147–169.

Kingston, P., and J. Fries. (1994). "Having a Stake in the System—The Sociopolitical Ramifications of Business and Homeownership." *Social Science Quarterly* 75(3), 679–686.

Krumm, R., and A. Kelly. (1989). "Effects of Homeownership on Household Savings." *Journal of Urban Economics* 26(3), 281–294.

Kusko, A. L., J. M. Poterba, and D. W. Wilcox. (1994). *Employee Decisions with Respect to 401(k) Plans: Evidence from Individual Level Data*. Working Paper No. 4635. Cambridge, Mass.: National Bureau of Economic Research.

Lee, C., and R. Amin. (1981). "Socioeconomic Factors, Intermediate Variables, and Fertility in Bangladesh." *Journal of Biosocial Science* 13, 179–188.

Lee, C., D. Culhane, and S. Wachter. (1999). "The Differential Impacts of Federally Assisted Housing Programs on Nearby Property Values: A Philadelphia Case Study." *Housing Policy Debate* 10(1), 75–93.

Levinson, D. (1989). *Family Violence in Cross-cultural Perspective*. Newbury Park, Calif.: Sage.

Lloyd, K. M., and S. J. South. (1996). "Contextual Influences on Young Men's Transition to First Marriage." *Social Forces* 74(3), 1097–1120.

Long, J., and S. Caudill. (1992). "Racial Differences in Homeownership and Housing Wealth, 1970–1986." *Economic Inquiry* 30(1), 83–100.

Madrian, B. C., and D. F. Shea. (2000). *The Power of Suggestion: Inertia in 401(k) Participation and Savings Behavior*. Working Paper No. 7682. Cambridge, Mass.: National Bureau of Economic Research.

Maital, S. (1986). "Prometheus Rebound: On Welfare-Improving Constraints." *Eastern Economic Journal* 12(3), 337–344.

Maital, S., and S. L. Maital. (1994). "Is the Future What It Used to Be? A Behavioral Theory of the Decline of Saving in the West." *Journal of Socio-Economics* 23(1/2), 1–32.

Massey, D., and L. Basem. (1992). "Determinants of Savings, Remittances, and Spending Patterns among United States Migrants in Four Mexican Communities." *Sociological Inquiry* 62, 185–207.

Mayer, N. (1981). "Rehabilitation Decisions in Rental Housing." *Journal of Urban Economics* 10, 76–94.

Mayer, S. (1997). *What Money Can't Buy: Family Income and Children's Life Chances*. Cambridge, Mass.: Harvard University Press.

McGarry, K., and R. Schoeni. (1995). "Transfer Behavior in the Health and Retirement Study: Measurement and the Redistribution of Resources within the Family." *Journal of Human Resources* 30, S184–S226.

McHugh, K. (1985). "Reasons for Migrating or Not." *Sociology and Sociological Research* 69(4), 585–589.

Midema, H., and H. Vos. (1999). "Demographic and Attitudinal Factors That Modify Annoyance from Transportation Noise." *Journal of the Acoustical Society of America* 105(6), 3336–3344.

Midgley, J. (1999). "Growth, Redistribution, and Welfare: Towards Social Investment." *Social Service Review* 77(1), 3–21.

Miller, C. J., and C. P. Montalto. (1998). "Comparison of Economic Status of Elderly Households: Nonmetropolitan versus Metropolitan Residence." *Family Economics and Nutrition Review* 11(4), 19–35.

Mirowsky, J., and C. Ross. (1999). "Economic Hardship across the Life Course." *American Sociological Review* 64(4), 548–569.

Modigliani, F., and R. Brumberg. (1954). "Utility Analysis and the Consumption Function: An Interpretation of Cross-Section Data." In *Post-Keynesian Economics*, ed. K. K. Kurihara. New Brunswick, N.J.: Rutgers University Press, 388–436.

Moore, A., S. Beverly, M. Schreiner, M. Sherraden, M. Lombe, E. Y.-N. Cho, L. Johnson, and R. Vonderlack. (2001). *Saving, IDA Programs, and Effects of IDAs: A Survey of Participants.* Research Report. St. Louis, Mo.: Center for Social Development, Washington University.

Moser, K., H. Pugh, and P. Goldblatt. (1990). "Mortality and Social Classification of Women." In *Longitudinal Study: Mortality and Social Organization*, ed. P. Goldblatt. OPCS, Series LS, No. 9. London: HMSO.

Mulder, C., and J. Smits. (1999). "First Time Home-Ownership of Couples—The Effect of Inter-generational Transmission." *European Sociological Review* 15(3), 323–337.

Mulder, C., and M. Wagner. (1998). "First-time Home-Ownership in the Family Life Course: A West German-Dutch Comparison." *Urban Studies* 35(4), 687–714.

Neale, W. C. (1987). "Institutions." *Journal of Economic Issues* 21(3), 1177–1206.

Neumark, D. (1995). "Are Rising Earnings Profiles a Forced-Savings Mechanism?" *The Economic Journal* 105, 95–106.

Noponen, H. (1992). "Loans and the Working Poor: A Longitudinal Study of Credit, Gender and the Household Economy." *International Journal of Urban and Regional Research* 16, 234–251.

North, D. (1990). *Institutions, Institutional Change, and Economic Performance.* Cambridge, Mass.: Cambridge University Press.

Oliver, M., and T. Shapiro. (1995). *Black Wealth/White Wealth: A New Perspective on Racial Inequality.* New York: Routledge.

Page-Adams, D. (1995). *Homeownership and Marital Violence.* Doctoral dissertation. St. Louis, Mo.: Washington University.

Page-Adams, D., D. Scanlon, S. Beverly, and T. McDonald. (2001). *Assets, Health, and Well-being of Children and Youth: What Is Expected from a CYSAPD?* Research Background Paper. St. Louis, Mo.: Center for Social Development, Washington University.

Page-Adams, D., and M. Sherraden. (1996). *What We Know about Effects of Asset Holding: Implications for Research on Asset-Based Antipoverty Initiatives.* Working Paper No. 96-1. St. Louis, Mo.: Center for Social Development, Washington University.

Page-Adams, D., and N. Vosler. (1996). "Predictors of Depression among Workers at the Time of a Plant Closing." *Journal of Sociology and Social Welfare* 23(4), 25–42.

Perin, C. (1977). *Everything in Its Place.* Princeton, N.J.: Princeton University Press.

Perkins, D., P. Florin, R. Rich, A. Wandersman, and D. Chavis. (1990). "Participation and the Social and Physical Environment of Residential Blocks: Crime and Community Context." *American Journal of Community Psychology* 18, 83–115.

Petersen, R. (1980). "Social Class, Social Learning, and Wife Abuse." *Social Service Review* 54, 390–406.

Pettit, B., S. McClanahan, and M. Hanratty. (1999). *Moving to Opportunity: Benefits and Hidden Costs.* Working Paper No. 98-11. Princeton, N.J.: Bendheim-Thoman Center for Research on Child Well-Being, Princeton University.

Pickvance, C. (1973). "Life-Cycle, Housing Tenure and Intra-Urban Residential Mobility: A Causal Model." *Sociological Review* 21(2), 279–297.

Poterba, J. M., S. F. Venti, and D. A. Wise. (1996). "How Retirement Saving Programs Increase Saving." *Journal of Economic Perspectives* 10(4), 91–112.

Potter, R., and J. Coshall. (1987). "Socio-economic Variations in Perceived Life Domain Satisfactions: A South West Wales Case Study." *Journal of Social Psychology* 127(1), 77–82.

Powers, E. T. (1998). "Does Means-Testing Welfare Discourage Saving? Evidence from a Change in AFDC Policy in the United States." *Journal of Public Economics* 68, 33–53.

Pritchard, M., B. Myers, and D. Cassidy. (1989). "Factors Associated with Adolescent Saving and Spending Patterns." *Adolescence* 24, 279–297.

Pugh, H., C. Power, P. Goldblatt, and S. Arber. (1991). "Women's Lung Cancer Mortality, Socioeconomic Status and Changing Smoking Patterns." *Social Science and Medicine* 32(10), 1105–1110.

Quanine, J. (1989). "Women and Nutrition: The Grameen Bank Experience." *Food and Nutrition Bulletin* 11, 64–66.

Raheim, S., and C. Alter. (1995). *The Final Evaluation Report: The Self-Employment Learning Project.* Washington, D.C.: Corporation for Enterprise Development.

Rakoff, R. (1977). "Ideology in Everyday Life: The Meaning of the House." *Politics and Society* 7, 85–104.

Robert, S., and J. House. (1996). "SES Differentials in Health by Age and Alternative Indicators of SES." *Journal of Aging and Health* 8(3), 359–388.

Rocha, C. (1997). "Factors That Contribute to Economic Well-Being in Female Headed Households." *Journal of Social Service Research* 23(1), 1–17.

Rodgers, B. (1991). "Socioeconomic Status, Employment, and Neurosis." *Social Psychiatry and Epidemiology* 26, 104–114.

Rohe, W., and V. Basolo. (1997). "Long-Term Effects of Homeownership on the Self-Perceptions and Social Interaction of Low-Income Persons." *Environment and Behavior* 29(6), 793–819.

Rohe, W., and M. Stegman. (1994a). "The Effects of Homeownership on the Self-Esteem, Perceived Control and Life Satisfaction of Low-Income People." *Journal of the American Planning Association* 60(2), 173–184.

Rohe, W., and M. Stegman. (1994b). "The Impact of Homeownership on the Social and Political Involvement of Low-Income People." *Urban Affairs Quarterly* 30(1), 152–172.

Rohe, W., and L. Stewart. (1996). "Home Ownership and Neighborhood Stability." *Housing Policy Debate* 9(1), 37–81.

Rosenbaum, J., and S. Popkin. (1991). "Employment and Earnings of Blacks Who Move to Middle-Class Suburbs." In *The Urban Underclass*, eds. C. Jencks and P. Petersen. Washington, D.C.: Brookings Institution Press.

Rossi, P., and E. Weber. (1996). "The Social Benefits of Homeownership: Empirical Evidence from National Surveys." *Housing Policy Debate* 7(1), 1–35.

Saegert, S., and G. Winkel. (1998). "Social Capital and the Revitalization of New York City's Distressed Inner City Housing." *Housing Policy Debate* 9(1), 17–60.

Saunders, P. (1978). "Beyond Housing Classes: The Sociological Significance of Private Property Rights in Means of Consumption." *International Journal of Urban and Regional Research* 18(2), 202–227.

Saunders, P. (1990). *A Nation of Homeowners.* London: Unwin Hyman.

Scanlon, E. (1997). "The Economic, Psychological and Social Effects of Home-ownership on Individuals and Households." Area of Specialization Statement, Doctoral Program. St. Louis, Mo.: George Warren Brown School of Social Work, Washington University.

Scanlon, E. (1998). "Low-Income Homeownership Policy as a Community Development Strategy." *Journal of Community Practice* 5(2), 137–154.

Scanlon, E. (2001). *Toward a Theory of Financial Savings and Child Well-Being: Implications for Research on a Children and Youth Saving Account Policy.* Research Background Paper. St. Louis, Mo.: Center for Social Development, Washington University.

Scanlon, E., and D. Page-Adams. (2001). "Effects of Asset Holding on Neighborhoods, Families, and Children: A Review of Research." In *Building Assets,* ed. R. Boshara. Washington, D.C.: Corporation for Enterprise Development.

Schreiner, M. (2004). *Measuring Savings.* Working Paper No. 04-08. St. Louis, Mo.: Center for Social Development, Washington University.

Schreiner, M., M. Sherraden, M. Clancy, E. Johnson, J. Curley, M. Grinstein-Weiss, M. Zhan, and S. Beverly. (2001). *Savings and Asset Accumulation in IDAs.* Research Report. St. Louis, Mo.: Center for Social Development, Washington University.

Schuler, S., and S. Hashemi. (1994). "Credit Programs, Women's Empowerment, and Contraceptive Use in Rural Bangladesh." *Studies in Family Planning* 25(2), 65–76.

Seidman, L. (2001). "Assets and the Tax Code." In *Assets for the Poor,* eds. T. Shapiro and E. N. Wolff. New York: Russell Sage Foundation, 324–356.

Sen, A. (1985). *Commodities and Capabilities.* Amsterdam: North-Holland Publishing Company.

Sen, A. (1993). "Capability and Well-Being." In *The Quality of Life,* eds. M. Nussbaum and A. Sen. Oxford, U.K.: Clarendon Press, 30–53.

Sen, A. (1999). *Democracy as Freedom.* New York: Knopf.

Shapiro, T. (2004). *The Hidden Cost of Being African American: How Wealth Perpetuates Inequality.* New York: Oxford University Press.

Shefrin, H. M., and R. H. Thaler. (1988). "The Behavioral Life-Cycle Hypothesis." *Economic Inquiry* 26, 609–643.

Sherraden, M. (1991). *Assets and the Poor: A New American Welfare Policy.* Armonk, N.Y.: M. E. Sharpe.

Sherraden, M. (2001). "Asset Building Policy and Programs for the Poor." In *Assets for the Poor: Benefits and Mechanisms of Spreading Asset Ownership,* eds. T. M. Shapiro and E. N. Wolff. New York: Russell Sage Foundation, 302–323.

Sherraden, M., S. Nair, S. Vasoo, N. T. Liang, and M. S. Sherraden. (1995). "Effects of Asset Accumulation among Members of Singapore's Central Provident Fund." Paper presented at the Seventh International Conference of the Society for the Advancement of Socio-Economics, April 7–9, Washington, D.C.

Sherraden, M., M. Schreiner, and S. Beverly. (2003). "Income, Institutions, and Saving Performance in Individual Development Accounts." *Economic Development Quarterly* 17(1), 95–112.

Sherraden, M. S., A. M. McBride, E. Johnson, S. Hanson, and F. Ssewamala. (2005). *Saving in Low-Income Households: Evidence from Interviews with Participants in the American Dream Demonstration.* Research Report. St. Louis, Mo.: Center for Social Development, Washington University.

South, S. J., K. D. Crowder, and K. Trent. (1998). "Children's Residential Mobility and Neighborhood Environment following Parental Divorce and Remarriage." *Social Forces* 77(2), 667–685.

South, S. J., and G. Spitze. (1986). "Determinants of Divorce over the Marital Life Course." *American Sociological Review* 51(4), 583–590.

Spilerman, S. (2004). "Young Couples in Israel: The Impact of Parental Wealth on Early Living Standards." *American Sociological Review* 110(1), 92–122.

Steinberger, P. (1981). "Political Participation and Community: A Cultural/ Interpersonal Approach." *Rural Sociology* 46(1), 17–19.

Stronks, K., H. van de Mheen, J. van de Bos, and J. Mackenbach. (1997). "The Interrelationship between Income, Health, and Employment Status." *International Journal of Epidemiology* 26(3), 592–600.

Tucker, J., J. Marx, and L. Long. (1998). "Moving On: Residential Mobility and Children's School Lives." *Sociology of Education* 7, 111–129.

U.S. Department of Housing and Urban Development. (1995). *Urban Policy Brief,* no. 2. Washington, D.C.: Author.

Varady, D. P. (1986). *Neighborhood Upgrading: A Realistic Assessment.* Albany, N.Y.: State University of New York Press.

Vitt, L. (1994). "Homeownership, Well-Being, Class and Politics: Perceptions of American Homeowners and Renters." Doctoral dissertation. Washington, D.C.: Department of Sociology, American University.

Williams, L., K. Mehta, and S. Lin. (1999). "Intergenerational Influence in Singapore and Taiwan: The Role of the Elderly in Family Decisions." *Journal of Cross Cultural Gerontology* 14(4), 291–322.

Wolff, E. N. (2001). "Recent Trends in Wealth Ownership, from 1983 to 1998." In *Assets for the Poor: Benefits and Mechanisms of Spreading Asset Ownership,* eds. T. M. Shapiro and E. N. Wolff. New York: Russell Sage Foundation, 34–73.

Yadama, G., and M. Sherraden. (1996). "Effects of Assets on Attitudes and Behaviors: Advance Test of a Social Policy Proposal." *Social Work Research* 20, 3–11.

Zhan, M., and M. Sherraden. (2003). "Assets, Expectations, and Children's Educational Achievement in Female-headed Households." *Social Service Review* 77(2), 191–211.

Ziliak, J. P. (1999). *Income Transfers and Assets of the Poor.* Discussion Paper No. 1202-99. Madison: Institute for Research on Poverty, University of Wisconsin.

Conclusion

Michael Sherraden

Inclusion in the American Dream: Assets, Poverty, and Public Policy is perhaps an optimistic title. It offers a vision of asset holding for the whole population, and suggests that public policy can help to make this possible. This is a lofty and progressive goal and a view of public policy that is perhaps against the current of our times. We live in an age characterized by weak political support for social policy, especially policy aimed at the poor, and a general rejection of government as a solution to major domestic challenges. In such times, is it realistic to suppose that the United States will move toward greater inclusion in asset-based policy? Is such optimism warranted, or is it misplaced?

Academic and policy developments of the past decade suggest that the vision of widespread asset holding, with the active influence of public policy, may, in fact, be a realistic goal. Progress in research has been notable. As demonstrated in this book, many scholars today are studying assets in relation to poverty and development. This is a new area of inquiry in advanced economies. In recent years, policies for progressive asset building, primarily in the form of individual development accounts (IDAs), have been enacted in most U.S. states and at the federal level. To be sure, many of these policies are for small demonstration programs, but they are widespread. As illustrated in this volume, universal, progressive policies are being proposed. For perspective, it is useful to bear in mind that such proposals were not being offered or discussed fifteen years ago.

Nonetheless, this is barely a beginning. In order to reach a truly inclusive asset-based policy, one that is universal and progressive, both a sound knowledge base and promising policy models will be necessary. The aim of this book has been to contribute to the knowledge base and suggest policy designs. We pause now to look back and assess these contributions. What do we learn from the social researchers and policy analysts in this book? What questions and challenges remain?

EMERGING SCHOLARSHIP AND POLICY

Foremost, it is apparent that new asset-based knowledge and policy are emerging. As the authors in this book demonstrate, there is a growing body of work in theory, evidence, analysis, and policy design. This body of work has developed far beyond a creative idea, a single intellectual agenda, or one policy proposal. Today, scholars and analysts are engaged in many different aspects of asset-based inquiry and application.

The term "asset-based" research and policy, which is now common in policy discussions, was not introduced until 1991 in *Assets and the Poor*. Today, studies of saving, asset accumulation, and related public policies are growing rapidly. This book's contributing authors are among the leading architects of this emerging body of knowledge and its application in asset-based policy. Emergence has been rapid, with growing scholarly interest, increasing and often bipartisan political support, and new funding streams for both research and policy.

These developments can also be viewed through the lens of research support. Funding for research on this topic did not exist in the early 1990s, then gradually became available from philanthropic foundations during that decade. Today, there is increasing public support for asset-based research. These developments may reflect a general pattern of public support for applied social research: Public support for research usually does not lead but, rather, follows policy. For example, it was not until asset-based policies (such as IDAs) actually existed that public funding became available to study them.

This pattern of applied innovation preceding extensive research funding imposes a high barrier of entry for any new field of applied social research. In short, it is hard to get started. Many promising ideas never find their footing. In the case of asset-based research and scholarship, the authors of chapters in this book have worked with determination to overcome this high initial barrier and establish an emergent body of work.

In a new area of scholarship, there are many questions to ask and a great deal of new ground to be plowed. The research and policy chapters in this book reflect these conditions and circumstances, and many of the studies and analyses are the first of a kind.

ASSETS, POLICY, AND DEVELOPMENT

Shanks's chapter 2 study of the Homestead Act serves to connect this "historical" policy with people living today. The underlying message of this work is that asset-based policy, unlike income support policy, has a long-term development agenda. Shanks is not able to say exactly how much people are better off if their ancestors were homesteaders, but few could doubt these effects. To provide only one example, both of my parents came from homesteading families in Kansas. Both farms were still in family possession until the mid-twentieth century. These farms raised both of my parents, and financial assets from the sale of these farms were passed forward across generations. This did not happen in Shanks's family, which is African American. Blacks benefited very little from the Homestead Act. In her family, farmland in the South was purchased, with great effort, in the nineteenth century; this is a common story among rural blacks in the South. However, Shanks's ancestors' property title was unclear, and their land was eventually taken away, similar to the experiences of many other black rural landowners, with little recourse for its return. Perhaps Shanks's study and these two contrasting family stories will help to remove any lingering doubts about the continuing relevance of the Homestead Act and public policies regarding property ownership in general. These policies have lasting influence across generations.

These examples also serve as reminders that the federal government historically has been—and still is today—deeply involved in the creation of asset inequality. Providing massive asset transfers via home mortgage interest tax deductions and retirement pensions accounts, which benefit wealthy, white Americans disproportionately, has effects on inequality that are no less profound and long-lasting than those of the Homestead Act.

ASSETS, INEQUALITY, AND RACE

This book was not intended to be about race. Nevertheless, the subject of asset holding is so intertwined with racial inequality in America that race emerges as a strong theme. Chapter 5, by Chiteji and Hamilton, and chapter 6, by Shapiro and Johnson, document the continuing disadvantages of opportunity among low-wealth households, particularly in relation to race. These two studies make clear the point that class and race in America are interconnected. In documenting the dynamics of class-race interconnections within families, these studies are important contributions. In these two chapters, readers will be able to look beyond the veneer of statistics, to peer into families and see how pressures, choices, and opportunities are created or not created. Chapter 7, by Scanlon and Adams, also raises the possibility of different effects of household wealth by race.

In general, race matters. When I make a public presentation on asset-based policy, I usually show a slide comparing income and asset inequality for whites and blacks. Whites in America have a median income that is about 1.5 times that of blacks, a large inequality. But whites have a median net worth that is about 10 times that of blacks, a huge inequality. The audience is invariably surprised by these fundamental data, as if this huge difference in ownership by race had not occurred to them. If assets represent potential for long-term development, then asset inequality by race may be the most fundamental aspect of racial inequality in America. Until the last few years, this has been largely overlooked in scholarship, and it is not yet commonly known among the general public.

DIRECTIONS FOR THEORY AND RESEARCH

Policy and political research, not well addressed in this book, require greater attention. We will need to know more about costs and outcomes of asset-based policy compared to other policy options. Also, we will need to know more about public opinion and political opportunities regarding potential for an inclusive asset-based policy.

However, in the long run, policy and political studies may not be the most important. John Maynard Keynes was probably correct in observing that, ultimately, it is ideas of thinkers, perhaps long dead, that drive policy. If inclusive asset-based policy is to find a stable footing, it will be due to theoretical specification and empirical knowledge in two areas: how savings and assets accumulate and how assets affect well-being.

Fortunately, recent advances in behavioral and institutional economics are contributing a great deal to the first area, how savings and assets accumulate. The Center for Social Development (CSD) at Washington University in St. Louis has taken one direction in theoretical specification of institutional theory, which may or may not prove to be productive. Other directions are possible, and many scholars are asking these questions. The chapters in this volume on savings by the poor (chapter 9, by Beverly and colleagues; chapter 16, by Smeeding; and chapter 10, by Schreiner and colleagues) add valuable empirical knowledge and theoretical insight to this growing body of knowledge.

One of the pillars of America's founding is the right to own property, with assumed benefits accruing to families and communities. Despite this bedrock social philosophy, there has not been an integrated effort to study effects of asset ownership. This is changing now, with contributions in this volume (chapter 2, by Shanks; chapter 6, by Shapiro and Johnson; and chapter 7, by Scanlon and Adams). This growing knowledge base on the effects of asset holding will inform and influence future investments in asset-based public policy.

In addition, this knowledge base may eventually force the same questions on income-based policy, for which positive effects have been more or less taken for granted. For example, we know little about whether income transfer policy affects psychological well-being, social interactions, or civic involvement. Whether income-based or asset-based policy leads to greater well-being does not have to be an assertion or an ideological matter; it can and should be an empirical matter.

APPLIED SOCIAL RESEARCH

A strength of this book is the bridging of research and policy. These studies are not "academic exercises"; instead, they are purposeful inquiries intended to inform policy. Many of the studies in this book are about existing policies or new policy demonstrations.

In the applied social sciences, studying an "intervention," although inevitably challenging, is the ideal source of knowledge for policies and programs. Intervention research requires asking a key question and specifying it theoretically, operationalizing the theory into a practical application, setting up the new project, making sure that it is administered successfully, and then studying the participants over time to see what happens to them. This research process is perhaps one hundred times more challenging—in terms of time, human resources, and financial resources—than doing a statistical analysis on an existing data set. Fortunately, for policy purposes, it can also be one hundred times more productive.

This volume contains two examples of such research: the study of extra credit savings by Beverly and her colleagues, in chapter 9, and chapter 10, on IDAs by Schreiner and his colleagues. Stegman and Faris then build off the IDA research in chapter 11 and ask about comparisons with non-IDA participants.

Other studies in applied social research are based on existing policies, and these also can be very productive. This book contains several strong examples. Caskey studies the use of financial services in chapter 8; Orszag and Greenstein study retirement pensions in chapter 13; Rideout studies the thrift savings plan in chapter 14; and Smeeding studies the Earned Income Tax Credit in chapter 16. These are valuable studies, based in real experience with clear policy implications.

TOWARD AN INCLUSIVE ASSET-BASED POLICY

The contributing authors and I hope that this book will create greater awareness of the extraordinary regressivity of current asset-based policy. If it accomplishes nothing more than that, it will have been worth the effort. Greater awareness of these upside-down policies may lead to a broader interest in changing policy, so that it is more universal and more progressive—the meaning of *inclusion* in this volume.

With growing recognition of the role of assets and wealth in long-term development, scholars and policy makers are creating new policy language. Today, we talk about "asset-based" research and policy, in contrast with "income-based" research and policy. As Midgley points out in chapter 3, larger policy objectives are sometimes called "social investment," in contrast with the terms "social support" or "social protection," commonly used in traditional policy discussion.

Although asset building is a new direction with new terms and new meanings, this does not suggest that support and protection in public policy should be reduced. Bernstein, in chapter 17, appropriately voices this concern. None of the other authors in this book would make the suggestion that income-based policy should be reduced. To promote and ensure well-being, both support and development are required. The heavily income-oriented welfare state has done the former but not the latter. The suggestion of this book is that a development agenda should be added to social policy as a complement to—not a replacement of—a support agenda.

In this regard, new measures of asset poverty will be required. Haveman and Wolff, in chapter 4, create, analyze, and discuss possible options for measures of asset poverty. This exercise is much more than academic. There is political power in measures. If asset poverty were regularly measured and reported, this in itself would make it more likely that policy would eventually be implemented to address asset poverty. In fact, at this writing, there are efforts on Capitol Hill to get the U.S. Census Bureau to begin using such measures.

To clarify, the aim of this body of work is not an antipoverty agenda. We are not seeking to help or to fix poor people. Rather, we are seeking to include the poor in asset-based policies that already exist, such as home ownership and retirement pension accounts, or will be created, for example, a universal children's savings account (CSA). This is a development agenda. We are aiming for universal policies that include everyone, while providing greater subsidies to the poor. In this regard, the principles and pathways laid out by Friedman and Boshara, in chapter 12, are a good place to start. Creating a universal CSA, as proposed in chapter 15 by Goldberg is a desirable option, and, in fact, at this writing, a bill for CSAs, the ASPIRE Act, has been introduced in both the House and Senate, with bipartisan cosponsors. Boshara and his colleagues at the New America Foundation have laid the groundwork for the ASPIRE Act. This uses the model of the thrift savings plan, as discussed by Rideout in chapter 14. In order to be universal, a savings *plan* is required. It will not be sufficient to create only saving products in the marketplace. (For clear articulation of this, I am indebted to Margaret Clancy at CSD, a coauthor of chapter 10, who sees similar possibilities in state college savings plans).

Looking to the future, it seems almost inevitable that asset-based discussions, research, and policy proposals will continue to expand. This is not merely a "program" idea, but a fundamentally different way to think about the purposes and possibilities of social policy. In fact, asset-based policies are growing rapidly in the United States and around the world. Quite likely, this is because these policies are a better fit with economies and labor markets in the post-Industrial era. This is not an ideological matter but a practical matter—governments are adopting policies that fit the economies and societies of the twenty-first century.

Unfortunately, changes toward asset-based policy to date have been mostly regressive. The poor are often excluded altogether, and even when included, they receive far less than an equal share of the benefits.

A basic policy principle going forward should be that *public benefits for asset building should be at least equal for everyone in dollar terms,* that is, everyone should receive the same amount. To be sure, I would prefer that the poor receive more—because I think this would be a more productive use of public resources—but I would accept the basic principle of equal benefits as a starting place. This principle would be a vast improvement over the exclusionary asset-based policies that exist today.

Index